Southern Literary Studies

SOUTHERN LITERARY STUDIES

Louis D. Rubin, Jr., Editor

A Season of Dreams: The Fiction of Eudora Welty
Alfred Appel, Jr.

The Hero with the Private Parts
Andrew Lytle

Hunting in the Old South: Original Narratives of the Hunters
Edited by Clarence Gohdes

Joel Chandler Harris: A Biography
Paul M. Cousins

John Crowe Ransom: Critical Essays and a Bibliography
Edited by Thomas Daniel Young

A Bibliographical Guide to the Study of Southern Literature
Edited by Louis D. Rubin, Jr.

Poe: Journalist and Critic
Robert D. Jacobs

Love, Boy: The Letters of Mac Hyman
Edited by William Blackburn

The Complete Works of Kate Chopin
Edited by Per Seyersted

Kate Chopin: A Critical Biography
Per Seyersted

Without Shelter: The Early Career of Ellen Glasgow
J. R. Raper

Southern Excursions: Essays on Mark Twain and Others
Lewis Leary

The Poetry of Randall Jarrell
Suzanne Ferguson

Death by Melancholy: Essays on Modern Southern Fiction
Walter Sullivan

The Sovereign Wayfarer: Walker Percy's Diagnosis of the Malaise
Martin Luschei

Literature and Society in Early Virginia, 1608–1840
Richard Beale Davis

The Question of Flannery O'Connor
Martha Stephens

Grace King of New Orleans: A Selection of Her Writings
Edited by Robert Bush

Grace King of New Orleans

Edited with Introduction and Notes
by ROBERT BUSH

GRACE KING OF NEW ORLEANS

A Selection of Her Writings

Louisiana State University Press
BATON ROUGE

ISBN 0–8071–0055–2
Library of Congress Catalog Card Number 72–96399

Manufactured in the United States of America
Printed by The Colonial Press Inc., Clinton, Massachusetts
Designed by Dwight Agner

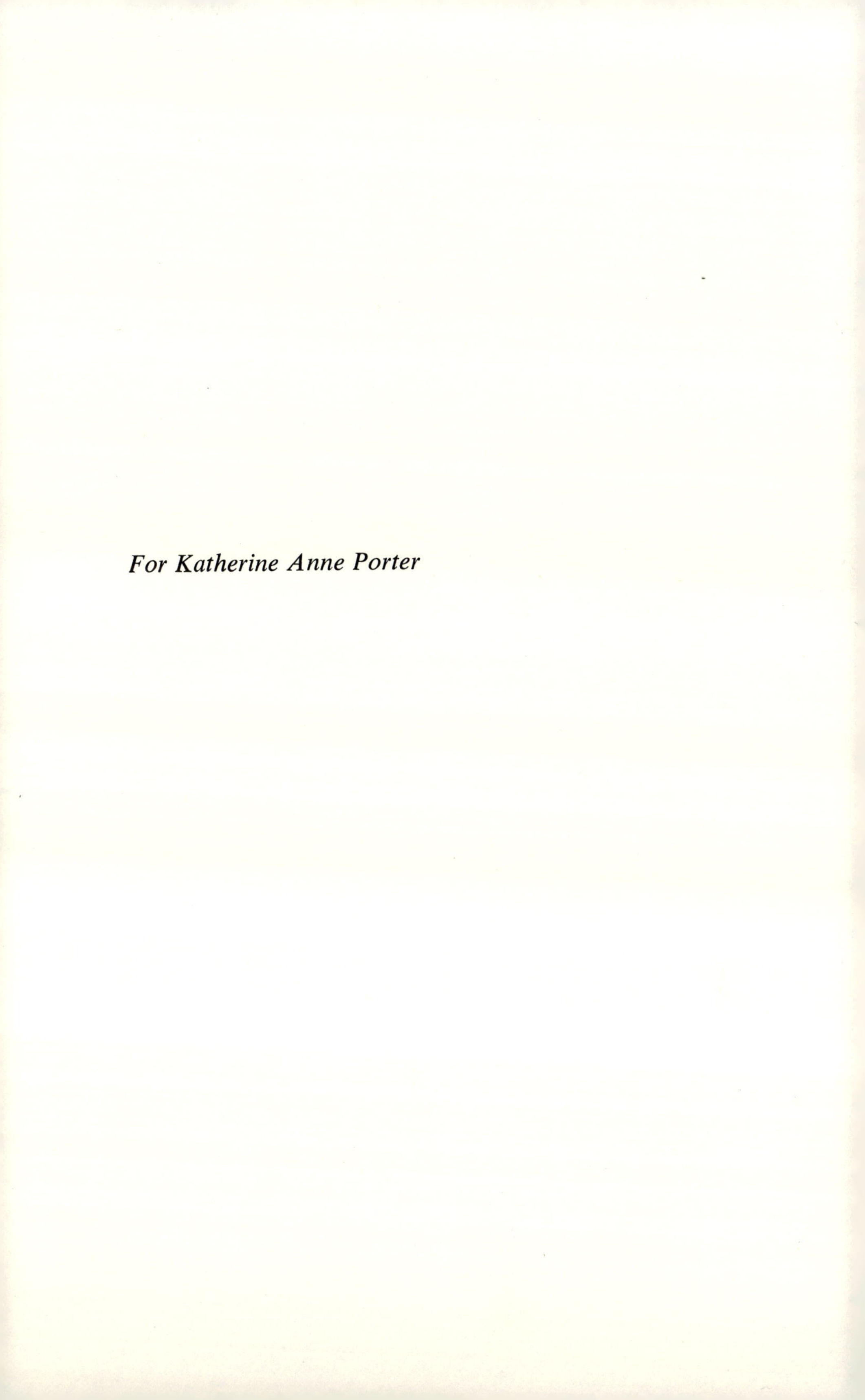

For Katherine Anne Porter

Contents

	Acknowledgments	xi
	A Note on the Texts	xiii
I	**Introduction**	3
II	**From *Memories of a Southern Woman of Letters***	33
III	**Monsieur Motte**	53
IV	**Bayou L'Ombre: An Incident of the War**	97
V	**From *Balcony Stories*** La Grande Demoiselle 133 / Anne Marie and Jeanne Marie 138 / A Crippled Hope 142 / The Little Convent Girl 150	131
VI	**Uncollected Stories** An Affair of the Heart 159 / The Evening Party 164 / A Quarrel with God 172 / Destiny 184 / Making Progress 197	157
VII	**From *The Pleasant Ways of St. Medard*** A Journey into the Far Country 209 / "It Was a Famous Victory" 232 / Jerry 244 / The San Antonios 256 / *From* Mademoiselle Coralie 270 / At the Villa Bella 280 / The Turning of the Road 290	207

VIII **History** 295

The Old Cabildo of New Orleans 297 / The Glorious Eighth of January 304

IX **Biography** 331

Mark Twain: First Impression 333 / Mark Twain: Second Impression 334 / Madame la Baronne Blaze de Bury 335 / Madame la Comtesse Tascher de la Pagerie 342 / Theo. Bentzon—Madame Th. Blanc 347 / Bernard de Marigny 352

X **Letters and Notebook Selections** 337

To Charles Dudley Warner, October 18, 1885 379 / To Charles Dudley Warner, November 22, 1885 379 / To May McDowell, May 31, 1885 379 / To Olivia L. Clemens, August 15, 1888 380 / To Mark Twain, September 5, 1888 382 / To Sarah Ann Miller King, February 28, 1892 383 / Notebook Selections, September 22, 1901 385 / To Edwin Anderson Alderman, February 11, 1903 386 / To Warrington Dawson, January 22, 1905 388 / To Warrington Dawson, March 15, 1906 389 / To Warrington Dawson, April 16, 1906 392 / To John R. Ficklen, November 27, 1906 393 / To John R. Ficklen, March 5, 1907 394 / To May McDowell, November 15, 1908 395 / To Robert Underwood Johnson, March 30, 1909 397 / To Fred Lewis Pattee, January 19, 1915 398 / To Carleton King, June 4, 1915 399 / To Edward Garnett, April 7, 1916 400 / To Edward Garnett, February 3, 1917 401 / To George W. Cable, October 14, 1917 402 / To Warrington Dawson, August 5, 1924 402 / To Leonidas Warren Payne, October 18, 1927 403 / To Warrington Dawson, November 4, 1930 404

Bibliographical Note 405

Acknowledgments

Much of the original material of this book has been transcribed from manuscripts of the Grace King Papers in the Department of Archives and Manuscripts, Louisiana State University, Baton Rouge. John M. Coxe, guardian of those papers, has kindly permitted me to publish selections from them. He has also consented to the editing and publishing of various writings of Grace King still under copyright. I am most grateful for his cooperation and his advice. Among former members of the Department of Archives, Mrs. Elsa B. Meier generously shared with me her knowledge of the papers; Dr. John M. Price discussed the historical background with me to my advantage. I am indebted to both for their contribution to the volume.

Dr. Mattie Russell of the William R. Perkins Library, Duke University, introduced me to the correspondence between Grace King and Warrington Dawson. I am grateful to her for this and to the library for permission to publish excerpts from those letters. Authorities of seven other libraries have kindly granted permission for publication of letters owned by them. These are listed in the headnote preceding the final section of the volume. Mrs. Sherwood Anderson has kindly consented to the publication of two letters from Sherwood Anderson to Grace King, both of which are deposited in the Newberry Library, Chicago. Edmund Wilson also permitted the publication of a letter of his to Grace King.

I am grateful to the following members of the Department of Romance Languages, Herbert H. Lehman College, for their assistance and advice in the interpretation of obscure allusions in French and Spanish: Professors Carmen de Zulueta and Nadine Savage.

Two grants in aid from funds of the City University of New York were helpful in defraying travel expenses of my research. One was a Faculty Research Award, the other a grant made through the Graduate Committee, Department of English, Herbert H. Lehman College. For the latter my thanks go to Professor Alice Griffin and other members of her committee.

Finally, I am indebted to Professor Louis D. Rubin, Jr., of the University of North Carolina for his early encouragement of this volume and for his helpful suggestions on its development.

Robert Bush

Herbert H. Lehman College
City University of New York
March, 1973

A Note on the Texts

The copy-text for each of the selections of this anthology has been determined by the first edition of each work in book form. The text for the story "Monsieur Motte," for example, is based not on the periodical publication but on the revised work as it appears as the first part of the volume *Monsieur Motte*. When the selection has not previously been collected in book form, the unique periodical edition has been used as copy-text. The particular date and place of publication for each of the selections is recorded in the headnote preceding the individual parts of this volume.

Emendations have been made in the individual texts to correct typographical errors and other errors that we can be reasonably sure the author would agree to. In the profile "Madame la Comtesse Tascher de la Pagerie," Grace King writes of the "Third Empire" repeatedly when she means the Second Empire. These instances have been emended. As for mechanics, early volumes of her fiction seem to be free of the eccentricities found in the 1916 edition of *The Pleasant Ways of St. Médard.* Early in her career Miss King admitted some weakness in matters of punctuation and stated her willingness to accept editorial revisions. Apparently such revisions were not made for her in *The Pleasant Ways.* In editing chapters from that novel the aim has not been to modernize punctuation but to emend when no valid reason existed for a given form. Several commas have been removed when they were without purpose, but certain capitalizations and hyphenations that appear quaint today have not been emended. Grace King used a series of three or four periods on occasion to indicate a break in dialogue or a pause in time. Although this device may be confused with editorial ellipsis, it has been retained and printed as in the original edition of *The Pleasant Ways.* No editorial ellipsis has been used in this volume except infrequently in the selections from the manuscript letters and notebooks and in the excerpts from reviews.

In the editing of the letters the policy has been to respect the constant use of the dash when it conveys spontaneity, but not when it seems to indicate the writer's pause for thought. The dash at the end of a sentence has been interpreted invariably as a rapidly written period. Frequently a period is followed by a dash in the manuscript; here the dash has been omitted.

Grace King of New Orleans

I INTRODUCTION

GRACE ELIZABETH KING (1851–1932) once enjoyed a modest reputation as one of the several fiction writers of the South who began publishing at the end of the Reconstruction period. Less well known than George W. Cable or Thomas Nelson Page, she was nevertheless highly praised by critics as eminent as William Dean Howells. During the period of the vogue of local-color fiction in the 1880s and 1890s her work appeared frequently in the pages of *Harper's* and *Century* magazines. By the time when that vogue faded around the turn of the century she had already established herself as a historian of the Louisiana territory in the tradition of François Xavier Martin and Charles Gayarré. In the nineteenth century her writing achieved a degree of national acceptance, but as time passed she produced less, and her reputation shrank into the realm of New Orleans and the state of Louisiana.

There are a number of reasons for rescuing her best work from oblivion. When her thirteen volumes are read forty years after her death, it becomes clear that she wrote with great perceptiveness in fiction about her own time and about the history of her city and region. One of her novels, *The Pleasant Ways of St. Médard*, and one of her histories, *New Orleans, the Place and the People*, are unqualified successes.

Among southern writers of her time she was one of the few who achieved excellence in both history and fiction; in her work the one strongly reinforces the other. All of her fiction is governed by the same seriousness of the social historian that Henry James insisted on in "The Art of Fiction," and much of her work is grounded on observed historical fact. Her earliest stories, "Monsieur Motte" and "Bonne Maman" (1886), are concerned with the affectionate relationships that still existed between black and white women after the days of slavery. In her novel *The Pleasant Ways of St. Médard* (1916), the subject is the reversal of social station that followed the war: the success of the unworthy, the poverty of the faithful. These stories and many that were published between them, derive from Grace King's ability to recognize the ironies of social change that left scars on her own life. As a member of a disfranchised patrician family she was most conscious of how defeat in war had created the topsy-turvy world of Reconstruction in which most of the established values and standards of society had been overturned.

Her irony was by no means limited to the defense of her own class. In "Monsieur Motte" it is the quadroon hairdresser who is caught in an undeserved position as a result of the caste system. Having spent much of her income supporting a white girl in a boarding school, Marcélite the hairdresser must maintain her anonymity lest she disgrace the girl whom she loves. When the revelation of the bounty of her generous heart is made, she is unnerved as if she had been discovered in a criminal act. "Oh, my God!" she cries in anguish, "I knew it would kill her! . . . To be supported by a nigger!" The terrifying critical light shed on the injustice of caste by the remark is comparable to Huckleberry Finn's "All right, then, I'll *go* to hell," when he decides to risk damnation by committing the crime of helping a slave escape.

Grace King was to become a good friend of Mark Twain, but there is little possibility that his fiction influenced her own. More likely the uses of irony by Maupassant in such a famous story as "Boule-de-suif" (1880) could have. Educated in a French Creole school in New Orleans, her cultural orientation was more French than English, although her family was of course English-speaking. She spoke and read French well, and in 1885, when she began to write seriously, she determined to use French novels as models (in spite of their "naughtiness") rather than either

English or American ones.[1] With such a background she bears a close resemblance to Kate Chopin, whose St. Louis education was French Creole and who was early inspired by her reading of Maupassant. Marveling at his stories, Mrs. Chopin wrote that "Here was life, not fiction; for where were the plots, the old fashioned mechanism and stage trapping that in a vague, unthinking way I had fancied were essential to the art of story making." [2] A similar disregard for plots and "stage trapping" is characteristic of Grace King's fiction at its best, and the two volumes that illustrate this uncontrived realism are *Balcony Stories* and *The Pleasant Ways of St. Médard.* The belief of both Mrs. Chopin and Miss King that their art was to portray "life, not fiction," accounts for their excellence. During a period when many American story writers were following the fashion of varnishing their little plots with local color, both women were exposed to the more sophisticated principles of the French, which enabled them to produce fiction of lasting quality.

Grace King was almost exclusively southern. Although she made strong friendships among northern intellectuals and recognized the importance of publishing her work in New York, she never lost the feeling that the South had first claim to her patriotism. When she was in France she made it clear that she was not just an American, but one from the South, which made a difference. She was representative of the new southern energies that flourished at the end of the Reconstruction era, but she was never a New South author with a fully conciliatory national spirit. She went through life keeping bright her childhood memories of the defiant burning of the cotton bales before the landing of Federal troops in New Orleans and of the indignities suffered by southern ladies under the tactless General Benjamin F. Butler, commander of the occupation forces of the city. The memory of the humiliation of Reconstruction, especially as it affected her own family, and the pride generated by the reversals of social position of the time, made her resist any temptation to feel a full sense of reunion or to embark on her career in the spirit of the New South. She could not

1 Grace King to her sister, May McDowell, July 14, 1885, in Grace King Papers, Department of Archives and Manuscripts, Louisiana State University, Baton Rouge.

2 Quoted by Per Seyersted in *Kate Chopin: A Critical Biography* (Oslo and Baton Rouge, 1969), 51.

imitate Joel Chandler Harris, who seemed to further reconciliation by flattering the North; nor could she possibly admit the justice of the northern cause as Cable did in his novel *Dr. Sevier* (1885). Although too much the patrician to approve of the corrupt governments of late nineteenth-century Bourbonism in Louisiana, she nevertheless belonged to and represented in literature the reestablishment of the political power of the upper-class whites, who were to maintain their conservative control until the time of the election of Huey P. Long to the governorship in 1928. Her attitude toward the Negro was both kindly and paternalistic, patronizing and apprehensive—a thoroughly conventional attitude according to her class and time.

It would be difficult to find an American author more deeply committed to her family than Grace King, and the experience of the King family during the crucial years of its existence from the Civil War to the end of the century was the experience of the intellectual and patrician South in microcosm. They were the haves before the war, the have-nots for more than a decade after. If fate gave them social position and luxury in the Old South period, it spurred them to recapture all those material and social values that were lost as a result of the war. The sensitive Grace King was the vessel for the family dignity, the one who keenly felt the necessity to improve the family position. She was about nine years old when her mother fled from occupied New Orleans with all her children and reached L'Embarras Plantation, near New Iberia and within Confederate lines. When the family returned four years later, they found themselves completely dispossessed of their city property and obliged to live in crowded quarters among working-class people opposite Jackson Barracks. The father, William Woodson King, reestablished his once thriving law practice only after years of labor and privation. The family lived at various temporary addresses in New Orleans until 1904, when the surviving children acquired a permanent home on Coliseum Place. Both parents were then dead, and the house would shelter one brother and the three unmarried sisters for the remainder of their lives. The purchase of the house seems a minor matter, but to Grace King it was of the highest importance in the history of this archetypal family. She recorded in her Notebook:

> To me it was of solemn significance—the great landmark of our lives—the attainment of what our Father worked so nobly

> for—the hope and prayer of Mimi [her mother] a permanent home for the family. What a track of life behind us; since the day that the family quitted their home under the compulsion of Butler's orders, leaving their furniture—pictures . . souvenirs—behind them . . . How we have struggled and worked—fallen down, gotten up again—to toil on . . striving with others—striving with the villainous temper of one another . . suffering what anguish of mind & heart—in the midnight hours of wakefulness—in consequence thereof—the home . . . we are where we were forty years ago! at the point from which the war drove us back.[3]

Those southern families who had lost the most in the war were not likely to assume the generous attitudes of many of the New South writers. The people of New Orleans who remembered General Butler's rule and had suffered from it were destined to live out their lives as conservatives with a suspicious eye on the Federal power that had disfranchised them. And it may be true that southern women of that era had longer memories of such sufferings than the men.

What the King family lacked in wealth, they made up for in cultivation and sociability. Even after the death of William Woodson King (1881) they continued to flourish as a lively southern household, known for their excellent table, a family interested in meeting intellectuals from all parts of the country. During the years of the Cotton Centennial Exposition (1884–1886) the city was on display with its new bid for economic growth, and the King family performed their more personal function on a cultural and social level. During these years New Orleans and the Kings were exposed to such figures as Julia Ward Howe, Joaquin Miller, Richard Watson Gilder, and Charles Dudley Warner. In the year 1884 the combination of forces was entirely favorable to the commencement of Grace King's literary career. The officious Mrs. Howe, in New Orleans to preside over the Women's Department of the Exposition, had revived a small literary discussion group known as the Pan Gnostics, to which Grace King belonged. A paper she read to the group, "The Heroines of Novels," was to become her first published

3 Notebook (MS in the Grace King Papers), November 17, 1904. The ellipses in this passage are authorial.

critical essay.[4] She met Richard Watson Gilder, editor of *Century Magazine,* at a dinner party during the carnival season, 1885, as she recounted the important moment many years later. On the way home Gilder questioned her about the hostility shown George W. Cable by his fellow citizens of New Orleans. One of Gilder's major achievements had been his sponsorship of Cable as a writer.

"I hastened to enlighten him," Grace King wrote, "to the effect that Cable proclaimed his preference for colored people over white and assumed the inevitable superiority—according to his theories—of the quadroons over the Creoles. He was a native of New Orleans and had been well treated by its people, and yet he stabbed the city in the back, as we felt, in a dastardly way to please the Northern press." [5] In an interview in 1923 she recalled the incident and analyzed her youthful outburst against Cable: "I abused him as only a New Orleans person could—not really abuse you know, it was a sense of resentment, of having our feelings hurt. I admired the Gilders immensely—Richard, Joseph, Jeannette, but I did not admire Cable and, being foolish and young, I said so. Of course I understood even then that he was a genius, but he did not understand the Creoles." [6]

Gilder, unconvinced by her emotional remarks in 1885, asked, "Why, if Cable is so false to you, why do not some of you write better?" She had no answer for him at the time, but later asked herself, "Why, why, do we not write our side? . . . Are we to submit to Cable's libels in resignation?" [7] The following morning she climbed to an attic room in her home on Rampart Street to begin her first story, "Monsieur Motte."

At the time of Gilder's challenge to Grace King in 1885 the career of Cable was in full flower, and the controversy over his accuracy as a critic of Louisiana Creoles and his judgment as a reformer was at its height. During the previous decade he had risen from obscurity to become internationally known as an interpreter of New Orleans as a city and the

4 New Orleans *Times-Democrat*, May 31, 1885.

5 Grace King, *Memories of a Southern Woman of Letters* (New York, 1932), 58–60. By "Creoles" Grace King referred to those people born in the Gulf States (or in Caribbean areas) of pure French or Spanish stock. This did not include the Louisiana "Cajuns," who had emigrated from Nova Scotia.

6 Louise Hubert Guyol, "A Southern Author in Her New Orleans Home," *Louisiana Historical Quarterly*, VI (July, 1923), 365.

7 *Memories of a Southern Woman of Letters*, 60–61.

South as a region. Grace King was strongly allied socially and intellectually to the Creole community. Her education had been in French-speaking, Catholic schools; her family's closest friend was the historian Charles Gayarré, whose influence on her opinions had been a strong one. Like him and many of her contemporaries, Miss King accepted the theory that Cable was an apostate who had betrayed his own people to please the northern press. This view was especially intense because Cable's liberal views began to be published at the end of the Reconstruction period when the former ruling class still smarted from the presence of uneducated black officials in carpetbagger governments. Grace King's outburst against Cable in 1885 should be judged within the emotional context of the post-Reconstruction era. Like most southerners who had known the war and its aftermath, she held loyalty to the tribe as a primary moral rule. Cable, whose mother had a New England background, had struggled between his sympathies for the South and his own personal conviction, and the latter had won out. Even so, his position was misunderstood by Miss King. No scholar today would think Cable so debased as to write "to please the Northern press." If anything, he wrote to arouse the northern reader to the realization that the North had "retreated from its uncomfortable dictational attitude and thrown the whole matter [the racial problem] over to the States of the South." [8] Even though the setting of his novel *The Grandissimes* (1880) is the early nineteenth century, its message is a strong condemnation of a rigid caste system based on the power of a ruling white class. In his essays in *The Silent South* it is clear that he had no intention of showing preference for blacks over whites, but of pointing out injustices in a society in which the whites made all the decisions in their own interest. He approved of neither miscegenation nor social integration. All he set forth was the ideal of political and judicial equality for all citizens. That principle was, of course, untenable in the South of 1885.

Although in disagreement on the questions of Creoles and Negroes, Cable and Grace King had much in common. They had both been reared in the plainness and simplicity of Presbyterianism, and like some other American Protestants they were attracted by the Catholic

8 George W. Cable, "The Freedman's Case in Equity," in *The Silent South* (New York, 1885), 2.

community more than by their own in their search for meaningful subject matter for fiction. There was certainly more individuality and often more sensuous appeal in the life of the Creoles than in that of the Protestant Americans. Because the quality of Creole life was closely related to continental European life, there was greater richness of complication possible in the stories that might be produced. The Negro, also, often a crude primitive in the English-speaking world, assumed the exotic combination of Africa and France in his Louisiana milieu. American authors had often despaired of the poverty of American life because of its sameness. James Fenimore Cooper was concerned with this flaw in his day, Henry James in his. The local colorists of midcentury and after seem to have felt this also, but instead of looking abroad for themes, they sought out what was still unstandardized in American life. The exploitation of Louisiana by the fiction writers—Cable, Hearn, Grace King, Kate Chopin, and Ruth McEnery Stuart—was a kind of answer to the James who went abroad in search of themes for fiction.

Grace King was well aware of Cable's role as the first author to make New Orleans internationally famous in his writings. She was, however, to be no imitator of Cable or any of the local colorists, with the possible exception of Lafcadio Hearn. There is little of the wish to celebrate a vanishing way of life in her writings, that evocation of the past one feels in Cable's *Old Creole Days* or in Sarah Orne Jewett's *The Country of the Pointed Firs.* In an era when a heavy use of dialect was expected in such stories, her infrequent use of it is marked. When she does use it, dialect is never allowed to inhibit the reading process as it sometimes does in the stories of Mary Noailles Murfree or Thomas Nelson Page. Coming somewhat late to local-color writing, Grace King determined to be a local realist rather than a local romanticist. Her settings tend to be within the time span of her own life, and her plots tend to be uncontrived actions that spring logically according to character and environment. Her earlier work is not without the sentiment that often accompanied local color, but after "Monsieur Motte" and "Bonne Maman," sentiment is judiciously restrained.

When she climbed the stairs to the attic room to begin "Monsieur Motte," she muttered to herself, "I'll show him!" the "him" meaning Gilder or Cable. Since she neither had made nor would make any public expression of her abhorrence of Cable's opinions, he could hardly have recognized that the story was an answer to him. Indeed, it is difficult to discern any direct answer to Cable in this or future stories; her disdain of any element of propaganda in fiction determined that. Her treatment of Creoles and Negroes is predictably different from Cable's. The setting of *The Grandissimes* in the early nineteenth century invited him to depict Creoles as cruel masters over suffering and sometimes enraged blacks. Miss King, writing about the Reconstruction period when Creole power was reduced, concentrated on the females of a boarding school, the mistresses and students and their relation to a former slave. Since the theme of "Monsieur Motte" is the extraordinary devotion of a quadroon to the child of her former master, Miss King expected her readers to infer that such devotion was the deserved reward of benign treatment on the part of the white family.

A similar theme was to appear in the long story "Bonne Maman" and in "Joe," one of the later balcony stories. There is little doubt that Miss King looked upon these portraits of good relationships between the races as an antidote to such melodramatic stories as that of Bras Coupé, the defiant, enslaved African prince of *The Grandissimes.* Notable also is her treatment of the former slave family in *The Pleasant Ways of St. Médard.* Here she recorded from family experience the pain by which a black family achieved their precarious independence. The faithful Jerry and Matilda return to New Orleans as servants of their former master. They are a mature couple, but their inexperienced daughters, vulnerable to the temptations of the city, fall to thievery. Grace King does not attempt to defend the antebellum social system; she is the sympathetic and somewhat melancholy interpreter of the sorrows of Jerry's family as she sees it disintegrate. Jerry himself finally leaves the Talbots, his former owners, not out of disloyalty but because he must find his family and reunite them as a free and independent group. The departure of Jerry is most significant: in that act he becomes an emblem of all freed blacks in their compulsion to break the bonds that held them to the whites.

The writing of "Monsieur Motte" was not her first attempt at fiction. Grace King had resolved to become a writer at the age of ten during the war years on the plantation. After her graduation from the Institut St. Louis she had attended the school of Heloise Cenas in New Orleans, where she had been rigorously trained in basic writing. After the death of her father in 1881 she felt the obligation to follow her brothers in a career, this time pressed by the hope of financial independence. She berated herself: "Was I a laggard? Was I incapable? And all my reading and preparation? Were they to go for nothing? Patience! Patience! The time will come. It has not come yet." [9] The time came with the Gilder challenge. And it was Gilder to whom she first submitted "Monsieur Motte"—anonymously through a bookseller. It was returned without comment.[10] Over a year later she had the good fortune to meet Charles Dudley Warner, who in the spring of 1885 was on a trip south for *Harper's Magazine.* He was then nationally known for his column in *Harper's*, for his editorials in the Hartford *Courant*, and for his familiar essays and travel writings. With his varied literary activities well publicized through his lectures about the country he had become a symbol of Gilded Age literary success. Grace King was an attractive woman in her early thirties, with curly reddish brown hair, a stylish woman whose mind at the time was concerned with what she was reading and what she was wearing. Her letters to her married sister, May McDowell, are a curious mélange of the progress of her wardrobe and the progress of her mind, who were the best dressmakers to patronize, and what were the most intellectual magazines to subscribe to.

In April, 1885, she met Warner at a party given by Maud Howe, Julia Ward Howe's daughter. She described a second meeting in a letter to May McDowell: "Maud gave another reception Wednesday evening. It was stupid in all but the opportunity it gave me of prosecuting my acquaintance with Charles Dudley Warner. I had dragged through a long evening talking 'scraps' . . . . But I watched my opportunity & snatched it when it came. Mr Warner made an engagement with me to call on the Gayarrés. This morning at 11 oc he came for me & we had a very nice time of it. He is about fifty—grey haired & bearded & married—but so clever, refined & original. Of course we are affinities & of course the fashionables are racing after him & he doesn't meet me any where & notice it—tant pis." [11] Grace King's "prosecuting" of her

9 *Memories of a Southern Woman of Letters*, 48.
10 *Ibid.*, 61, 62.
11 Grace King to May McDowell, April 11, 1885, in Grace King Papers.

acquaintance with Warner was an event that shows her use of social talent to fulfill her own professional destiny. With the help of her family's hospitality and her own charm she established herself as one of his closest friends. The assistance he was to give her at the beginning of her career was immense. He arranged for the publication of "Monsieur Motte" in the *New Princeton Review.* Thereafter he saw that *Harper's Magazine* was usually open to her contributions. His advice to her about reading was invaluable: he served as a kind of intellectual advisor, guiding her to important reading from Plato to Herbert Spencer. She in turn was grateful for his sponsorship, and she genuinely admired him. She wrote May McDowell that "When I see how beautifully he writes, I am quite aghast at my great familiarity with him. In one respect I was more intimate with him than with any man in my life before; & he declared that he never would believe that in three weeks he could have become so attached to a stranger as to grieve for days over the prospect of a separation. . . . After all Warner's encouragement, I am as bold as a lion—& if I make a failure it will be an audacious one." [12]

In her thirty-fourth year the excitement of her friendship for the older celebrity brought a new drive to her life. She now felt bold enough to believe in the possibility of her success. By September of 1885 she had sent "Monsieur Motte" to him with the feeling that she would take a rejection of the story as an indication that she was perhaps wasting her time trying to write. She wrote May McDowell that "he will be the Supreme Court which shall regulate my entrée to or dismissal from the literary world." [13] During the period of suspense she wrote him: "I felt like a young lady in a novel when your letter came today—and *almost* hesitated to open it. Confessions of poverty, both of pocket and intellect, are not pleasant food for recollection—and ever since I sent you all that stuff, I have been feeling as I shall on Judgement Day when Montaigne says 'Le livre de notre conscience sera lu a haute voix devant toute la compagnie.' [14] You see, I wanted you to know frankly all I had done in the way of writing—bad, as well or more particularly than good. I am thankful the exposé is over. Now, don't you worry about Monsieur

12 King to McDowell, May 9, 1885, *ibid.*
13 King to McDowell, September 8, 1885, *ibid.*
14 The book of our conscience will be read aloud before all the company of heaven.

Motte—if no one else finds it good I shall be satisfied with your opinion and my own endeavor to call attention at least to some of those relations brought on by slavery, honorable to all concerned. It seems to me, white as well as black women have a sad showing in what some people call romance. I am very tired, and I should think others are too, of these local stories, but as I recollect little things, I think I shall try and write them. If no one else does it better, one of these days they may prove a pleasant record and serve to bring us all nearer together blacks and whites." [15]

Shortly thereafter Warner wrote that he had submitted her story to Professor William M. Sloane, editor of the *New Princeton Review*, and that it had been accepted with a proviso that certain changes be made, especially a shortening of the introduction. Grace King wrote with excitement and gratitude: "Your letter which came yesterday was an overwhelming surprise for me. I never dared hope that you would find others to reiterate your good opinion of Monsieur Motte. Undoubtedly it is a great honor to get in the new review, one which counterbalances far, any pecuniary advantage possible elsewhere. You have indeed acted, not as a friend but a loving relation—and I hope to prove, for I cannot write it, my fatihful love and gratitude to you. I am too much of a woman not to dwell more on the sentiment that you cared enough for me to take so much trouble—than on the immense practical advantage your intermediation has been to me. I should on the contrary be better pleased if a critical hand should prime away my fault. Such corrections would be of immense service to me; I am afraid of my English—and general criticisms are hard to apply with effect. I would not like any changes which would alter the pure disinterestedness of Marcélite's devotion. The friend I showed it to here wanted me to give a cause such as saving her from the auction block—but I felt this was gross and untrue to my conception. Great instances of devotion were found among even the worst treated slaves; I love to dwell on this, what I would call, holy passion of the Negro women, for it serves to cancel those other grosser ones, with which they are really victimised by their blood. And besides I think it highly honorable to the Southern women that they could be so served and loved by slaves. Do you recollect how finely Goethe puts it?

15 Grace King to Charles Dudley Warner, September 17, 1885, in Grace King Papers.

'Fidelity in this case is the effort of a noble soul struggling to become equal with one exalted above it.' "[16]

The anonymous "Monsieur Motte" was well received. Warner wrote with enthusiasm, telling her that "One paper said it was a 'selection' from foreign contemporary fiction. The N.Y. Tribune had (ten) lines of hearty praise. The N.Y. Post attributes it to Cable, The Springfield Republican to Mr. Janvier.[17] The Boston Herald . . . said it was the sort of fiction found in the 'Revue des deux Mondes,' and that we ought to have more of it. All my friends, who have read it, think it very strong, vigorous, pathetic, and wonderful in giving pictures with a few strokes of the pen." [18]

In February, 1886, William M. Sloane wrote Grace King that he wanted another installment or another story about the same characters, but he suggested that the setting be a plantation. She then set out to write the second story, "On the Plantation," almost on order. Warner urged her to write two more stories, each with the same time duration as the first two—forty-eight hours. The completed series was her first volume, *Monsieur Motte*, published by Armstrong and Company in 1888.

The year 1885, when she was thirty-four, was the great divide in Grace King's life. Had there been no Cotton Centennial Exposition, no visiting editors, no contempt for Cable, no challenge from Gilder, no encouragement from Warner, and no need for money, she might never have entered the larger world she became a part of. The 1885 career launching led to a visit to New England, a major step in her cosmopolitan education. She was invited by Charles Dudley Warner and his wife to visit Hartford in June, 1887. As a young author she had the opportunity to meet the members of the Nook Farm community, living in some affluence from their literary labors. Entertained with kindness and a degree of lavishness, she was quick to respond in gratitude; but the memory of the sufferings of the Reconstruction South was always with her and in perpetual contrast with the easy life of her northern hosts. She had high respect for Joseph Twichell, the pastor, and wrote of him, "Like

16 King to Warner, October 4, 1885, *ibid.*

17 Thomas Allibone Janvier (1849–1913), American author known for his sketches of life in New York and southern France.

18 Warner to King, January 5, 1886, in Grace King Papers.

all the other good friends at Hartford, he seemed to strive to smooth away any hard feeling I might have about the war. Reconstruction, which was also war, they never mentioned." She was conscious of her symbolic posture in a partially alien land. The vision of the figure of Harriet Beecher Stowe, now eccentric and senile, gliding about the grounds of the Warners' home, prompted her to admit that she had not read *Uncle Tom's Cabin*: "It was not allowed to be even spoken of in our house!" But she was fascinated by the sight of Mrs. Stowe "in spite of her hideous, black, dragon-like book that hovered on the horizon of every Southern child." [19]

At a dinner given by Mark Twain and his wife, General Lucius Fairchild, commander in chief of the Grand Army of the Republic, defended passionately his recent speech condemning President Cleveland for the gesture of returning Confederate battle flags. Grace King's contempt for Fairchild was unbounded, and the Clemenses were embarrassed that they had honored two such intense champions of opposite causes at the same dinner. Taken by the Warners and the Clemenses to visit Frederick E. Church's remarkable home Olana, she was excited by the highland landscape and the sumptuousness of the Victorian Moorish house overlooking the Hudson because such romantic settings were quite unknown in her part of the country.[20] Even the wealth of the Yale campus inspired her exclamations. But her delight on such occasions was muted by the recollection of southern poverty, which northern wealth seemed to intensify; and her usual conclusion was that the South was neverthless richer than the North in spiritual values.

In an early notebook, Grace King confessed, "I detest the North as a whole—the climate, the people the atmosphere—the social and other [institutions?]—the very scenery loses with me, when I see the sign of human habitation there. Out of a vast region of dislike arise exceptions however—exceptions whom I love—in whom no critical assiduity of mine can detect aught but what is admirable—most admirable. I love the South as a whole—at the very name warmth brightness, [sun?] and beauty start up before me—and yet when I think of the individuals there

19 King, *Memories*, 76–78.

20 See Robert Bush, "Grace King and Mark Twain," *American Literature*, XLIV (March, 1972), 33–36.

Grace King

are . . . in it that I detest—nowhere are found less admirable characters—men and women." [21] The northern exceptions she was thinking of were certainly those who showed sympathy not so much for herself as for the patrician South she stood for. Warner had been confirmed as one of these when he published the kind of essay she approved of on the South.[22] Later Hamilton Wright Mabie and Henry Mills Alden would earn similar positions in her affections. Professor Thomas Lounsbury of Yale was in her eyes the ideal former Federal officer because of his sympathetic attitude toward the South after his service in Virginia.

Among northerners it was the masculine mind she seemed attracted to. She knew women like Annie Fields and Sarah Orne Jewett, but never intimately. Only Olivia Clemens, among northern women, became a true confidant of hers. The charming, refined Livy, who was thoroughly domestic and made no pretense to be an intellectual, delighted in her letters and after the death of her daughter Susy in 1896 poured out her emotions to Grace King. The Clemenses, having left Hartford, were undecided about returning. Grace King advised them to go back to their permanent home, at the same time adding her personal misgivings about life among the affluent of the Gilded Age: "I do not conceal from myself—a moment—that Hartford is itself—to me—the most perfect expression of American Philistinism—that I ever came across. I thought when I was there—among your old friends—that I never met more uninteresting people in my life—of a more boring form of uninterestingness." Even the Warners, in retrospect, she came to see as examples of too much success and too much wealth: "Ah my dear!" she wrote Livy, "they show me, the want—the actual want—of a grief—in a loss in their lives. They have grown old in increasing prosperity—they have *succeeded*—and they are typically American in their enjoyment of it. As the children say—they 'show off.' " [23]

As her vision of the world broadened she inevitably felt the need for an exposure to Europe. Grace King's Europe was almost exclusively

21 Notebook, 1886–1901 (MS in Grace King Papers).

22 Charles Dudley Warner, "Impressions of the South," *Harper's*, LXXI (September, 1885), 546–52.

23 Grace King to Olivia Clemens, December 6, 1899, in Bancroft Library, University of California, Berkeley.

Paris. She traveled widely on three different European trips, but she lived and worked in Paris for many months at a time. Paris as a cultural home was the direction of her Creole education. Her first trip began in the fall of 1891 and ended in the fall of 1892. It was made with all the enthusiasm we should expect of a former student of the Institut St. Louis. She was armed with sufficient funds of her own earning, a commendable reputation as one of the new fiction writers of the South, a good knowledge of German, and a command of French. After a brief stay in England she and her sister Annie gravitated toward Paris.

Few American writers have been so well prepared for Paris as Grace King; from the beginning of her residence there she felt that she belonged: "Paris is a great place," she wrote her brother Branch, "but, New Orleans is very much like it. By carrying New Orleans out to its highest possible expression of wealth and beauty . . . and turning a French opera matinée loose in every corner, you can have an idea of what the mother of New Orleans is. Nan and I try to feel strange but we can't. Everything seems so natural, so what we are accustomed to. Even the grand buildings and magnificent places do not dazzle us." [24] Paris became a setting in which to write and learn. She began her book on Bienville, founder of New Orleans, using the Bibliothèque Nationale for research. She completed her series of *Balcony Stories.* But discipline was difficult when she shared her room with her sister: "I get Nan to sit in the corner of the room and turn her back to me & keep very quiet—& so I manage to write. I almost went wild though first, before I thought of this arrangement." [25] Then Paris became the ideal place for the practicing author: "I find this a delightful place to work—strange to say; I never heard of any one before coming to Paris to work—but there is inspiration everywhere, and one can always count upon long, quiet, morning hours. I believe I enjoy the Museum of the Louvre, and the old Sorbonne, and the walks along the Seine more than anything." [26] In the spring of 1892, while waiting for the Bibliothèque Nationale to open after the Easter holidays, she thought of writing a novel. She wrote Charles Dudley Warner, "I am going to try my hand at something on the

24 Grace King to Branch King, November 29, 1891, in Grace King Papers.
25 Grace King to May McDowell, November 29, 1891, *ibid.*
26 MS Letter fragment, undated, *ibid.*

American life here in Paris. I wish I could make a novel of it—but I am about convinced that I have not the large construction ability, necessary for a novel."[27] She attended the theater frequently—once for a performance of *Andromaque*, followed by a lecture on Racine by Brunetière. She was drawn to Brunetière's critical leadership because of his conservatism and his insistence on the moral basis for literature. She attended other lectures, the most notable one by Renan in the last year of his life.

Through a letter of introduction from Annie Fields, Grace King met her most important French friend, Marie Thérèse Blanc, who wrote under the pen name of Th. Bentzon. Madame Blanc had been a protégée of George Sand, whose style she had emulated in a series of novels. When Grace King met her she had long been associated with the *Revue des Deux Mondes* as critic and translator. She had written one of the earliest (1872) critical essays in French on Mark Twain as humorist, and she had translated for French readers "The Celebrated Jumping Frog of Calaveras County."[28]

Madame Blanc admired Grace King as a person and as author; in 1893 she would translate portions of her stories for an article on the new southern writers.[29] The Victorian Grace King could admire Madame Blanc because she believed her an anomaly among French women of letters: her novels were as impeccable as her personal history, and her intellectual interests embraced the English-speaking world with unusual sympathy. Madame Blanc's salon was a relatively important one that attracted the sincere and moral rather than the rich and snobbish or the unprincipled. It was in her home that Grace King met a good selection of French intellectuals. One of these, who became a close friend, was the Baronne Blaze de Bury, an elderly Scotswoman and widow of a French nobleman. She appealed to Grace King because her talk reflected her acquaintance with European political leaders since the days of

27 King to Warner, April 10, 1892, *ibid.*

28 Th. Bentzon, "*Les humoristes américains*: I. Mark Twain," *Revue des Deux Mondes*, C (Part II, 1872), 313–35. See also Mark Twain, "Private History of the 'Jumping Frog Story,'" *North American Review*, CLVIII (April, 1894), 451; Bush, "Grace King and Mark Twain," 46–48.

29 Th. Bentzon, "*Les romanciers du Sud en Amérique*," *Revue des Deux Mondes*, CXVI (1893), 652–83.

Metternich. Madame Blanc and the Baronne were the feminine side of *L'Union pour l'action morale,* a movement in the Paris of the 1890s that attempted to revive the spiritual and moral power of France. Paul Desjardins and Ferdinand Brunetière were the literary moguls within the group. Pastor Charles Wagner (1852–1918), an Alsatian Protestant minister, attracted a congregation that sought the new moral energy through religion. A man of peasant origin, he preached a philosophy of Christian love without dogma. His call for the life of simplicity and the love of nature, suggesting the ideas of Thoreau, attracted Grace King. She saw in Wagner the answer to what was to her the flaw of modern French civilization—its materialism and corruption. In 1903 she would provide a biographical introduction to the American edition of his popular work, *The Simple Life.*

Grace King's first European year proved her remarkable talent for international friendship and her ability to act as an intellectual influence. Among the French and the English, she championed the little known Lafacadio Hearn and the completely unknown Sidney Lanier, whom she considered the most original of American poets. She wrote a series of articles for *Harper's Bazar* that introduced the French personalities she had met to American readers. She also contributed a number of the introductions to Charles Dudley Warner's multivolume *Library of the World's Best Literature* (1896–1897). These were brief articles on Vigny, Baudelaire, Mérimée, Michelet, Lamennais, Édouard Rod, Melchior de Vogüé, and Paul Desjardins, most of which were inspired by her year in France and her personal acquaintance with the last three.

When she returned to the United States after a month spent with the Clemenses in their villa outside Florence, she must have realized the immense value of the year to her. While she was abroad, *Tales of a Time and Place* (1892) had been completed and published, and the first edition of *Balcony Stories* was being completed for publication in the following year. These two volumes include much of the short fiction for which she would be remembered, and they witness Grace King's growth in technique over a period of several years. The stories of the earlier collection are long, detailed narratives written in a consciously literary style. The best of these is "Bayou L'Ombre" because of its power to evoke the wartime plantation experience—a poetic memory of the emotions of time past. It concerns the arrival of a gunboat on the bayou and the bringing of a touch of excitement to the remote community. The plot is of little consequence, but the story contains one of Grace King's most memorable scenes—the bringing of the news of freedom to the black laundresses at work on the banks of the bayou.

Miss King's shift from such long stories to the relatively short, compact *Balcony Stories* may have been determined partly by the demands of *Century Magazine* for which they were written. It is also true that the taste for detailed local fiction had begun to decline in the 1890s. Grace King had developed her own taste for a brevity in which much was left to be inferred by the reader. Her prose style became less learned and pretentious, more relaxed; a colloquial tone pervades the book in imitation of the manner of the lady raconteurs who told such stories on the galleries of New Orleans houses in the warm evenings of summer. For her narrator she seems to have applied to prose Wordsworth's principle of selecting "the language really spoken by men." The result is not the usual attempt to efface the narrator but to emphasize her immediacy as a conveyor of the vitality of the story.

Balcony Stories shows a noticeable influence of French realism. "A Crippled Hope" suggests Flaubert's "Un coeur simple" in that it is a portrait of a commonplace servant woman whose life story is unified by the spirit of caring for others. "Anne Marie and Jeanne Marie" is concerned with two elderly peasant sisters in New Orleans, but the realism of the commonplace is centered on character rather than place. In a Norman French setting the two women might have been a subject for Maupassant.

The five-year period from 1893 to 1898 marks Grace King's effort to establish herself as a historian of the territory and state of Louisiana. Her interest in this subject dated from her early education and it was fostered by the very close friendship between her family and Charles Gayarré. She was thoroughly familiar with his accomplishment in this field and that of his predecessors, but her approach to history was to be her own. She first wrote the biography of a Canadian who had made history—*Jean Baptiste le Moyne, sieur de Bienville* (1893). The only book on the founder of both Mobile and New Orleans, it presents the history of the struggle for survival of the French colony as in large part the work of one hero. She next collaborated with Professor H. R. Ficklen of Tulane on *A History of Louisiana* (1894), primarily intended as a school text. And then followed *New Orleans, the Place and the People* (1895), written for a series of municipal histories then being published by the Macmillan Company. The book is a model for such histories, and it succeeds in a way that the best of nineteenth-century history succeeds: it is well grounded in fact but written with a grace and vitality to appeal to all intelligent readers. As in her fiction of the period a narrator speaks to us with the rhythm and the intimacy of one speaking, a learned narrator who conveys the fullness of her enthusiasm and her delight. The city's panoramic story unfolds rapidly before us with a wealth of sensuous detail. In this, her best historical work, her aim was clearly to present the past as vividly to the reader's imagination as she had recreated it in her own through the labor of research. She dedicated the book to Gayarré, whose recent death at the age of ninety seemed the symbolic end of nineteenth-century Creole civilization. His burial at St. Louis Cemetery is the concluding event. "Thus it is," she wrote at the end, "that one beholden to him for a long life's endowment of affection, help, and encouragement, judges it meet that a chronicle begun under his auspices, to which he contributed so richly from his memory, and of whose success he was so tenderly solicitous, should end, as it began, with a tribute to his memory and name."

De Soto and His Men in the Land of Florida (1898) was her final serious volume of history. In fiction also the end of the century marked a slowing of production. In the final years of the century Grace King published a series of excellent stories that were left uncollected. They include "An Affair of the Heart" (1894), "A Quarrel with God" (1897), and "Destiny" (1898). But after "Making Progress" (1901), her stories and historical articles appeared only infrequently. One of the reasons for the decline of her literary production may be that she had exhausted her major supply of ideas. Another was the series of deaths in her family circle and among her close friends. Charles Dudley Warner died in 1900, her brother Will and her literary advisor George C. Préot in 1901. Her mother's death in 1903 was the heaviest of blows, leaving her desolate for more than a year. The death of Branch, her eldest brother and head of the family, occurred in 1905. Many years later she attributed the falling off of her earlier energy to these bereavements. Recalling the loss of her mother and her brother Branch, she wrote George W. Cable that "Life has been so dark without them—that I have not written anything worth while since they left us." [30] The death of Branch was an almost unbearable catastrophe to his three unmarried sisters. Grace King explained to Robert Underwood Johnson, "A great bereavement & sorrow is driving us away—hoping for a 'surcease' in complete change." [31] The sisters sailed for Europe in January, 1906, where they remained for about two and a half years. It was a period of importance to Grace King for her literary friendships, but one scarcely marked by the prolific authorship of the earlier stay in Europe.

The greater part of her time was spent in Paris or Meudon, although she also traveled in England, Belgium, and Switzerland. She renewed the friendships she had made during the earlier period and spent a long time at Meudon during the last illness of Madame Blanc. She continued to bring out new editions of the books that brought her a small income: *Balcony Stories* and *New Orleans, the Place and the People* and her books for schools, the *History of Louisiana* and the recent *Stories from Louisiana History* (1905). In spite of Robert Underwood Johnson's requests for more balcony stories for *Century Magazine*, she wrote little short fiction. After she returned home she lived for twenty-four years, but in that time she produced relatively few stories and articles and only two novels, one of which may be her masterpiece.

Grace King spent a longer time writing *The Pleasant Ways of St. Médard*, and a longer time finding a publisher for it, than any of her books. Early in the century George P. Brett of the Macmillan Company urged Grace King to write a romance of the Reconstruction period. He no doubt had in mind such best sellers that exploited the sensational side of the era as Thomas Nelson Page's *Red Rock* (1898) or Thomas Dixon's *The Leopard's Spots* (1902). When she met Page in the early 1920s, she told him of her failure to produce the acceptable long novel because the publishers wanted love stories. "I know, I know," he said. "That was the

30 Grace King to George W. Cable, October 14, 1917, in George W. Cable Collection, Tulane University Library.

31 Grace King to Robert Underwood Johnson, January 15, 1906, in the *Century* Collection, New York Public Library.

fault they found with one of my novels. And I had to remedy it to get it published. Now I tell you what to do; for I did it! Just rip the story open and insert a love story. It is the easiest thing to do in the world. Get a pretty girl and name her Jeanne, that name always takes! Make her fall in love with a Federal officer and your story will be printed at once! The publishers are right; the public wants love stories. Nothing easier than to write them. You do it! You can do it! Don't let your story fail!" [32]

But she was not the sort to bow to what the public wanted. She was an honest realist and in *The Pleasant Ways of St. Médard* an autobiographical realist. To her the Reconstruction period was one of cruel memories of economic struggle and humiliation rather than love stories between northerners and southerners or repressive measures of one race against another. She resisted Brett's request for a romance and began her unromantic novel in the hope that it would partially satisfy him. She rewrote the novel five times trying to suit him, a process that, she said, "consumed years of my life & bled me of spirit & energy." The novel still met with rejection. The manuscript gathered dust for several years until 1913, when she took a trip to England with other members of her family. She left the manuscript with an agent in London, who passed it to Edward Garnett, the critic. He was deeply impressed, but he allowed years to pass before he published his views on the novel. In an article for the *Atlantic Monthly* for February, 1916, he mentioned it with the highest praise, assuming that by that time it must have been published. After discussing Willa Cather's *O Pioneers!* he wrote: "Even higher, in its literary art, must we rank Grace King's *The Pleasant Ways of St. Médard*, a story rare in its historical significance. This poignant lament for the South, at the close of the Civil War, rehearses a woman's lingering memories of the charm and grace of the New Orleans atmosphere, and of the poignant humiliation suffered by a ruined family. Will not its exquisite shades of feeling, delicate in vibrating sadness, give this novel a permanent place as an American literary classic?"

Grace King was elated. She wrote him that "Your praise of The Pleasant Ways of St. Médard has created quite a sensation here in New Orleans. I am constantly asked about it and even new orders for the

32 *Memories of a Southern Woman of Letters*, 378.

book have been sent to me." She added what was perhaps quite true, that "your praise is the greatest compliment my writing has ever received." [33] She hoped that this would change the attitude of Mr. Brett, but it did not; and perhaps he was commercially wise since the novel would make few profits even when it was published by Henry Holt and Company in 1916. There were three small printings, and despite the inconspiciuous sales, the notices it received were rewarding. A reviewer in the *Dial*, Chicago, took issue with Garnett's calling the book a "lament"; the tone to him was a positive one: "These sketches have the charm of 'Il Penseroso' rather than the bitterness of woe. And out of the ruins of health, and wealth, and aristocratic assurance rises Character in these pages—indomitable, indestructible. Such a result is not a defeat, it is the highest victory attainable by humanity. I close this volume with a sense of elation—with that intellectual salute that moral victories receive." [34]

An equally perceptive reviewer in the *New York Times Book Review* also recognized Grace King's tendency to reject standard narrative technique in her emphasis on character: "She cares little . . . for the story as a story, that she wishes to tell, and she is interested in what her people do or say or think only as it furnishes a means for the portrayal of them, for making them seem living, feeling, suffering, enjoying beings. . . . She is contemptuous, too, of the artful aid of dramatic situations, the reader's suspense, and cumulative interest. But she can make a character alive in a single sentence, she can paint it with subtle shadings, she can make it respond to its surroundings with every faint minor chord or sharp, high note of human suffering or joy. And not only can she thus depict individuals, but equally subtle and effective is her pen when it is busied with a social order, a community, a regime." [35]

The Pleasant Ways is as genuine a picture of the true tenor of life in the Reconstruction South as we have. It is a moving document of the struggle of a white family to reestablish itself and, in the chapter "Jerry," the struggle of a black family to face the precarious world of independence.

33 Grace King to Edward Garnett, February 16, 1916, Academic Center Library, University of Texas, Austin.

34 *Dial*, Chicago, September 21, 1916.

35 *New York Times Book Review* (August 27, 1916).

Early in 1917 George W. Cable wrote Grace King an appreciative note on *The Pleasant Ways*, which she answered with genuine warmth and friendliness (See p. 402). In 1915, when she heard him speak before the Louisiana Historical Society she had lost much of her animosity toward him. Her account of the reading he gave suggests that, like other New Orleanians that evening, she was ready to be reconciled with the charming old man who had done so much to bring fame to the city: "Many of us never dreamed the day would come when we would shake hands with Cable. He told us a little story of a Confederate who served in the war and was wounded. It was beautifully written and really the most compelling little incident I have ever heard. The hall was packed. When he finished everybody stood up, and I never heard such applause. I am so glad that at last he got that compliment from New Orleans. He deserved it, not only as tribute to his genius, but as compensation for the way we had treated him. I am glad. He is an old man, very picturesque, very sad, with beautiful manners." [36]

Her sincerity here is unquestioned, but as Edmund Wilson has pointed out in *Patriotic Gore*, she does not mention this conciliatory attitude of her later years in her *Memories of a Southern Woman of Letters.*[37] Why did she choose to leave the hatchet unburied in the final statement of her career? The answer may be found in the ambivalent attitudes that she held toward all the forces that worked to the making of her personality. She loved her family deeply, but never hesitated to quarrel with her brothers or sisters; she disliked the North, but made some of her best friends there and depended on them to promote her career; she loved the South, but had strong misgivings about the thoughtlessness of southern men to women; she loved France but saw it steeped in corruption. From the beginning she admired Cable for his ability, but condemned him for what she considered his disloyalty to his own people. She might let her admiration for Cable's ability show itself in a passing interview, but she may have thought that such admiration in her autobiography would neutralize the outrage that first drove her to her pen. Take away her emotional drive of 1884 and you take away much of Grace King's own symbolic character. For Cable had indeed failed to conform to the ideal

36 Guyol, "A Southern Author in Her New Orleans Home," 372.
37 Edmund Wilson, *Patriotic Gore* (New York, 1962), 575.

of the white patrician, who wished to maintain his power. Grace King's refusal to agree with Richard Watson Gilder had been a solemn and symbolic act, and if she later called herself young and foolish in making an emotional statement against Cable, she did not mean to say that she retracted the essential outrage. Her career itself had been generated by that fine anger, and she never really changed her mind, although she might well have been moved to applaud the aged Cable in New Orleans.

Late in her career she published *Creole Families of New Orleans* (1921), an unusual attempt to interpret the history of the city in the experience of the distinguished French and Spanish families who were its leaders in the eighteenth and nineteenth centuries. This is the study of how the generations of a small number of families flourished and contributed to the development of New Orleans before the Creole culture was gradually overwhelmed by the growth of the great American city. One of her best portraits is that of Bernard de Marigny, a man who never achieved national prominence but who remained the ideal Creole of his era, the representative man of early New Orleans. Marigny was at once the committed public official, the planter, the soldier, and the man who knew how to live well and entertain with lavishness. He was the favorite aristocrat of early nineteenth-century Louisiana. In her profiles of the various worthies of this volume, Grace King raised the tedious study of genealogy, or facts about the dead, to the status of living history and literature.

In spite of the quality of *The Pleasant Ways of St. Médard* and *Creole Families*, they did not receive the mild national and even international recognition of her early writing. Her final novel, *La Dame de Sainte Hermine* (1924), a historical romance about a woman sent against her will to New Orleans in the eighteenth century, was generally ignored. It was the kind of competent fiction that might have become successful in the 1890s or perhaps in the 1930s. The novel was as good as many successful ones of those two eras, and no one could say that the author was not a major authority on the historical background of her subject. But the apparent failure of *Sainte Hermine* was another of the series of disappointments by which she measured out the years of the twentieth century.

There was one major compensation, and that was the high regard in which her own city and state held her. Because she represented so well the Louisiana establishment (which George W. Cable did not), she attained a kind of recognition as literary heroine of the state. During the twenties few of her books were purchased or read in New Orleans, an irony of which she had long been aware; nevertheless, she was well known on all levels of the intellectual life of Louisiana. She had written texts for the students; she was a patroness and occasional lecturer at Tulane University, from which she had received an honorary degree in 1915; Louisiana State University named a dormitory in her honor. She had been for many years one of the driving forces of the Louisiana Historical Society.

Grace King had always considered the social side of the literary life of the highest importance. She was one of the small number of American women who have had the salon sense, who have fostered literary thought in a community and have kept respectable society from going to seed intellectually. To the end of her life she was known for her Friday afternoons that attracted interesting New Orleanians or interesting outsiders to her Greek revival house on Coliseum Place, with its columned galleries and its high-ceilinged drawing room with elaborate Victorian rosewood furniture and dazzling prisms. She had not learned the salon idea in France from Madame Blanc or the Baronne Blaze de Bury; in her youth it had flourished on a small scale in New Orleans as a part of its own French tradition.

In her seventies Grace King was a figure of the genteel past in a city that in the 1920s was attracting some of the most vigorous modern writers. She then stood as a learned sybil whom it was doubtless a pleasure to meet and consult over a cup of tea. As Charles Dudley Warner had insisted in years past, she had her prejudices. She took an immediate dislike to Joseph Hergesheimer, whom she privately scorned as a writer for the *Saturday Evening Post.* Once, looking at the furnishings of the King drawing room, he offended her by asking, "Where did you pick up all these beautiful old things?" [38] Just as easily she might befriend younger authors and invite them to tea or dinner to see what they were made of. Both Sherwood Anderson and Edmund Wilson met

38 Edmund Wilson to Robert Bush, July 20, 1970.

her during these latter days of her career. When she invited him for tea, Sherwood Anderson wrote somewhat shyly: "I should have called upon you before but that I was somewhat afraid. You see I thought you might possibly think me terrible since I have often been pictured as being.

"On the other hand I have admired you as a sincere craftsman and have thought it too bad that people really interested in the same elusive crafts should not have met.

"The tea idea frightens me a little. Before I say anything definite about it may I not come to call on you." [39]

Apparently he called on her and presented one of his recent volumes, probably *A Story Teller's Story* (1924). She was extravagant in her praise of the work, calling it "overwhelming." "You have a pen of iron," she wrote, "& you use it like a giant. The reviewers are right in their estimate of you. Poignantly sad & marvelously beautiful. I must read it over again. What a book! What a book!" [40] He answered:

> I am sure you cannot know how much pleasure your kind little note gave me. We, of a younger generation of writers in America, have been such truculent fellows. There has been so much of meeting flair with flair.
>
> Always however I have known and loved a gentler tribe of the ink party here—of which you, in my mind, have always been one—and have hoped some day to merit what would make me acceptable to gentler people too.
>
> I thank you more than you can perhaps realize for liking my book and telling me so charmingly.[41]

In 1926 through their mutual friend Lyle Saxon, Grace King met Edmund Wilson, whom she invited to dinner; but he sent his regrets since it was the very day he had planned to leave New Orleans. In a letter he reassured her, "Altogether I left New Orleans with the greatest reluctance!—I can't tell you how much I enjoyed your book; I believe I learned more about the South from it—not merely from the point of view

39 Sherwood Anderson to Grace King, November 24, 1924, in Grace King Papers.

40 King to Anderson, undated, *ca.* December, 1924, in the Sherwood Anderson Papers, Newberry Library, Chicago.

41 Anderson to King, December 11, 1924, in Grace King Papers.

of information but from that of dramatic communication of the spirit and ideas of society—than from any other book I've read." [42] He referred to *New Orleans, the Place and the People.*

In the late 1920s, when Grace King was partially forgotten outside Louisiana, Macmillan and Company took some interest in her forthcoming memoirs. Her experience went back to the Civil War and the occupation of New Orleans. She had had important friends in Charles Gayarré, Charles Dudley Warner, Mark Twain, Frederick E. Church, Julia Ward Howe, Joaquin Miller, Hamilton Wright Mabie, Henry Mills Alden, and Madame Blanc. She had met many other figures like Augustin Daly, William Gillette, and William Dean Howells. There would be a value in her comments on these personalities from her southern vantage point. She had a wealth of materials for a volume of literary memoirs, which she labored to complete before her time ran out, for the book was published posthumously as she herself seems to have feared. *Memories of a Southern Woman of Letters* (1932) has since served frequently as a source of biographical information. As autobiography it attempts to tell the reader more about Grace King's friends than about herself, and this apparently was her aim in writing it.

The volume was received as the swan song it was, the recollections of a representative of the genteel world that was largely in eclipse in 1932. Unfortunately it was not the brilliant work it might have been; it brought out the polite side of Grace King the lady rather than the perceptive and critical writer at her best. At least two reviewers mentioned that her comments on the important people she had met were conventional. Jonathan Daniels spoke of her building a "book of shadows" which were resurrected "in politeness but seldom into life." He admired her early narrative of the escape from New Orleans, but added, "In her descriptions of men and places, she is both hurried and stereotyped. All must go in." [43] The *Times Literary Supplement* objected that "she is so enthusiastic about everyone she knows that her pages rather lack salt." [44] Agnes Repplier found similar fault with the volume, but having written of Philadelphia with the affection and knowledge that Grace King wrote

42 Edmund Wilson to Grace King, April 11, 1926, in Grace King Papers.
43 Jonathan Daniels, *Saturday Review of Literature*, IX (September 10, 1932), 88.
44 *Times Literary Supplement* (December 8, 1932), 945.

of New Orleans, she paid her the final high compliment of her career: "Of her own work she speaks with modesty and reserve; yet it merited the enthusiasm with which it was received. Her stories were well-written, and deal with a world she knew. Her 'New Orleans' is as good a piece of municipal history as any American writer has given us. It has never been superseded, and is not likely to be superseded by anything better." [45]

The Creole city that had maintained much of its individuality by resisting total Americanization since 1803, was the place for which Grace King had held a lifelong affection. Ever since the disaster of conquest and the ordeal of Federal occupation the city had been an object for her strongest sympathies. It had been her grand theme, and in portraying its life she had set forth her affectionate and defiant personality. When she was in Paris in 1892 Grace King met the elderly Comtesse Tascher de la Pagerie, whom she saw as a vital and enduring relic of the court of Louis Napoleon. She wrote later that although the men of the Second Empire were dead and forgotten, "Not so the women. The cup of sorrow, on the contrary, contains a drop of immortality for women, and it is not too much to say of them that there are but few who after disaster do not live for the betterment of the worldly reputation of the cause for which they suffered." [46] The parallel with the emotional drive of her own life must have been quite evident to her when she wrote the lines. Her city had known disaster during her sensitive childhood. As a youth she experienced the consequences of that disaster, and the creative energies of her maturity were spent defending the character of New Orleans and upholding the quality of its traditions.

45 *Commonweal*, XVII (November 16, 1932), 83.
46 *Harper's Bazar*, XXVI (September 20, 1893), 807.

II FROM *MEMORIES OF A SOUTHERN WOMAN OF LETTERS*

THE MOST VALUABLE part of Grace King's reminiscences is the beginning, in which she recalls the impact of the events of May, 1862, when the Union navy arrived at New Orleans to force the city to submit to occupation. In preparation for this the Confederate powers had put the torch to hundreds of bales of cotton along the wharves to prevent them and other supplies from falling to the enemy. The young girl of ten, watching from the bedroom window, terrified by the sounds of explosions within the city and the sight of the fires, could conceive of the approach of the enemy only in terms of the pictures of slaughter she had seen in an illustrated Bible.

Two other future American authors witnessed the beginning of Federal occupation from separate points of view, but both were young men who could analyze the events more objectively than the girl. George W. Cable, still a civilian in New Orleans, closed up the office where he was employed and went to the riverside to observe the burning cotton. He describes this event as a historian would—the hundreds of drays bringing the cotton, the glare from miles of flame along the wharves. He observed that the Louisianians within the city were distraught and angry, convinced that their cause had been betrayed. When the Federal forces arrived he saw two Union naval officers walk without guards through a hostile, jeering mob to City Hall to demand the surrender of the city. To Cable, who could be objective despite his Confederate sympathies, "It was one of the bravest deeds I ever saw done." [1]

John William DeForest, a Union army captain, describes the reception as a mixed one. There were sneers and curses from the "roughs," but several people showed respect for the flag and indicated their loyalty. He saw "a handsome, grey-whiskered gentleman and a very handsome lady, evidently his daughter, study our faces sympathetically and then salute the flag with an expression of solemn joy." [2] The loyalty to the North on the part of this couple may have suggested to him the theme of his novel *Miss Ravenel's Conversion from Secession to Loyalty* (1867). Cable would serve in the Confederate army, but in the years that followed he would assume a fully conciliatory attitude toward the Union. Grace King, whose girlhood would be marked by the privations of war, was to nourish through life her piety, in the sense of *pietas*, her unchanging fidelity to family, to New Orleans, and to the South.

1 George W. Cable, "New Orleans before the Capture," *Century*, XXIX (January, 1885), 922.

2 John William DeForest, *A Volunteer's Adventure: A Union Captain's Record of the Civil War*, ed. James H. Croushore (New Haven, 1946), 18–19.

The past is our only real possession in life. It is the one piece of property of which time cannot deprive us; it is our own in a way that nothing else in life is. It never leaves our consciousness. In a word, we are our past; we do not cling to it, it clings to us.

Innumerable filaments of memory fasten it to us, and we go through life with them dangling behind us. The memories do not date merely from our childhood. They go back far beyond our experience, out of sight of it, to fasten upon parents and grandparents. Blessed are the children who have parents and grandparents who can relate the stories of their own pasts and so connect the younger with the older memories, lighting a taper to the imagination that never goes out, no matter what extinguishes the great lights of acquired memories, but that, on the contrary, flickers away persistently until, as by a miracle, with time these filaments increase in brilliance and color, so that at the end of a long life we see them shining through the vista of years like beacons.

Many a grandmother and grandfather are still carrying such tapers set alight by their grandmothers and grandfathers, and will live in their illumination to the end of their lives.

I was particularly blessed in this regard. My mother, a charming raconteuse, witty and inexhaustible in speech, never displayed these qualities so well as when talking to her children. We were never beyond or above that entertainment. "Tell us about when you were a little girl," was our prayer to her, and she loved to do so, dropping into our minds the never-forgetable picture of a pale little girl with white hair and eyes ever reddened by sties, always sickly but always full of fun, and quick to see the funny side of her little life; the only Protestant in the school where she was a day boarder, picking up French as she went along, conforming in everything to her Creole and Catholic mates, even to allowing herself to be prepared for her first communion, when at last she felt forced to acknowledge the truth. "But, *mon père*, I am a Protestant!"

"What a pity," said the good priest placidly, and dropped her from the class.

She drank wine for breakfast and practised her piano on Sunday as though she too were a good little Creole. Her handsome, good-natured father, who did not mind breaking rules, would have it that she must go to the theater with him every night, his wife not being fond of the theater. Of course nothing pleased her more. She saw all the famous actors of the day who came to New Orleans: the elder Booth, Macready, McCullough, the beautiful Alice Placide; and she met the famous impresario, Caldwell,[3] who knew all the plays and all the actors and actresses and impersonated their rôles delightfully. And of all this she told her children. Everything happened to her so beautifully. She never forgot anything funny or pleasant that had come to her; and her children never found anything that happened to them worth while, so tame and listless their lives seemed in contrast.

The grandmother's stories were quite different. Huguenot by descent, she came from Georgia, of an austere family. Her memories and stories were never amusing; but they were interesting. All about the Revolutionary War, and General Marion, who was related to her mother; and of Continental soldiers, and jayhawkers, and the sinfulness of New Orleans when she came to the city as a bride, fresh from the piety and civilization of Georgia, which she represented—for so she remembered it—as an earthly paradise.

The home in which memory began to make their first gatherings was a plain dwelling of the usual prosperous American lawyer. It seemed ordinary in comparison with the rich houses of the neighborhood, set in the midst of great gardens. But it had a distinct personality in memory. It was three stories high, with broad galleries in front. There were a good garden and grass plot with a back yard, provided with the usual dependencies of the time, servants' quarters of course, outhouses, a gigantic cistern, and a great cellar of plastered brick.

The first story of the house was devoted to a large drawing-room, called "the parlor," whose folding doors opened into the dining room, with its huge sideboard, and its long table in the center. The walls were plentifully supplied with pictures in gilt frames. A majestic-looking bookcase packed with books stood opposite the sideboard.

The upper stories held the bedrooms of the family and of the French governess, who was made one of us. The rooms of the father and mother, the front rooms of the second floor, were always held in awe by the children, and we avoided them as much as possible.

3 Both Junius Brutus Booth (1796–1852) and William Charles Macready (1793–1873) were English. John Edward McCullough (1832–85), known for Shakespearean roles, was Irish. Alice Placide, niece of Henry Placide, was well known in New York following the Civil War. James H. Caldwell (1793–1863) built and managed the St. Charles Theatre, New Orleans, in 1853.

The third story dwells in a bright light always—the grandmother's apartment—her realm and the children's. The rooms, large and commodious, seem in memory plain and bare. The room used as the nursery had none of the prettiness of the modern nursery. Two plain little beds, some chairs, and a table furnished all that at that time was deemed necessary—for boys. The little girls were kept in the room of the grandmother. They slept in what was then known as a "trundle-bed," that was by day rolled, or trundled, under the great mahogany bed of the grandmother.

The furniture of this room all came from the grandmother's home in Georgia—the square-looking bureau, with its small mirror and glass handles to the drawers; a cavernous-looking *armoire*, a treasure cave of precious relics. On the walls hung the portraits of the dead-and-gone grandfather, a handsome man of about forty, with the pleasant face of a father who would take his little girl every night to the theater with him, and who loved the good things to eat and drink that played a part in the spirited stories about him.

Far away in a dark corner, on the floor, was a taper floating in its bowl of oil. Its wick flaring up and down during the dreadful black nights used to frighten the little girls in their trundle-beds, who imagined it was the eye of God watching them!

After we were waked in the morning and dressed, the good grandmother would range us on our knees alongside her bed and make us say our prayers in unison, standing behind us to correct at the first mistake. How she managed it I cannot say, but she made us feel that God was listening to us, and that He could and would make us the good children we petitioned to be, and bless our long list of relatives carefully recited, winding up with the general petition for "all our kind friends." After our prayers we would read a verse in the Bible, standing beside a low table, each spelling out the words of the Great Book. On Sundays a little catechism was added to these rites, and the verse of a hymn; and then we were sent to Sunday school.

The light filaments that hold this memory seem to break here, and evening comes dangling down to us. We go to bed; the lights are put out; and we are left to ourselves. The heavy tread of the father sounds downstairs, and his sonorous voice. He and the mother go to the upper gallery for their after-dinner talk; and black night hides all the rest.

Here memory yields a never-to-be-forgotten picture. I recall standing one evening at the side window of Grandmother's room looking at surging flames rising higher and higher through black smoke, up into the sky. Alarm bells were ringing all over the city, crowds were running through the streets below, shouting and screaming. The flames would die down every now and then, only to start up fiercer than ever, lighting up the heavens. The city shook with explosions. I knew, but only vaguely, that the city was being prepared for surrender to the "enemy," as Grandmother called our foes. Their gunboats were crowding up the river, so I heard round about me. All the shipping on the river was being set on fire, and the cotton in the warehouses and presses; and barrels of whisky were being broken open and the whisky poured into the gutters.

I looked with stupid interest out of the window. Will they kill us all when they take the city, I wondered vaguely, recalling pictures of captured cities of the Bible, where men and women were cut through with spears and swords, and children were dashed against walls. But the window was firmly closed, and the children were put to bed by a nurse, quietly and methodically as usual.

By morning only a heavy smoke covered the heavens. That night the parents talked in subdued tones on the upper front gallery. Grief and humiliation made their faces look strange and different.

Another memory comes. The enemy were in possession of the city. Squads of soldiers marched through the streets, with guns on their shoulders. The children and servants peeped through the windows at them. The "enemy!" Curious things to us. Our elders talked in low voices inside closed rooms. Neighbors slipped in and out of the back gate and up the servants' staircase.

All lessons were stopped—the governess was among the talkers in the closed rooms. Children were kept strictly within doors. Not a child was allowed to play in the front yard, although the weather was fine and the sun shone brilliantly. Mamma was pale and excited; Grandmamma, calm and dignified, expressing complete reliance on God.

Some days—it might have been a week—later one of the squads of soldiers marching through the street stopped at our house, entered the gate and the front door without ringing, and walked up-stairs behind an officer in glittering uniform, who was consulting a list in his hand.

Mamma went to meet him, I as usual holding to her dress. She held her head stiff and high, and spoke haughtily. The officer, holding his head as stiffly, told her that the house was to be searched as it had been reported to headquarters that there were arms concealed in great quantities in it. Assenting, she herself opened the door of her bed-chamber and stood quietly by while her *armoire* and bureau drawers were opened and the contents thrown on the floor.

The officer asked for my father, and was told that he was not at home. The sanctuary of the grandmother was gone through, and the soldiers, staring, searched down-stairs.

My mother, quite herself by this time, called the two little boys to her and told them in a low voice to go at once to their father's office and tell him what had happened.

Memory holds to the picture of them. The two little tow-headed fellows standing before her in their short pants as she gave them the message, stolid, cool, and intelligent, walking out of the room afterwards with perfect self-possession. They gave their message, the sentinels at the gate letting them pass without a look at them.

My father did not come home again, but escaped from the city that night.

A long, dreary time passed, days that memory did not take notice of, but what afterward, as we learned, were used by the "enemy" in taking possession of the city. The flames and smoke were quenched on the levee. There were no more secret talks behind closed doors. The neighbors stayed at home, and their children also. An attempt was made to resume lessons, but the governess was forced to go home, and she stayed there. The grandmother became more dignified and serious than ever; the mother more excited and animated.

At last one day there came into the house in the dark of the evening a visitor whom the children knew as one of the dependents of the mother, who had maintained an army of them, shabby old people whom we did not like. This one, however, was a favorite. She was always good-natured, her handsome face dimpling with fun and good humor. Her poverty seemed to bring her a lot of funny stories that she loved to tell. She was a working woman, but did not show it. Energetic, strong, and hearty, the occasion had come for her to make a return for past favors, and she had a suggestion to make in the family councils.

My mother had to leave the city to join my father in the Confederacy, but she could not leave without a passport from the power in possession. Her one-time dependent was now in easy circumstances, well dressed, and, according to her story, influential at headquarters. The story was amusing.

As soon as the city fell, she saw her opportunity to open a boarding-house for Federal officers. Handsome houses, well furnished, abandoned by their owners, were numerous and cheap. She made her choice, secured what she required, and according to her plans filled her house with officers who for her beautiful rooms and luxurious table well furnished with wine were willing to pay the high price she asked. One of the officers was a handsome, stout quartermaster, devoted to the pleasures of the table. He soon became her devoted.

Her proposition to my mother was very simple—to coax a passport out of this officer. She was positive she could do it; and she did, bringing the paper to my mother a day or two later—but with a dreadful condition attached. Certain necessary formalities must be obtained from the Commanding General! [4] The influence of the friend ended with the quartermaster. My mother had to undertake the rest of the task.

Impossible! But impossible also to stay in New Orleans under military rule with nothing but Confederate money. My grandmother offered herself for the mission, but she was delicate and old—at least sixty at that time, plain and simple and uncompromising. No, she would not do for such a mission. My mother must do it, and she could do it. She was not afraid of anything or anybody, and she, if anyone, could face the Commanding General in his headquarters. In short, she eventually attempted that which was really a descent into the lower regions, an interview with the Prince of Darkness himself! My mother, who indeed knew not fear, only abhorrence of the enemy, really accomplished her purpose.

We children watched her set out, dressed carefully as for church—silk dress, mantilla, pretty bonnet—it had big pink roses and was tied under the chin with wide light-green ribbon—lace veil, and parasol, her head held high, and the usual bright smile on her face.

She returned looking just the same. We rushed to band around her while she related her adventure to the grandmother. When she had come to the dreadful abode of the Ogre, as the General was currently called, she boldly walked past the sentinel at the door, and by the sentinel at the foot of the stairway, and as boldly walked past the sentinel at the door of the office, which was the great front room of the handsome, confiscated house, and sent in her name by another sentinel, asking to see the General on business. The man who took the message looked doubtfully and sympathetically at her, as did the sentinel at the door of the room.

Sitting behind a great table with his pistols on it, the portentous figure

4 General Benjamin Franklin Butler (1818–93) was military governor of New Orleans, May–December, 1862.

of the Ogre scowled at her. In a loud, rough voice he asked her name, and when she gave it, he broke out in a tirade against her husband in the Confederacy and all men like him who had run away from the city. She took the abuse standing, and then in a pleasant society voice stated her business, which started him off again on his famous dictum about "she-adders." She turned in the midst of it and calmly told the sentinel to bring her a chair. He did it, to her surprise. She sat down and prepared to listen comfortably to her scolding. But the General curtly dismissed her with an emphatic refusal of her request. She arose with a polite smile and bow and left the room.

Outside the door stood an officer in full uniform, another general. Easily and courteously he spoke to her, listened to her request, and promised to send the papers she required; which he did in the course of the day.

The narrative finished, the preparations for departure began. Trunks were bought and packed, the children taking hand in the doing, each contributing something, a toy, a picture book, to take into THE CONFEDERACY.

However, the great event thrusting itself up in memory is not the excitement of the preparations, but the departure itself. How dark and mysterious and full of apprehension it was! Even Grandmamma showed nervousness. The night was dark. In the dimly lighted street two carriages stood before the garden gate, and at a little distance the cart for the trunks. Neighbors and friends thronged about us as we left the house. The sentinel withdrew to a distance. The older children were lifted up into the carriage. Mamma and Grandmamma followed and took their seats. The two Negro maids and the younger children and the baby were put into the other carriage, and after them baskets and bundles of all sorts. As we were driving away, someone thrust into my hand a rag doll "for you to play with," and then we were off. The doll, ugly, heavy, and cumbersome, was hideously dressed, but I eagerly clasped it to my bosom, and day and night kept it in my arms, loving it as only little girls love ugly dolls. By the time we reached the plantation, its seams had begun to open, and we found that it was stuffed with Confederate money, large and small bills, with an address to some soldier in the army of North Louisiana. The money was sent to him, and I never had another doll!

The house was left dark and gloomy, with the doors wide open. Nothing could be seen in the garden, but the perfume of the yellow jasmine came to us in farewell.

We drove through dark and ugly streets to the levee and stopped at a landing where a steamboat was moored, with steam up. The river was black, and we children were frightened. We clung to the carriage and had to be lifted out bodily by "hands" from the boat, who carried us up the gang-plank and the steep steps to the deck and deposited us in a large cabin. The rest of the family followed close after us. Grandmamma was given a chair, and we children clustered around her closely. I can see her plainly, sad and dignified in her dark dress and black silk mantilla, veil thrown back and bonnet strings tied under the chin.

Mamma was elsewhere, busy about the trunks which had been brought up and placed at the other end of the boat. The Negro nurses had disappeared into the cabins, with the babies. A bell rang and the steamboat started, the paddles moving noiselessly. The lights were turned down. We could barely see one another. Suddenly a shot rang out. We all started!

"What's that?" demanded Grandmamma sternly.

"Confederate guerrillas," was the careless answer of the Captain, standing near.

"But they might hit us and kill us!" exclaimed Grandmamma.

"Oh, no! We are out of the range of their rifles. They always shoot at us when we leave the city; but they never hit us."

Nevertheless, Grandmamma gathered us all around her and held us as we steamed along through the firing that was kept up for some time. We were frightened, but as I recollect it, we did not whimper, although we knew that we might be sent to Heaven by one of the rifle shots.

The little boys wriggled away and went off to stand by Mamma, who was watching the trunks being searched. They were rudely pulled open, and their contents thrown on the floor, while she was cross-questioned by the young officer in charge.

Suddenly from the end of the boat came loud voices in expostulation, prayers, and even sobs, interrupted by my mother's gentle supplications. Contraband had been found in one of the trunks belonging to the two handsome, gay Creole ladies who had come on the boat just after us. They were prettily dressed, and in their vivacious way were most attractive. But as the boat was slowly turned into the bank of the river, their supplications were changed to cries of abuse and vituperation. The boat was inexorably stopped at the bank, and the ladies, now sobbing violently, were put ashore with their trunks.

My mamma, who had given her word of honor not to take contraband articles into the Confederacy, was not disturbed about her emptied trunks, but came back to us terribly wrought up over the fate of the Creole ladies landed so ruthlessly in the black night on a bare river bank. The officer, the mate who had given the order, was as indifferent to her as he had been to the Creole ladies.

After this we were all put to bed without being undressed, and we fell asleep. In the gray dawn we were taken up out of our beds, stood upon the floor, and marched to where Mamma and Grandmamma stood with the Negro maids and the babies. We felt the boat turning in toward the bank of the river. A bump that nearly threw us off our feet announced the landing, and we all moved out of the cabin on to the deck and clambered down the little companionway to the broad lower deck that lay alongside the muddy bank, the yellow water of the river running between. Nothing more than this could be seen, for it was still dark. The skies were black over us, and it began to rain.

Planks were put out, and Mamma was led across by the Captain. The little girls were carried over by the crew, the Captain taking the little boys by the hand.

While we were crossing on one plank, our luggage, trunks, baskets, and two barrels were taken over on the other, rolling alongside of us. Mamma stood on the bank to count them, the Captain still at her side.

"But those—those barrels—do not belong to me!" she exclaimed, pointing to the barrels being quickly rolled to land.

The Captain pressed her arm significantly. "Hush!" he whispered. "Hurry up there," he shouted in his loud voice, followed by the voice of the little steamboat mate who shouted at the crew, cursing and hurrying them. But Mamma said the Captain bent to her ear and whispered so that she alone could hear, "I am a Confederate!"

It was one of Mamma's best stories in her long after-life, a story that she embellished and improved in her own inimitable way, that during the darkest hours of the Confederacy, when the levees had been cut as a means of defense against invasion, and when fevers were raging on the plantation and all the medicines had given out, with of course no hope of getting more through the deed of contraband established by the enemy, she, needing flour, opened the barrel that was not hers, and inside found securely packed in the flour a miraculous store of all the medicine she needed—quinine, calomel, morphine, blue mass, etc., and underneath a store of precious chloroform, whose value to the Confederacy could not be expressed in earthly terms. The chloroform was instantly dispatched to the nearest camp with the over-supply of other drugs, a God-sent and mystifying blessing.

The boat backed out and left us. Nothing was to be seen around us but a great stretch of bare fields from which the cane had been cut. The heavy clouds overhead began to drop their moisture in a soft drizzle of rain. Grandmamma, with a hopeless look on her face, ordered the maids to keep the babies well covered up.

"We are on some plantation," said Mamma cheerfully. "If we could only get across the fields!" She looked about anxiously and finally added, "I see someone! A cane cart and Negroes!" We all looked where she pointed. Far, far away, forms could be seen, tiny moving figures.

Mamma began to call. The children joined with her in their squealing voices. The maids raised their musical "halloo—oo!" No response from the minute figures at work. Then Grandmamma, with a resolute hand, undid her mantilla and waved it. Everyone then waved something. At last, slowly and sluggishly, a cane cart advanced towards us. When it came near, the driver, a heavy-footed, muddy Negro, got down from it. Mamma questioned him, but could get nothing out of him to help us. She finally drew her purse out of her pocket and paid him to go to the "big house" and tell his master about us.

Again we waited in the mud and rain. Then across the fields came a carriage, driven rapidly, followed by two cane carts. The master of the plantation, a genial, ebullient Creole, who was on horseback, came forward as if to greet old friends. There was no time to talk. We were loaded into the carriage, the luggage and maids into the cane carts, and were driven briskly down an avenue of oaks to a splendid-looking white house. It was now barely daylight, but the ladies of the house were waiting on the gallery to welcome us. Black coffee was passed to the elders as soon as we entered the hallway, and there was hot milk for the children, and with this hospitality all possible exclamations of commiseration and sympathy. We were led upstairs into two handsome bedrooms all prepared, with fires burning in the grates.

As soon as breakfast was over—it was a long-drawn-out meal on account of Mamma's interesting talk—arrangements were made for the continuation of our journey, in spite of the kind urgings to stay two or three days until we were all rested. But Mamma was firm, she must get to the plantation and deliver her charge to her husband, who had laid his commands upon her when he left the city, "Join me as soon as you can on the plantation."

She had but a vague idea about how to get there, knowing only that she must get to Bayou Plaquemine[5] and there take a boat to the plantation. A carriage and a cane cart were therefore engaged from a neighboring small plantation. They arrived during the morning. The servants and larger children were put into the cane cart, together with the luggage. The rest of us were stowed in the carriage, which was drawn by only one horse.

Our route lay up the river, on the great road inside the high levee, which was like a wall between us and the water. The rain had stopped, the wind blew clear from the north, and the ground had dried. As the cart lumbered on, we children were let out and allowed to run along on the top of the levee where there was a small path. This was great fun for the two boys and the two little girls. Sometimes we came to great pecan trees shedding their nuts on the ground. We gathered them and carried them to the carriage, and poured them into Mamma's lap. She enjoyed our fun as much as we did, and would have joined in but for the baby on her lap. Grandmamma even smiled and revived in the bright sunlight.

That night we came to another great plantation, where we drove into the broad avenue confidently and were taken in as at the first plantation, like old friends, and treated hospitably. The next morning was a repetition of the day before, except that we went faster, Mamma vetoing the dallying by the wayside to please the children. Then the weather grew sharply cold, and the sky dark and threatening. We were all looking forward impatiently, and the children crossly, to our night's rest. Our good old Negro driver passed small houses and plantations, and drove on until he reached the long avenue of trees that led to some great residence. But as we drove up we saw that there were no lights in the house. The windows were all closed, and also the great front doors. The driver got out and rapped on the door. There was no response. Not only were there no lights anywhere around the house, but no signs of life. The Negro quarters in the distance were bright and active enough, however. Mamma directed the driver to go there and fetch someone to her. He returned with the housekeeper, the servant of confidence. She explained that the master and mistress had gone away and left everything in her charge. She had locked up the house and was living in the "quarters."

Mamma demanded hospitality for the night. The woman hesitated. Mamma insisted imperiously, offering to pay for her trouble in opening

5 Bayou Plaquemine, Iberville Parish, was a distributary of the Mississippi at Plaquemine, whence it flowed to Grand River. It is now part of a waterway.

the house. Both the Negro drivers joined in, explaining our story, and how we were journeying to the ferry. She listened to them and finally agreed to accede to their persuasions; but, she explained, there was no food to be had. By this time we were unloaded from the carriage and standing on the porch. After a long time the front door was opened, and the woman stood there with a lighted candle in her hand. She was a good-looking Negro woman, neatly dressed, tall, and dignified. Taking Mamma aside, she told her in a low voice that the master and mistress and all the family had fled from the house in a panic after the death of one of the children from scarlet fever. This staggered Mamma and shook her courage. But Grandmamma intervened and asked if the house had been aired and scrubbed since the death.

"Oh, yes, Madam, I saw to that. The child died over a week ago, and we have kept the windows all open till today."

"Then," said Grandmamma decidedly, "we can go in and stay tonight without fear."

"But we have no food to give you!"

"You have hominy and milk; give us that."

We sat in the empty and deserted house, around a long, bare dining-room table, and silently ate our boiled hominy and milk. Then we were hurried off to rooms in the rear of the house and put to bed in cold sheets over which our clothes and cloaks were heaped.

Mamma had us up by daylight and ready for a start. It was bitterly cold, and we shivered miserably until the good Negro woman gave us great cups of hot milk. She was visibly uneasy and strangely serious until we got away.

The drive ended at midday at a kind of hotel facing the river, a plain, uncomfortable-looking place which, however, furnished us a good luncheon. Mamma heard here that the ferry had been burned in a recent raid by the enemy, and that she could not cross the river. This was a terrible disappointment. However, she discounted it by going at once, with the two little boys at her heels, to interview the man who owned the ferry. He confirmed the bad news and took her to the landing to show her the ferry—a long, flat boat, propelled with long oars by two men standing in the prow. It had in truth been burned.

But, as Mamma pointed out, it had been burned only at one end; and, she asked, why could we not all be put at the good end and so cross the river? The old ferryman looked at her in dismayed astonishment and shook his head.

"It might be possible," he said at length, "but I would be afraid to take the responsibility."

"I will risk it!" said Mamma. And then and there she made a bargain with him for our transfer.

Grandmamma shook her head and warned against it; but Mamma was firm. Our luggage was put in the good end of the boat and our party lined up behind it.

As the boat started, the burned end trailed in the water, whose ripples swept over it.

Two trips were made, Mamma crossing each time, back and forth. Her courage was rewarded by getting us all over safely, and the boatmen were rewarded generously for their good efforts.

We landed at a little town at the mouth of Bayou Plaquemine, a crowd of men standing around and looking in wonderment at us.

Mamma, whose wits never left her, asked for a very prominent lawyer who lived in the town. His name was well known, and a messenger was soon dispatched for him. His office was near at hand, and in a few moments he appeared, a tall, handsome man, with iron-gray hair and moustache.

Mamma explained our problem to him. His answer was prompt and definite. He would take charge of everything and would see that we should get to the plantation in safety.

Another night was spent on a plantation whose hospitality made a great impression on us. It was the largest and richest plantation in Louisiana.

The next morning arrangements were completed, and we were conveyed to a landing on the bank of a little bayou where two barges were waiting for us.

We were stowed away carefully, and started with the sure promise of reaching the plantation by nightfall. Our stalwart rowers bent their bare backs to their oars, and we started.

After the Mississippi River, the little bayou seemed no larger than a ditch. The cypress trees were thick on the banks, their long gray moss dropping almost to our heads.

Grandmamma sat in the stern of the barge, we children on the seat in front, then came the nurses and the babies. Mamma's seat was in the bow, where she could see and dominate. The luggage was in the other barge, which sank, under its load, far down in the water. The rowing was strong and steady, and we cut through the stream rapidly.

The prospect of soon being at the end of our troubles raised our spirits, and we were all laughing and chatting gayly when we came to the end of the bayou, and to the lake out of which it extended. There, on the smooth, sun-flecked surface, rode a steamboat! At the sight, a fearful silence fell upon us. The oarsmen paused, as if in a panic, and murmured their wonderment that the Yankees could have got past the town in the night.

"Go on! Go on!" commanded Mamma. "They cannot hurt us. We have passports!"

The oars dipped into the water again and our boat steered straight for the steamboat that lay across the channel. As soon as the officers saw us, we were signaled to come alongside. The boat seemed crowded with men—but they wore the gray uniform! We were safe!

As soon as we were within speaking distance, an officer questioned us —who we were—where we came from—where we were going.

This was Mamma's opportunity. She told them not only what they wanted to know, but a great deal else besides. All the news from New Orleans and what was happening under the Federal occupation, her interview with General Butler, her triumphant success in getting out of the city, telling them about our trip up the river, and, in fact, everything about us.

The officer listened with the keenest interest. Others joined him, until the side of the boat was lined with a delighted audience. They laughed at Mamma's good stories, about the women in the city, of how they would not walk under the Federal flag, and when the soldiers stationed for the purpose seized them by the arm and forcibly led them under its bright folds, they put up their parasols and lifted their skirts. On and on Mamma talked, enjoying herself as she always did when she had a good audience.

But at length our oarsmen dropped their oars again in the water and we pushed away. Grandmamma, who was a passionate newspaper reader and had brought from the city a bag full of papers, had the inspiration to hand them out to the news-famishing Confederates. They seized upon them with vociferous thanks and rushed off to read them. The officer had explained that they were only a scouting party sent out on some military quest from their camp in the swamp. We parted with an exuberant overflow of good feeling in which even the children participated.

The great round lake—it was, in fact, named "Round Lake" [6]—ended in another short bayou, which in its turn flowed, if bayous can be said to flow, into another lake, called Lake Long, which connected with another bayou, the bayou of our plantation.

By the time we entered Lake Long, the sun was sinking in a great splendor of golden and red light. We were rowing across, when with a sudden jar our skiff stopped. We had run on a shallow! In vain the oarsmen pulled to get off it; we seemed but to settle down the firmer. The skiff behind came up alongside. It too stuck fast! The oarsmen shook their heads, stood up, and all together in one boat used their oars as poles and put out all their strength in the effort to break away from the soft muddy bottom that held us fast. All of us strained, unconsciously, with them. It was in vain. Then the sun went down. For a few minutes the twilight lasted, but we could not get our boats released.

"Do you think we can get off tonight?" asked Mamma.

The oarsmen shrugged their shoulders and shook their heads doubtfully.

"But we cannot stay here all night!" she exclaimed. "Get out and see if you can't push the skiff off the bar!"

They did so. But the more they pushed, the tighter it held.

Grandmamma ordered the nurses to come closer to her, where she could spread her large shawl over the children. We crouched down at her feet and clasped our hands over her knees while she covered us with another shawl.

We were terribly serious, but not at all frightened. We knew why. Grandmamma was relying upon God for help, and secretly praying to Him. This strengthened us; we had the same confidence in her that she had in God. And she had told us often how He had stood by her and helped her through the terrible moments of her life. She was looking up with her eyes fixed upon the stars that seemed dropping down almost on top of us.

The darkness came on, blacker and thicker. The huge cypress trees on the shore of the lake seemed to advance upon us, closing us in. We little girls laid our heads upon Grandmamma's lap and closed our eyes. We were afraid of the terrible trees!

"Call! Call! Shout for help!" ordered Mamma. "Maybe someone will hear you!"

6 Round Lake is in St. Martin Parish, between Donaldsonville and New Iberia.

And the men raised their great voices, which made us feel even more afraid. But we all joined in, following Mamma's example.

"Whoo! Whooee! Whooeee!" went our cry of distress.

But the darkness only grew denser, the stars dropping closer, and the awful trees getting nearer. The servants said they could hear the alligators swimming around us, and the turtles dropping from their logs into the water.

Mamma grew angry and began scolding the oarsmen who, in truth, were as keen to get out of the lake as she was. There were no habitations on the bank to get help from, evidently no swampers or fishermen anywhere within sound of our voices.

"Oh, if God would only help us!" we little ones prayed, reinforcing Grandmamma's petitions, as we were trying to help the halloo of the oarsmen. "Only God can help us," she whispered, overwhelmed, herself, at the disaster that had overtaken us.

Everyone gave up hope, and we settled down for the night. All except Mamma. God, Himself, was not more vigilant than she.

"Listen! I hear something! Listen! Shout again as loud as you can!" And louder than ever our men shouted.

Faint, faint, far away, came a mere whisper of a cry. Then the blessed relief of the sound of oar-locks.

"Someone is coming! Someone is coming!" screamed Mamma in excitement. Our hearts stopped beating as we listened.

Yes! Yes! Someone is coming! Hailing us nearer and nearer as we listened.

"Mistress, is that you?" called out a Negro.

"Yes, yes! Here we are!" Mamma's voice choked, filled with tears of excitement.

"Master sent us. We thought we heard someone calling, and he sent us to look for you."

"Your master? Your master?" called Mamma.

"Yes, Ma'am. He's just come to the plantation. He was expecting you."

Grandmamma gave a great sigh of relief. God had not failed her. It seemed easy enough now to get over the bar and row down our bayou to the plantation; so easy that memory only holds the event and what happened afterwards—the landing at the gunwales in front of the house, being lifted and carried up the high levee where Papa stood waiting for us. After that the good supper, big fires, and soft, warm beds, where sleep came for the children to the pleasant tune of talk over what was past, at the end of which Papa related his story.

With his patience and courage gone, we heard, he lay discouraged on a hard cot in a rough kind of tavern, hopeless for news of his family, when he heard an interruption in the next room, a boisterous party of young soldiers stopping for a meal. The laughing and talking were unendurable to his nerves, when all at once he heard what made him listen, the account of a lady from New Orleans in a skiff full of children and luggage, which they had stopped, crossing the lake. The lady was wonderful with her relating of conditions in New Orleans—soldiers—Ben Butler—and all sorts of funny happenings in the captured and supposedly unhappy city. Papa sat up in his cot to listen better. Then he bounded into the next room where the young men were talking.

"That was my wife! No one could tell that story but she!"

He questioned the soldiers, got all the information he needed, jumped upon his horse, and rode through the swamp to the plantation. When night fell and still the boats did not arrive, he sent out the best oarsmen on the place in the largest skiffs to see what had happened. Fires were made and supper was prepared. And this, ever afterwards, was one of Mamma's best stories.

Mamma and Grandmamma took off their fine bonnets, and after rolling their wide strings, laid them away on the top shelf of an *armoire.* Four years later they took them out and put them on again, and the servants and children were dressed in their best clothes for the return trip to the city, but not as they had come; a little steamboat was sent for us by Papa, who had already gone to the city.

III MONSIEUR MOTTE

HER FIRST published story, "Monsieur Motte," won Grace King recognition as one of the promising new writers of the South in the late 1880s. When the story was published with three sequels, the volume received its highest praise from William Dean Howells, who wrote, in effect, that it was not the garden variety of local-color fiction, which he did not respect. He called it "a striking example of the unconscious expression of the life of a community, without the slightest effort on the part of the writer to make that life visible by exaggeration of peculiarities. There was no question here of the truth of dialect or the external characterizations of the race; the author wrote out of her own experience; this was a life she knew so thoroughly that she was not trying to exploit it in telling her story. The result, as we know, was as perfect a representation of Creole conditions and social life as Hawthorne ever made of New England. And the two results were produced exactly in the same way. Neither author used 'local color' as a varnish." [1]

One of the defects of the story in its original version in the *New Princeton Review* (January, 1886) was an excessive use of French phrases intended to give the illusion that the characters were speaking French. But the effect was that the characters spoke English decorated with the affectation of French phrases. Grace King improved the story by greatly

1 "The Editor's Study," *Harper's Magazine*, LXXXV (June, 1892), 156.

reducing these for the published volume *Monsieur Motte* (New York: Armstrong and Company, 1888). It is the revised version that has been used as copy-text for the present edition. To connect her story with its sequel she added a transitional passage of some length, which has not been included here.

It was near mid-day in June. A dazzling stream of vertical sun-rays fell into the quadrangular courtyard of the Institute St. Denis, and filled it to suffocation with light and heat. The flowers which grew in little beds, dotting the gray-flagged surface, bowed their heads under their leaves for shelter.

A thin strip of shadow, stretching from the side of the schoolhouse, began to creep over the garden, slowly following the sun in its progress past the obtruding walls of neighboring buildings, until he should disappear behind a certain square steeple far off in the distance; then the shade would entirely cover the yard; then the stars would be coming out, languid and pale; and then the fragrance of oleander and jasmine, travelling from yard to yard, would burden the air, soothing the senses in order to seduce the imagination.

Along the narrow shaded strip, quite filling it up, moved a class of girls in Indian file, their elbows scraping against the rugged bricks of the wall as they held their books up to the openings of their sun-bonnets. A murmur of rapidly articulated words, like the murmur of boiling water in a closed kettle, came from the leaves of their books, while from their hidden lips dropped disjointed fragments of "l'Histoire de France."

The foundation, as well as key-stone, of St. Denisian education, it was but natural that the examination in "l'Histoire de France, par D. Lévi Alvares, père," should fill the last days of the scholastic term; and as a prize in that exercise set the brightest crown upon the head of the victor, it was not strange that it should be conducted with such rigidity and impartiality as to demoralize panic-stricken contestants whose sex usually warranted justice in leaving one eye at least unbound.

Under the circumstances, a trust in luck is the most reliable source of comfort. If experience proved anything, if the study of the history of France itself made one point clear, it was the dependence of great events on trifles, the unfailing interposition of the *inattendu,* and, consequently, the utter futility of preparation. The graduating class of 1874 turned their pages with clammy fingers, and repeated mechanically, with unwearied tongues, any passage upon which Fate should direct their eyes; none dared be slighted with impunity, the most insignificant being perhaps the very one to trip them up; the most familiar, the traitor to play them false.

A laggard church clock in the neighborhood gave them each eleven separate, distinct shocks. It warned them that two minutes and a half had already been consumed on the road from one class-room to the other, and reminded them of Monsieur Mignot's diabolical temper.

A little girl, also in a large sun-bonnet, with a placard marked *"Passe-Partout"* around her neck, turned an angle of the building suddenly and threw the nervous ranks into dire confusion; the books went down, the bonnets up.

"Seigneur! qu'est-ce que c'est?"

"*Ma chère!* how you frightened me!"

"*Mon Dieu!* I thought it was Monsieur Mignot!"

"I am trembling all over!"

"I can hardly stand up!"

"Just feel how my heart beats!"

"You had better hurry up, *mes enfants,*" replied the little one, in the patronizing tone of personal disinterestedness; "it is past eleven."

"But we don't know one word," they groaned in unison,—"not one single word."

"Ah, bah! you are frightened, that's all; you always say that." She gave one of them a good-natured push in the direction of the door about which they were standing in distressful hesitation.

"I tell you, old Mignot is in a horrible temper. *Il a fait les quatre cents coups* in our class; threw his inkstand at Stéphanie Morel's head."

The door, with startling coincidence, was violently pulled open at these words, and a gray-haired, spectacled old gentleman thrust out an irate face in quest of his dilatory class. Thrown by the catastrophe into a state of complete nescience of all things historical, from Clovis to Napoleon, the young ladies jerked off their sun-bonnets and entered the room, while the little girl escaped at full speed. A drowsy, quiet, peaceful half-hour followed in the yard,—a surprising silence for the centre of a busy city, considering the close proximity of two hundred school-girls. It was a mocking contrast to the scene of doubt, hesitation, and excitement on the other side of the closed door,—a contrast advantageous to the uneducated happiness of the insects and flowers.

A door-bell rang; not the bell of the pretty little gate which admitted visitors to the rose-hedged, violet-bordered walk leading to Madame's *antichambre,* but the bell of the capacious *porte-cochère* which was reserved for the exits and entrances of scholars and domestics. After a carefully measured pause, the ring was repeated, then again, and again.

The rusty organ of intercommunication squeaked and creaked plaintively after each disturbance as if forced from a sick-bed to do painful and useless service. A gaunt, red-haired woman finally came out in obedience to the summons, with an elaboration of slowness which the shuffling sabots clearly betrayed to the outsider, as evidenced by a last superfluous, unnecessarily energetic pull of the bell-knob.

She carefully unrolled her sleeves as she sauntered along, and stood until she loosened the cord which reefed her dress to an unconventional height. Then she opened the *grille* and looked out.

"Ah, je le savais bien," she muttered, with strong Gascon accent.

There was a diminutive door cut into the large gate. It looked, with its coat of fresh paint, like a barnacle on the weather-beaten exterior. Opening with the facility of greased hinges, it was an unavoidable compromise between the heavy cypress timber and iron fastenings, prescribed by the worldly, or heavenly, experience of St. Denis as the proper protection of a young ladies' boarding-school, and the almost incessant going and coming which secluded feminity and excluded shops made necessary.

"But I can't get in there!" said a woman outside.

"Tant pis." And the little door was closed.

"But I must come in with my basket."

A shrug of the shoulders was the only reply through the *grille.*

"It is Mamzelle Marie's toilet for the exhibition."

The little gate was again held open.

"Don't you see I can't get in there?"

"Ça m'est égal."

A snort of exasperation was heard on the outside, and a suppressed *"C'est un peu fort!"*

"Will you open the big gate for me so that I can bring in Mamzelle Marie's dress?"

No answer.

"Well, then, I shall ring at Madame's bell."

The white woman did not lack judgment. She was maintaining her own in a quarrel begun years ago; a quarrel involving complex questions of the privileges of order and the distinctions of race; a quarrel in which hostilities were continued, year by year, with no interruptions of courtesy or mitigation by truce. This occasion was one of the perquisites of Jeanne's position of *femme de ménage,*—slight compensation enough when compared to the indignities put upon her as a white woman, and the humiliations as a sensitive one by *"cette négresse Marcélite."* But the duration of triumph must be carefully measured. Marcélite's ultimatum, if carried out, would quickly reverse their relative positions by a bonus to Marcélite in the shape of a reprimand to Jeanne. She allowed her foe, however, to carry her basket in the hot sun as far as the next bell, and even waited until she put her hand on it before the iron bar fell and the massive structure was allowed to swing open.

"*Ristocrate!*" she muttered, without looking at either woman or basket.

"*Canaille!*" whispered the other, with her head thrown back and her nose in the air.

Glancing at the line of shade in the yard to see how near it was to twelve o'clock, for want of other accommodation Marcélite went into an open arbor, put her basket on the floor, and wiped her face with a colored foulard handkerchief. "*Fait chaud mo dit toi,*" she said aloud in creole, her language for self-communion. She pulled her skirts out on each side, and sat down with a force that threatened the stability of the bench; then, careless of creeping and crawling possibilities, leaned her head back against the vine-covered wall. The green leaves formed a harmonious frame for the dark-brown face, red and yellow *tignon,* and the large gold ear-rings hanging beneath two glossy *coques* of black wool. Her features were regular and handsome according to the African type, with a strong, sensuous expression, subdued but not obliterated. Her soft black eyes showed in their voluptuous depths intelligence and strength and protecting tenderness. Her stiff purple calico dress settled in defining folds about her portly limbs. A white kerchief was pinned over her untrammelled bosom; her large, full, supple waist was encircled by the strings of her apron, which were tied in a careful bow at her side.

Besides the large basket, she carried on her arm a small covered one, which, if opened, would reveal her calling to be that of hairdressing. She was the hairdresser of the school, and as such, the general *chargée d'affaires, confidente,* messenger, and adviser of teachers and scholars. Her discretion was proven beyond suspicion. Her judgement, or rather her intuition, was bold, quick, and effective. In truth, Marcélite was as indispensable as a lightning-rod to the boarding-school, conducted as it was under the austere discipline of the old régime. Her smooth, round hands and taper fingers had been polished by constant friction with silken locks; her familiar, polite, gentle, servile manners were those contracted during a courtly life of dependent intimacy with superiors. It was said that her basket carried other articles besides combs, brushes, and cosmetics, and that her fingers had been found preferable to the post-office for the delivery of certain implicative missives written in the prose or verse of irresistible emotion. Even without her basket, any one, from her hands, gait, and language, would recognize a hairdresser of the élite, while in New Orleans, in the *Quartier Créole,* there was hardly a man, woman, or child who did not call her by name: Marcélite Gaulois.

She lifted a palmetto fan, bound and tied to her waist with black ribbon, and holding it up between her and observation, betook herself in quiet and privacy to slumber,—a nap of delicious relaxation, so gentle that the bite of a mosquito, the crawling of an ant, an incipient snore, startled it; but so tenacious that the uplifted hand and dropping head resettled themselves without breaking its delicate filaments. A little, thin, rusty-voiced bell had now one of its three important daily announcements to make,—Recreation Time. From all over the city came corroborative evidence of the fact, by chronometers, some a little ahead and some a little behind meridian. This want of unanimity proclaimed the notorious and distressing difference of two minutes and a half between Church and State,—a difference in which the smallest watch in the school could not avoid participation.

It was the same little girl with the *"Passe-Partout"* who published the truce to study. The rope of the bell and she were both too short, so she had to stand on tiptoe and jerk it in little quick jumps. The operation involved a terrible disproportion between labor invested and net profit, for which nothing but the gladsome nature of her mission, and the honorary distinction implied in it, could have compensated her. A moment of stillness, during which both the rope and the little girl quieted themselves, and then, a shower of little girls fell into the yard,—all of them little girls, but not all of them children, and as much alike as drops of different colored water.

They were all dressed in calico dresses made in the same way, with very full, short skirts, and very full, short waists, fastened, matron-fashion, in front. They all wore very tight, glossy, fresh, black French kid boots, with tassels or bows hanging from the top. With big sun-bonnets, or heavily veiled hats on their heads, thick gloves on their hands, and handkerchiefs around their necks, they were walking buttresses against the ardent sun. They held their lunch baskets like bouquets, and their heads as if they wore crowns. They carried on conversations in sweet, low voices, with interrupting embraces and apostrophic tendernesses:—

"Chère!"

"Chérie!"

"Ange!"

"M'amie!"

They had a grace of ease, the gift of generations; a self-composure and polish, dating from the cradle. Of course they did not romp, but promenaded arm in arm, measuring their steps with dainty particularity; moving the whole body with rhythmic regularity, displaying and acquiring at the same time a sinuosity of motion. Their hair hung in plaits so far below their waists that it threatened to grow into a measuring-tape for their whole length.

The angular Jeanne appeared, holding a waiter at arm's-length over her head. She had no need to cluck or chirp; the sound of her sabots was enough to call around her in an instant an eager brood of hungry boarders, jumping and snatching for their portion of lunch. There was the usual moment of obstruction over the point of etiquette whether they should take their own piece of bread and butter or receive it from Jeanne. The same useless sacrifice of a test slice was made, and the obstinate servant had to give in with the same consolatory satisfaction of having been again true to her fixed principle to make herself as disagreeable as possible under any circumstances that the day might bring forth. There is great field for choice, even in slices of bread and butter. The ends, or knots of the loaves, split longitudinally, offer much more appetizing combinations of crust and crumb than the round inside slices. Knots, however, were the prerogative of the big girls; inside slices the grievance of the little ones. To-day, *"comme toujours,"* as they said, with a shrug, the primary classes had to take what was left them. But their appetite was so good, they ate their homely fare with so much gusto, that the day scholars looked on enviously and despised their own epicurean baskets, which failed to elicit such expectations and never afforded them similar gratification.

À la fin des fins! The door which concealed the terrible struggle going on with the history of France was opened. All rushed forward for news, with eager sympathy. It was a dejected little army that filed out after so protracted a combat, with traces of tears in their eyes and all over their flushed cheeks. Tired and nervous, not one would confess to a ray of hope. Certainty of defeat had succeeded to certainty of failure. The history of France, with its disastrous appliances of chronology, dynasties, conquests, and revolutions, had gained, according to them, a complete and unquestioned victory.

"Marie Modeste, look at Marcélite," said one of the girls, hailing the diversion.

The *bonne* was coming out of the garden-house with her basket. One of the graduating class rushed forward to meet her, and both together disappeared in the direction of the dormitory stairway. "It is her toilette for the exhibition," was whispered, and curious eyes followed the basket invested with such preternatural importance. "They say *le vieux* is going to give her a superb one."

The *Grand Concert Musicale et Distribution de Prix* was to take place the next evening. All parents and friends had, for two weeks, been invited to "assist" by their presence. This annual fête was pre-eminently *the* fête of St. Denis. It was the goal of the scholastic course, the beginning of vacation, and the set term to the young ladies' aspirations if not ambition. A fair share of books, laurel crowns, in green and gold paper, and a possible real gold medal was with them the end if not the aim of study from the opening of the school in September. Personally they could not imagine any state or condition in life when knowledge of French history would be a comfort or cosmography an assistance; but prizes were so many concrete virtues which lasted fresh into grandmotherhood. *Noblesse oblige,* that the glory of maternal achievements be not dimmed in these very walls where their mothers, little creoles like themselves, strove for laurel crowns culled from the same imperishable tree in Rue Royale.

Marcélite followed Marie through the dormitory, down the little aisle, between the rows of beds with their veils of mosquito netting, until they came to the farthest corner; which, when one turned one's back to the rest of the chamber, had all the seclusion and "sociability" of a private apartment. The furniture, however, did not include chairs, so Marie seated herself on the side of the bed, and, taking off her bonnet, awaited Marcélite's pleasure to initiate her into the delightful mysteries of the basket.

She wondered where Marcélite had picked up the artistic expedient of heightening the effect by playing on the feelings of the spectator; and she wondered if carrying that basket up the stairs had really tired those strong shoulders and made her so dreadfully hot; and if it were really necessary that each one of those thousand pins should be quilted into the front of that white kerchief; and if Marcélite had made a vow not to open her mouth until she got out the last pin; and if—

She was naturally nervous and impatient, and twisted and turned ceaselessly on the bed during the ordeal of assumed procrastination. Her black eyes were oversized for her face, oversized and overweighted with expression; and most of the time, as to-day, they were accompanied by half-moon shadows which stretched half-way down her cheek. Over her forehead and temples the hieroglyphic tracery of blue veins might be seen, until it became obscured under the masses of black hair whose heavy plaits burdened the delicate head and strained the slender neck. The exterior of a girl of seventeen! That frail mortal encasement which precocious inner life threatens to rend and destroy. The appealing languor, the uncomplaining lassitude, the pathetic apathy, the transparent covering through which is seen the growth of the woman in the body of the child.

Marcélite saw upon the bed the impatient figure of a petulant girl, wild for the sight of her first *toilette de bal.* There lay on the bed, in reality, a proud, reserved, eager, passionate spirit, looking past toilettes, past graduating, past studies and examinations; looking from the prow of an insignificant vessel into the broad prospect, so near, so touching near, reserved for her, and all girls of seventeen,—that unique realm called "Woman's Kingdom."

Romances and poetry had been kept from her like wine and spices. But the flowers bloomed, and music had chords, and moonlight rays, and were the bars of the school never so strong, and the rules never so rigid, they could not prevent her heart from going out toward the rays, nor from listening to the music, nor from inhaling the breath of the flowers. And what they said is what they always say to the girl of seventeen. It is the love-time of life, when the heart first puts forth its flowers; and what boarding-school can frustrate spring? Her mouth, like her eyes, was encircled with a shadow, faint, almost imperceptible, as was the timid suggestion of nascent passion which it gave to the thin, sad lips.

She was four years old when she came to this school; so Marcélite told her, for she could not remember. Now she was seventeen. She looked at the strong, full maturity of Marcélite. Would she, Marie, ever be like that? Had Marcélite ever been like her? At seventeen, did she ever feel this way? This—oh, this longing! Could Marcélite put her finger on the day, as Marie could, when this emotion broke into her heart, that thought into her brain? Did Marcélite know the origin of blushes, the cause of tremors? Did Marcélite ever pray to die to be relieved from vague apprehensions, and then pray to live in the faith of some great unknown but instinctive prophecy?

She forbore to ask. If Marcélite had had a mother!—But did girls even ask their mothers these things? But she had no mother! Good, devoted, loyal as she was, Marcélite was not a mother—not her mother. She had stopped at the boundary where the mother ceases to be a physical and becomes a psychical necessity. The child still clung to Marcélite, but the young woman was motherless. She had an uncle, however, who might become a father.

"*Là!*" Marcélite had exhausted her last devisable subterfuge, and made known her readiness to begin the show.

"*Là! mon bébé! là, ma mignonne!* what do you think of that?" She turned it around by the belt; it seemed all covered over with bubbles of muslin and frostings of lace.

"Just look at that! Ah ha! I thought you would be astonished! You see that lace? *Ça c'est du vrai,* no doubt about that,—real Valenciennes. You think I don't know real lace, *hein?* and *mousseline des Indes?* You ask Madame Treize—you know what she said? 'Well, Marcélite, that is the prettiest pattern of lace and the finest piece of muslin I almost ever saw.' Madame Treize told me that herself; and it's true, for I know it myself."

"Madame Treize, Marcélite?"

Madame Treize was the *on ne peut plus* of New Orleans for fashion and extravagance.

"Yes, Madame Treize. Who do you think was going to make your dress, *hein?* Madame *N'importe-qui?*

"Marcélite, it must have cost so much!"

"*Eh bien,* it's all paid for. What have you got to do with that? All you have got to do is to put it on and wear it. Oh, *mon bébé! ma petite chérie!*"—what tones of love her rich voice could carry,—"if it had cost thousands and thousands of dollars it would not be too fine for you, nor too pretty."

"But, Marcélite, I will be ashamed to wear it; it is too beautiful."

But the eyes sparkled joyfully, and the lips trembled with delightful anticipations.

"Here's the body! You see those bows? That was my taste. I said to myself, 'She must have blue ribbon bows on the shoulder,' and I went back and made Madame Treize put them on. Oh, I know Madame Treize; and Madame Treize, she knows me!"

"And the shoes, Marcélite?"

Hands and voice fell with utter disgust.

"Now you see, Mamzelle, you always do that. Question, question,

question, all the time. Why didn't you wait? Now you have spoiled it all, —all the surprise!"

"Pardon, Marcélite, I did not mean; but I was afraid you had forgotten—"

"Oh, *mon bébé!* when did Marcélite ever forget anything you wanted?"

Marie blushed with shame at a self-accusation of ingratitude.

"*Ma bonne* Marcélite! I am so impatient, I cannot help it."

A bundle of shoes was silently placed in her lap.

"White satin boots! Mar-cé-lite! White satin boots for me? Oh, I can't believe it! And I expected black leather!—how shall I ever thank my uncle for them; and all this? How can I ever do it?"

The radiant expression faded away from the nurse's face at these words.

"Oh, but I know it was your idea, Marcélite! My good, kind, dear Marcélite! I know it was all your idea. He never could have thought of all these beautiful things,—a man!"

She put her arms around the *bonne's* neck and laid her head on the broad, soft shoulder, as she used to do when she was a little, little girl.

"Ah, Marcélite, my uncle can never be as kind to me as you are. He gives me the money, but you—"

She felt the hands patting her back and the lips pressed against her hair; but she could not see the desperate, passionate, caressing eyes, "savoring" her like the lips of an eager dog.

"Let us try them on," said Marcélite.

She knelt on the floor and stripped off one shoe and stocking. When the white foot on its fragile ankle lay in her dark palm, her passion broke out afresh. She kissed it over and over again; she nestled it in her bosom; she talked baby-talk to it in creole; she pulled on the fine stocking as if every wrinkle were an offence, and slackness an unpardonable crime. How they both labored over the boot,—straining, pulling, smoothing the satin, coaxing, urging, drawing the foot! What patience on both sides! What precaution that the glossy white should meet with no defilement! Finally the button-holes were caught over the buttons, and to all intents and purposes a beautiful, symmetrical, solidified satin foot lay before them.

"Too tight?"

It might have been a question, but it sounded more like the laying of a doubt.

"Too tight! just look!"

The little toes made a vigorous demonstration of contempt and denial.

"I can change them if they are."

"Do you want me to wear sabots like Jeanne?"

"They will stretch, anyhow."

Marcélite preferred yielding to her own rather than to another's conviction, even when they both were identical.

The boots were taken off, rolled in tissue-paper, and put away in the *armoire,* which was now opened to its fullest extent to receive the dress.

Marie leaned against the pillow of the bed and clasped her hands over her head. She listened dreamily and contentedly to her praises thrown off by Marcélite's fluent tongue. What would the reality be, if the foretaste were so sweet?

"I wonder what he will say, Marcélite?"

"Qui ça?"

"My uncle. Do you think he will be pleased?"

"What makes you so foolish, *bébé?*"

"But that's not foolish, Marcélite."

"Hum!"

"Say, Marcélite, do you think he will be satisfied?"

"Satisfied with what?"

"Oh, you know, Marcélite,—satisfied with me."

The head was thrust too far into the *armoire* for an immediate answer.

"How can I tell, Mamzelle?"

"Mamzelle! Mamzelle! Madame Marcélite!"

"Well then, *bébé.*"

"Anyway, he will come to the concert—*Hein,* Marcélite?"

"What is it, Zozo?"

"My uncle; he is coming to the concert, isn't he?"

Marcélite shrugged her shoulders; her mouth was filled with pins.

"*Ma bonne!* do not be so mean; tell me if he is coming, and what he said."

"Poor gentleman! he is so old."

"Did he tell you that?"

Marie laughed; this was a standing joke between them.

"But, my child, what do you want him to say? You bother me so with your questions, I don't know what I am doing."

"But, Marcélite, it is only natural for me to want him to come to the concert and see me in my pretty dress that he gave me."

"Well, when one is old and sick—"

"Sick! ah, you did not tell me that."

"But I tell it to you all the time!"

"Oh, Marcélite!"

There is no better subject on which to exercise crude eloquence than the delinquencies of laundresses. A heinous infraction had been committed against the integrity of one of Marie's garments, and Marcélite threatened to consume the rest of the day in expressions of disgust and indignation.

"So he is *not* coming to the concert?" the girl demanded, excitedly.

"Ah! there's the bell; you had better run quick before they send for you."

"No, I am excused until time to practise my duet. Marcélite,"—the voice lost its excited tone and became pleading, humble, and timid,—"Marcélite, do you think my uncle will like me?"

"*Mon Dieu!* yes, yes, yes."

"*Mais ne t'impatiente pas, ma bonne,* I can't help thinking about it. He has never seen me—since I was a baby, I mean—and I don't recollect him at all, at all. Oh, Marcélite! I have tried so often, so often to recall him, and my *maman*"—she spoke it as shyly as an infant does the name of God in its first prayer. "If I could only go just one little point farther back, just that little bit"—she measured off a demi-centimetre on her finger—"but impossible. Maybe it will all come back to me when I see him, and the house, and the furniture. Perhaps if I had been allowed to see it only once or twice, I might be able to remember something. It *is* hard, Marcélite, it is very hard not even to be able to recollect a mother. To-morrow evening!"—she gave a long, long sigh,—"only to-morrow evening more!"

The depravity of the washerwoman must have got beyond even Marcélite's powers of description, for she had stopped talking, but held her head inside the shelf.

"One reason I want him to come to the concert is to take me home with him. In the first place, Madame wouldn't let me go unless he came for me; and—and I want the girls to see him; they have teased me so much about him. I believe, Marcélite, that if my graduating were put off one day longer, or if my uncle did not come for me to-morrow evening, I would die. How foolish! Just think of all these years I have been here, summer after summer, the only boarder left during vacation! I didn't seem to mind it then, but now it's all different; everything has become so different this last year."

The tears had been gathering in her eyes for some time, and she had been smearing them with her finger off the side of her face to escape Marcélite's notice; but now they came too fast for that, so she was forced to turn over and hide her face flat in the pillow.

"Crying, *mon bébé?* What is the matter with you—oh, oh!—you do not feel well! something you do not like about your toilette, *hein?* Tell Marcélite, *chérie;* tell your *bonne.* There! there!"

Sobs were added to tears, until she seemed in conflict with a tornado of grief. She pressed her head tighter and tighter against the pillow to stifle the noise, but her narrow, high shoulders shook convulsively, and her feet twisted and turned, one over the other, in uncontrollable agitation. Marcélite stood by her side, a look of keen torture on her emotional face. If the child had only been larger, or stronger! if she did not writhe so helplessly before her! if she had fought less bravely against the rending sobs! Ah! and if the shrouded form of a dead mother had not intervened with outstretched arms and reproachful eyes fixed upon Marcélite. She could hold out no longer, but fell on her knees by the bed, and clasped her arms around the little one to hold her quiet. With her face on the pillow, and her lips close to the red, burning ear, she whispered the soothing tendernesses of a maternal heart. There was a balsam which never failed: a story she had often told, but which repetition had only made more difficult, more hesitating; to-day the words fell like lead,—about the father Marie had never seen, the mother she had never known, the home-shelter of her baby years, beyond even her imagination, and the guardian uncle, the question of whose coming to the concert had so excited her.

"Is Marie Modeste here?" asked a little voice through a far-off door.

Marie started. "Yes." Her voice was rough, weak, and trembling.

"They want you for the '*Cheval de Bronze.*' "

She sat up and let the nurse smooth her hair and bathe her face, keeping her lips tightly shut over the ebbing sobs.

"Thank you, Marcélite. Thank you for everything—for my beautiful dress, and my shoes; and thank my uncle too, and try and persuade him to come to-morrow evening, won't you, Marcélite? Do not tell him about my crying, though. Oh, I want to go home so much, and to see him! You know if you want you can get him to come. Won't you promise me, *ma bonne?*"

"You know I would kill myself for you, *mon bébé.*"

The good little Paula was waiting outside the door. Uncontrollable tears are too common in a girls' school to attract attention. They were crises which, though not to be explained, even the smallest girl understood intuitively, and for which were tacitly employed convenient conventional excuses.

"The *concours* was very difficult, *chère?*"

"Yes, very difficult."

"And Monsieur Mignot is so trying. I think he gets more *exigeant* every day."

And they kissed each other sympathetically on the stairway.

"Grand Dieu Seigneur!" groaned Marcélite, when Marie had left the room, holding her head with both hands. "What am I going to do now! I believe I am turning fool!"

Life was changing from a brilliant path in white muslin dresses to a hideous dilemma; and for once she did not know what to do. A travail seemed going on in her brain; her natural strength and audacity had completely oozed away from her. She began a vehement monologue in creole, reiterating assertions and explanations, stopping short always at one point.

"My God! I never thought of that."

She looked towards the ceiling with violent reproaches to the *bon Dieu, doux Jésus,* and *Sainte-Vierge.* Why had they left her alone to manage this? They knew she was a "nigger, nigger, nigger" (trying to humiliate and insult herself). Why hadn't they done something? Why couldn't they do something now? And all she had done for them, and that ungrateful patron saint, the recipient of so much attention, so many favors! She never had asked them anything for herself, thank God! Marcélite could always manage her own affairs without the assistance of any one. But her *bébé,* for whom she had distinctly prayed and burned candles, and confessed and communed, and worked, and toiled, and kept straight! She clasped her flesh in her sharp, long nails, and the pain did her good. She could have dashed her head against the wall. She would gladly have stripped her shoulders to the lash, if—if it would do any good. She would kill herself, for the matter of that, but what would that prevent or remedy? The church was not far off, perhaps a miracle! But what miracle can avert the inevitable? She shoved her empty basket under the bed and went out upon the covered gallery that spanned the garden and led to Madame Lareveillère's bedchamber.

The quadrangle lay half overspread now by shadow. The gay *insouciante* flowers moved gently in an incipient breeze, the umbrella top of the little summer-house warded the rays from the benches beneath, and kept them cool and pleasant. Her own face was not more familiar, more matter-of-fact to Marcélite, and yet she saw in the yard things she had never remarked before. There was a different expression to it all. Flowers, summer-house, even the gray flags, depressed her and made her sad; as if they, or she, were going to die soon. She caught the balustrade in her hand, but it was not vertigo. What was it, then, that made her feel so unnatural and everything so portentous? This morning, life was so comfortable and small, everything just under her hand. She was mistress of every day, and night was the truce, if not the end of all trouble. But to-day had united itself to past and future in such a way that night was but a transparent veil that separated but could not isolate them one from the other. Time was in revolt against her; her own powers betrayed her; flight was impossible, resistance useless, death, even, futile.

What was the matter with her head, anyhow? She must be *voudoued.* If she could only feel as she did this morning! The slatternly Jeanne shuffled underneath on her way to the bell, an augur of ill-omen. She would go and see Madame Lareveillère.

Madame (as she was commonly called) sat at her *secrétaire* writing. Her pen, fine pointed as a cambric needle, scratched under her fingers as if it worked on steel instead of paper. She was very busy, transferring the names from a list before her into the gilt-edged prize-books piled up in glowing heaps all around her. A strict observer would have noticed many inaccuracies which would have invalidated any claim to correctness on the part of her copy. There were not only liberties taken with the prize itself, but entire names were involved in transactions which the original list by no means warranted. These inaccuracies always occurred after consultation of another list kept in Madame's little drawer,—a list whose columns carried decimals instead of good and bad marks for lessons. A single ray of light, filtered through various intermedial shades and curtains, had been manœuvred so as to fall on the small desk at a safe distance from Madame's sensitive complexion. At difficult calculations, she would screw up her eyes and peer at both lists brought into the focus of illumination, then would sink back into obscurity for advisory reflection.

There are so many calculations to be made, so many fine distinctions drawn, in a distribution of prizes! No one but a schoolmistress knows the mental effort requisite for the working out of an equation which sets good and bad scholars against good and bad pay. Why could not the rich girls study more, or the poor less? Oh, the simple beauty of strict, injudicious impartiality! Cursed be the inventor or originator of these annual rehearsals, where every one was rewarded except the rewarder!

On occasions like these any interruption is a deliverance; Madame heard with glad alacrity a knock at the door.

"*Ah! c'est toi,* Marcélite!"

Marcélite represented another matter of yearly consideration, another question of paramount importance, a suspensive judgment, involving, however, Madame alone. With the assistance of the hairdresser, many years ago (the date is not essential, and women are sensitive about such things), the principal of the Institut St. Denis had engaged in one of those struggles against Time to which pretty unmarried women seem pledged during a certain period, the fighting age, of their lives. It was purely a defensive struggle on her part, and consisted in a protest against that uglifying process by which women are coaxed into resignation to old age and death. So far, she had maintained her own perfectly; and Time, for all the progress he had made in the sweet, delicate face of Eugénie Lareveillère, might just as well have been tied for ten years past to one of the four posts of the bedstead. The musical concert and distribution of prizes and its consequent indispensable new toilette furnished an excellent date for an annual review and consultation, when old measures were discussed, new ones adopted, and the next campaign planned. Madame, however, did not feel this year the same buoyant courage, the same irrepressible audacity as heretofore. In fact, there was a vague suspicion in her breast, hitherto unacknowledged, that in spite of facial evidence she herself, *dans son intérieur,* was beginning to grow the least, little, tiny bit old. She felt like capitulating with the enemy, and had almost made up her mind to surrender—her hair. *"L'incertitude est le pire des maux, jusqu'au moment où la réalité nous fait regretter l'incertitude."*[2] Should the conditions be proven too hard for mortal beauty, she could at least revolt again. Thank heaven! over there in Paris worked devoted emissaries for women, and the last word had not yet been said by the artists of hair-dyes and cosmetics.

"*Eh, bien, qu'en dis-tu,* Marcélite?"

The artistically arranged head, with its curls and puffs and frisettes clustered like brown silken flowers above the fair skin, was directly in the line of Marcélite's vision. Who would have suspected that these were but transplanted exotics from the hot head of foreign youth? that under their

2 A slightly inaccurate version of an epigram by Alphonse Karr (1808–90). *"Le pire des maux"* should read *"le pire de tous les maux."*

adorning luxuriance lay, fastened by inflexible hairpins, the legitimate but deposed possessors of this crown? But they were old, gray, almost white, and Madame was suggesting for them a temporary and empirical resurrection. That head which daily for years she had moulded according to her comprehension of fashion; that inert little ball for which Marcélite, in her superb physical strength, had almost felt a contempt,—she looked at it now, and, like the flowers in the garden, it was changed to her, was pregnant with subtle, portentous meaning. She was beginning faintly to suspect the truth. All this buzzing, whirling, thought, fear, calculation, retrospection, and prevision, which had come into her great, big, strong head only an hour ago, had been going on in this little, fragile, delicate handful of skull for years, ever since it was born. She saw it now, she knew it,—the difference between Madame's head and hers, between a consciousness limited by eternity and one limited by a nightly sleep, between an intelligence looking into immortality and one looking into the eyes of a confessor.

The room would have been quite dark but for that one useful ray which, after enlightening the path of distributive justice for Madame, fell on and was absorbed by a picture opposite. Out of the obscurity arose one by one the features of the bedchamber,—the supreme model of bedchambers in the opinion of the impressionable loyalists of St. Denis; a bedchamber, the luxury of which could never be surpassed, the mysterious solemnity never equalled; a bed-chamber, in fact, created to satisfy the majestic coquettishness of the autocratic superior of an aristocratic school for girls.

Indistinct, undefined, vague fragments of color struggled up through the floor of sombre carpet. The windows, made to exclude the light, were draped with mantles of lace and silk hanging from gigantic, massive, convoluted gilt cornices. The grand four-posted mahogany bedstead, with its rigging of mosquito-netting and cords and tassels, looked like some huge vessel that by accident had lodged in this small harbor. So stupendous, so immeasurable, so gloomily, grandly, majestically imposing, this dark, crimson-housed bedstead looked in the small, dimly-lighted room, that little girls sent on occasional messages to Madame felt a tremor of awe at the sight of it, and understood instinctively, without need of explanation or elucidation, that here, indeed, was one of those *lits de justice* which caused such dismay in the pages of their French history. The bureau with its laces and ribbons, its cushions, essence-bottles, jewel-cases, *vide-poches,* and little galleried étagères full of gay reflections for the mirror underneath, was as coquettish, as volatile, as petulant an article of furniture as was ever condemned to bedchamber companionship with a *lit de justice.*

The *prie-dieu* in front of the altar granted the occupant an encouraging view into all the visible appliances for stimulating faith in the things not seen. The willing heart, as by an ascending scale, rose insensibly from the humanity to the divinity of sacrifice and suffering: reliquaries, triply consecrated beads, palms, and crucifixes, pictures of sainted martyrs and martyresses (who contradicted the fallacious coincidence of homeliness and virtue), statuettes, prayer-books, pendent flasks of holy water, and an ecclesiastical flask of still holier liquid, impregnated with miraculous promises. A taper, in a red globe, burned with subdued effulgence below it all. Ghastly white and black bead wreaths, hanging under faded miniatures, set the bounds of mural consecration, and kept Madame mournfully reminded of her deceased husband and mother.

Marcélite stood, like a threatening idol, in the centre of the room, her eyes glaring through the gloom with fierce doggedness. Her feet were planted firmly apart, her hands doubled up on her high, round, massive hips. The cords of her short, thick neck stood out, and her broad, flexible nostrils rose and fell with passion. Her untamed African blood was in rebellion against the religion and civilization whose symbols were all about her in that dim and stately chamber,—a civilization which had tampered with her brain, had enervated her will, and had duped her with false assurances of her own capability.

She felt a crushing desire to tear down, split, destroy, to surround herself with ruins, to annihilate the miserable little weak devices of intelligence, and reassert the proud supremacy of brute force. She longed to humiliate that meek Virgin Mother; and if the form on the crucifix had been alive she would have gloated over his blood and agony. She thirsted to get her thin, taper, steel-like fingers but once more on that pretty, shapely, glossy head.

"*Pauvre petite chatte!* I shall miss her very much; you know, Marcélite, it seems only a year or two since you brought her here a little baby, and now she is a young lady of seventeen. Thirteen years ago! What a *chétive* little thing she was! You were as much of a scholar here then as she; you had to stay with her so much. You have been a faithful nurse to her, *ma bonne femme.* A mother could not have been more devoted, and very few would have done all you have for that child. Ah! that's a thing money can never pay for,—love. I hope Marie will always remember what you have been to her, and repay it with affection. But she will; she is a good girl,—a good, good girl, *pauvre petite!* It is Monsieur Motte, though, who should give you a handsome present, something really valuable. I would like to know what he would have done for a *bonne* for his niece without you. You remember that summer when she had the fever? Eh, well, she would have died but for you; I shall never forget her sad little face and her big black eyes. You know, her mother must see all that; I can never believe, Marcélite, that a mother cannot come back, sometimes, to see her children, particularly a little girl—"

Marcélite listened with head averted. Her hands had fallen from her hips, her mouth slowly relaxed, and the lips opened moist and red. As if drawn by strains of music, she came nearer and nearer Madame's chair.

"She was always such a quiet little thing, *ma foi!*" Madame's reminiscence was an endless chain. "I used to forget her entirely; but now she is going away, I know I shall miss her, yes, very much. I hope the world will be kind to her. She will be handsome, too, some day, when she does not have to study so hard, and can enjoy the diversions of society a little. By the time she is twenty you will see she will be *une belle femme.* Ah, Monsieur Motte, you will be satisfied, *allez!*"

The little pen commenced scratching away again, and this time registered the deed of prize of French history to *l'élève,* Marie Modeste Motte.

Marcélite, with wistful eyes, listened for some more of the soft, sweet tones. She made the movement of swallowing two or three times to get the swelling and stiffness out of her throat.

"Mamzelle Marie, too, she will be sorry to leave Madame." Her voice was thick and unsteady.

"Oh no, girls are always glad to quit school. Very naturally, too. When one is young, one does not like to stay indoors and study, when there is so much outside,—dancing, music, beaux." A sigh interrupted Madame. "It is all past for me now, but I can recollect how I felt when I was seventeen. *A propos,* Marcélite, did you give my invitation to Monsieur Motte?"

"Yes, Madame."

The answer came after an interval of hesitation. At one moment Marcélite's eyes flashed as if she would brave all results and refuse to respond.

"And what did he say?"

"He—he sent his compliments to Madame."

Madame looked around to see what the good-natured *coiffeuse* meant by such sullen tones. "Yes; but did he say he would come to the concert? I wanted particularly to know that."

"He is so old, Madame."

"*Là, là,* the same old excuse! I am so tired of it."

"But when one is old, Madame."

"Ah, bah! I do not believe he is too old for his own pleasure. I know men; old age is a very convenient excuse at times."

Marcélite appeared to have no reply at the end of her ready tongue.

"But this time he must come, *par exemple!* even if he is so old. I think he might subject himself to some little inconvenience and trouble to see his niece graduate. He has not put himself out much about her for twelve or thirteen years."

"God knows! Madame."

"God knows? *Mais,* Marcélite, how silly you talk! Don't you see that Monsieur Motte must come to-morrow night, at least to take Marie home? God does know, and so should he."

Marcélite spoke as if galvanized by an inspiration. "Perhaps he wants Miss Marie to stay another year, Madame; you see, she is so young, and—and—there is so much to learn, *enfin.*"

"He wants that, does he? he wants that! Ah, *l'égoïste!* That is like a man; oh, I know them, like *a b c.* No, if Marie is not too young to graduate, she is not too young to leave school; and besides, if she had not learned everything, how could she graduate? There is an end to learning, *enfin.* You tell Monsieur Motte that. But no, *tiens,* it is better I shall write it."

She seized some note-paper and put her message in writing with the customary epistolary embellishment of phrase at the expense of sincerity and truth.

"I hope he will be kind to her, and look out for a good *parti* for her. Of course she will have a *dot,*—his only relative. Did you not tell me she was his only relative, Marcélite? He has absolutely no one else besides her?"

"No, Madame."

"Well, then, she will get it all when he dies, unless"—with a shrug—"I do not know; one is never sure about men."

Madame bethought herself of the time, and looked at her watch just as Marcélite, by a sudden resolution, made a desperate movement towards her.

"Nearly three o'clock! I must go and make my *tour. Au revoir, ma bonne.* Be sure and give Monsieur Motte my note, and come early to-morrow morning; and do not forget to think about what I told you, you know." She tapped her head significantly and left the room. On the short passage to the *Salle des Classes* she put off her natural manner, and assumed the conventional disguise supposed to be more fitting her high position. When the door opened and the little girls started up to drop their courtesies, and their *"Je vous salue, Madame,"* her stately tread and severe mien could hardly have been distinguished from those of her predecessor, the aristocratic old *réfugiée* from the Island of St. Domingo.

After dinner, when the shadow had entirely enveloped the yard, and the fragrance of the oleander and jasmine had fastened itself on the air, the girls were allowed their evening recreation. Relieved from the more or less restraining presence of the day scholars, the boarders promenaded in the cordial intimacy of home life. The laughter of the children in the street, the music of the organs (there seemed to be one at each corner), the gay jingle of the ice-cream cart came over the wall to them. Tomorrow there would be no wall between them and the world,—the great, gay, big world of New Orleans. The thought was too exhilarating for their fresh blood; they danced to the music and laughed to the laughter outside, they kissed their hands to invisible friends, and made *révérences* and complimentary speeches to the crescent moon up in the blue sky. The future would soon be here now! only to-morrow evening,—the future, which held for them a *début* in society, a box at the opera, beautiful toilettes, balls, dancing, music. No more study, routine, examinations, scoldings, punishments, and bread-and-butter lunches. The very idea of it was intoxicating, and each girl felt guilty of a maudlin effusion of sentiment and nonsense to her best friend. A "best friend" is an institution in every girls' school. Every class-book when opened would direct you to a certain page on which was to be found the name of *"celle que j'aime,"* or *"celle que j'adore,"* or *"mon amie chérie,"* or *"ma toute dévouée."* The only source of scandal that flourished in their secluded circle was the formation or disrupting of these ties through the intermeddling officiousness of *"rapporteuses"* and *"mauvaises langues."* But the approaching dissolution of all ties drew them together, each one to each one's best friend, and, as usual, the vows exchanged became more fervent and passionate just before breaking. Marcélite was outside, leaning against the wall. Close over her head hung the pink oleanders through their green leaves, and on their strong perfume was wafted the merry voices of the boarders. How glad, how happy they were! She could hear her *bébé* above the others, and, strange to say, her laughter made her sadder even than her tears to-day. She lifted up her black, passionate face. If she could only see them! if she could look over the wall and catch one more glimpse of the girl whom as a baby she had held to her bosom, and whom she had carried in her arms through that gate when . . . *"Ah, mon Dieu, ayez pitié de moi, pauvre négresse!"*

"Dansez, chantez," they were singing and making a *ronde.* She heard some one at the gate,—Jeanne, probably, coming out. She turned her back quickly and walked away around the corner, making the tour of the square. When she turned the corner coming the other way, she was quite out of breath with walking so fast; as there was no one in the street, she increased her pace to a run, and reached the oleanders panting; but all was now still inside; the boarders had been summoned to supper. She stretched her arms out and leaned her head against the rough bricks. She turned and looked at the sky; her eyes gleamed through her tears like the hot stars through the blue air. She moved away a few steps, hesitated, returned; then went again, only to be drawn back under the oleanders. She sat down close to the wall, threw her apron over her head, and drew her feet up out of the way of the passers-by.

Daylight found her still there. When the early carts began to pass, laden for the neighboring market, she rose stiff and sore and walked in the direction of the river, where the morning breeze was just beginning to ripple the waters and drive away the fog.

The great day of the concert began very early. Fête days always get up before the sun. The boarders in the dormitory raised their heads from their pillows and listened to the pushing and dragging going on underneath them: the men arranging the chairs for that night. Their heads, done up in white paper *papillotes,* looked like so many blanched porcupines. This was one of the first of those innumerable degrees of preparation by which they expected to transform themselves into houris of loveliness by concert-time. As there can be no beauty without curls, in a school-girl's opinion, and as a woman's first duty is to be beautiful, they felt called upon to roll lock after lock of their hair around white paper, which was then twisted to the utmost limit of endurance; and on occasions when tightness of curl is regulated by tightness of twist, endurance may safely be said to have no limits. Fear of the unavoidable ensuing disappointment forced Marie to renounce, reluctantly, beauty in favor of discretion. When her companions saw the omission, they screamed in dismay.

"Oh, Marie!"

"Ah! Why didn't you put your hair up?"
"What a pity!"
"And you won't have curls for this evening?"
"Do it now!"
"*Mais je t'assure,* it will curl almost as tight."
"Let me do it for you, *chère.*"
"No, me."
"But it is better to have it a little *frisé,* than straight, so."

Marie, from practice accomplished in excuses, persisted that she had a *migraine.*

"Oh, *la migraine,* poor thing!"
"I implore you, don't be ill to-night."
"Try my *eau de Cologne.*"
"No, my *eau sédative* is better."
"Put this on your head."
"Tie this around your neck."
"Carry this in your pocket."
"Some water from Notre Dame de Lourdes."
"Some smelling-salts."

Madame Lareveillère opened *her* eyes that morning as from an unsuccessful experiment. She cared little about sleep as a restorative, but it was invaluable to her in this emergency as a cosmetic.

Jeanne brought in her morning cup of coffee, with the news that the men had almost finished in the *Salle de Concert.*

"*C'est bon;* tell Marcélite to come as soon as she is ready."

The eyes closed again on the pillow in expectation of speedy interruption. But sleep, the coquette, courted and coaxed in vain all night, came now with blandishment, lullaby, and soft caress, and fastened the already heavy lids down over the brown eyes, and carried the occupant of the big bed away out on pretty dreams of youth and pleasure; away, beyond all distractions, noises, interruptions; beyond the reach of matutinal habits, duties, engagements, rehearsals, prizes; beyond even the practising of the "*Cheval de Bronze*" on four pianos just underneath her. She slept as people sleep only on the field of battle or amid the ruins of broken promises; and thanks to her exalted position, she slept undisturbed.

"*Mais,* come in *donc,* Marcélite!" she exclaimed, as a perseverant knocking at the door for the past five minutes had the effect of balancing her in a state of uncertain wakefulness. "You are a little early this morning, it seems."

She rubbed her hands very softly over her still-closed eyes; that last dream was so sweet, so clinging, what a pity to open them!

"It is not Marcélite; it is I,—Madame Joubert."

"You! Madame Joubert!"

The excellent, punctilious, cold, austere, inflexible French teacher by her bedside!

"I thought it was Marcélite."

She still was hardly awake.

"No, it is I."

"But what is the matter, Madame Joubert?"

"It is twelve o'clock, Madame."

"Twelve o'clock! Impossible!"

"You hear it ringing, Madame."

"But where is Marcélite?"

"Marcélite did not come this morning."

"Marcélite did not come this morning!" She was again going to say "Impossible!" but she perceived Madame Joubert's head, and was silent.

Instead of her characteristic, formal, but conventionally fashionable coiffure, Madame Joubert had returned to, or assumed, that most primitive and innocent way of combing her hair, called *la sauvagesse.* Unrelieved by the soft perspective of Marcélite's handiwork, her plain, prominent features stood out with the savage boldness of rocks on a shrubless beach. "How frightfully ugly!" thought Madame Lareveillère.

"Marcélite did not come this morning? Why?"

"How should I know, Madame?"

"She must be ill; send Jeanne to see."

"I did that, Madame, five hours ago; she was not in her room."

"But what can have become of her?"

Madame Joubert had early in life eliminated the consideration of supposititious cases from the catalogue of her salaried duties; but she answered gratuitously,—

"I cannot imagine, Madame."

"But I must have some one to comb my hair."

"The music-teacher is waiting for you. The French professor says he will be here again in a half-hour; he has been here twice already. Madame Criard says that it is indispensable for her to consult you about the choruses."

"*Mais, mon Dieu!* Madame Joubert, I must have a hairdresser!"

Madame Joubert waived all participation in this responsibility by continuing her communication.

"The girls are all very tired; they say they will be worn out by to-night if they are kept much longer. *They* have been up ever since six o'clock."

"I know, I know, Madame Joubert; it was an accident. I also was awake at six o'clock. *J'ai fait la nuit blanche.* Then I fell asleep again. Ah! that miserable Marcélite! I beg of you, tell Jeanne to go for some one, no matter whom—Henriette, Julie, Artémise. I shall be ready in a moment."

In a surprisingly short while she was quite ready, all but her hair, and stood in her white muslin peignoir, tied with blue ribbons, before her toilette, waiting impatiently for some one to come to her assistance.

How terrible it is not to be able to comb one's own hair! Her hands had grown completely unaccustomed to the exercise of the comb and brush.

"Madame," said Jeanne at the door, "I have been everywhere. I cannot find a hairdresser at home; I have left word at several places, and Madame Joubert says they are waiting for you."

What could she do? She looked in the glass at her gray, spare locks; she looked on her toilette at her beautiful brown curls and plaits. "How in the world did Marcélite manage to secure all *that* on *this?*"

There was a knock at the door.

"Perhaps that was a hairdresser!" She hastened to unfasten it.

"Madame," said a little girl, trying to speak distinctly, despite a nervous shortness of breath, "Madame Joubert sent me to tell you they were waiting."

"Very well, *mon enfant*, very well. I am coming."

"I shall be a greater fright than Madame Joubert," she murmured to herself.

The drops of perspiration disfiguring the clear tissue of the muslin peignoir were the only visible results of her conscientious efforts.

"I will never be able to fix my hair."

There was another knock at the door, another "Madame Joubert *vous fait dire*," etc.

"Tell Madame Joubert I am coming in a moment."

How impatient Madame Joubert was this morning. Oh for Marcélite!

She knew nothing about hair, that was evident; but she remembered that she knew something about lace. Under the pressure of accelerating summonses from Madame Joubert, she fashioned a fichu, left on a chair from last night, into a very presentable substitute for curls and puffs.

"*Mais ce n'est pas mal, en effet,*" she muttered. Hearing the sound of footsteps again in the corridor, she rushed from the mirror and met the messenger just as her hand was poised to give a knock at the door. The "*Sa . . . lu . . . t! mois de va . . . can . . . ces!*" and the "*Vi . . . er . . . ge, Ma . . . ri . . . e*" had been chorused and re-chorused; the "*Cheval de Bronze*" had been hammered into durable perfection; the solos and duos, dialogues and scenes, the salutatory and valedictory had been rehearsed *ad nauseam.*

Madame finally dismissed the tired actors, with the recommendation to collect all their *petites affaires*, so that their trunks could be sent away very early the next morning.

"I suppose Marcélite will be sure to come this evening?" she asked Madame Joubert.

"Oh, *that* is sure, Madame," Madame Joubert replied, as if this were one of the few rules of life without exceptions; and Madame Lareveillère believed her as confidently as if Noël and Chapsal[3] had passed upon her answer, and the *Dictionnaire de l'Académie*[4] had indorsed it.

The girls scattered themselves all over the school, effacing with cheerful industry every trace of their passage through the desert of education. "*Dieu merci! that* was all past." Marie had emptied her desk of everything belonging to her except her name, dug out of the black lid with a dull knife. That had to remain, with a good many other Marie Modeste Mottes on the different desks that had harbored her books during her sojourn in the various classes. This was all that would be left of her in the rooms where she had passed thirteen years of her life. The vacant teacher's desk, the throne of so many tyrants (the English teachers were all hateful!); the white walls with their ugly protecting dado of black; the rows of pegs, where the hats and cloaks hung; the white marble mantel, with its carving of naked cherubs, which the stove had discreetly clothed in soot,—she could never forget them. Sitting in her future home, the house of her uncle, she knew that these homely objects would come to her memory, as through sunset clouds of rose and gold.

3 Charles-Pierre Chapsal (1788–1858), in collaboration with Jean-François-Michel Noël (1755–1841), published the *Grammaire française* (1823), which remained the authority on French usage throughout the nineteenth century.

4 The *Dictionnaire de l'Académie française*, the traditional authority on the language of polite society, first published in 1694 and revised frequently up to 1935.

"What will you do when you quit school, Marie?" her companions would ask, after detailing with ostentatious prolixity their own pleasant prospects.

"Ah, you know that depends entirely upon my uncle," she would reply, shrugging her thin shoulders under her calico waist.

This rich old uncle, an obstinate recluse, was the traditional *le vieux* of the school.

"How is *le vieux* to-day?" they would call to Marcélite.

"Give my love to *le vieux*."

"*Dis donc*, why doesn't *le vieux* take Marie away in the summer?"

"Did you see the beautiful *étrennes le vieux* has sent Marie?"

"They say he has sent her a superb toilette for the exhibition, made at Madame Treize's, and white satin boots."

Her trunk had been brought down with the others, and placed at her bedside. What more credible witness than a coffin or a trunk? It stood there as it might have stood thirteen years ago, when her baby wardrobe was unpacked. Her dear, ugly, little, old trunk! It had belonged to her mother, and bore three faded M's on its leather skin. She leaned her head against the top as she knelt on the floor before it to pack her books. How much that trunk could tell her if it could only speak! If she were as old as that trunk, she would have known a father, a mother, and a home! She wrinkled her forehead in a concentrated effort to think a little farther back; to push her memory just a little,—a little beyond that mist out of which it arose. In vain! The big bell at the gate, with its clanging orders, remained the boundary of consciousness.

And Marcélite did not come, not even when the lamps were lighted, to comb their hair, fasten their dresses, and tie their sashes; did not even come at the very end to see how their toilettes became them. The young ladies had waited until the last moment, dressed to the last pin, taken their hair out of the last *papillote*, and then looked at one another in despair, indignation, and grief.

"Just look at my head, I ask you!"

"But mine is worse than yours."

"I shall never be able to do anything with mine."

"The more I brush, the more like a *nègre* I look."

"Ah, Marie, how wise you were not to put your hair in *papillotes!*"

"And all that trouble for nothing, *hein!*"

"And the pain."

"I didn't sleep a wink last night."

"See how nice Marie looks with her hair smoothly plaited."

"I will never forgive Marcélite."

"Nor I."

"Nor I."

"Nor I."

Marie's heart sank when she thought how difficult it would be for Marcélite to efface this disappointment from the remembrance of her clients; and she felt guilty, as being in a measure responsible for it all. Marcélite was evidently detained, or prevented from coming, by preparations for Marie's return. Who knows?—perhaps the eccentric old uncle had something to do with it! Madame Joubert positively refused to mitigate the injury or condone the offence by the employment of another hairdresser. As she had commenced, so she closed the day *à la sauvagesse;* and so she determined to wear her hair to the end of her life, maintaining, locically, that what one hairdresser had done, all were liable to do; life should never serve this disappointment to her a second time: she would employ no more of them.

The being deserted in a critical moment by a trusted servitor, dropped without warning by a confidante, left with an indifference, which amounted to heartlessness, to the prying eyes and gossiping tongue of a stranger,—this, not the mere trivial combing, was what isolated and distinguished Madame Lareveillère in her affliction. The question had been lifted beyond material consequences. Morally, it approached tragic seriousness. Marcélite would naturally have suggested, whether she thought so or not, that the color of the new gray moire-antique was a trifle *ingrate*, and Madame at least might have had the merit of declining propitiatory compromises between it and her complexion. . . . Julie was an idiot, there was no doubt about that; and the length of her tongue was notorious. By to-morrow evening the delicate mysteries of the youthful-looking Madame Lareveillère's toilette would be unveiled to satisfy the sensational cravings of her malicious patronesses.

The young ladies were placed on a high platform of steps, and rose tier above tier like flowers in a horticultural show,—the upper classes at the top and the best-looking girls well in the centre, as if the product of their beauty as well as their study went to the credit of the institute. When anything particular arrested their attention they whispered behind their fans, and it was as if a hive of bees had been let loose; when they laughed it was like a cascade rippling from step to step; when they opened their white, blue, and rose-colored fans (school-girls always do the same thing at the same time) and fluttered them, then it was like a cloud of butterflies hovering and coquetting about their own lips.

The *Externes* were radiant in toilettes unmarred by accident or omission; the flattering compliments of their mirrors at home had turned their heads in the direction of perfect self-content. Resignation was the only equivalent the unfortunate *Internes* could offer in extenuation of the unfinished appearance of their heads.

"*Mais, dis donc, chère*, what is the matter with your hair?"

"Marcélite did not come."

"Why, *doudouce*, how could you allow your hair to be combed that way?"

"Marcélite did not come."

"*Chérie*, I think your hair is curled a little tight this evening."

"I should think so; that *diable* Marcélite did not come."

"*Mon Dieu*, look at Madame Joubert *à la sauvagesse!*"

"And Madame *à la grande maman!*"

"Marcélite did not come, you see."

Not only was the room filled, but an eager audience crowded the yard and peeped in through the windows. The stairways, of course, were filled with the colored servants, an enthusiastic, irrepressible *claque*. When it was all over, and the last *bis* and *encore* had subsided, row after row of girls was gleaned by the parents, proud possessors of such shawlfuls of beauty, talent, and prizes. Marie's class, the last to leave, were picked off one by one. She helped the others to put on their wraps, gather up their prizes, and kissed one after another good-by.

Each man that came up was, by a glance, measured and compared with her imaginary standard. "He is too young." "He is too fat." "I hope he is not that cross-looking one." "Maybe it is he." "What a funny little one that is!" "Ah, he is very nice-looking!" "Is it he?" "No, he is Corinne's father." "I feel sure he is that ugly, disagreeable one." "Ah, here he is at last! at last!" "No; he only came to say good-night to Madame." "He is afraid of the crowd." "He is waiting outside." "He is at the gate in a carriage." "After all, he has only sent Marcélite." "I saw her here on the steps a while ago." She looked at the steps, they were deserted. There was but one person left in the room besides herself; Madame and her suite had gone to partake of their yearly exhibitional refreshments,—lemonade and *masse-pain*, served in the little parlor. Her uncle must be that man. The person walked out after finding a fan he had returned to seek.

She remained standing so by the piano a long while, her gold crown on her head, her prizes in her arms, and a light shawl she had thoughtfully provided to wear home. Home! She looked all around very slowly once more. She heard Jeanne crossing the yard, but before the servant could enter the door, the white muslin dress, blue sash, and satin boots had bounded into the darkness of the stairway. The white-veiled beds which the night before had nestled the gay *papilloted* heads were deserted and silent in the darkness. What a shelter the darkness was! She caught hold of the bedpost, not thinking, but feeling. Then Madame Joubert came tripping across the gallery with a candle, on her way to bed. The prizes and shawl dropped to the floor, and Marie crouched down close behind the bar. "Oh, God," she prayed, "keep her from seeing me!" The teacher after a pause of reflection passed on to her room; the child on the floor gave herself up to the full grief of a disappointment which was not childish in its bitterness. The events of the evening kept slipping away from her while the contents of her previous life were poured out with never-ending detail, and as they lay there, before and all around her, she saw for the first time how bare, how denuded, of pleasure and comfort it had been. What had her weak little body not endured in patient ignorance? But the others were not ignorant,—the teachers, Marcélite, her uncle! How had they imposed upon the orphan in their hands! She saw it now, and she felt a woman's indignation and pity over it. The maternal instinct in her bosom was roused by the contemplation of her own infancy. "Marcélite! Marcélite!" she called out, "how could you? for you knew, you knew it all!" The thought of a mother compelled to leave her baby on such an earth, the betrayal of the confidence of her own mother by her uncle, drew the first tears from her eyes. She leaned her head against the side of her bed and wept, not for herself, but for all women and all orphans. Her hand fell on the lace of her dress, and she could not recall at first what it was. She bounded up, and with eager, trembling fingers tearing open the fastenings, she threw the grotesque masquerade, boots and all, far from her on the floor, and stood clasping her naked arms over her panting breast; she had forgotten the gilt wreath on her head. "If she could die then and there! that would hurt her uncle who cared so little for her, Marcélite who had deserted her!" Living she had no one, but dead, she felt she had a mother. Before getting into bed, she mechanically fell on her knees, and her lips repeated the formula of a prayer, an uncorrected, rude tradition of her baby days, belonging to the other side of her memory. It consisted of one simple petition for her own welfare, but the blessings of peace, prosperity, and eternal salvation of her uncle and Marcélite were insisted upon with pious determination.

"I know I shall not sleep, I cannot sleep." Even with the words she sank into the oblivion of tired nature at seventeen years; an oblivion which blotted out everything,—toilette, prizes scattered on the floor, graduation, disappointment, and discomfort from the gilt-paper crown still encircling her black plaits.

"Has Marcélite come?" demanded Madame, before she tasted her coffee.

"Not yet, Madame."

"I wonder what has become of her?"

Jeanne sniffed a volume of unspeakable probabilities.

"Well, then, I will not have that *sotte* Julie; tell her so when she comes. I would rather dress myself."

"Will Madame take her breakfast alone, or with Madame Joubert?"

The pleasure of vacation was tempered by the companionship of Madame Joubert at her daily meals,—a presence imposed by that stern tyrant, common courtesy.

"Not to-day, Jeanne; tell Madame Joubert I have *la migraine*. I shall eat breakfast alone."

"And Mamzelle Marie Modeste?"

"Marie Modeste!"

"Yes, Madame; where must she take her breakfast?"

The Gasconne's eyes flamed suddenly from under her red lashes and her voice ventured on its normal loud tones in these sacred precincts.

"It's a shame of that negress! She ought to be punished well for it, too, ha! Not to come for that poor young lady last night; to leave her in that big dormitory all by herself; and all the other young ladies to go home and have their pleasure, and she all by herself, just because she is an orphan. You think she doesn't feel that, *hein?* If I had known it I would have helped her undress, and stayed with her, too; I would have slept on the floor,—a delicate little nervous thing like that; and a great, big, fat, lazy, good-for-nothing quadroon like Marcélite. *Mais c'est infâme!* It is enough to give her *des crises*. Oh, I would not have done that! *tenez*, not to go back to France would I have done that. And when I got up this morning, and saw her sitting in the arbor, so pale, I was frightened myself—I—"

"What is all this you are telling me? Jeanne, Jeanne, go immediately;

run, I tell you—run and fetch that poor child here. *Ah, mon Dieu!* egoist that I am to forget her! *Pauvre petite chatte!* What must she think of me?"

She jumped out of bed, threw on a wrapper, and waited at the door, peeping out.

"*Ma fille;* I did not know—Jeanne has just told me."

The pale little figure made an effort to answer with the old pride and indifference.

"It seems my uncle—"

"*Mais qu'est-ce que c'est donc, mon enfant?* Do not cry so! What is one night more in your old school? It is all my fault; the idea that I should forget you,—leave you all alone while we were enjoying our lemonade and *masse-pain!* But why did you not come to me? Oh! oh! if you cry so, I shall think you are sorry not to leave me; besides, it will spoil your pretty eyes."

"If Marcélite had only come—"

"Ah, my dear! do not speak of her! do not mention her name to me. We are *quittes* from this day; you hear me? We are *quittes*. But Marie, my child, you will make yourself ill if you cry so. Really, you must try and compose yourself. What is it that troubles you so? Come here, come sit by me; let me confess you. I shall play that I am your *maman*. There, there, put your head here, my *bébé*, so. Oh, I know how you feel. I have known what disappointment was; but *enfin*, my child, that will all pass; and one day, when you are old and gray-headed like me, you will laugh well over it."

The tender words, the caresses, the enfolding arms, the tears that she saw standing in the august schoolmistress's eyes, the sympathetic movement of the soft, warm bosom,—her idea of a mother was not a vain imagining. This was it; this was what she had longed for all her life. And she did confess to her,—confessed it all, from the first childish trouble to the last disappointment. Oh, the delicious relief of complete, entire confession to a sympathetic ear!

The noble heart of Madame, which had frittered itself away over puny distributions of prizes and deceiving cosmetics, beat young, fresh, and impulsive as in the days when the gray hairs were *châtains clairs*, and the cheeks bloomed natural roses. Tears fell from her eyes on the little black head lying so truthful, so confiding on her bosom. *Grand Dieu!* and they had been living thirteen years under the same roof,—the poor, insignificant, abandoned, suffering little Marie, and the gay, beautiful, rich, envied Madame Lareveillère! This was their first moment of confidence. Would God ever forgive her? Could she ever forgive herself? How good it feels to have a child in your arms! so. She went to the stand by her bed and filled a small gilded glass with *eau des carmes* and water.

"There, drink that, my child; it will compose you. I must make my toilette; it is breakfast-time. You see, *ma fille*, this is a lesson. You must not expect too much of the men; they are not like us. Oh, I know them well. They are all *égoïistes*. They take a great deal of trouble for you when you do not want it, if it suits them; and then they refuse to raise their little finger for you, though you get down on your knees to them. Now, there's your uncle. You see he has sent you to the best and most expensive school in the city, and he has dressed you well,—oh, yes, very well; look at your toilette last night! real lace; I remarked it. Yet he would not come for you and take you home, and spare you this disappointment. I wrote him a note myself and sent it by Marcélite."

"He *is* old, Madame," said Marie, loyally.

"Ah, bah! *Plus les hommes sont vieux plus ils sont méchants*. Oh, I have done that so often; I said, 'If you do not do this, I will not do that.' And what was the result? They did not do this, and I had *tout simplement et bonnement* to do that. I write to Monsieur Motte, 'Your niece shall not leave the Pension until you come for her;' he does not come, and I take her to him. *Voilà la politique féminine*."

After breakfast, when they had dressed, bonneted, and gloved themselves, Madame said,—

"*Ma foi!* I do not even know where the old Diogène lives. Do you remember the name of the street, Marie?"

"No, Madame; somewhere in the *Faubourg d'en bas*."

"Ah, well! I must look for it here."

She went to the table and quickly turned over the leaves of a ledger.

"Marie Modeste Motte, niece of Monsieur Motte. *Mais, tiens*, there is no address!"

Marie looked with interest at her name written in red ink.

"No; it is not there."

"*Ah, que je suis bête*. It is in the other one. This one is only for the last ten years. There, *ma fille*, get on a chair; can you reach that one? No, not that, the other one. How warm it is! You look it out for me!"

"I do not see any address here either, Madame."

"Impossible! There must be an address there. True, nothing but Marie Modeste Motte, niece of Monsieur Motte, just like the other one. Now, you see, that's Marcélite again; that's all her fault. It was her duty to give that address thirteen years ago. In thirteen years she has not had the time to do that!"

They both sat down warm and vexed.

"I shall send Jeanne for her again!"

But Jeanne's zeal had anticipated orders.

"I have already been there, Madame; I beat on her door, I beat on it as hard as I could, and the neighbors opened their windows and said they didn't think she had been there all night."

"Well, then, there is nothing for me to do but send for Monsieur le Notaire! Here, Jeanne; take this note to Monsieur Goupilleau."

All unmarried women, widows or maids, if put to the torture, would reveal some secret, unsuspected sources of advisory assistance,—a subterranean passage for friendship which sometimes offers a retreat into matrimony,—and the last possible wrinkle, the last resisting gray hair is added to other female burdens at the death of this secret counsellor or the closing up of the hidden passage. Therefore, how dreadful it is for women to be condemned to a life of such logical exactions where a reason is demanded for everything, even for a *statu quo* affection of fifteen years or more. Madame Lareveillère did not possess courage enough to defy logic, but her imagination and wit could seriously embarrass its conclusions. The *raison d'être* of a Goupilleau in her life had exercised both into athletic proportions.

"An old friend, *ma mignonne;* I look upon him as a father, and he treats me just as if I were his daughter. I go to him as to a confessor. And a great institute like this requires so much advice,—oh, so much! He is very old,—as old as Monsieur Motte himself. We might just as well take off our things; he will not come before evening. You see, he is so discreet, he would not come in the morning for anything in the world. He is just exactly like a father, I assure you, and very, very old."

The graduate and young lady of a day sat in the rocking-chair, quiet, almost happy. She was not in the home she had looked forward to; but Madame's tenderness, the beautiful room in its soothing twilight, and the patronizing majesty of the *lit de justice* made this a very pleasant abiding place in her journey,—the journey so long and so difficult from school to her real home, from girlhood to real young ladyhood. It was nearly two days now since she had seen Marcélite. How she longed for her, and what a scolding she intended to give her when she arrived at her uncle's, where, of course, Marcélite was waiting for her. How silly she had acted about the address! But, after all, procrastination is so natural. As for Madame, Marie smiled as she thought how easily a reconciliation could be effected between them, *quittes* though they were.

It is hard to wean young hearts from hoping and planning; they will do it in the very presence of the angel of death, and with their shrouds in full view.

Monsieur Goupilleau came: a Frenchman of small stature but large head. He had the eyes of a poet and the smile of a woman.

The prelude of compliments, the tentative flourish to determine in which key the ensuing variation on their little romance should be played, was omitted. Madame came brusquely to the *motif,* not personal to either of them.

"Monsieur Goupilleau, I take pleasure in presenting you to Mademoiselle Marie Motte, one of our young lady graduates. *Mon ami,* we are in the greatest trouble imaginable. Just imagine, Monsieur Motte, the uncle of mademoiselle could not come for her last night to take her home. He is so old and infirm," added Madame, considerately; "so you see mademoiselle could not leave last night: I want to take her home myself—a great pleasure it is, and not a trouble, I assure you, Marie—but we do not know where he lives."

"Ah! you have not his address."

"No, it should be in the ledger; but an accident,—in fact, the laziness of her *bonne,* who never brought it, not once in thirteen years."

"Her *bonne?*"

"Yes, her *bonne* Marcélite; you know Marcélite *la coiffeuse;* what, you do not know Marcélite, that great, fat—"

"Does Marcélite know where he lives?"

"But of course, my friend, Marcélite knows, she goes there every day."

"Well, send for Marcélite."

"Send for Marcélite! but I have sent for Marcélite at least a dozen times! she is never at her room. Marcélite! ha! my friend, I am done with Marcélite. What do you think? After combing my hair for fifteen years! —fifteen years, I tell you—she did not come yesterday at all, not once; and the concert at night! You should have seen our heads last night! we were frights—frights, I assure you!"

It was a poetical license, but the eyes of Monsieur Goupilleau disclaimed any such possibility for the head before him.

"Does not mademoiselle know the address of her uncle?"

"Ah, *that,* no. Mademoiselle has been a *pensionnaire* at the Institut St.

Denis for thirteen years, and she has never been anywhere except to church; she has seen no one without a chaperon; she has received no letter that has not passed through Madame Joubert's hands. Ah! for that I am particular, and it was Monsieur Motte himself who requested it."

"Then you need a directory."

"A what?"

"A directory."

"But what is that,—a directory?"

"It's a volume, Madame, a book containing the addresses of all the residents of the city."

"*Quelle bonne idée!* If I had only known that! I shall buy one. Jeanne! Jeanne! run quick, *ma bonne*, to Morel's and buy me a directory."

"Pardon, Madame, I think it would be quicker to send to Bâle's, the *pharmacien* at the corner, and borrow one. Here, Jeanne, take my card."

"*A la bonne heure!* now we shall find our affair."

But the M's, which started so many names in the directory, were perfectly innocent of any combination applicable to an old uncle by the name of Motte.

"You see, your directory is no better than my books!"

Monsieur Goupilleau looked mortified, and shrugged his shoulders. "He must live outside the city limits, Madame."

"Marcélite always said, 'in the *Faubourg d'en bas.*' "

Jeanne interrupted stolidly: "Monsieur Bâle told me to bring the book right back; it is against his rules to lend it out of his store."

"Here, take it! take it! Tell him I am infinitely obliged. It was of no use, any way. Ah, *les hommes!*"

"Madame," began Monsieur Goupilleau in precautionary deprecation.

A sudden noise outside,—apparently an assault at the front door; a violent struggle in the antechamber!

"*Grand Dieu!* what can that be!" Madame's lips opened for a shrill *Au secours! Voleurs!* but seeing the notary rush to the door, she held him fast with her two little white hands on his arm.

"*Mon ami*, I implore you!"

The first recognition; the first expression of a fifteen years' secret affection! The first thrill (old as he was) of his first passion! But danger called him outside; he unloosed the hands and opened the door.

A heavy body propelled by Jeanne's strong hands fell on the floor of the room, accompanied by a shower of leaves from Monsieur Bâle's directory.

"*Misérable! Infâme! Effrontée!* Ah, I have caught you! *Scélérate!*"

"Marcélite!"

"Marcélite!"

"Marcélite?"

"Sneaking outside the gate! Like an animal! like a thief! like a dog! Ha! I caught you well!"

The powerful arms seemed ready again to crush the unresisting form rising from the floor.

"Jeanne! hush! How dare you speak to Marcélite like that? Oh, *ma bonne*, what is the matter with you?"

Shaking, trembling, she cowered before them silent.

"Ah! she didn't expect me, *la fière négresse!* Just look at her!"

They did, in painful, questioning surprise. Was this their own clean, neat, brave, honest, handsome Marcélite,—this panting, tottering, bedraggled wretch before them, threatening to fall on the floor again, not daring to raise even her eyes?

"Marcélite! Marcélite! who has done this to you! Tell me, tell your *bébé*, Marcélite."

"Is she drunk?" whispered Madame to the notary.

Her *tignon* had been dragged from her head. Her calico dress, torn and defaced, showed her skin in naked streaks. Her black woolly hair, always so carefully packed away under her head-kerchief, stood in grotesque masses around her face, scratched and bleeding like her exposed bosom. She jerked herself violently away from Marie's clasp.

"Send them away! Send them away!" she at last said to Monsieur Goupilleau, in a low, unnatural voice. "I will talk to you, but send them all away."

Madame and Marie immediately obeyed his look; but outside the door Marie stopped firmly.

"Madame, Marcélite can have nothing to say which I should not hear—"

"Hush—" Madame put her finger to her lips; the door was still a little open and the voices came to them.

Marcélite, from the corner of her bleared eyes, watched them retire, and then with a great heave of her naked chest she threw herself on the floor at the notary's feet.

"Master! Oh master! Help me!"

All the suffering and pathos of a woman's heart were in the tones, all the weakness, dependence, and abandonment in the words.

The notary started at the unexpected appeal. His humanity, his manhood, his chivalry, answered it.

"*Ma fille*, speak; what can I do for you?"

He bent over her as she lay before him, and put his thin, white, wrinkled hand on her shoulder, where it had burst through her dress. His low voice promised the willing devotion of a saviour.

"But don't tell my *bébé*, don't let her know. My God! it will kill her! She's got no uncle—no Monsieur Motte! It was all a lie. It was me,—me a nigger, that sent her to school and paid for her—"

"You! Marcélite! You!"

Marcélite jumped up and tried to escape from the room. Monsieur Goupilleau quickly advanced before her to the door.

"You fooled me! It was you fooled me!" she screamed to Madame. "God will never forgive you for that! My *bébe* has heard it all!"

Marie clung to her; Monsieur Goupilleau caught her by the arm.

"Marcélite! It was you,—you who sent me to school, who paid for me! And I have no uncle?"

Marcélite looked at the notary,—a prayer for help. The girl fell in a chair and hid her face in her hands.

"Oh, my God! I knew it would kill her! I knew it would! To be supported by a nigger!" She knelt by the chair. "Speak to me, Mamzelle Marie. Speak to me just once! Pardon me, my little mistress! Pardon me! I did not know what I was doing; I am only a fool nigger, anyhow! I wanted you to go to the finest school with ladies, and—and—oh! my *bébé* won't speak to me; she won't even look at me."

Marie raised her head, put both hands on the nurse's shoulders, and looked her straight in the eyes.

"And that also was all a lie about"—she sank her trembling voice—"about my mother?"

"That a lie! That a lie! 'Fore God in heaven, that was the truth; I swear it. I will kiss the crucifix. What do you take me for, Mamzelle Marie? Tell a lie about—"

Marie fell back in the chair with a despairing cry.

"I cannot believe any of it."

"Monsieur! Madame! I swear to you it's the truth! God in heaven knows it is. I wouldn't lie about that,—about my poor dead young mistress. Monsieur! Madame! tell Miss Marie for me; can't you believe me?" She shrieked in desperation to Monsieur Goupilleau.

He came to her unhesitatingly. "I believe you, Marcélite." He put his hand again on her shoulder; his voice faltered, "Poor Marcélite!"

"God bless you, master! God bless you for that. Let me tell you; you believe me when my *bébé* won't. My young mistress, she died; my young master, he had been killed in the war. My young mistress was all alone by herself, with nobody but me, and I didn't take her poor little baby out of her arms till she was dead, as she told me. *Mon bébé, mon bébé!* don't you know that's the truth? Can't you feel that's the truth? You see that; she will never speak to me again. I knew it; I told you so. I heard her last night, in that big room, all by herself, crying for Marcélite. Marcélite! my God! I was afraid to go to her, and I was just under a bed; you think that didn't 'most kill me?" She hid her face in her arms, and swayed her body back and forth.

"Marcélite," said Monsieur Goupilleau. The voice of the champion trembled, and his eyes glistened with tears at the distress he had pledged himself to relieve. "Marcélite, I believe you, my poor woman; I believe you. Tell me the name of the lady, the mother of Mademoiselle."

"Ha! her name! I am not ashamed to tell her name before anybody. Her name! I will tell you her name." She sprang to her feet. "You ask anybody from the Paroisse St. Jacques if they ever heard the name of Mamzelle Marie Modeste Viel and Monsieur Alphonse Motte. That was the name of her mother and her father, and I am not ashamed of it that I shouldn't tell, ha! Yes, and I am Marcélite Gaulois, and when my mother was sold out the parish, who took me and brought me up, and made me sleep on the foot of her bed, and fed me like her own baby, *hein?* Mamzelle Marie Viel's mother, and Mamzelle was the other baby; and she nursed us like twins, *hein?* You ask anybody from the Paroisse St. Jacques. They know; they can tell you."

Marie stood up.

"Come, Marcélite, let us go. Madame, Monsieur—" She evidently struggled to say something else, but she only reiterated, "I must go; we must go; come, Marcélite, let us go."

No one would have remarked now that her eyes were too old for her face.

"Go? My Lord! Where have you *got* to go to?"

"I want to go home to Marcélite; I want to go away with her; come, Marcélite, let us go. Oh! don't you all see I can't stay here any longer? Let me go! Let me go!"

"Go with me! Go to my home! A white young lady like you go live with a nigger like me!"

"Come, Marcélite; please come; go with me; I don't want to stay here."

"You stand there! You hear that! Monsieur! Madame! You hear that!"

"Marcélite, I want to go with you; I want to live with you; I am not too good for that."

"What! You don't think you ain't white! Oh, God! Strike me dead!"

She raised her naked arms over her head, imploring destruction.

"Marcélite, *ma fille*, do not forget, I have promised to help you. Marcélite, only listen to me a moment. Mademoiselle, do not fear; Mademoiselle shall not leave us. I shall protect her; I shall be a father to her—"

"And I," said Madame, drawing Marie still closer to her,—"I shall be her mother."

"Now, try, Marcélite," continued Monsieur Goupilleau,—"try to remember somebody, anybody who knows you, who knew your mistress; I want their names. Anybody, anybody will do, my poor Marcélite! Indeed, I believe you; we all believe you; we know you are telling the truth; but is there not a person, even a book, a piece of paper, anything, you can remember?"

He stood close to her; his head did not reach above her shoulders, but his eyes plead into her face as if petitioning for his own honor; and then they followed the hands of the woman fumbling, feeling, passing, repassing inside her torn dress-waist. He held his hands out,—the kind tender little hands that had rested so gently on her bruised black skin.

"If I have not lost it, if I have not dropped it out of my gown since last night—I never have dropped it, and I have carried it round inside my body now for seventeen years; but I was 'most crazy last night—"

She put a small package all wrapped up in an old bandanna handkerchief in his hands.

"I was keeping that for my *bébé;* I was going to give it to her when she graduated, just to remind her of her own mother. She gave it to me when she died."

It was only a little worn-out prayer-book, but all filled with written papers and locks of hair and dates and certificates,—frail fluttering scraps that dropped all over the table, but unanswerable champions for the honor of dead men and the purity of dead women.

"*Par la grâce de Dieu!*" exclaimed the notary, while the tears fell from his eyes on the precious relics, discolored and worn from bodily contact. Marie sank on her knees by the table, holding Marcélite tight by the hand.

"*Par la grâce de Dieu!* Nothing is wanting here,—nothing, nothing except the forgiveness of this good woman, and the assurances of our love and gratitude. And they say," turning to Madame, he hazarded the bold step of taking both her hands in his,—"they say," recollecting the tender pressure on his arm, he ventured still further,—"they say, Eugénie, that the days of heroism are past, and they laugh at our romance!"

IV BAYOU L'OMBRE: AN INCIDENT OF THE WAR

TALES OF A TIME AND PLACE, Grace King's second collection of fiction, is a series of five long stories with settings of the Civil War and Reconstruction eras. In "Bayou L'Ombre" Miss King constructed a tale based on her own recollections of life in the country at the very end of the war period. It is closely autobiographical, the name echoing Bayou L'Embarras, on which the family plantation was situated. Grace King's uncle, E. T. King, an active guerrilla leader, was probably the model for Beau, the young man of the story. The three girls resemble the patriotic King sisters, and names of the black women in the laundry scene are names of plantation slaves. The plot is subordinate to the primary interest of the story: the impact of the war on the peaceful domestic scene.

"Bayou L'Ombre" first appeared in *Harper's Magazine*, LXXV (July, 1887), 266–83. The copy-text on which the present text is based is the version in *Tales of a Time and Place* (New York: Harper and Brothers, 1892).

Of course they knew all about war—soldiers, flags, music, generals on horseback brandishing swords, knights in armor escalading walls, cannons booming through clouds of smoke. They were familiarized with it pictorially and by narrative long before the alphabet made its appearance in the nursery with rudimentary accounts of the world they were born into, the simple juvenile world of primary sensations and colors. Their great men, and great women, too, were all fighters; the great events of their histories, battles; the great places of their geography, where they were fought (and generally the more bloody the battle, the more glorious the place); while their little chronology—the pink-covered one—stepped briskly over the centuries solely on the names of kings and sanguinary saliencies. Sunday added the sabbatical supplement to week-day lessons, symbolizing religion, concreting sin, incorporating evil, for their better comprehension, putting Jehovah himself in armor, to please their childish faculties—the omnipotent Intervener of the Old Testament, for whom they waved banners, sang hymns, and by the brevet title, "little *soldiers* of the cross," felt committed as by baptism to an attitude of expectant hostility. Mademoiselle Couper, their governess, eased the cross-stitching in their samplers during the evenings, after supper, with traditions of "le grand Napoléon," in whose army her grandfather was a terrible and distinguished officer, le Capitaine Césaire Paul Picquet de Montignac; and although Mademoiselle Couper was most unlovable and exacting at times, and very homely, such were their powers of sympathetic enthusiasm even then that they often went to bed envious of the possessor of so glorious an ancestor, and dreamed fairy tales of him whose gray hair, enshrined in a brooch, reposed comfortably under the folds of mademoiselle's fat chin—the hair that Napoleon had looked upon!

When a war broke out in their own country they could hardly credit their good-fortune; that is, Christine and Régina, for Lolotte was still a baby. A wonderful panorama was suddenly unfolded before them. It was their first intimation of the identity of the world they lived in with the world they learned about, their first perception of the existence of an entirely novel sentiment in their hearts—patriotism, the *amour sacré de la patrie*, over which they had seen mademoiselle shed tears as copiously as her grandfather had blood. It made them and all their little companions feel very proud, this war; but it gave them a heavy sense of responsibility, turning their youthful precocity incontinently away from books, slates, and pianos towards the martial considerations that befitted the hour. State rights, Federal limits, monitors and fortresses, proclamations, Presidents, recognitions, and declarations, they acquired them all with facility, taxing, as in other lessons, their tongue to repeat the unintelligible on trust for future intelligence. As their father fired his huge after-dinner bombs, so they shot their diminutive ammunition; as he lighted brands in the great conflagration, they lighted tapers; and the two contending Presidents themselves did not get on their knees with more fervor before their colossal sphinxes than these little girls did before their doll-baby presentment of "Country." It was very hard to realize at times that histories and story-books and poetry would indeed be written about them; that little flags would mark battles all over the map of their country—the country Mademoiselle Couper despised as so hopelessly, warlessly insignificant; that men would do great things and women say them, teachers and copy-books reiterate them, and children learn them, just as they did of the Greeks and Romans, the English and French. The great advantage was having God on their side, as the children of Israel had; the next best thing was having the finest country, the most noble men, and the bravest soldiers. The only fear was that the enemy would be beaten too easily, and the war cease too soon to be glorious; for, characteristic of their sex, they demanded nothing less than that their war should be the longest, bloodiest, and most glorious of all wars ever heard of, in comparison with which even "le grand Napoleon" and his Capitaine Picquet would be effaced from memory. For this were exercised their first attempts at extempore prayer. God, the dispenser of inexhaustible supplies of munitions of war, became quite a different power, a nearer and dearer personality, than "Our Father," the giver of simple daily bread, and He did not lack reminding of the existence of the young Confederacy, nor of the hearsay exigencies they gathered from the dinner-table talk.

Titine was about thirteen, Gina twelve, and Lolotte barely eight years old, when this, to them, happy break in their lives occurred. It was easily comprehensible to them that their city should be captured, and that to escape that grim ultimatum of Mademoiselle Couper, "*passées au fil de l'épée*," they should be bundled up very hurriedly one night, carried out of their home, and journey in troublesome roundabout ways to the plantation on Bayou l'Ombre.

That was all four years ago. School and play and city life, dolls and fêtes and Santa Claus, had become the property of memory. Peace for them hovered in that obscurity which had once enveloped war, while "'61," "'62," "'63," "'64," filled immeasurable spaces in their short past. Four times had Christine and Régina changed the date in their diaries—the last token of remembrance from Mademoiselle Couper—altering the numerals with naïve solemnity, as if under the direction of the Almighty himself, closing with conventional ceremony the record of the lived-out twelve months, opening with appropriate aspirations the year to come. The laboriously careful chronicle that followed was not, however, of the growth of their bodies advancing by inches, nor the expansion of their minds, nor of the vague forms that began to people the shadowland of their sixteen and seventeen year old hearts. Their own budding and leafing and growing was as unnoted as that of the trees and weeds about them. The progress of the war, the growth of their hatred of the enemy, the expansion of the *amour sacré* germ—these were the confidences that filled the neatly-stitched foolscap volumes. If on comparison one sister was found to have been happier in the rendition of the common sentiment, the coveted fervor and eloquence were plagiarized or imitated the next day by the other, a generous emulation thus keeping the original flame not only alight, but burning, while from assimilating each other's sentiments the two girls grew with identity of purpose into identity of mind, and effaced the slight difference of age between them.

Little Lolotte responded as well as she could to the enthusiastic exactions of her sisters. She gave her rag dolls patriotic names, obediently hated and loved as they required, and learned to recite all the war songs procurable, even to the teeming quantities of the stirring "Men of the South, our foes are up!" But as long as the squirrels gambolled on the fences, the blackbirds flocked in the fields, and the ditches filled with fish; as long as the seasons imported such constant variety of attractions—persimmons, dewberries, blackberries, acorns, wild plums, grapes, and muscadines; as long as the cows had calves, the dogs puppies, the hogs pigs, and the quarters new babies to be named; as long as the exasperating negro children needed daily subjugation, regulation, and discipline—the day's measure was too well filled and the night's slumber too short to admit of her carrying on a very vigorous warfare for a country so far away from Bayou l'Ombre—a country whose grievances she could not understand.

But—there were no soldiers, flags, music, parades, battles, or sieges. This war was altogether distinct from the wars contained in books or in Mademoiselle Couper's memory. There was an absence of the simplest requirements of war. They kept awaiting the familiar events for which they had been prepared; but after four years the only shots fired on Bayou l'Ombre were at game in the forest, the only blood shed was from the tottering herds of Texas beeves driven across the swamps to them, barely escaping by timely butchery the starvation they came to relieve, and the only heroism they had been called upon to display was still going to bed in the dark. Indeed, were it not that they knew there was a war they might have supposed that some malignant fairy had transported them from a state of wealth and luxury to the condition of those miserable Hathorns, the pariahs of their childhood, who lived just around the corner from them in the city, with whom they had never been allowed to associate. If they had not so industriously fostered the proper feelings in their hearts, they might almost have forgotten it, or, like Lolotte, been diverted from it by the generous overtures of nature all around them. But they kept on reminding each other that it was not the degrading want of money, as in the Hathorns' case, that forced them to live on salt meat, corn-bread, and sassafras tea, to dress like the negro women in the quarters, that deprived them of education and society, and imprisoned them in a swamp-encircled plantation, the prey of chills and fever; but it was for love of country, and being little women now, they loved their country more, the more they suffered for her. Disillusion might have supervened to disappointment and bitterness have quenched hope, experience might at last have sharpened their vision, but for the imagination, that ethereal parasite which fattens on the stagnant forces of youth and garnishes with tropical luxuriance the abnormal source of its nourishment. Soaring aloft, above the prosaic actualities of the present, beyond the rebutting evidence of earth, was a fanciful stage where the drama of war such as they craved was unfolded; where neither homespun, starvation, overflows, nor illness were allowed to enter; where the heroes and heroines they loved acted roles in all the conventional glitter of costume and conduct, amid the dazzling pomps and circumstances immortalized in history and romance. Their hearts would bound and leap after these phantasms, like babes in nurses' arms after the moon, and would almost burst with longing, their ripe little hearts, Pandora-boxes packed with passions and pleasures for a lifetime, ready to spring open at a touch! On moonlit nights in summer, or under the low gray clouds of winter days, in the monotony of nothingness about them, the yearning in their breasts was like that of hunting dogs howling for the unseen game. Sometimes a rumor of a battle "out in the Confederacy" would find its way across the swamps to them, and months afterwards a newspaper would be thrown to them from a passing skiff, some old, useless, tattered, disreputable, journalistic tramp, garrulous with mendacities; but it was all true to them, if to no one else in the world—the factitious triumphs, the lurid glories, the pyrotechnical promises, prophecies, calculations, and Victory with the laurel wreath always in the future, never out of sight for an instant. They would con the fraudulent evangel, entranced; their eyes would sparkle, the blood color their cheeks, their voices vibrate, and a strange strength excite and nerve their bodies. Then would follow wakeful nights and restless days; Black Margarets, Jeanne d'Arcs, Maids of Saragossa, Katherine Douglases, Charlotte Cordays,[1] would haunt them like the goblins of a delirium; then their prayers would become imperious demands upon Heaven, their diaries would almost break into spontaneous combustion from the incendiary material enmagazined in their pages, and the South would have conquered the world then and there could their hands but have pointed the guns and their hearts have recruited the armies. They would with mingled pride and envy read all the names, barely decipherable in the travel-stained record, from the President and Generals in big print to the diminishing insignificance of smallest-type privates; and they would shed tears, when the reaction would come a few days later, at the thought that in the whole area of typography, from the officers gaining immortality to the privates losing lives, there was not one name belonging to them; and they would ask why, of all the families in the South, precisely their father and mother should have no relations, why, of all the women in the South, they should be brotherless.

There was Beau, a too notorious guerilla captain; but what glory was to be won by raiding towns, wrecking trains, plundering transports, capturing couriers, disobeying orders, defying regulations? He was almost as obnoxious to his own as to the enemy's flag.

1 Black Margaret is not identified; "Maid of Saragossa" was Marí Augustín, a defender of the city against the French during the siege, 1808–1809. See Byron, *Childe Harold*, I (53–56). Lady Katherine Douglas in 1436 at Blackfriars Monastery, Perth, heroically held off the assassins of King James I of Scotland by thrusting her arm where the bolt of the door was missing. Charlotte Corday was the assassin of Marat.

Besides, Beau at most was only a kind of a cousin, the son of a deceased step-sister of their father's; the most they could expect from him was to keep his undisciplined crew of " 'Cadians," Indians, and swampers away from Bayou l'Ombre.

"Ah, if we were only men!" But no! They who could grip daggers and shed blood, they who teemed with all the possibilities of romance or poetry, they were selected for a passive, paltry contest against their own necessities; the endurance that would have laughed a siege to scorn ebbing away in a never-ceasing wrangle with fever and ague—willow-bark tea at odds with a malarious swamp!

It was now early summer; the foliage of spring was lusty and strong, fast outgrowing tenderness and delicacy of shade, with hints of maturity already swelling the shape. The day was cloudless and warm, the dinner-hour was long past, and supper still far off. There were no appetizing varieties of menu to make meals objects of pleasant anticipation; on the contrary, they had become mournful effigies of a convivial institution of which they served at most only to recall the hours, monotonously measuring off the recurring days which passed like unlettered mileposts in a desert, with no information to give except that of transition. To-day the meal-times were so far apart as to make one believe that the sun had given up all forward motion, and intended prolonging the present into eternity. The plantation was quiet and still; not the dewy hush of early dawn trembling before the rising sun, nor the mysterious muteness of midnight, nor yet the lethargic dulness of summer when the vertical sun-rays pin sense and motion to the earth. It was the motionless, voiceless state of unnatural quietude, the oppressive consciousness of abstracted activity, which characterized those days when the whole force of Bayou l'Ombre went off into the swamps to cut timber. Days that began shortly after one midnight and lasted to the other; rare days, when neither horn nor bell was heard for summons; when not a skiff, flat-boat, nor pirogue was left at the "gunnels;" * when old Uncle John alone remained to represent both master and men in the cares and responsibilities devolving upon his sex. The bayou lived and moved as usual, carrying its deceptive depths of brackish water unceasingly onward through the shadow and sunshine, rippling over the opposite low, soft banks, which seemed slowly sinking out of sight under the weight of the huge cypress-trees growing upon it. The long stretch of untilled fields back of the house, fee-

* "Gunnels," floating wharf [Grace King's note].

bly kept in symmetrical proportion by crumbling fences, bared their rigid, seedless furrows in despairing barrenness to the sun, except in corner spots where a rank growth of weeds had inaugurated a reclamation in favor of barbarism. The sugar-house, superannuated and decrepit from unwholesome idleness, tottered against its own massive, smokeless chimney; the surrounding sheds, stables, and smithy looked forsaken and neglected; the old blind mule peacefully slept in the shade of his once flagellated course under the corn-mill. Afar off against the woods the huge wheel of the draining-machine rose from the underbrush in the big ditch. The patient buzzards, roosting on the branches of the gaunt, blasted gum-tree by the bayou, would raise their heads from time to time to question the loitering sun, or, slowly flapping their heavy wings, circle up into the blue sky, to fall again in lazy spirals to their watch-tower, or they would take short flights by twos and threes over the moribund plantation to see if dissolution had not yet set in, and then all would settle themselves again to brood and sleep and dream, and wait in tranquil certainty the striking of their banqueting hour.

The three girls were in the open hall-way of the plantation house, Christine reading, Régina knitting, both listlessly occupied. Like everything else, they were passively quiet, and, like everything else, their appearance advertised an unwholesome lack of vitality, an insidious anamorphosis from an unexplained dearth or constraint. Their meagre maturity and scant development clashed abnormally with the surrounding prodigality of insensible nature. Though tall, they were thin; they were fair, but sallow; their gentle deep eyes were reproachful and deprived-looking. If their secluded hearts ventured even in thought towards the plumings natural to their age, their coarse, homely, ill-fitting garments anathematized any coquettish effort or naïve expression of a desire to find favor. Like the fields, they seemed hesitating on the backward path from cultivation. Lolotte stood before the cherry-wood armoire that held the hunting and fishing tackle, the wholesome receptacle of useful odds and ends. Not old enough to have come into the war with preconceptions, Lolotte had no reconciliations or compromises to effect between the ideal and the real, no compensations to solicit from an obliging imagination, which so far never rose beyond the possibilities of perch, blackbirds, and turtle eggs. The first of these occupied her thoughts at the present moment. She had made a tryst with the negro children at the draining-machine this afternoon. If she could, unperceived, abstract enough tackle from the armoire for the crowd, and if they could slip away from the quarters, and she evade the surveillance of Uncle John, there would be a diminished number of "brim" and "goggle-eye" in the ditch out yonder, and such a notable addition to the plantation supper to-night as would crown the exploit a success, and establish for herself a reputation above all annoying recollections of recent mishaps and failures. As she tied the hooks on to the lines she saw herself surrounded by the acclaiming infantile populace, pulling the struggling perch up one after the other; she saw them strung on palmetto thongs, long strings of them; she walked home at the head of her procession; heard Peggy's exclamations of surprise, smelt them frying, and finally was sitting at the table, a plate of bones before her, the radiant hostess of an imperial feast.

"Listen!" Like wood-ducks from under the water, the three heads rose simultaneously above their abstractions. "Rowlock! Rowlock!" The eyes might become dull, the tongue inert, and the heart languid on Bayou l'Ombre, but the ears were ever assiduous, ever on duty. Quivering and nervous, they listened even through sleep for that one blessed echo of travel, the signal from another and a distant world. Faint, shadowy, delusive, the whispering forerunner of on-coming news, it overrode the rippling of the current, the hooting of the owls, the barking of dogs, the splash of the gar-fish, the grunting of the alligator, the croaking of frogs, penetrating all turmoil, silencing all other sounds. "Rowlock! Rowlock!" Slow, deliberate, hard, and strenuous, coming upstream; easy, soft, and musical, gliding down. "Rowlock! Rowlock!" Every stroke a very universe of hope, every oar frothing a sea of expectation! Was it the bayou or the secret stream of their longing that suggested the sound today? "Rowlock! Rowlock!" The smouldering glances brightened in their eyes, they hollowed their hands behind their ears and held their breath for greater surety. "Rowlock! Rowlock!" In clear, distinct reiteration. It resolved the moment of doubt.

"Can it be papa coming back?"

"No; it's against stream."

"It must be swampers."

"Or hunters, perhaps."

"Or Indians from the mound."

"Indians in a skiff?"

"Well, they sometimes come in a skiff."

The contingencies were soon exhausted, a cut-off leading travellers far around Bayou l'Ombre, whose snaggy, rafted, convoluted course was by universal avoidance relegated to an isolation almost insulting. The girls, listening, not to lose a single vibration, quit their places and advanced to the edge of the gallery, then out under the trees, then to the levee, then to the "gunnels," where they stretched their long, thin, white necks out of their blue and brown check gowns, and shaded their eyes and gazed down-stream for the first glimpse of the skiff—their patience which had lasted months fretting now over the delay of a few moments.

"At last we shall get some news again."

"If they only leave a newspaper!"

"Or a letter," said Lolotte.

"A letter! From whom?"

"Ah, that's it!"

"What a pity papa isn't here!"

"Lolotte, don't shake the gunnels so; you are wetting our feet."

"How long is it since the last one passed?"

"I can tell you," said Lolotte—"I can tell you exactly: it was the day Lou Ann fell in the bayou and nearly got drowned."

"You mean when you both fell in."

"I didn't fall in at all; I held on to the pirogue."

The weeping-willow on the point below veiled the view; stretching straight out from the bank, it dropped its shock of long, green, pliant branches into the water, titillating and dimpling the surface. The rising bayou bore a freight of logs and drift from the swamps above; rudely pushing their way through the willow boughs, they tore and bruised the fragile tendrils that clung to the rough bark, scattering the tiny leaves which followed hopelessly after in their wake or danced up and down in the hollow eddies behind them. Each time the willow screen moved, the gunnels swayed under the forward motion of the eager bodies of the girls.

"At last!"

They turned their eyes to the shaft of sunlight that fell through the plantation clearing, bridging the stream. The skiff touched, entered, and passed through it with a marvellous revelation of form and color, the oars silvering and dripping diamonds, arrows and lances of light scintillating from polished steel, golden stars rising like dust from tassels, cordons, buttons, and epaulets, while the blue clouds themselves seemed to have fallen from their empyrean heights to uniform the rowers with their own celestial hue—blue, not gray!

"Rowlock! Rowlock!" What loud, frightful, threatening reverberations of the oars! And the bayou flowed on the same, and the cypress-trees gazed stolidly and steadfastly up to the heavens, and the heavens were serenely blue and white! But the earth was sympathetic, the ground shook and swayed under their feet; or was it the rush of thoughts that made their heads so giddy? They tried to arrest one and hold it for guidance, but on they sped, leaving only wild confusion of conjecture behind.

"Rowlock! Rowlock!" The rudder headed the bow for the gunnels.

"Titine! Gina! Will they kill us all?" whispered Lolotte, with anxious horror.

The agile Lou Ann, Lolotte's most efficient coadjutor and Uncle John's most successful tormentor, dropped her bundle of fishing-poles (which he had carefully spread on his roof to "cure"), and while they rolled and rattled over the dry shingles she scrambled with inconceivable haste to her corner of descent. Holding to the eaves while her excited black feet searched and found the top of the window that served as a step, she dropped into the ash-hopper below. Without pausing, as usual, to efface betraying evidences of her enterprise from her person, or to cover her tracks in the wet ashes, she jumped to the ground, and ignoring all secreting offers of bush, fence, or ditch, contrary to her custom, she ran with all the speed of her thin legs down the shortest road to the quarters. They were, as she knew, deserted. The doors of the cabins were all shut, with logs of wood or chairs propped against them. The chickens and dogs were making free of the galleries, and the hogs wallowed in peaceful immunity underneath. A waking baby from a lonely imprisoned cradle sent cries for relief through an open window. Lou Ann, looking neither to the right nor the left, slackened not her steps, but passed straight on through the little avenue to the great white-oak which stood just outside the levee on the bank of the bayou.

Under the wide-spreading, moss-hung branches, upon the broad flat slope, a grand general washing of the clothes of the small community was in busy progress by the women, a proper feminine consecration of this purely feminine day. The daily irksome routine was broken, the men were all away, the sun was bright and warm, the air soft and sweet. The vague recesses of the opposite forest were dim and silent, the bayou played under the gunnels in caressing modulations. All furthered the hearkening and the yielding to a debonair mood, with disregard of concealment, license of pose, freedom of limb, hilarity, conviviality, audacities of heart and tongue, joyous indulgence in freak and impulse, banishment of thought, a return, indeed, for one brief moment to the wild, sweet ways of nature, to the festal days of ancestral golden age (a short retrogression for them), when the body still had claims, and the mind concessions, and the heart owed no allegiance, and when god and satyr eyes still might be caught peeping and glistening from leafy covert on feminine midsummer gambols. Their skirts were girt high around their broad full hips, their dark arms and necks came naked out of their low, sleeveless, white chemise bodies, and glistened with perspiration in the sun as if frosted with silver. Little clouds of steam rose from the kettles standing around them over heaps of burning chips. The splay-legged battling-boards sank firmer and firmer into the earth under the blows of the bats, pounding and thumping the wet clothes, squirting the warm suds in all directions, up into the laughing faces, down into the panting bosoms, against the shortened, clinging skirts, over the bare legs, out in frothy runnels over the soft red clay corrugated with innumerable toe-prints. Out upon the gunnels the water swished and foamed under the vigorous movements of the rinsers, endlessly bending and raising their flexible, muscular bodies, burying their arms to the shoulders in the cool, green depths, piling higher and higher the heaps of tightly-wrung clothes at their sides. The water-carriers, passing up and down the narrow, slippery plank-way, held the evenly filled pails with the ease of coronets upon their heads. The children, under compulsion of continuous threats and occasional chastisement, fed the fire with chips from distant wood-piles, squabbling for the possession of the one cane-knife to split kindlers, imitating the noise and echoing with absurd fidelity the full-throated laughter that interrupted from time to time the work around the wash-kettles.

High above the slop and tumult sat old Aunt Mary, the official sick-nurse of the plantation, commonly credited with conjuring powers. She held a corn-cob pipe between her yellow protruding teeth, and her little restless eyes travelled inquisitively from person to person as if in quest of professional information, twinkling with amusement at notable efforts of wit, and with malice at the general discomfiture expressed under their gaze. Heelen sat near, nursing her baby. She had taken off her kerchief, and leaned her uncovered head back against the trunk of the tree; the long wisps of wool, tightly wrapped in white knitting-cotton, rose from irregular sections all over her elongated narrow skull, and encircled her wrinkled, nervous, toothless face like some ghastly serpentine chevelure.

"De Yankees! de Yankees! I seed 'em—at de big house! Little mistus she come for Uncle John. He fotched his gun—for to shoot 'em."

Lou Ann struggled to make her exhausted breath carry all her tidings. After each item she closed her mouth and swallowed violently, working her muscles until her little horns of hair rose and moved with the contortions of her face.

"An' dey locked a passel o' men up in de smoke-house—Cornfedrits."

The bats paused in the air, the women on the gunnels lifted their arms out of the water, those on the gang-plank stopped where they were; only the kettles simmered on audibly.

Lou Ann recommenced, this time finishing in one breath, with the added emphasis of raising her arm and pointing in the direction from whence she came, her voice getting shriller and shriller to the end:

"I seed 'em. Dey was Yankees. Little mistus she come for Uncle John; he fotched his gun for to shoot 'em; and they locked a passel o' men up in de smoke-house—Cornfedrits."

The Yankees! What did it mean to them? How much from the world outside had penetrated into the unlettered fastnesses of their ignorance? What did the war mean to them? Had Bayou l'Ombre indeed isolated both mind and body? Had the subtle time-spirit itself been diverted from them by the cut-off? Could their rude minds draw no inferences from the gradual loosening of authority and relaxing of discipline? Did they neither guess nor divine their share in the shock of battle out there? Could their ghost-seeing eyes not discern the martyr-spirits rising from two opposing armies, pointing at, beckoning to them? If, indeed, the water-shed of their destiny was forming without their knowledge as without their assistance, could not maternal instinct spell it out of the heart-throbs pulsing into life under their bosoms, or read from the dumb faces of the children at their breast the triumphant secret of their superiority over others born and nourished before them?

Had they, indeed, no gratifications beyond the physical, no yearnings, no secret burden of a secret prayer to God, these bonded wives and mothers? Was this careless, happy, indolent existence genuine, or only a fool's motley to disguise a tragedy of suffering? What to them was the difference between themselves and their mistresses? their condition? or their skin, that opaque black skin which hid so well the secrets of life, which could feel but not own the blush of shame, the pallor of weakness.

If their husbands had brought only rum from their stealthy midnight excursions to distant towns, how could the child repeat it so glibly—"Yankees—Cornfedrits?" The women stood still and silent, but their eyes began to creep around furtively, as if seeking degrees of complicity in a common guilt, each waiting for the other to confess comprehension, to assume the responsibility of knowledge.

The clear-headed children, profiting by the distraction of attention from them, stole away for their fishing engagement, leaving cane-knife and chips scattered on the ground behind them. The murmuring of the bayou seemed to rise louder and louder; the cries of the forsaken baby, clamorous and hoarse, fell distinctly on the air.

"My Gord A'mighty!"

The exclamation was uncompromising; it relieved the tension and encouraged rejoinder.

"My Lord!—humph!"

One bat slowly and deliberately began to beat again—Black Maria's. Her tall, straight back was to them, but, as if they saw it, they knew that her face was settling into that cold, stern rigidity of hers, the keen eyes beginning to glisten, the long, thin nostrils nervously to twitch, the lips to open over her fine white teeth—the expression they hated and feared.

"O-h! o-h! o-h!"

A long, thin, tremulous vibration, a weird, haunting note: what inspiration suggested it?

"Glo-o-ry!"

Old Aunt Mary nodded her knowing head affirmatively, as if at the fulfilment of a silent prophecy. She quietly shook the ashes out of her pipe, hunted her pocket, put it in, and rising stiffly from the root, hobbled away on her stick in the direction of her cabin.

"Glo-o-ry!"

Dead-arm Harriet stood before them, with her back to the bayou, her right arm hanging heavy at her side, her left extended, the finger pointing to the sky. A shapely arm and tapering finger; a comely, sleek, half-nude body; the moist lips, with burning red linings, barely parting to emit the sound they must have culled in uncanny practices. The heavy lids drooped over the large sleepy eyes, looking with languid passion from behind the thick black lashes.

"Glo-o-ry!" It stripped their very nerves and bared secret places of sensation! The "happy" cry of revival meetings—as if midnight were coming on, salvation and the mourners' bench before them, Judgment-day and fiery flames behind them, and "Sister Harriet" raising her voice to call them on, on, through hand-clapping, foot-stamping, shouting, groaning, screaming, out of their sins, out of their senses, to rave in religious inebriation, and fall in religious catalepsy across the floor at the preacher's feet. With a wild rush, the hesitating emotions of the women sought the opportune outlet, their hungry blood bounding and leaping for the mid-day orgy. Obediently their bodies began the imperceptible motion right and left, and the veins in their throats to swell and stand out under their skins, while the short, fierce, intense responsive exclamations fell from their lips to relieve their own and increase the exaltation of the others.

"Sweet Christ! sweet Christ!"

"Take me, Saviour!"

"Oh, de Lamb! de Lamb!"

"I'm a-coming! I'm a-coming!"

"Hold back, Satan! we's a-catching on!"

"De blood's a-dripping! de blood's a-dripping!"

"Let me kiss dat cross! let me kiss it!"

"Sweet Master!"

"Glo-o-ry! Fre-e-dom!" It was a whisper, but it came like a crash, and transfixed them; their mouths stood open with the last words, their bodies remained bent to one side or the other, the febrile light in their eyes burning as if from their blood on fire. They could all remember the day when Dead-arm Harriet, the worst worker and most violent tongue of the gang, stood in the clearing, and raising that dead right arm over her head, cursed the overseer riding away in the distance. The wind had been blowing all day; there was a sudden loud crack above them, and a limb from a deadened tree broke, sailed, poised, and fell crashing to her shoulder, and deadening her arm forever. They looked instinctively now with a start to the oak above them, to the sky—only moss and leaves and blue and white clouds. And still Harriet's voice rose, the words faster, louder, bolder, more determined, whipping them out of their awe, driving them on again down the incline of their own passions.

"Glory! Freedom! Freedom! Glory!"

"I'm bound to see 'em! Come along!"

Heelen's wild scream rang shrill and hysterical. She jerked her breast from the sucking lips, and dropped her baby with a thud on the ground. They all followed her up the levee, pressing one after the other, slipping in the wet clay, struggling each one not to be left behind. Emmeline, the wife of little Ben, the only yellow woman on the place, was the last. Her skirt was held in a grip of iron; blinded, obtuse, she pulled forward, reaching her arms out after the others.

"You stay here!"

She turned and met the determined black face of her mother-in-law.

"You let me go!" she cried, half sobbing, half angry.

"You stay here, I tell you!" The words were muttered through clinched teeth.

"You let me go, I tell you!"

"Glory! Freedom!"

The others had already left the quarters, and were on the road. They two were alone on the bank now, except Heelen's baby, whimpering under the tree; their blazing eyes glared at each other. The singing voices grew fainter and fainter. Suddenly the yellow face grew dark with the surge of blood underneath, the brows wrinkled, and the lips protruded in a grimace of animal rage. Grasping her wet bat tightly with both hands, she turned with a furious bound, and raised it with all the force of her short muscular arms. The black woman darted to the ground; the cane-knife flashed in the air and came down pitilessly towards the soft fleshy shoulder. A wild, terrified scream burst from Emmeline's lips; the bat dropped; seizing her skirt with both hands, she pulled forward, straining her back out of reach of the knife; the homespun tore, and she fled up the bank, her yellow limbs gleaming through the rent left by the fragment in the hand of the black woman.

The prisoners were so young, so handsome, so heroic; the very incarnation of the holy spirit of patriotism in their pathetic uniform of brimless caps, ragged jackets, toeless shoes, and shrunken trousers—a veteran equipment of wretchedness out of keeping with their fresh young faces. How proud and unsubdued they walked through the hall between the file of bayonets! With what haughty, defiant eyes they returned the gaze of their insultingly resplendent conquerors! Oh, if girls' souls had been merchantable at that moment! Their hands tied behind their backs like runaway slaves! Locked up in the smoke-house! that dark, rancid, gloomy, mouldy depot of empty hogsheads, barrels, boxes, and fetid exhalations.

They were the first soldiers in gray the girls had ever seen; their own chivalrous knights, the champions of their radiant country. What was the story of their calamity? Treacherously entrapped? Overpowered by numbers? Where were their companions—staring with mute, cold, upturned faces from pools of blood? And were these to be led helplessly tethered into captivity, imprisoned; with ball and chain to gangrene and disgrace their strong young limbs, or was solitary confinement to starve their hearts and craze their minds, holding death in a thousand loathsome, creeping shapes ever threateningly over them?

The smoke-house looked sinister and inimical after its sudden promotion from keeper of food to keeper of men. The great square white-washed logs seemed to settle more ponderously on the ground around them, the pointed roof to press down as if the air of heaven were an emissary to be dreaded; the hinges and locks were so ostentatiously massive and incorruptible. What artful, what vindictive security of carpenter and locksmith to exclude thieves or immure patriots!

The two eldest girls stood against the open armoire with their chill fingers interlaced. Beyond the wrinkled back of Uncle John's copperas-dyed coat before them lay the region of brass buttons and blue cloth and hostility; but they would not look at it; they turned their heads away; the lids of their eyes refused to lift and reveal the repugnant vision to them. If their ears had only been equally sensitive!

"And so you are the uncle of the young ladies? Brother of the father or mother?" What clear, incisive, nasal tones! Thank Heaven for the difference between them of the voice at least!

The captain's left arm was in a sling, but his hand could steadily hold the note-book in which he carefully pencilled Uncle John's answers to his minute cross-examination—a dainty, fragrant, Russia-leather note-book, with monogram and letters and numbers emblazoned on the outside in national colors. It had photographs inside, also, which he would pause and admire from time to time, reading the tender dedications aloud to his companions.

"And the lady in the kitchen called mammy? She is the mother, I guess?"

"P-p-p-peggy's a nigger, and my mistresses is white," stuttered Uncle John.

"Ah, indeed! Gentlemen in my uniform find it difficult to remember these trifling distinctions of color."

What tawdry pleasantry! What hypocritical courtesy! What exquisite ceremony and dainty manual for murderous dandies!

"Ef-ef-ef-ef I hadn't done gone and forgot dem caps!"

Uncle John stood before his young mistresses erect and determined, his old double-barrel shotgun firmly clasped in his tremulous hands, his blear, bloodshot eyes fearlessly measuring the foe. If it were to be five hundred lashes on his bare back under the trees out there (terms on which he would gladly have compromised), or, his secret fear, a running noose over one of the branches, or the murderous extravagance of powder and shot for him, he had made up his mind, despite every penalty, to fulfil his duty and stand by his word to Marse John. Ever since the time the little crawling white boy used to follow the great awkward black boy around like a shadow, John had made a cult of Marse John. He had taught him as a child to fish, hunt, trap birds, to dress skins, knit gloves, and play cards on the sly, to fight cocks on Sunday, to stutter, to cut the "pigeon wing" equal to any negro in the State—and other personal accomplishments besides. He had stood by him through all his scrapes as a youth, was valet to all his frolics as a young man, and now in his old age he gardened for him, and looked after the young ladies for him, stretching or contracting his elastic moral code as occasion required; but he had never deceived him nor falsified his word to him. He knew all about the war: Marse John had told him. He knew what Marse John meant when he left the children to him, and Marse John knew what to expect from John. He would treat them civilly as long as they were civil, but his gun was loaded, both barrels with bullets, and—

"Ef-ef-ef-ef I hadn't done gone and forgot dem caps!"

There was his powder-horn under one arm, there was his shot-flask filled with the last batch of slugs under the other; but the caps were not in his right-hand coat-pocket, they were in his cupboard, hidden for safety under a pile of garden "truck."

The busy martins twittered in and out of their little lodge under the eaves of the smoke-house. Régina and Christine were powerless to prevent furtive glances in that direction. Could the *prisoners* hear it inside? Could *they* see the sun travelling westward, crack by crack, chink by chink, in the roof? Could they feel it sinking, and with it sinking all their hopes of deliverance? Or did they hope still?

Maidens had mounted donjon towers at midnight, had eluded Argus-eyed sentinels, had drugged savage blood-hounds, had crossed lightning-flashed seas, had traversed robber-infested forests; whatever maidens had done they would do, for could ever men more piteously implore release from castle keep than these gray-clad youths from the smoke-house? And did ever maiden hearts beat more valiantly than theirs? (and did ever maiden limbs tremble more cowardly?) Many a tedious day had been lightened by their rehearsal of just such a drama as this; they had prepared roles for every imaginable sanguinary circumstance, but prevision, as usual, had overlooked the unexpected. The erstwhile feasible conduct, the erstwhile feasible weapons, of a Jeanne d'Arc or Charlotte Corday, the defiant speeches, the ringing retorts—how inappropriate, inadequate, here and now! If God would only help them! but, like the bayou, the cypresses, and the blue sky, He seemed to-day eternally above such insignificant human necessities as theirs.

Without the aid of introspection or the fear of capital punishment, Lolotte found it very difficult to maintain the prolonged state of rigidity into which her sisters had frozen themselves. All the alleviations devised during a wearisome experience of compulsory attendance on plantation funerals were exhausted in the course of this protracted, hymnless, prayerless solemnity. She stood wedged in between them and the armoire which displayed all its shelves of allurements to her. There were her bird-traps just within reach; there was the fascinating bag of nux-vomica root —crow poison; there was the little old work-box filled with ammunition, which she was forbidden to touch, and all the big gar-fish lines and harpoons and decoy-ducks. There were her own perch lines, the levy she had raised in favor of her companions; they were neatly rolled, ready to tie on the rods, only needing sinkers; and there was the old Indian basket filled with odds and ends, an unfailing treasure of resource and surprise. She was just about searching in it for sinkers when this interruption occurred.

The sky was so bright over the fields! Just the evening to go fishing, whether they caught anything or not. If the enemy would only hurry and go, there might still be time; they would leave, they said, as soon as mammy cooked them something to eat. She had seen mammy chasing a chicken through the yard. She wondered how the nice, fat little round "doodles" [2] were getting on in their tin can under the house; she never had had such a fine box of bait; she wondered if the negro children would go all the same without her; she wondered if she could see them creeping down the road. How easy she could have got away from Uncle John! Anything almost would do for sinkers—bits of iron, nails; they had to do since her father and Uncle John made their last moulding of bullets. She thought they might have left her just one real sinker simply as a matter of distinction between herself and the little darkies. Her eyes kept returning to the Indian basket, and if she stopped twisting her fingers one over the other but a moment they would take their way to rummaging among the rusty contents.

"Glory! Freedom!"

In came the negresses, Bacchantes drunk with the fumes of their own hot blood, Dead-arm Harriet, like a triumphant sorceress, leading them,

2 Doodles or doodle-bugs, the larvae of various insects, especially the ant lion, are used for bait.

waving and gesticulating with her one "live" arm, all repeating over and over again the potent magical words, oblivious of the curious looks of the men, their own exposure, the presence of their mistresses, of everything but their own ecstasy.

"Freedom! Master! Freedom!"

Christine and Régina raised their heads and looked perplexed at the furious women in the yard, and the men gazing down to them.

What was the matter with them? What did they mean? What was it all about?

"Freedom! Freedom!"

Then light broke upon them; their fingers tightened in each other's clasp, and their cheeks flushed crimson.

"How dared they? What insolence! What—"

The opposite door stood open; they rushed across the hall and closed it between them and the humiliating scene. This, this they had not thought of, this they had never read about, this their imagination in wildest flights had not ventured upon. This was not a superficial conflict to sweep the earth with cannons and mow it with sabres; this was an earthquake which had rent it asunder, exposing the quivering organs of hidden life. What a chasm was yawning before them! There was no need to listen one to the other; the circumstances could wring from the hearts of millions but one sentiment, the tongue was left no choice of words.

"Let them go! let them be driven out! never, never to see them again!"

The anger of outraged affection, betrayed confidence, abandoned trust, traitorous denial, raged within them.

These were their servants, their possessions! From generation to generation their lives had been woven together by the shuttle of destiny. How flimsy and transparent the fabric! how grotesque and absurd the tapestry, with its vaunted traditions of mutual loyalty and devotion! What a farce, what a lying, disgusting farce it had all been! Well, it was over now; that was a comfort—all over, all ended. If the hearts had intergrown, they were torn apart now. After this there was no return, no reconciliation possible! Through the storm of their emotions a thought drifted, then another; little detached scenes flitted into memory; familiar gestures, speeches, words, one reminiscence drawing another. Thicker and thicker came little episodes of their pastoral existence together; the counter interchanges of tokens, homely presents, kind offices, loving remembrances; the mutual assistance and consolation in all the accidents of life traversed together, the sicknesses, the births, the deaths; and so many thousand trivial incidents of long, long ago—memory had not lost one—down to the fresh eggs and the pop-corn of that very morning; they were all there, falling upon their bruised hearts.

In the hearts of the women out there were only shackles and scourges. What of the long Sundays of Bible-reading and catechism, the long evenings of woodland tales; the confidences; the half-hours around the open fireplaces when supper was cooking, the potatoes under their hillocks of ashes, the thin-legged ovens of cornbread with their lids of glowing coals, the savory skillets of fried meat, the— Was it indeed all of the past, never again to be present or future? And those humble, truthful, loving eyes, which had looked up to them from the first moment of their lives: did they look with greater trust up to God Himself? It was all over, yes, all over! The color faded from their faces, the scornful resolution left their lips; they laid their faces in their hands and sobbed.

"Do you hear, Titine?" Lolotte burst into the room. "They are all going to leave, every one of them; a transport is coming to-night to take them off. They are going to bundle up their things and wait at the steamboat-landing; and they are not going to take a child, and not a single husband. The captain says the government at Washington will give them the nicest white husbands in the land; that they ought to be glad to marry them. They carried on as if they were drunk. Do you believe it, Titine? Oh, I do wish Jeff Davis would hurry up and win!"

The door opened again; it was Black Maria, still holding the cane-knife in her hand. She crossed the room with her noiseless barefooted tread, and placed herself behind them. They did not expect her to say anything; Black Maria never talked much; but they understood her, as they always did.

Her skirts were still tied up, her head-kerchief awry; they saw for the first time that the wool under it was snow-white.

Black Maria! They might have known it! They looked at her. No! She was not! She was not negro, like the others. Who was she? What was she? Where did she come from, with her white features and white nature under her ebon skin? What was the mystery that enveloped her? Why did the brain always torture itself in surmises about her? Why did she not talk as the others did, and just for a moment uncover that coffin heart of hers? Why was she, alone of all the negroes, still an alien, a foreigner, an exile among them? Was she brooding on disgrace, outrage, revenge? Was she looking at some mirage behind her—a distant equatorial country, a princely rank, barbaric state, some inherited memory transmitted by that other Black Maria, her mother? Who was the secret black father whom no one had discovered? Was it, as the negroes said, the Prince of Darkness? Who was her own secret consort, the father of Ben? What religion had she to warrant her scornful repudiation of Christianity? What code that enabled her to walk as if she were free through slavery, to assume slavery now when others hailed freedom, to be loyal in the midst of treason?

"Look!" Lolotte came into the room, and held up a rusty, irregular piece of iron. "I found this in the old Indian basket where I was looking for sinkers. Don't you see what it is? It is the old key of the smoke-house, and I am going to let those Confederates out." She spoke quietly and decidedly. There was something else in the other hand, concealed in the folds of her dress. She produced it reluctantly. It was the gun-wrench that filled so prominent a part in her active life—always coveting it, getting possession of it, being deprived of it, and accused unfailingly for its every absence and misplacement. "You see, it is so convenient; it screws so nicely on to everything," she continued, apologetically, as she demonstrated the useful qualification by screwing it on to the key. "There! it is as good as a handle. All they've got to do is to slip away in the skiff while the others are eating. And I would like to know how they can ever be caught, without another boat on the place! But oh, girls"—her black eyes twinkled maliciously—"what fools the Yankees are!"

If the Federals, as they announced, were only going to remain long enough for the lady in the kitchen to prepare them something to eat, the length of their stay clearly rested in Peggy the cook's hands, as she understood it. She walked around her kitchen with a briskness rarely permitted by her corpulent proportions, and with an intuitive faith in the common nature of man regardless of political opinion, she exerted her culinary skill to the utmost. She knew nothing of the wholesale quarreling and fighting of a great war, but during her numerous marital experiments, not counting intermittent conjugalities for twenty-five years with Uncle John, she had seen mercy and propitiation flow more than once after a good meal from the most irate; and a healthy digestion aiding, she never despaired of even the most revengeful. The enemy, in her opinion, were simply to be treated like furious husbands, and were to be offered the best menu possible under the trying circumstances. She worked, inspired by all the wife-lore of past ages, the infiltrated wisdom that descends to women in the course of a world of empirical connubiality, that traditionary compendium to their lives by which they still hope to make companionship with men harmonious and the earth a pleasant abiding-place. With minute particularity Peggy set the table and placed the dishes. The sun was now sinking, and sending almost horizontal rays over the roof of the smoke-house, whose ugly square frame completely blocked the view of the dining-room window. Peggy carefully drew the red calico curtain across it, and after a moment's rehearsal to bring her features to the conventional womanly expression of cheerful obtuseness to existing displeasure, she opened the dining-room door.

Gina and Lolotte stood close under the window against the dwelling, looking at the locked door of the smoke-house before them, listening to the sounds falling from the dining-room above. Once in the skiff, the prisoners were safe; but the little red curtain of the window fluttering flimsily in the breeze coquetted with their hopes and the lives of three men. If the corners would but stay down a second! Titine and Black Maria were in front, busy about the skiff. Peggy's culinary success appeared, from the comments of the diners, to be complimentary to her judgment. But food alone, however, does not suffice in the critical moments of life; men are half managed when only fed. There was another menu, the ingredients of which were not limited or stinted by blockade of war. Peggy had prepared that also; and in addition to the sounds of plates, knives, forks, and glasses, came the tones of her rich voice dropping from a quick tongue the *entremets* of her piquant imagination. The attention in the room seemed tense, and at last the curtain hung straight and motionless.

"Now! now!" whispered Gina. "We must risk something."

Woman-like, they paused midway and looked back; a hand stretched from the table was carelessly drawing the curtain aside, and the window stared unhindered at the jail.

Why had they waited? Why had they not rushed forward immediately? By this time their soldiers might have been free! They could hear Peggy moving around the table; they could see her bulky form push again and again across the window.

"Mammy! Mammy!"

Could she hear them? They clasped their hands and held their faces up in imploring appeal. The sun was setting fast, almost running down the west to the woods. The dinner, if good, was not long. It all depended upon Peggy now.

"Mammy! Mammy!" They raised their little voices, then lowered them in agony of apprehension. "Mammy, do something! Help us!"

But still she passed on and about, around the table, and across the window, blind to the smoke-house, deaf to them, while her easy, familiar voice recited the comical gyrations of "old Frizzly," the half-witted hen, who had set her heart against being killed and stewed, and ran and hid, and screamed and cackled, and ducked and flew, and then, after her silly head was twisted off, "just danced, as if she were at a ' 'Cadian' ball, all over the yard."

It would soon be too late! It was, perhaps, too late now!

Black Maria had got the skiff away from the gunnels, but they might just as well give it up; they would not have time enough now.

"Mammy!" The desperate girls made a supreme effort of voice and look. The unctuous black face, the red bead ear-rings, the bandanna head-kerchief, appeared at the window with "old Frizzly's" last dying cackle. There was one flashing wink of the left eye.

Her nurslings recognized then her *pièce de résistance oratoire*—a side-splitting prank once played upon her by another nursling, her pet, her idol, the plague of her life—Beau.

Who could have heard grating lock or squeaking hinges through the boisterous mirth that followed? Who could have seen the desperate bound of the three imprisoned soldiers for liberty through that screen of sumptuous flesh—the magnificent back of Mammy that filled to overlapping the insignificant little window?

They did not wait to hear the captain's rapturous toast to Peggy in sassafras tea, nor his voluble protestations of love to her, nor could they see him in his excitement forgetting his wounded arm, bring both clinched fists with a loud bravo to the table, and then faint dead away.

"I knew it!"

"Just like him!"

"Take him in the air—quick!"

"No, sir! You take him in there, and put him on the best bed in the house." Peggy did not move from the window, but her prompt command turned the soldiers from the door in the hall, and her finger directed them to the closed bed-chamber.

Without noticing Christine standing by the open window, they dropped their doughty burden—boots, spurs, sword, epaulets, and all—on the fresh, white little bed, the feather mattress fluffing up all around as if to submerge him.

"Oh, don't bother about that; cut the sleeve off!"

"Who has a knife?"

"There."

"That's all right now."

"He's coming round."

"There's one nice coat spoiled."

"Uncle Sam has plenty more."

"Don't let it drip on the bed."

"Save it to send to Washington—trophy—wet with rebel blood."

The captain was evidently recovering.

"You stay here while I keep 'em eating," whispered Peggy, authoritatively, to Christine.

Titine trembled as if she had an ague.

"How could they help seeing the tall form of Black Maria standing in the prow of the boat out in the very middle of the bayou? Suppose she, Titine, had not been there to close the window quick as thought? Suppose instead of passing through her room she had run through the basement, as she intended, after pushing off the skiff?"

Rollicking, careless, noisy, the soldiers went back to their interrupted meal, while the boat went cautiously down the bayou to the meeting place beyond the clearing.

"How far was Black Maria now?" Titine opened the window a tiny crack. "Heavens! how slowly she paddled! lifting the oar deliberately from side to side, looking straight ahead. How clear and distinct she was in the soft evening light! Why did she not hurry? why did she not row? She could have muffled the oars. But no, no one thought of that; that was always the way—always something overlooked and forgotten. The soldiers could finish a dozen dinners before the skiff got out of sight at this rate. Without the skiff the prisoners might just as well be locked still in the smoke-house. Did he on the bed suspect something, seeing her look out this way?" She closed the window tight.

"How dark the room was! She could hardly see the wounded man. How quiet he was! Was he sleeping, or had he fainted again? In her bed! her enemy lying in her bed! his head on her pillow, her own little pillow, the feverish confidant of so many sleepless nights! How far were they now on the bayou? She must peep out again. Why, Maria had not moved! not moved an inch! Oh, if she could only scream to her! if she were only in the skiff!

"How ghastly pale he looked on the bed! his face as white as the coverlet, his hair and beard so black; how changed without his bravado and impertinence! And he was not old, either; not older than the boys in gray. She had fancied that age and ugliness alone could go with violence and wrong. How much gold! how much glitter! Why, the sun did not rise with more splendor of equipment. Costumed as if for the conquest of worlds. If the Yankees dressed their captains this way, what was the livery of their generals? How curious the sleeveless arm looked! What a horrible mark the gash made right across the soft white skin! What a scar it would leave! What a disfigurement! And this, this is what men call love of country!"

On Saturday nights sometimes, in the quarters, when rum had been smuggled in, the negroes would get to fighting and beating their wives, and her father would be sent for in a hurry to come with his gun and separate them. Hatchets, axes, cane-knives—anything they would seize, to cut and slash one another, husbands, wives, mothers, sons, sisters, brothers; but they were negroes, ignorant, uneducated, barbarous, excited; they could not help it; they could not be expected to resist all at once the momentum of centuries of ancestral ferocity. But for white men, gentlemen, thus furiously to mar and disfigure their own mother-given bodies! All the latent maternal instinct in her was roused, all the woman in her revolted against the sacrilegious violence of multilation. "Love of country to make her childless, or only the mother of invalids! This was only one. What of the other thousands and hundreds of thousands? Are men indeed so inexhaustible? Are the pangs of maternity so cheap? Are women's hearts of no account whatever in the settlement of disputes? O God! cannot the world get along without war? But even if men want it, even if God permits it, how can the women allow it? If the man on the bed were a negro, she could do something for his arm. Many a time, early Sunday mornings, Saturday night culprits had come to her secretly, and she had washed off the thick, gummy blood, and bandaged up their cuts and bruises; they did not show so on black skin. . . . This man had a mother somewhere among the people she called 'enemies;' a mother sitting counting day by day the continued possession of a live son, growing gray and old before that terrible next minute ever threatening to take her boy and give her a corpse. Or perhaps, like her own, his mother might be dead. They might be friends in that kingdom which the points of the compass neither unite nor divide; together they might be looking down on this quarrelling, fighting world; mothers, even though angels, looking, looking through smoke and powder and blood and hatred after their children. Their eyes might be fixed on this lonely little spot, on this room. . . ." She walked to the bed.

The blood was oozing up through the strips of plaster. She stanched and bathed and soothed the wound as she well knew how with her tender, agile fingers, and returned to the window. Maria had disappeared now; she could open the window with impunity. The trackless water was flowing innocently along, the cooling air was rising in mist, the cypress-trees checked the brilliant sky with the filigree and net-work of their bristly foliage. The birds twittered, the chickens loitered and dallied on their way to roost. The expectant dogs were lying on the levee waiting for the swampers, who, they ought to know, could not possibly return before midnight. And Molly was actually on time this evening, lowing for mammy to come and milk her; what was the war to her? How happy and peaceful it all was! What a jarring contrast to swords and bayonets! Thank God that Nature was impartial, and could not be drilled into partisanship! If humanity were like Nature! If—if there had been no war! She paused, shocked at her first doubt; of the great Circumstance of her life it was like saying, "If there had been no God!"

As she stood at the window and thought, all the brilliant coloring of her romantic fantasies, the stories of childhood, the perversions of education, the self-delusions, they all seemed to fade with the waning light, and with the beautiful day sink slowly and quietly into the irrevocable past. "Thank God, above all, that it is a human device to uniform people into friends and enemies! The heart (her own felt so soft and loving)—the heart repudiates such attempts of blue and gray; it still clings to Nature, and belongs only to God." She thought the wound must need tending again, and returned to the bed. The patient, meanwhile, went in and out of the mazes of unconsciousness caused by weakness.

"Was that really he on this foamy bed? What a blotch his camp-battered body made down the centre of it! It was good to be on a bed once more, to look up into a mosquito-bar instead of the boughs of trees, to feel his head on a pillow. But why did they put him there? Why did they not lay him somewhere on the floor, outside on the ground, instead of soiling and crumpling this lily-white surface?"

He could observe his nurse through his half-closed lids, which fell as she approached the bed, and closed tight as she bent above him. When she stood at the window he could look full at her. "How innocent and unsuspecting she looked!" The strained rigidity had passed away from her face. Her transparent, child-like eyes were looking with all their life of expression in the direction of the bed, and then at something passing in her own mind. "Thank Heaven, the fright had all gone out of them!

How horrible for a gentleman to read fear in the eyes of a woman! Her mind must be as pure and white, yes, and as impressionable, too, as her bed. Did his pesence lie like a blot upon it also? How she must hate him! how she must loathe him! Would it have been different if he had come in the other uniform—if he had worn the gray? would she then have cared for him, have administered to him? How slight and frail she was! What a wan, wistful little face between him and the gloomy old bayou! He could see her more plainly now since she had opened the window and let in the cool, fragrant air. There was no joyous development of the body in her to proclaim womanhood, none of the seductive, confident beauty that follows coronation of youth; to her had only come the care and anxiety of maturity. This—this," he exclaimed to himself, "is the way women fight a war." Was she coming this way? Yes. To the bed? Hardly. Now she was pressing against it, now bending over him, now dropping a cooling dew from heaven on his burning arm, and now—oh, why so soon?—she was going away to stand and look out of the window again.

The homely little room was filled with feminine subterfuges for ornament, feminine substitutes for comfort. How simpie women are! how little they require, after all! only peace and love and quiet, only the impossible in a masculine world. What was she thinking of? If he could only have seen the expression of her eyes as she bent over him! Suppose he should open his and look straight up at her? but no, he had not the courage to frighten her again. He transplanted her in his mind to other surroundings, her proper surroundings by birthright, gave her in abundance all of which this war had deprived her, presented to her assiduous courtiers, not reckless soldiers like himself, but men whom peace had guided in the lofty sphere of intellectual pursuits. He held before her the sweet invitations of youth, the consummations of life. He made her smile, laugh.

"Ah!"—he turned his face against the pillow—"had that sad face ever laughed? Could any woman laugh during a war? Could any triumph, however glorious, atone for battles that gave men death, but left the women to live? This was only one; how many, wan and silent as she, were looking at this sunset—the sunset not of a day, but a life? When it was all over, who was to make restitution to them, the women? Was any cost too great to repurchase for them simply the privilege of hoping again? What an endless chain of accusing thoughts! What a miserable conviction tearing his heart! If he could get on his knees to her, if he could kiss her feet, if he could beg pardon in the dust—he, a man for all men, of her, a woman for all women. If he could make her his country, not to fight, but to work for, it . . ."

She came to his side again, she bent over him, she touched him.

Impulsive, thoughtless, hot-headed, he opened his eyes full, he forgot again the wounded arm. With both hands he stayed her frightened start; he saw the expression of her eyes bending over him.

"Can you forgive me? It is a heartless, cowardly trick! I am not a Yankee; I am Beau, your cousin, the guerilla."

The door of the smoke-house opened, the escaped soldiers ran like deer between the furrows of Uncle John's vegetable garden, where the waving corn leaves could screen them; then out to the bank of the bayou—not on the levee, but close against the fence—snagging their clothes and scratching their faces and hands on the cuckleburs;[3] Lolotte in front, with a stick in her hand, beating the bushes through habit to frighten the snakes, calling, directing, animating, in excited whispers; Régina in the rear, urging, pressing, sustaining the young soldier lagging behind, but painfully striving with stiffened limbs to keep up with the pace of his older, more vigorous companions. Ahead of them Black Maria was steadily keeping the skiff out in the current. The bayou narrowed and grew dark as it entered between the banks of serried cypress-trees, where night had already begun.

Régina looked hurriedly over her shoulder. "Had they found out yet at the house? How slowly she ran! How long it took to get to the woods! Oh, they would have time over and over again to finish their dinner and catch them. Perhaps at this very moment, as she was thinking of it, some forgotten article in the skiff was betraying them! Perhaps a gun might even now be pointing down their path! Or, now! the bullet could start and the report come too late to warn them."

She looked back again and again.

From the little cottage under the trees the curtains fluttered, but no bayonet nor smooth-bore was visible.

She met her companion's face, looking back also, but not for guns—for her. "If it had been different! If he had been a visitor, come to stay; days and evenings to be passed together!" The thought lifting the sulphurous war-clouds from her heart, primitive idyls burst into instantaneous fragrant bloom in it like spring violets. He was not only the first soldier in gray she had ever seen, but the first young man; or it seemed so to her.

3 A cucklebur is a variant of cuckold-bur or cocklebur.

Again she looked back.

"How near they were still to the house! how plainly they could yet be seen! He could be shot straight through the back, the gray jacket getting one stain, one bullet-hole, more, the country one soldier less. Would they shoot through a woman at him? Would they be able to separate them if she ran close behind him, moving this way and that way, exactly as he did? If she saw them in time she could warn him; he could lie flat down in the grass; then it would be impossible to hit him."

Increasing and narrowing the space between them at the hest of each succeeding contradictory thought, turning her head again and again to the house behind her, she lost speed. Lolotte and the two men had already entered the forest before she reached it. Coming from the fields, the swamps seemed midnight dark. Catching her companion's hand, they groped their way along, tripped by the slimy cypress knees that rose like evil gnomes to beset and entangle their feet, slipping over rolling logs, sinking in stagnant mire, noosed by the coils of heavy vines that dropped from unseen branches overhead. Invisible wings of startled birds flapped above them, the croaking of frogs ebbed and flowed around them, owls shrieked and screamed from side to side of the bayou. Lolotte had ceased her beating; swamp serpents are too sluggish to be frightened away. In the obscurity, Black Maria could be dimly seen turning the skiff to a half-submerged log, from which a turtle dropped as if ballasted with lead. A giant cypress-tree arrested them; the smooth, fluted trunk, ringed with whitish water-marks, recording floods far over their heads; where they were scrambling once swam fish and serpents. The young soldier turned and faced her, the deliverer, whose manœuvres in the open field had not escaped him.

She had saved him from imprisonment, insult, perhaps death—the only heir of a heroic father, the only son of a widowed mother; she had restored him to a precious heritage of love and honor, replaced him in the interrupted ambitious career of patriotic duty; she had exposed her life for him—she was beautiful. She stood before him, panting, tremulous, ardent, with dumb, open red lips, and voluble, passionate eyes, and with a long scratch in her white cheek from which the blood trickled. She had much to say to him, her gray uniformed hero; but how in one moment express four years—four long years—and the last long minutes. The words were all there, had been rushing to her lips all day; her lips were parted; but the eager, overcrowded throng were jammed on the threshold; and her heart beat so in her ears! He could not talk; he could not explain. His companions were already in the boat, his enemies still in gunshot. He bent his face to hers in the dim light to learn by heart the features he must never forget—closer, closer, learning, knowing more and more, with the eager precocity of youth.

Bellona must have flown disgusted away with the wings of an owl, Columbia might have nodded her head as knowingly as old Aunt Mary could, when the callow hearts, learning and knowing, brought the faces closer and closer together, until the lips touched.

"I shall come again; I shall come again. Wait for me. Surely I shall come again."

"Yes! Yes!"

Black Maria pushed the skiff off. "Rowlock! Rowlock!" They were safe and away.

A vociferous group stood around the empty gunnels. Uncle John, with the daring of desperation, advanced, disarmed as he was, towards them.

"I-I-I-I don't keer ef you is de-de-de President o' de United States hisself, I ain't gwine to 'low no such cussin' an' swearin' in de hearin' o' de-de-de young ladies. Marse John he-he-he don't 'low it, and when Marse John ain't here I-I-I don't 'low it."

His remonstrance and heroic attitude had very little effect, for the loud talk went on, and chiefly by ejaculation, imprecation, and self-accusation published the whole statement of the case; understanding which, Uncle John added his voice also:

"Good Gord A'mighty! Wh-wh-what's dat you say? Dey—dey—dey Yankees, an' you Cornfedrits? Well, sir, an' are you Marse Beau—you wid your arm hurted? Go 'long! You can't fool me; Marse Beau done had more sense en dat. My Gord! an' dey wuz Yankees? You better cuss —cussin's about all you kin do now. Course de boat's gone. You'll never ketch up wid 'em in Gord's world now. Don't come along arter me about it? 'Tain't my fault. How wuz I to know? You wuz Yankees enough for me. I declar', Marse Beau, you ought to be ashamed o' yourself! You wanted to l'arn dem a lesson! I reckon dey l'arnt you one! You didn't mean 'em no harm! Humph! dey've cut dey eye-teeth, dey have! Lord! Marse Beau, I thought you done knowed us better. Did you really think we wuz a-gwine to let a passel o' Yankees take us away off our own plantation? You must done forgot us. We jes cleaned out de house for 'em, we did—clo'es, food, tobacco, rum. De young ladies 'ain't lef' a mossel for Marse John. An'—an'—an' 'fore de good Gord, my gun! Done tuck my gun away wid 'em! Wh-wh-wh-what you mean by such doin's? L-l-look here, Marse Beau, I don't like dat, nohow! Wh-wh-what! you tuck my gun and gin it to de Yankees? Dat's my gun! I done had dat gun twenty-five year an' more! Dog-gone! Yes, sir, I'll cuss—I'll cuss ef I wants to! I 'ain't got no use for gorillas, nohow! Lem me 'lone, I tell you! lem me 'lone! Marse John he'll get de law o' dat! Who's 'sponsible? Dat's all I want to know—who's 'sponsible? Ef-ef-ef-ef— No, sir; dar ain't nary boat on de place, nor hereabouts. Yes, sir; you kin cross de swamp ef you kin find de way. No, sir—no, sir; dar ain't no one to show you. I ain't gwine to leave de young ladies twell Marse John he comes back. Yes, I reckon you kin git to de cut-off by to-morrow mornin', ef you ain't shot on de way for Yankees, an' ef your company is fool enough to wait for you. No, sir, I don't know nothin' 'bout nothin'; you better wait an' arsk Marse John. . . . My Gord! I'm obleeged to laugh; I can't help it. Dem fool nigger wimen a-sittin' on de brink o' de byer, dey clo'es tied up in de bedquilts, an' de shotes an' de pullits all kilt, a-waitin' for freedom! I lay dey'll git freedom enough to-night when de boys come home. Dey git white gentlemen to marry 'em! Dey'll git five hundred apiece. Marse Beau, Gord 'll punish you for dis—He surely will. I done tole Marse John long time ago he oughter sell dat brazen nigger Dead-arm Harriet, an' git shet o' her. Lord! Lord! Lord! Now you done gone to cussin' an' swearin' again. Don't go tearin' off your jackets an' flingin' 'em at me. We don't want 'em; we buys our clo'es—what we don't make. Yes, Marse John 'll be comin' along pretty soon now. What's your hurry, Marse Beau? Well, so long, ef you won't stay. He ain't got much use for gorillas neither, Marse John hain't."

The young officer wrote a few hasty words on a leaf torn from the pretty Russia-leather notebook, and handed it to the old darky. "For your Marse John."

"For Marse John—yes, sir; I'll gin hit to him soon 's he comes in."

They had dejectedly commenced their weary tramp up the bayou; he called him back, and lowered his voice confidentially: "Marse Beau, when you captured dat transport and stole all dem fixin's an' finery, you didn't see no good chawin' tobacco layin' round loose, did you? Thanky! thanky, child! Now I looks good at you, you ain't so much changed sence de times Marse John used to wallop you for your tricks. Well, good-bye, Marse Beau."

On the leaf were scrawled the words:

"All's up! Lee has surrendered.—BEAU."

V FROM *BALCONY STORIES*

THE ORIGINAL edition of *Balcony Stories* contained thirteen tales, of which four are printed in this section. This collection maintained a popularity over a period of years. A second edition appeared in 1914 and a third in 1925 with an additional two stories. As Grace King's most representative volume of short fiction, several of these stories have appeared in anthologies of southern literature.

Most of the collection are realistic narratives about Louisiana Creoles, two are about Negro slaves, and one, "The Little Convent Girl," is a variation on the theme of mixed blood. This is a story that bears comparison with Sherwood Bonner's "A Volcanic Interlude" (1880) or with George W. Cable's " 'Tite Poulette" (1879) and "Madame Delphine" (1881). "The Little Convent Girl" avoids the problem of miscegenation, but centers on the tragedy of a girl's first knowledge that her mother is black. The treatment is delicately sympathetic; the action is seen from the point of view of the captain of the ship on which the girl comes to meet her mother. She herself never speaks, and it is this complete silence that gives the story a poignancy that makes it memorable. Grace King had learned that what is left unsaid in a short story is often more eloquent than what is stated directly.

The four balcony stories of this volume appeared in *Century Magazine* as follows: "La Grande Demoiselle," XLIV (January, 1893), 323–27; "Anne Marie and Jeanne Marie," XLVI (July, 1893), 372–74; "A

Crippled Hope," XLVI (July, 1893), 374–79; "The Little Convent Girl," XLVI (August, 1893), 547–51. Copy-text for the four stories was the volume *Balcony Stories* (New York: Century, 1893). Later editions were by Graham, New Orleans, 1914 and by Macmillan, New York, 1925.

La Grande Demoiselle

That was what she was called by everybody as soon as she was seen or described. Her name, besides baptismal titles, was Idalie Sainte Foy Mortemart des Islets. When she came into society, in the brilliant little world of New Orleans, it was the event of the season, and after she came in, whatever she did became also events. Whether she went, or did not go; what she said, or did not say; what she wore, and did not wear—all these became important matters of discussion, quoted as much or more than what the president said, or the governor thought. And in those days, the days of '59, New Orleans was not, as it is now, a one-heiress place, but it may be said that one could find heiresses then as one finds type-writing girls now.

Mademoiselle Idalie received her birth, and what education she had, on her parents' plantation, the famed old Reine Sainte Foy place, and it is no secret that, like the ancient kings of France, her birth exceeded her education.

It was a plantation, the Reine Sainte Foy, the richness and luxury of which are really well described in those perfervid pictures of tropical life, at one time the passion of philanthropic imaginations, excited and exciting over the horrors of slavery. Although these pictures were then often accused of being purposely exaggerated, they seem now to fall short of, instead of surpassing, the truth. Stately walls, acres of roses, miles of oranges, unmeasured fields of cane, colossal sugar-house—they were all there, and all the rest of it, with the slaves, slaves, slaves everywhere, whole villages of negro cabins. And there were also, most noticeable to the natural, as well as to the visionary, eye—there were the ease, idleness, extravagance, self-indulgence, pomp, pride, arrogance, in short the whole enumeration, the moral *sine qua non,* as some people considered it, of the wealthy slaveholder of aristocratic descent and tastes.

What Mademoiselle Idalie cared to learn she studied, what she did not she ignored; and she followed the same simple rule untrammeled in her eating, drinking, dressing, and comportment generally; and whatever discipline may have been exercised on the place, either in fact of fiction, most assuredly none of it, even so much as in a threat, ever attainted her sacred person. When she was just turned sixteen, Mademoiselle Idalie made up her mind to go into society. Whether she was beautiful or not, it is hard to say. It is almost impossible to appreciate properly the beauty of the rich, the very rich. The unfettered development, the limitless choice of accessories, the confidence, the self-esteem, the sureness of expression, the simplicity of purpose, the ease of execution—all these produce a certain effect of beauty behind which one really cannot get to measure length of nose, or brilliancy of eye. This much can be said: there was nothing in her that positively contradicted any assumption of beauty on her part, or credit of it on the part of others. She was very tall and very thin with small head, long neck, black eyes, and abundant straight black hair,—for which her hair-dresser deserved more praise than she,—good teeth, of course, and a mouth that, even in prayer, talked nothing but commands; that is about all she had *en fait d'ornements,* as the modistes say. It may be added that she walked as if the Reine Sainte Foy plantation extended over the whole earth, and the soil of it were too vile for her tread. Of course she did not buy her toilets in New Orleans. Everything was ordered from Paris, and came as regularly through the custom-house as the modes and robes to the milliners. She was furnished by a certain house there, just as one of a royal family would be at the present day. As this had lasted from her layette up to her sixteenth year, it may be imagined what took place when she determined to make her début. Then it was literally, not metaphorically, *carte blanche,* at least so it got to the ears of society. She took a sheet of note-paper, wrote the date at the top, added, "I make my début in November," signed her name at the extreme end of the sheet, addressed it to her dressmaker in Paris, and sent it.

It was said that in her dresses the very handsomest silks were used for linings, and that real lace was used where others put imitation,—around the bottoms of the skirts, for instance,—and silk ribbons of the best quality served the purposes of ordinary tapes; and sometimes the buttons were of real gold and silver, sometimes set with precious stones. Not that she ordered these particulars, but the dressmakers, when given *carte blanche* by those who do not condescend to details, so soon exhaust the outside limits of garments that perforce they take to plastering them inside with gold, so to speak, and, when the bill goes in, they depend upon the furnishings to carry out a certain amount of the contract in justifying the price. And it was said that these costly dresses, after being worn once or twice, were cast aside, thrown upon the floor, given to the negroes—

anything to get them out of sight. Not an inch of the real lace, not one of the jeweled buttons, not a scrap of ribbon, was ripped off to save. And it was said that if she wanted to romp with her dogs in all her finery, she did it; she was known to have ridden horseback, one moonlight night, all around the plantation in a white silk dinner-dress flounced with Alençon. And at night, when she came from the balls, tired, tired to death as only balls can render one, she would throw herself down upon her bed in her tulle skirts,—on top, or not, of the exquisite flowers, she did not care,—and make her maid undress her in that position; often having her bodices cut off her, because she was too tired to turn over and have them unlaced.

That she was admired, raved about, loved even, goes without saying. After the first month she held the refusal of half the beaux of New Orleans. Men did absurd, undignified, preposterous things for her; and she? Love? Marry? The idea never occurred to her. She treated the most exquisite of her pretenders no better than she treated her Paris gowns, for the matter of that. She could not even bring herself to listen to a proposal patiently; whistling to her dogs, in the middle of the most ardent protestations, or jumping up and walking away with a shrug of the shoulders, and a "Bah!"

Well! Every one knows what happened after '59. There is no need to repeat. The history of one is the history of all. But there was this difference—for there is every shade of difference in misfortune, as there is every shade of resemblance in happiness. Mortemart des Islets went off to fight. That was natural; his family had been doing that, he thought, or said, ever since Charlemagne. Just as naturally he was killed in the first engagement. They, his family, were always among the first killed; so much so that it began to be considered assassination to fight a duel with any of them. All that was in the ordinary course of events. One difference in their misfortunes lay in that after the city was captured, their plantation, so near, convenient, and rich in all kinds of provisions, was selected to receive a contingent of troops—a colored company. If it had been a colored company raised in Louisiana it might have been different; and these negroes mixed with the negroes in the neighborhood,—and negroes are no better than whites, for the proportion of good and bad among them,—and the officers were always off duty when they should have been on, and on when they should have been off.

One night the dwelling caught fire. There was an immediate rush to save the ladies. Oh, there was no hesitation about that! They were seized in their beds, and carried out in the very arms of their enemies; carried away off to the sugar-house, and deposited there. No danger of their doing anything but keep very quiet and still in their *chemises de nuit,* and their one sheet apiece, which was about all that was saved from the conflagration—that is, for them. But it must be remembered that this is all hearsay. When one has not been present, one knows nothing of one's own knowledge; one can only repeat. It has been repeated, however, that although the house was burned to the ground, and everything in it destroyed, wherever, for a year afterward, a man of that company or of that neighborhood was found, there could have been found also, without search-warrant, property that had belonged to the Des Islets. That is the story; and it is believed or not, exactly according to prejudice.

How the ladies ever got out of the sugar-house, history does not relate; nor what they did. It was not a time for sociability, either personal or epistolary. At one offensive word your letter, and you, very likely, examined; and Ship Island for a hotel, with soldiers for hostesses! Madame Des Islets died very soon after the accident—of rage, they say; and that was about all the public knew.

Indeed, at that time the society of New Orleans had other things to think about than the fate of the Des Islets. As for *la grande demoiselle,* she had prepared for her own oblivion in the hearts of her female friends. And the gentlemen,—her *preux chevaliers,*—they were burning with other passions than those which had driven them to her knees, encountering a little more serious response than "bahs" and shrugs. And, after all, a woman seems the quickest thing forgotten when once the important affairs of life come to men for consideration.

It might have been ten years according to some calculations, or ten eternities,—the heart and the almanac never agree about time,—but one morning old Champigny (they used to call him Champignon) was walking along his levee front, calculating how soon the water would come over, and drown him out, as the Louisianians say. It was before a seven-o'clock breakfast, cold, wet, rainy, and discouraging. The road was knee-deep in mud, and so broken up with hauling, that it was like walking upon waves to get over it. A shower poured down. Old Champigny was hurrying in when he saw a figure approaching. He had to stop to look at it, for it was worth while. The head was hidden by a green barege veil, which the showers had plentifully besprinkled with dew; a tall, thin figure. Figure! No; not even could it be called a figure: straight up and down, like a finger or a post; high-shouldered, and a step—a step like a plowman's. No umbrella; no—nothing more, in fact. It does not sound so peculiar as when first related—something must be forgotten. The feet —oh, yes, the feet—they were like waffle-irons, or frying-pans, or anything of that shape.

Old Champigny did not care for women—he never had; they simply did not exist for him in the order of nature. He had been married once, it is true, about a half century before; but that was not reckoned against the existence of his prejudice, because he was *célibataire* to his finger-tips, as any one could see a mile away. But that woman *intrigué'd* him.

He had no servant to inquire from. He performed all of his own domestic work in the wretched little cabin that replaced his old home. For Champigny also belonged to the great majority of the *nouveaux pauvres.* He went out into the rice-field, where were one or two hands that worked on shares with him, and he asked them. They knew immediately; there is nothing connected with the parish that a field-hand does not know at once. She was the teacher of the colored public school some three or four miles away. "Ah," thought Champigny, "some Northern lady on a mission." He watched to see her return in the evening, which she did, of course; in a blinding rain. Imagine the green barege veil then; for it remained always down over her face.

Old Champigny could not get over it that he had never seen her before. But he must have seen her, and, with his abstraction and old age, not have noticed her, for he found out from the negroes that she had been teaching four or five years there. And he found out also—how, is not important—that she was Idalie Sainte Foy Mortemart des Islets. *La grande demoiselle!* He had never known her in the old days, owing to his uncomplimentary attitude toward women, but he knew of her, of course, and of her family. It should have been said that his plantation was about fifty miles higher up the river, and on the opposite bank to Reine Sainte Foy. It seemed terrible. The old gentleman had had reverses of his own, which would bear the telling, but nothing was more shocking to him than this—that Idalie Sainte Foy Mortemart des Islets should be teaching a public colored school for—it makes one blush to name it—seven dollars and a half a month. For seven dollars and a half a month to teach a set of—well! He found out where she lived, a little cabin—not so much worse than his own, for that matter—in the corner of a field; no companion, no servant, nothing but food and shelter. Her clothes have been described.

Only the good God himself knows what passed in Champigny's mind on the subject. We know only the results. He went and married *la grande demoiselle.* How? Only the good God knows that too. Every first of the month, when he goes to the city to buy provisions, he takes her with him —in fact, he takes her everywhere with him.

Passengers on the railroad know them well, and they always have a chance to see her face. When she passes her old plantation *la grande demoiselle* always lifts her veil for one instant—the inevitable green barege veil. What a face! Thin, long, sallow, petrified! And the neck! If she would only tie something around the neck! And her plain, coarse cottonade gown! The negro women about her were better dressed than she.

Poor old Champignon! It was not an act of charity to himself, no doubt cross and disagreeable, besides being ugly. And as for love, gratitude!

Anne Marie and Jeanne Marie

Old Jeanne Marie leaned her hand against the house, and the tears rolled down her cheeks. She had not wept since she buried her last child. With her it was one trouble, one weeping, no more; and her wrinkled, hard, polished skin so far had known only the tears that come after death. The trouble in her heart now was almost exactly like the trouble caused by death; although she knew it was not so bad as death, yet, when she thought of this to console herself, the tears rolled all the faster. She took the end of the red cotton kerchief tied over her head, and wiped them away; for the furrows in her face did not merely run up and down—they ran in all directions, and carried her tears all over her face at once. She could understand death, but she could not understand this.

It came about in this way: Anne Marie and she lived in the little red-washed cabin against which she leaned; had lived there alone with each other for fifty years, ever since Jeanne Marie's husband had died, and the three children after him, in the fever epidemic.

The little two-roomed cabin, the stable where there used to be a cow, the patch of ground planted with onions, had all been bought and paid for by the husband; for he was a thrifty, hard-working Gascon, and had he lived there would not have been one better off, or with a larger family, either in that quarter or in any of the red-washed suburbs with which Gascony has surrounded New Orleans. His women, however,—the wife and sister-in-law,—had done their share in the work: a man's share apiece, for with the Gascon women there is no discrimination of sex when it comes to work.

And they worked on just the same after he died, tending the cow, digging, hoeing, planting, watering. The day following the funeral, by daylight Jeanne Marie was shouldering around the yoke of milk-cans to his patrons, while Anne Marie carried the vegetables to market; and so on for fifty years.

They were old women now,—seventy-five years old,—and, as they expressed it, they had always been twins. In twins there is always one lucky and one unlucky one: Jeanne Marie was the lucky one, Anne Marie the unlucky one. So much so, that it was even she who had to catch the rheumatism, and to lie now bedridden, months at a time, while Jeanne Marie was as active in her sabots as she had ever been.

In spite of the age of both, and the infirmity of one, every Saturday night there was some little thing to put under the brick in the hearth, for taxes and license, and the never-to-be-forgotten funeral provision. In the husband's time gold pieces used to go in, but they had all gone to pay for the four funerals and the quadrupled doctor's bill. The women laid in silver pieces; the coins, however, grew smaller and smaller, and represented more and more not so much the gain from onions as the saving from food.

It had been explained to them how they might, all at once, make a year's gain in the lottery; and it had become their custom always, at the end of every month, to put aside one silver coin apiece, to buy a lottery ticket with—one ticket each, not for the great, but for the twenty-five-cent, prizes. Anne Marie would buy hers round about the market; Jeanne Marie would stop anywhere along her milk course and buy hers, and they would go together in the afternoon to stand with the little crowd watching the placard upon which the winning numbers were to be written. And when they were written, it was curious, Jeanne Marie's numbers would come out twice as often as Anne Marie's. Not that she ever won anything, for she was not lucky enough to have them come out in the order to win; they only came out here and there, singly: but it was sufficient to make old Anne Marie cross and ugly for a day or two, and injure the sale of the onion-basket. When she became bedridden, Jeanne Marie bought the ticket for both, on the numbers, however, that

Anne Marie gave her; and Anne Marie had to lie in bed and wait, while Jeanne Marie went out to watch the placard.

One evening, watching it, Jeanne Marie saw the ticket-agent write out the numbers as they came on her ticket, in such a way that they drew a prize—forty dollars.

When the old woman saw it she felt such a happiness; just as she used to feel in the old times right after the birth of a baby. She thought of that instantly. Without saying a word to any one, she clattered over the *banquette* as fast as she could in her sabots, to tell the good news to Anne Marie. But she did not go so fast as not to have time to dispose of her forty dollars over and over again. Forty dollars! That was a great deal of money. She had often in her mind, when she was expecting a prize, spent twenty dollars; for she had never thought it could be more than that. But forty dollars! A new gown apiece, and black silk kerchiefs to tie over their heads instead of red cotton, and the little cabin new red-washed, and soup in the pot, and a garlic sausage, and a bottle of good, costly liniment for Anne Marie's legs; and still a pile of gold to go under the hearth-brick—a pile of gold that would have made the eyes of the defunct husband glisten.

She pushed open the picket-gate, and came into the room where her sister lay in bed.

"Eh, Anne Marie, my girl," she called in her thick, pebbly voice, apparently made purposely to suit her rough Gascon accent; "this time we have caught it!"

"Whose ticket?" asked Anne Marie, instantly.

In a flash all Anne Marie's ill luck ran through Jeanne Marie's mind; how her promised husband had proved unfaithful, and Jeanne Marie's faithful; and how, ever since, even to the coming out of her lottery numbers, even to the selling of vegetables, even to the catching of the rheumatism, she had been the loser. But above all, as she looked at Anne Marie in the bed, all the misery came over Jeanne Marie of her sister's not being able, in all her poor old seventy-five years of life, to remember the pressure of the arms of a husband about her waist, nor the mouth of a child on her breast.

As soon as Anne Marie had asked her question, Jeanne Marie answered it.

"But your ticket, *Coton-Maï!*" *

* *Coton-Maï* is an innocent oath invented by the good, pious priest as a substitute for one more harmful [Grace King's note].

"Where? Give it here! Give it here!" The old woman, who had not been able to move her back for weeks, sat bolt upright in bed, and stretched out her great bony fingers, with the long nails as hard and black as rake-prongs from groveling in the earth.

Jeanne Marie poured the money out of her cotton handkerchief into them.

Anne Marie counted it, looked at it; looked at it, counted it; and if she had not been so old, so infirm, so toothless, the smile that passed over her face would have made it beautiful.

Jeanne Marie had to leave her to draw water from the well to water the plants, and to get her vegetables ready for next morning. She felt even happier now than if she had just had a child, happier even than if her husband had just returned to her.

"Ill luck! *Coton-Maï!* Ill luck! There's a way to turn ill luck!" And her smile also should have beautified her face, wrinkled and ugly though it was.

She did not think any more of the spending of the money, only of the pleasure Anne Marie would take in spending it.

The water was low in the well, and there had been a long drought. There are not many old women of seventy-five who could have watered so much ground as abundantly as she did; but whenever she thought of the forty dollars and Anne Marie's smile she would give the thirsting plant an extra bucketful.

The twilight was gaining. She paused. "*Coton-Maï!*" she exclaimed aloud. "But I must see the old woman smile again over her good luck."

Although it was "my girl" face to face, it was always "the old woman" behind each other's back.

There was a knot-hole in the plank walls of the house. In spite of Anne Marie's rheumatism they would never stop it up, needing it, they said, for light and air. Jeanne Marie slipped her feet out of her sabots and crept easily toward it, smiling, and saying "*Coton-Maï!*" to herself all the way. She put her eye to the hole. Anne Marie was not in the bed, she who had not left her bed for two months! Jeanne Marie looked through the dim light of the room until she found her.

Anne Marie, in her short petticoat and nightsack, with bare legs and feet, was on her knees in the corner, pulling up a plank, hiding—peasants know hiding when they see it—hiding her money away—away—away from whom?—muttering to herself and shaking her old grayhaired head. Hiding her money away from Jeanne Marie!

And this was why Jeanne Marie leaned her head against the side of the house and wept. It seemed to her that she had never known her twin sister at all.

A Crippled Hope

You must picture to yourself the quiet, dim-lighted room of a convalescent; outside, the dreary, bleak days of winter in a sparsely settled, distant country parish; inside, a slow, smoldering log-fire, a curtained bed, the infant sleeping well enough, the mother wakeful, restless, thought-driven, as a mother must be, unfortunately, nowadays, particularly in that parish, where cotton worms and overflows have acquired such a monopoly of one's future.

God is always pretty near a sick woman's couch; but nearer even than God seems the sick-nurse—at least in that part of the country, under those circumstances. It is so good to look through the dimness and uncertainty, moral and physical, and to meet those little black, steadfast, all-seeing eyes; to feel those smooth, soft, all-soothing hands; to hear, across one's sleep, that three-footed step—the flat-soled left foot, the tiptoe right, and the padded end of the broomstick; and when one is so wakeful and restless and thought-driven, to have another's story given one. God, depend upon it, grows stories and lives as he does herbs, each with a mission of balm to some woe.

She said she had, and in truth she had, no other name than "little Mammy"; and that was the name of her nature. Pure African, but bronze rather than pure black, and full-sized only in width, her growth having been hampered as to height by an injury to her hip, which had lamed her, pulling her figure awry, and burdening her with a protuberance of the joint. Her mother caused it by dropping her when a baby, and concealing it, for fear of punishment, until the dislocation became irremediable. All the animosity of which little Mammy was capable centered upon this unknown but never-to-be-forgotten mother of hers; out of this hatred had grown her love—that is, her destiny, a woman's love being her destiny. Little Mammy's love was for children.

The birth and infancy (the one as accidental as the other, one would infer) took place in—it sounds like the "Arabian Nights" now!—took place in the great room, caravansary, stable, behind a negro-trader's auction-mart, where human beings underwent literally the daily buying and selling of which the world now complains in a figure of speech—a great, square, dusty chamber where, sitting cross-legged, leaning against the wall, or lying on foul blanket pallets on the floor, the bargains of to-day made their brief sojourn, awaiting transformation into the profits of the morrow.

The place can be pointed out now, is often pointed out; but no emotion arises at sight of it. It is so plain, so matter-of-fact an edifice that emotion only comes afterward in thinking about it, and then in the reflection that such an edifice could be, then as now, plain and matter-of-fact.

For the slave-trader there was no capital so valuable as the physical soundness of his stock; the moral was easily enough forged or counterfeited. Little Mammy's good-for-nothing mother was sold as readily as a vote, in the parlance of to-day; but no one would pay for a crippled baby. The mother herself would not have taken her as a gift, had it been in the nature of a negro-trader to give away anything. Some doctoring was done,—so little Mammy heard traditionally,—some effort made to get her marketable. There were attempts to pair her off as a twin sister of various correspondencies in age, size, and color, and to palm her off, as a substitute, at migratory, bereaved, overfull breasts. Nothing equaled a negro-trader's will and power for fraud, except the hereditary distrust and watchfulness which it bred and maintained. And so, in the even balance between the two categories, the little cripple remained a fixture in the stream of life that passed through that back room, in the fluxes and refluxes of buying and selling; not valueless, however—rely upon a negro-trader for discovering values as substitutes, as panaceas. She earned her nourishment, and Providence did not let it kill the little animal before the emancipation of weaning arrived.

How much circumstances evoked, how much instinct responded, belongs to the secrets which nature seems to intend keeping. As a baby she had eyes, attention, solely for other babies. One cannot say while she was still crawling, for she could only crawl years after she should have been walking, but, before even precocious walking-time, tradition or the old gray-haired negro janitor relates, she would creep from baby to baby to play with it, put it to sleep, pat it, rub its stomach (a negro baby, you know, is all stomach, and generally aching stomach at that). And before she had a lap, she managed to force one for some ailing nursling. It was then that they began to call her "little Mammy." In the transitory population of the "pen" no one stayed long enough to give her another name; and no one ever stayed short enough to give her another one.

Her first recollection of herself was that she could not walk—she was past crawling; she cradled herself along, as she called sitting down flat, and working herself about with her hands and her one strong leg. Babbling babies walked all around her,—many walking before they babbled,—and still she did not walk, imitate them as she might and did. She would sit and "study" about it, make another trial, fall; sit and study some more, make another trial, fall again. Negroes, who believe that they must give a reason for everything even if they have to invent one, were convinced that it was all this studying upon her lameness that gave her such a large head.

And now she began secretly turning up the clothes of every negro child that came into that pen, and examining its legs, and still more secretly examining her own, stretched out before her on the ground. How long it took she does not remember; in fact, she could not have known, for she had no way of measuring time except by her thoughts and feelings. But in her own way and time the due process of deliberation was fulfilled, and the quotient made clear that, bowed or not, all children's legs were of equal length except her own, and all were alike, not one full, strong, hard, the other soft, flabby, wrinkled, growing out of a knot at the hip. A whole psychological period apparently lay between that conclusion and—a broom-handle walking-stick; but the broomstick came, as it was bound to come,—thank heaven!—from that premise, and what with stretching one limb to make it longer, and doubling up the other to make it shorter, she invented that form of locomotion which is still carrying her through life, and with no more exaggerated leg-crookedness than many careless negroes born with straight limbs display. This must have been when she was about eight or nine. Hobbling on a broomstick, with, no doubt, the same weird, wizened face as now, an innate sense of the fitness of things must have suggested the kerchief tied around her big head, and the burlap rag of an apron in front of her linsey-woolsey rag of a gown, and the bit of broken pipe-stem in the corner of her mouth, where the pipe should have been, and where it was in after years. That is the way she recollected herself, and that is the way one recalls her now, with a few modifications.

The others came and went, but she was always there. It wasn't long before she became "little Mammy" to the grown folks too; and the newest inmates soon learned to cry: "Where's little Mammy?" "Oh, little Mammy! little Mammy! Such a misery in my head [or my back, or my stomach]! Can't you help me, little Mammy?" It was curious what a quick eye she had for symptoms and ailments, and what a quick ear for suffering, and how apt she was at picking up, remembering, and inventing remedies. It never occurred to her not to crouch at the head or the foot of a sick pallet, day and night through. As for the nights, she said she dared not close her eyes of nights. The room they were in was so vast, and sometimes the negroes lay so thick on the floor, rolled in their blankets (you know, even in the summer they sleep under blankets), all snoring so loudly, she would never have heard a groan or a whimper any more than they did, if she had slept, too. And negro mothers are so careless and such heavy sleepers. All night she would creep at regular intervals to the different pallets, and draw the little babies from under, or away from, the heavy, inert impending mother forms. There is no telling how many she thus saved from being overlaid and smothered, or, what was worse, maimed and crippled.

Whenever a physician came in, as he was sometimes called, to look at a valuable investment or to furbish up some piece of damaged goods, she always managed to get near to hear the directions; and she generally was the one to apply them also, for negroes always would steal medicines most scurvily one from the other. And when death at times would slip into the pen, despite the trader's utmost alertness and precautions,—as death often "had to do," little Mammy said,—when the time of some of them came to die, and when the rest of the negroes, with African greed of eye for the horrible, would press around the lowly couch where the agonizing form of a slave lay writhing out of life, she would always to the last give medicines, and wipe the cold forehead, and soothe the clutching, fearsome hands, hoping to the end, and trying to inspire the hope that his or her "time" had not come yet; for, as she said, "Our time doesn't come just as often as it does come."

And in those sad last offices, which somehow have always been under reproach as a kind of shame, no matter how young she was, she was always too old to have the childish avoidance of them. On the contrary, to her a corpse was only a kind of baby, and she always strove, she said, to make one, like the other, easy and comfortable.

And in other emergencies she divined the mysteries of the flesh, as other precocities divine the mysteries of painting and music, and so become child wonders.

Others came and went. She alone remained there. Babies of her babyhood—the toddlers she, a toddler, had nursed—were having babies themselves now; the middle-aged had had time to grow old and die. Every week new families were coming into the great back chamber; every week they passed out: babies, boys, girls, buxom wenches, stalwart youths, and the middle-aged—the grave, serious ones whom misfortune had driven from their old masters, and the ill-reputed ones, the trickish, thievish, lazy, whom the cunning of the negro-trader alone could keep in circulation. All were marketable, all were bought and sold, all passed in one door and out the other—all except her, little Mammy. As with her lameness, it took time for her to recognize, to understand, the fact. She could study over her lameness, she could in the dull course of time think out the broomstick way of palliation. It would have been almost better, under the circumstances, for God to have kept the truth from her; only—God keeps so little of the truth from us women. It is his system.

Poor little thing! It was not now that her master *could* not sell her, but he *would* not! Out of her own intelligence she had forged her chains; the lameness was a hobble merely in comparison. She had become too valuable to the negro-trader by her services among his crew, and offers only solidified his determination not to sell her. Visiting physicians, after short acquaintance with her capacities, would offer what were called fancy prices for her. Planters who heard of her through their purchases would come to the city purposely to secure, at any cost, so inestimable an adjunct to their plantations. Even ladies—refined, delicate ladies—sometimes came to the pen personally to back money with influence. In vain. Little Mammy was worth more to the negro-trader, simply as a kind of insurance against accidents, than any sum, however glittering the figure, and he was no ignorant expert in human wares. She can tell it; no one else can for her. Remember that at times she had seen the streets outside. Remember that she could hear of the outside world daily from the passing chattels—of the plantations, farms, families; the green fields, Sunday woods, running streams; the camp-meetings, corn-shuckings, cotton-pickings, sugar-grindings; the baptisms, marriages, funerals, prayer-meetings; the holidays and holy days. Remember that, whether for liberty or whether for love, passion effloresces in the human being—no matter when, where, or how—with every spring's return. Remember that she was, even in middle age, young and vigorous. But no; do not remember anything. There is no need to heighten the coloring.

It would be tedious to relate, although it was not tedious to hear her relate it, the desperations and hopes of her life then. Hardly a day passed that she did not see, looking for purchases (rummaging among goods on a counter for bargains), some master whom she could have loved, some mistress whom she could have adored. Always her favorite mistresses were there—tall, delicate matrons, who came themselves, with great fatigue, to select kindly-faced women for nurses; languid-looking ladies with smooth hair standing out in wide *bandeaux* from their heads, and lace shawls dropping from their sloping shoulders, silk dresses carelessly held up in thumb and finger from embroidered petticoats that were spread out like tents over huge hoops which covered whole groups of swarming piccaninnies on the dirty floor; ladies, pale from illnesses that she might have nursed, and over-burdened with children whom she might have reared! And not a lady of that kind saw her face but wanted her, yearned for her, pleaded for her, coming back secretly to slip silver, and sometimes gold, pieces into her hand, patting her turbaned head, calling her "little Mammy" too, instantly, by inspiration, and making the negro-trader give them, with all sorts of assurances, the refusal of her. She had no need for the whispered "Buy me, master!" "Buy me, mistress!" "You'll see how I can work, master!" "You'll never be sorry, mistress!" of the others. The negro-trader—like hangmen, negro-traders are fitted by nature for their profession—it came into his head—he had no heart, not even a negro-trader's heart—that it would be more judicious to seclude her during these shopping visits, so to speak. She could not have had any hopes then at all; it must have been all desperations.

That auction-block, that executioner's block, about which so much has been written—Jacob's ladder, in his dream, was nothing to what that block appeared nightly in her dreams to her; and the climbers up and down—well, perhaps Jacob's angels were his hopes, too.

At times she determined to depreciate her usefulness, mar her value, by renouncing her heart, denying her purpose. For days she would tie her kerchief over her ears and eyes, and crouch in a corner, strangling her impulses. She even malingered, refused food, became dumb. And she might have succeeded in making herself salable through incipient lunacy, if through no other way, had she been able to maintain her rôle long enough. But some woman or baby always was falling into some emergency of pain and illness.

How it might have ended one does not like to think. Fortunately, one does not need to think.

There came a night. She sat alone in the vast, dark caravansary—alone for the first time in her life. Empty rags and blankets lay strewn over the floor, no snoring, no tossing in them more. A sacrificial sale that day had cleared the counters. Alarm-bells rang in the streets, but she did not know them for alarm-bells; alarm brooded in the dim space around her, but she did not even recognize that. Her protracted tension of heart had made her fear-blind to all but one peradventure.

Once or twice she forgot herself, and limped over to some heap to relieve an imaginary struggling babe or moaning sleeper. Morning came. She had dozed. She looked to see the rag-heaps stir; they lay as still as corpses. The alarm-bells had ceased. She looked to see a new gang enter the far door. She listened for the gathering buzzing of voices in the next room, around the auction-block. She waited for the trader. She waited for the janitor. At nightfall a file of soldiers entered. They drove her forth, ordering her in the voice, in the tone, of the negro-trader. That was the only familiar thing in the chaos of incomprehensibility about her. She hobbled through the auction-room. Posters, advertisements, papers, lay on the floor, and in the torch-light glared from the wall. Her Jacob's ladder, her stepping-stone to her hopes, lay overturned in a corner.

You divine it. The negro-trader's trade was abolished, and he had vanished in the din and smoke of a war which he had not been entirely guiltless of producing, leaving little Mammy locked up behind him. Had he forgotten her? One cannot even hope so. She hobbled out into the street, leaning on her nine-year-old broomstick (she had grown only slightly beyond it; could still use it by bending over it), her head tied in a rag kerchief, a rag for a gown, a rag for an apron.

Free, she was free! But she had not hoped for freedom. The plantation, the household, the delicate ladies, the teeming children,—broomsticks they were in comparison to freedom, but,—that was what she had asked, what she had prayed for. God, she said, had let her drop, just as her mother had done. More than ever she grieved, as she crept down the street, that she had never mounted the auctioneer's block. An ownerless free negro! She knew no one whose duty it was to help her; no one knew her to help her. In the whole world (it was all she had asked) there was no white child to call her mammy, no white lady or gentleman (it was the extent of her dreams) beholden to her as to a nurse. And all her innumerable black beneficiaries! Even the janitor, whom she had tended as the others, had deserted her like his white prototype.

She tried to find a place for herself, but she had no indorsers, no recommenders. She dared not mention the name of the negro-trader; it banished her not only from the households of the whites, but from those of the genteel of her own color. And everywhere soldiers sentineled the streets—soldiers whose tone and accent reminded her of the negro-trader.

Her sufferings, whether imaginary or real, were sufficiently acute to drive her into the only form of escape which once had been possible to friendless negroes. She became a runaway. With a bundle tied to the end of a stick over her shoulder, just as the old prints represent it, she fled from her homelessness and loneliness, from her ignoble past, and the heart-disappointing termination of it. Following a railroad track, journeying afoot, sleeping by the roadside, she lived on until she came to the one familiar landmark in life to her—a sick woman, but a white one. And so, progressing from patient to patient (it was a time when sick white women studded the country like mile-posts), she arrived at a little town, a kind of a refuge for soldiers' wives and widows. She never traveled further. She could not. Always, as in the pen, some emergency of pain and illness held her.

That is all. She is still there. The poor, poor women of that stricken region say that little Mammy was the only alleviation God left them after Sheridan passed through; and the richer ones say very much the same thing—

But one should hear her tell it herself, as has been said, on a cold, gloomy winter day in the country, the fire glimmering on the hearth; the overworked husband in the fields; the baby quiet at last; the mother uneasy, restless, thought-driven; the soft black hand rubbing backward and forward, rubbing out aches and frets and nervousness.

The eyelids droop; the firelight plays fantasies on the bed-curtains; the ear drops words, sentences; one gets confused—one sleeps—one dreams.

The Little Convent Girl

She was coming down on the boat from Cincinnati, the little convent girl. Two sisters had brought her aboard. They gave her in charge of the captain, got her a state-room, saw that the new little trunk was put into it, hung the new little satchel up on the wall, showed her how to bolt the door at night, shook hands with her for good-by (good-bys have really no significance for sisters), and left her there. After a while the bells all rang, and the boat, in the awkward elephantine fashion of boats, got into mid-stream. The chambermaid found her sitting on the chair in the state-room where the sisters had left her, and showed her how to sit on a chair in the saloon. And there she sat until the captain came and hunted her up for supper. She could not do anything of herself; she had to be initiated into everything by some one else.

She was known on the boat only as "the little convent girl." Her name, of course, was registered in the clerk's office, but on a steamboat no one thinks of consulting the clerk's ledger. It is always the little widow, the fat madam, the tall colonel, the parson, etc. The captain, who pronounced by the letter, always called her the little con*vent* girl. She was the beau-ideal of the little convent girl. She never raised her eyes except when spoken to. Of course she never spoke first, even to the chambermaid, and when she did speak it was in the wee, shy, furtive voice one might imagine a just-budding violet to have; and she walked with such soft, easy, carefully calculated steps that one naturally felt the penalties that must have secured them—penalties dictated by a black code of deportment.

She was dressed in deep mourning. Her black straw hat was trimmed with stiff new crape, and her stiff new bombazine dress had crape collar and cuffs. She wore her hair in two long plaits fastened around her head tight and fast. Her hair had a strong inclination to curl, but that had been taken out of it as austerely as the noise out of her footfalls. Her hair was as black as her dress; her eyes, when one saw them, seemed blacker than either, on account of the bluishness of the white surrounding the pupil. Her eyelashes were almost as thick as the black veil which the sisters had fastened around her hat with an extra pin the very last thing before leaving. She had a round little face, and a tiny pointed chin; her mouth was slightly protuberant from the teeth, over which she tried to keep her lips well shut, the effort giving them a pathetic little forced expression. Her complexion was sallow, a pale sallow, the complexion of a brunette bleached in darkened rooms. The only color about her was a blue taffeta ribbon from which a large silver medal of the Virgin hung over the place where a breastpin should have been. She was so little, so little, although she was eighteen, as the sisters told the captain; otherwise they would not have permitted her to travel all the way to New Orleans alone.

Unless the captain or the clerk remembered to fetch her out in front, she would sit all day in the cabin, in the same place, crocheting lace, her spool of thread and box of patterns in her lap, on the handkerchief spread to save her new dress. Never leaning back—oh, no! always straight and stiff, as if the conventual back board were there within call. She would eat only convent fare at first, notwithstanding the importunities of the waiters, and the jocularities of the captain, and particularly of the clerk. Every one knows the fund of humor possessed by a steamboat clerk, and what a field for display the table at meal-times affords. On Friday she fasted rigidly, and she never began to eat, or finished, without a little Latin movement of the lips and a sign of the cross. And always at six o'clock of the evening she remembered the angelus, although there was no church bell to remind her of it.

She was in mourning for her father, the sisters told the captain, and she was going to New Orleans to her mother. She had not seen her mother since she was an infant, on account of some disagreement between the parents, in consequence of which the father had brought her to Cincinnati, and placed her in the convent. There she had been for twelve years, only going to her father for vacations and holidays. So long as the father lived he would never let the child have any communication with her mother. Now that he was dead all that was changed, and the first thing that the girl herself wanted to do was to go to her mother.

The mother superior had arranged it all with the mother of the girl, who was to come personally to the boat in New Orleans, and receive her child from the captain, presenting a letter from the mother superior, a facsimile of which the sisters gave the captain.

It is a long voyage from Cincinnati to New Orleans, the rivers doing their best to make it interminable, embroidering themselves *ad libitum* all over the country. Every five miles, and sometimes oftener, the boat would stop to put off or take on freight, if not both. The little convent girl, sitting in the cabin, had her terrible frights at first from the hideous noises attendant on these landings—the whistles, the ringings of the bells, the running to and fro, the shouting. Every time she thought it was shipwreck, death, judgment, purgatory; and her sins! her sins! She would drop her crochet, and clutch her prayer-beads from her pocket, and relax the constraint over her lips, which would go to rattling off prayers with the velocity of a relaxed windlass. That was at first, before the captain took to fetching her out in front to see the boat make a landing. Then she got to liking it so much that she would stay all day just where the captain put her, going inside only for her meals. She forgot herself at times so much that she would draw her chair a little closer to the railing, and put up her veil, actually, to see better. No one ever usurped her place, quite in front, or intruded upon her either with word or look; for every one learned to know her shyness, and began to feel a personal interest in her, and all wanted the little convent girl to see everything that she possibly could.

And it was worth seeing—the balancing and *chasséing*[1] and waltzing of the cumbersome old boat to make a landing. It seemed to be always attended with the difficulty and the improbability of a new enterprise; and the relief when it did sidle up anywhere within rope's-throw of the spot aimed at! And the roustabout throwing the rope from the perilous end of the dangling gang-plank! And the dangling roustabouts hanging like drops of water from it—dropping sometimes twenty feet to the land, and not infrequently into the river itself. And then what a rolling of barrels, and shouldering of sacks, and singing of Jim Crow songs, and pacing of Jim Crow steps; and black skins glistening through torn shirts, and white teeth gleaming through red lips, and laughing, and talking and—bewildering! entrancing! Surely the little convent girl in her convent walls never dreamed of so much unpunished noise and movement in the world!

The first time she heard the mate—it must have been like the first time woman ever heard man—curse and swear, she turned pale, and ran quickly, quickly into the saloon, and—came out again? No, indeed! not with all the soul she had to save, and all the other sins on her conscience. She shook her head resolutely, and was not seen in her chair on deck again until the captain not only reassured her, but guaranteed his reassurance. And after that, whenever the boat was about to make a landing, the mate would first glance up to the guards, and if the little convent girl

1 *Chasséing:* making or performing a *chassé,* a dance movement consisting of quick, gliding steps.

was sitting there he would change his invective to sarcasm, and politely request the colored gentlemen not to hurry themselves—on no account whatever; to take their time about shoving out the plank; to send the rope ashore by post-office—write him when it got there; begging them not to strain their backs; calling them mister, colonel, major, general, prince, and your royal highness, which was vastly amusing. At night, however, or when the little convent girl was not there, language flowed in its natural curve, the mate swearing like a pagan to make up for lost time.

The captain forgot himself one day: it was when the boat ran aground in the most unexpected manner and place, and he went to work to express his opinion, as only steamboat captains can, of the pilot, mate, engineer, crew, boat, river, country, and the world in general, ringing the bell, first to back, then to head, shouting himself hoarser than his own whistle—when he chanced to see the little black figure hurrying through the chaos on the deck; and the captain stuck as fast aground in midstream as the boat had done.

In the evening the little convent girl would be taken on the upper deck, and going up the steep stairs there was such confusion, to keep the black skirts well over the stiff white petticoats; and, coming down, such blushing when suspicion would cross the unprepared face that a rim of white stocking might be visible; and the thin feet, laced so tightly in the glossy new leather boots, would cling to each successive step as if they could never, never make another venture; and then one boot would (there is but that word) hesitate out, and feel and feel around, and have such a pause of helpless agony as if indeed the next step must have been wilfully removed, or was nowhere to be found on the wide, wide earth.

It was a miracle that the pilot ever got her up into the pilot-house; but pilots have a lonely time, and do not hesitate even at miracles when there is a chance for company. He would place a box for her to climb to the tall bench behind the wheel, and he would arrange the cushions, and open a window here to let in air, and shut one there to cut off a draft, as if there could be no tenderer consideration in life for him than her comfort. And he would talk of the river to her, explain the chart, pointing out eddies, whirlpools, shoals, depths, new beds, old beds, cut-offs, caving banks, and making banks, as exquisitely and respectfully as if she had been the River Commission.

It was his opinion that there was as great a river as the Mississippi flowing directly under it—an underself of a river, as much a counterpart of the other as the second story of a house is of the first; in fact, he said they were navigating through the upper story. Whirlpools were holes in the floor of the upper river, so to speak; eddies were rifts and cracks. And deep under the earth, hurrying toward the subterranean stream, were other streams, small and great, but all deep, hurrying to and from that great mother-stream underneath, just as the small and great overground streams hurry to and from their mother Mississippi. It was almost more than the little convent girl could take in: at least such was the expression of her eyes; for they opened as all eyes have to open at pilot stories. And he knew as much of astronomy as he did of hydrology, could call the stars by name, and define the shapes of the constellations; and she, who had studied astronomy at the convent, was charmed to find that what she had learned was all true. It was in the pilot-house, one night, that she forgot herself for the first time in her life, and stayed up until after nine o'clock. Although she appeared almost intoxicated at the wild pleasure, she was immediately overwhelmed at the wickedness of it, and observed much more rigidity of conduct thereafter. The engineer, the boiler-men, the firemen, the stokers, they all knew when the little convent girl was up in the pilot-house: the speaking-tube became so mild and gentle.

With all the delays of river and boat, however, there is an end to the journey from Cincinnati to New Orleans. The latter city, which at one time to the impatient seemed at the terminus of the never, began, all of a sudden, one day to make its nearingness felt; and from that period every other interest paled before the interest in the immanence of arrival into port, and the whole boat was seized with a panic of preparation, the little convent girl with the others. Although so immaculate was she in person and effects that she might have been struck with a landing, as some good people might be struck with death, at any moment without fear of results, her trunk was packed and repacked, her satchel arranged and rearranged, and, the last day, her hair was brushed and plaited and smoothed over and over again until the very last glimmer of a curl disappeared. Her dress was whisked, as if for microscopic inspection; her face was washed; and her finger-nails were scrubbed with the hard convent nail-brush, until the disciplined little tips ached with a pristine soreness. And still there were hours to wait, and still the boat added up delays. But she arrived at last, after all, with not more than the usual and expected difference between the actual and the advertised time of arrival.

There was extra blowing and extra ringing, shouting, commanding, rushing up the gangway and rushing down the gangway. The clerks, sitting behind tables on the first deck, were plied, in the twinkling of an eye, with estimates, receipts, charges, countercharges, claims, reclaims, demands, questions, accusations, threats, all at topmost voices. None but steamboat clerks could have stood it. And there were throngs composed of individuals every one of whom wanted to see the captain first and at once: and those who could not get to him shouted over the heads of the others; and as usual he lost his temper and politeness, and began to do what he termed "hustle."

"Captain! Captain!" a voice called him to where a hand plucked his sleeve, and a letter was thrust toward him. "The cross, and the name of the convent." He recognized the envelop of the mother superior. He read the duplicate of the letter given by the sisters. He looked at the woman—the mother—casually, then again and again.

The little convent girl saw him coming, leading some one toward her. She rose. The captain took her hand first, before the other greeting, "Good-by, my dear," he said. He tried to add something else, but seemed undetermined what. "Be a good little girl—" It was evidently all he could think of. Nodding to the woman behind him, he turned on his heel, and left.

One of the deck-hands was sent to fetch her trunk. He walked out behind them, through the cabin, and the crowd on deck, down the stairs, and out over the gangway. The little convent girl and her mother went with hands tightly clasped. She did not turn her eyes to the right or left, or once (what all passengers do) look backward at the boat which, however slowly, had carried her surely over dangers that she wot not of. All looked at her as she passed. All wanted to say good-by to the little convent girl, to see the mother who had been deprived of her so long. Some expressed surprise in a whistle; some in other ways. All exclaimed audibly, or to themselves, "Colored!"

It takes about a month to make the round trip from New Orleans to Cincinnati and back, counting five days' stoppage in New Orleans. It was a month to a day when the steamboat came puffing and blowing up to the wharf again, like a stout dowager after too long a walk; and the same scene of confusion was enacted, as it had been enacted twelve times a year, at almost the same wharf for twenty years; and the same calm, a death calmness by contrast, followed as usual the next morning.

The decks were quiet and clean; one cargo had just been delivered, part of another stood ready on the levee to be shipped. The captain was there waiting for his business to begin, the clerk was in his office getting his books ready, the voice of the mate could be heard below, mustering the old crew out and a new crew in; for if steamboat crews have a single principle,—and there are those who deny them any,—it is never to ship twice in succession on the same boat. It was too early yet for any but roustabouts, marketers, and church-goers; so early that even the river was still partly mist-covered; only in places could the swift, dark current be seen rolling swiftly along.

"Captain!" A hand plucked at his elbow, as if not confident that the mere calling would secure attention. The captain turned. The mother of the little convent girl stood there, and she held the little convent girl by the hand. "I have brought her to see you," the woman said. "You were so kind—and she is so quiet, so still, all the time, I thought it would do her a pleasure."

She spoke with an accent, and with embarrassment; otherwise one would have said that she was bold and assured enough.

"She don't go nowhere, she don't do nothing but make her crochet and her prayers, so I thought I would bring her for a little visit of 'How d' ye do' to you."

There was, perhaps, some inflection in the woman's voice that might have made known, or at least awakened, the suspicion of some latent hope or intention, had the captain's ear been fine enough to detect it. There might have been something in the little convent girl's face, had his eye been more sensitive—a trifle paler, maybe, the lips a little tighter drawn, the blue ribbon a shade faded. He may have noticed that, but— And the visit of "How d' ye do" came to an end.

They walked down the stairway, the woman in front, the little convent girl—her hand released to shake hands with the captain—following, across the bared deck, out to the gangway, over to the middle of it. No one was looking, no one saw more than a flutter of white petticoats, a show of white stockings, as the little convent girl went under the water.

The roustabout dived, as the roustabouts always do, after the drowning, even at the risk of their good-for-nothing lives. The mate himself jumped overboard; but she had gone down in a whirlpool. Perhaps, as the pilot had told her whirlpools always did, it may have carried her through to the underground river, to that vast, hidden, dark Mississippi that flows beneath the one we see; for her body was never found.

VI UNCOLLECTED STORIES

THE UNCOLLECTED stories of Grace King are not numerous. After the most productive period of her writing career, 1885 to 1895, she wrote more slowly, and short stories appeared only sporadically. Less than twenty stories and novellas were written in the last thirty-seven years of her life, from 1895 to 1932. The unique editions on which the stories of this section are based are as follows: "An Affair of the Heart," *Harper's Magazine*, LXXXVIII (April, 1894), 796–99; "The Evening Party," *Harper's Magazine*, LXXXIX (July, 1894), 192–95; "A Quarrel with God," *Outlook*, LV (March 6, 1897), 687–94; "Destiny," *Harper's Magazine*, XCVI (March, 1898), 541–48; "Making Progress," *Harper's Magazine*, CII (February, 1901), 423–30.

An Affair of the Heart

Life is like a sugar-plantation: it is never without something to worry about. An old sugar-planter must be excused for using such a homely, near-to-hand metaphor. The time was when he could have compared life to the great and mysterious and unknown with the best of them, in literature and out of it. But, what with the river, and fertilizers, and triple effects,[1] and stubble, and seed-cane, and droughts, and rains, and duty, and bounty, and commission merchants, and trusts, and Chinese, Italians, and negroes, and boiler-makers, and sugar-makers, and railroads, and steamboats, and mules, and cultivators, and road-machines, and always some old debt to pay off and a new one to contract, not only his figures of speech, but his thoughts, had become so involved in his life that even his imagination had given up soaring, to plod along in the daily routine with common-sense.

Indeed, on a plantation there is no time to think or feel about anything but the plantation. And yet life has some claims, which, be the crops what they may, must be presented some time. There is birth, there is death; and between these extremes, these termini, there is—nay, there must be—love or loves. Love! of all things for a harassed planter, in the midst of preparations for rolling, to have to think about!

He shaded his eyes from the lamp with one hand, and pretended to be smoking, but he was covertly looking at his daughter.

Of what use is it to describe a person? What difference does it make to the outside world, the color of the eyes, the hair—the qualities of the nose, the mouth? At any rate, all that is of so little importance to a man looking at his only daughter! One would hesitate to write, even if one knew it to a certainty, how an only daughter appears in the eyes of a father; what he felt when he was looking so at her. For, to tell the truth, the situation was a little intense between them.

Not that she seemed to feel it. Oh no! Not the least in the world. She

1 After the juice of the cane is steam-heated, it is allowed to settle, skimmed, decanted, and evaporated. The evaporation is effected in a triple-stage vacuum apparatus. The vapor arising from the boiling juice in the first stage passes into the heating pipes in the second stage. In the third stage the juice is thickened and further evaporated in a vacuum pan.

sat close to the lamp, doing her embroidery—red cross-stitch initials on towels, like the good little housewife she was. The light of the lamp played over her hair, and the sun itself could hardly have shone more tenderly upon it—at least so it seemed to the father, looking covertly at her. When she raised her eyes to thread her needle, always casting a glance at her father, he could detect in them not an expression of anything but cross-stitch and affection for him.

She was talking to him, fast and excitedly, for she was always so interested in interesting him that she could not help getting excited over it.

"—And then, after all those preliminaries, the great news came out; she told me of her engagement—an engagement only since last week. I could not help a scream. 'What! Him!' And although she is my best friend, papa, I could not help just a little movement of the heart against her. Fortunately I could conceal it under my surprise;. . . . but fancy, papa, to marry him!"

It would seem that no surprise could have concealed the contempt of her tone and air.

"But . . ."

"Oh, papa! As usual, you are going to defend her choice. You always defend the choice of young girls."

"But . . ."

"But ask yourself what there is in him! Of an insignificance—an insignificance that would appall an ant! And his age! Young to disgust!"

"But . . ."

"Oh, I do not say she is old. She is a year younger than I; and he, twenty-one; but to marry a man—a baby, I call it—of twenty-one—"

"But . . ."

"Ah, but, papa! Let me finish before you begin to annihilate me with your arguments! And then, what does he do? A—a—a" (oh, the depreciation of her tone!) "lawyer!"

"But . . ."

"Oh, he has prospects; I grant you that; his father is justice of the Supreme Court. But, papa, to marry a lawyer, you must confess—"

"But . . ."

"Oh, I do not say that I did not find the same objections last year when Theresa married her little doctor. Marry a doctor! Good heavens!"

"But . . ."

"He was older—yes—than this specimen of Marie's; but so commonplace! As commonplace as bread! And do you remember how tightly he held your hand when he shook it? It was an experience! I have never liked Theresa since."

"But . . ."

"Now, papa, do not play the innocent, and ask for reasons! When a thing happens, it happens, and I cannot see that reasons make it any better. Reasons are only excuses, that is all. As if I should ask myself for reasons why I should dislike Theresa! I do not believe now that I ever liked her seriously."

"But . . ."

"How could I tell whom she was going to marry when at school? We agreed so well about everything else that I thought we agreed about that too. Like Josephine. At school there was no one I took more pleasure in talking with than Josephine. Like me, always her first choice for a man was Richard Cœur de Lion, then Godefroi de Bouillon, then all the rest—Philippe Auguste, Francis I., Bayard, Du Guesclin, Saladin, and all like them. And we agreed perfectly well about those we disliked, as men—Cincinnatus, Brutus, Alfred the Great, George Washington."

"But . . ."

"Oh, papa! You do not suppose, oh, really, that any girl could love George Washington? That is, after he became George Washington. No! After every lesson in American history Josephine and I used to lie awake in our beds at night, and run the risk of punishment, just to talk about how much we hated him, and how glad we were that we had not to be Mrs. Washington. Just think, papa, how he looked? And he must have been of a stiffness! I should have felt like running and hiding behind a door whenever I heard him coming if I had been the deceased Mrs. Washington. Oh! I would just as soon have married the Professor of Mathematics . . . as Josephine wanted to do. Yes, that was the reason they took her away from school before her graduation. After having loved Richard Cœur de Lion, to want to marry the Professor of Mathematics!"

"But . . ."

"Oh, he was married when she first went to school, but he lost his wife, and of course they could not send him away immediately. He did not look like George Washington, though; he looked like St. François Xavier, only he had six children. Ah me!"

"But . . ."

"It has always seemed to me very curious that a young girl should be born with all of her ideas. Oh, they must be born with them! Where could they get them otherwise?—we are brought up with such particularity; never a forbidden book; never a suspected companion; never a pleasure, even, that had not received a prize of innocence. And what becomes of these ideas? All of a sudden they leave, they go somewhere; . . . and we marry, no matter whom! . . . Not I, though, I promise you! My ideas, I have them there," tapping her heart. "No; bravery, heroism, gallantry, a temper that stands nothing! fortitude, chivalry—they still exist for me! And your doctors, your lawyers, your professors, your clerks, your—"

"But . . ."

"But, papa, I say they do! What do you know? You are not a woman, you! It is not a question with you of— Oh no! You do not understand the question at all."

"But . . ."

"The only one outside of a woman who understands that is God. That is why women, even the worst, do not deny God. They know in their hearts that since they exist, He must exist."

"But . . ."

"Oh, you know, I only count upon what women know by the heart; what they know by the head does not amount to much. What they know by the heart is the juice as it exists in the cane, the living, growing juice; what they know by the head is that cane juice squeezed out, and steam-trained, and clarified, and triple-effect, and—what?—made into sugar, to be adulterated, and given into the hands of those highwaymen of the Trust."

"But . . ."

"Oh yes. They are highwaymen. Men are what their principles are, and the principles of the Trust! . . . When I think of it! . . . And it will be this year like last; . . . and the next year like this; . . . and—"

"But . . ."

"No! I have no hope, papa! No hope! Oh, if thinking could destroy the enemies of sugar they would have been destroyed long ago, I promise you! . . . What do you suppose I am thinking of all day long, and all night? Oh yes! all night, when I hear you sleeping, and snoring too, though you deny it . . . Sometimes, at night that way, I feel, yes, I feel like Charlotte Corday."

"But . . ."

"No! She is not one of my heroines; but I understand her so well!

When it gets to the last point, and a woman does not know what to do, then she feels she must do something."

"But . . ."

"I don't know, papa, what you call the last point . . . In fact, I do not know what it is myself. Every year there seems to be a new last point, worse than the last one."

"But . . ."

"Last year it was putting everything in machinery, and this year, the bounty being taken off—"

"But . . ."

"Oh, they will take it off, be sure of that! They hate us so in Washington! Legislation! Ah, bah! They help those they like in Washington well enough!"

"But . . ."

"Don't tell me I do not read the papers. I read them every day . . . I read them too much . . . It is enough only to read the newspapers to make one revolutionary, when it should be all the other way."

"But . . ."

"Oh, papa, you are not a judge! You go only by your own experience. You have a good crop this year. You can grind. You are on this side the river, in fact . . . As for me, I must judge by the experience of others. My own experience, what is it?—serving, servants."

"But . . ."

"If you say one should stay inside his own experience, oh, papa, how egoistic that would be! Then everybody would be like you, would have good crops, would be able to grind this year—would be on this side the river, in fact . . . Instead of which— As for me . . . I can live only with the unlucky, only on the other side the river. I see nothing but what is over there: those broken levees; those destroyed fields; those ruined roads; the fallen cabins; the tottering sugar-house; the beautiful garden planted by one's great-great-grandmother, desolate; the fine old house, with wave-marks on it . . . And then . . . the mortgage, the big debt; . . . and all the work, the work, the work—"

"But . . ."

"Oh, papa, you have said yourself that working that plantation had been a labor such as—such as— Oh, I can never get over that night! The levee must break, the levee must break, every one said. This side of the river or that, the levee must break! And the patrol riding up and down,

. . . the torches flying along between the bonfires, . . . and every planter with his gang! . . . Ah! we worked that night as if the opposite side of the river held our worst enemies . . . Every shovelful of earth to strengthen us hurt them! And I, I prayed, and made vows for our side, this side, as I sent out the hot coffee to you all in front, . . . and I watched the lights and bonfires on the other side the river . . . Suddenly the lights all came together, . . . then they ran far, far apart, . . . a roar —a great bonfire went out! Oh, my heavens! It had broken on the other side . . . right opposite . . . on the place of— Oh God! If it had only been ours! . . . Oh, papa! let me alone! What have I said? I have said nothing . . . Papa, let me alone! Go away! I have not said anything! I have not said anything! Only let me cry, papa! Crying signifies nothing! Oh, papa! papa!"

At last throwing her arms around him, and hiding her face close under his.

The Evening Party

"What a sight! Is it not beautiful! Ah! There is nothing I enjoy so much as the happiness of the young!"

Now that the critical moment of the evening was over for her, the company all arrived, and in so far compromised socially, it was impossible for the hostess longer to restrain her self-satisfaction, or suppress her desire for the flattery which had formed so delightful an anticipation during her preparation for the soirée. The remark was, however, felt by the critical to be a little premature for good taste.

The responses were, under the circumstances, compulsory. "Indeed, a beautiful party!" "A beautiful evening!" "Such beautiful flowers!" "So beautifully arranged!" "A beautiful bouquet of young girls!" "Such beautiful toilets!"

The first lady had paid the compliment that came easiest and most natural to her; the rest, either from imitation, or from lack of imagination, or because they had not presence of mind enough for discrimination, repeated the current adjective.

The occasion, as no one ignored, was rather critical: the initial attempt in society of people whose wealth was always the first item in the enumeration of their qualities. The issue had been made on the birthday of the only daughter. The whole of society seemed willing to participate in the experiment. One could look nowhere without seeing friends and the young sons and daughters of friends.

The young people were dancing in the large drawing-room on the other side of the hall. On this side was a small parlor in which the mammas sat. There were enough papas in attendance to fill up some card-tables in an adjoining room, which, in virtue of a writing-table and a bookcase, was called and thought to be a library. The silence of whist reigned in there, but in the parlor conversation rose and fell in irregular tides, rising at one moment to the clear distinctness in which discretions are to be said and heard of any one; sinking at another to the low monotone of indiscretions, when opinions may at any moment be misled into gossip.

"I am not so sure about these affairs for young girls," began a mamma in an ebbing voice, after the last outburst, reassuring herself by a glance at the receding figure of the hostess. "There are advantages, but there are disadvantages too."

This lady's opinion, however, seemed to have some damaging disqualifications attached to it, as if, for instance, her own circumstances prevented her giving a party.

"If a young girl is a great beauty or a great heiress—"

An elderly lady, who had evidently been neither, was about to furnish a commentary, but a nervous, energetic mamma, with a woman's intuition divining the argument, answered it before it was spoken: "But a great deal depends upon the mothers. Look at Céleste; her daughters were neither beauties nor heiresses; and with other disqualifications," shrugging her shoulders, "yet she married three of them."

"Ah, but she was Céleste! Where is she now? In the dancing-room, superintending, managing, devising, arranging. I predict it she will do for her nieces just what she has done for her daughters."

"Ah, well! At that expense!"

"That is true," a timid, belated respondent got in her word with a sigh of self-depreciation. "The mother, after all, is the important thing."

"After, or in default of the *dot.* At least, that is what my husband says."

This authority did not appear to be unimpeachable, or the taste of introducing it into a circle where each one, to say the least, had some claim to a similar infallible director.

"I wonder, Marie"—the last speaker, feeling the condemnation of the pause, sought to relieve it by a diversion—"if you object to evening parties, that you brought your daughter here."

Her malice was detected at once, and frustrated by brute strength, as it were.

"Really, that Marron plays too mechanically! I think it very pernicious having him play so everywhere; it will have an effect on the music of the young ones."

"You are right, my dear. He is already influencing them. The other day I heard Idéo at her piano: 'tam, ta, ta! tam, ta, ta!' 'But, my darling,' I cried, 'what possesses you? I thought it was a horse, playing with his hoofs!' 'I am playing like Marron, mamma,' she said; 'listen. It sounds just like him!' And, in fact, she played exactly like the perambulating piano in the street."

"I sometimes despair about the music." This mamma showed the care-worn face and the carelessly worn toilet of the many-childrened. "You labor and strive from the moment a child can sit alone on a piano stool, and the first time your back is turned, Heaven knows what bad habit is going to creep in!"

"That is true. It is a continual dipping up of water with a sieve. And then, too, there seems so much luck in it all! It is enough to discourage any one."

"That is the hardest thing about children—the education; all the rest in comparison is a farce."

"Yes, and when it comes to results, to the grand and final result, it is hard to tell the difference between the real education and the imitation."

"It will be like lace. In old times a lady thought it a disgrace, a misalliance, as it were, to wear imitation; now—" She perceived herself that this was venturing on delicate ground, and so instinctively paused, adding the always convenient—"At least it appears so."

"But even the imitation is better than the absolutely—nothing," braving her fear that the hostess might overhear.

"Yes, as we used to say when the negroes made their grotesque attempts at manners and language: it shows goodwill at least, and is meant to be a compliment to us."

"When it comes to that, we are, all of us, only imitations—that is, I confess only to myself—a poor imitation and cheap."

Only one who could have afforded it would have ventured to say that, and so the remark had no force.

But this line of conversation was felt to have painful possibilities too, and so the topic was changed again. It is almost impossible to keep a general conversation on safe grounds in an assemblage where all know one another. There seems to be no subject absolutely innocent.

The music stopped, and the dancers had an intermission for a promenade.

The young girls were only too willing to extend it into the parlor, and even among the whist tables, for the pleasurable excitement of seeing themselves looked at.

The expression of the mammas while the procession lasted! Such lightning glances of comparison, ill-concealed triumph, and still more ill-concealed defeats! How carefully, how painfully had they prepared for show! Each separate physical attribute the recipient of particular effort! The hair let down its full length when it was long and thick, and so artistically fastened up when deficient! And crimped and curled! Even naturally curling and undulating hair passed through the irons. Thin bodies were rounded with puffings of lace and tulle; the prettiness of full ones was as tenderly bared. Small feet were enhanced, large ones condoned; even the eyebrows evidenced a reference to the ideal which prefigures a woman's destiny in the world. The nervous mothers could not forbear calling their daughters to them to retie a bow, smooth or fluff the hair. The difference between girl and girl, both as to looks and dressing, was painfully apparent, and one could not help becoming impressed with what imagination was not needed to intensify into a crucial moment. Indeed, in some of the still ingenuous faces themselves could be read the discouragement of the *éclaircissement* which comparison and competition had brought about to a hitherto intact satisfaction of self and dress. And the ones who suffered thus in their own eyes were frankly regarded by the others as innocent victims to a mother's incompetency.

The mamma of such a one gave a sigh, and essayed by indirection to relieve her feelings.

"Valentine is really wonderful; her children always have on something new!"

"Oh, of course! We can always confidently expect that of her. Who ever saw her but running a race after the fashions? She would break her neck rather than not keep up with them. Let me tell you what happened the other day. Some lady, in the most casual manner in the world, happened to remark in her presence that in a letter from Paris it was mentioned that children were wearing little capes. Valentine did not know the lady who was speaking, and had never heard of the person who wrote the letter; but she went home immediately from that parlor, sent out her maid to Holmes's[2] for the stuff, and by the next morning all her children were wearing short capes, just like the children in Paris."

"My sister told me," contributed another—the music and dancing were well under way again now—"that one day, when she went on some affair to Valentine's, she found her ripping out all the pleats in every skirt in the house. She had just heard that pleats were no longer fashionable. She was so busy that she really could not talk to my sister."

"Perhaps she was right," confessed the discouraged mamma. "One must think so when one sees her family. It seems to me that for women it is the most profitable use for time and money in the world—dressing. It is so important!"

"And there are so many obstacles in the way of it! I mean good dressing."

"Unless one is—" A glance gave the address: the hostess. "They say their wealth is enormous—e-nor-mous!" increasing the quantity of it into something monstrous by this simple device of separating and prolonging the syllables of the adjective.

"Or why should we be here?" asked the sharp tongue, the never-failing discount on the society of women.

"And the daughter will have a 'parti' of her own choosing."

"When one thinks of it one is forced to ask one's self the valuation, not of principle, not of morality, but of common honesty in the world."

"I think the churches ought to attack it."

"Oh, the churches!"

In a community where religion obtains at least a conventional recognition, there could be no rejoinder to this so tactful as a feigned deafness to it.

And then the conversation, as it had done before several times, subdivided, each topic branching off to itself, the groups subdividing also, each woman holding fast to some little proprietary argument, and to the determination of making it heard, following her chosen topic—music or dressmakers or fashions or children, religion, wealth—and so making new pairings. The lady who had neither been an heiress nor a beauty,

2 Holmes's is an important New Orleans department store.

still pursuing the continuation of her idea, charged with it upon her sofa companion, without looking even to see who she was.

"As I was trying to explain— What, it's you, Louise?"

"Yes, it's I!"

"I have not noticed you here before?"

"Oh! There are so many here," as usual, giving the clew to her own self-effacement.

"But—it looks very well, very well indeed—" forgetting her idea about society, the lady looked through her eye-glasses at Louise's dress.

"If it passes unobserved, that is sufficient, as you told us."

"It must be sufficient; that is all about it. You have a daughter to bring into society; if you stay at home until you get the money to dress fine—like—" There was no need to be more explicit, the allusion always hit the mark this evening.

"Yes; my husband could have made money too, if—"

"Any one could, my dear—any one could. It requires only brute strength of conscience."

"But—it is very beautiful here."

Louise, in her faded, rusty black gown, with its stiff new white ruchings at neck and sleeves, looked up at the glittering splendor about her as if from the depths of some immeasurable abysm.

"Yes; so, so. But where is your daughter? Where is Louisette?"

" 'Sette? Oh, she was put in the room with the dancers when I was put here."

"Come, let us hunt her up; let us see what she is doing."

The stir of their moving off attracted the notice of the others, and all the buzzing, scattered conversation immediately forsook its separate topics to hive on their backs.

"What a resurrection!"

"An exhumation, rather!"

"My heavens! Are they still in the world?"

"Oh, I heard weeks ago that everybody who was anybody, even in name, was to be invited!"

"They do show great energy, these—" looking around cautiously.

"Well, we must keep up with the procession," said the lady who quoted her husband.

"Poor thing! But what can she do in society?"

"But what can she do out of it?"

"That is the question."

And this ramified into an argument which unfolded all the entertainments of the whole carnival, with commentaries, biographical, narrative, and critical, upon all the givers, and upon many of the recipients of them. In the midst of it Louise and her cicerone returned to find the young girl they were seeking standing before them, dropped, as it were, from heaven, or at least come from no one noticed where.

She was one of the thin ones, over whom the muslin and lace had to be puffed. She whispered something in the ear of her mother.

"What! Want to go home!" The mother, without thinking, expressed her astonishment aloud.

The daughter blushed sensitively, for in her mother's astonishment was revealed also a naïve horror, not to say anguish.

"But, my child!" in a whisper. "The supper! It is going to be magnificent! Don't you want to wait for supper? It should be ready soon now!"

"What! Is she not amusing herself?"

"Is she ill?"

"Isn't she fond of dancing?"

"Some one should have found a partner for her."

"It is a pity to go home so soon now."

"In fact, the evening seems very long to me too."

"Yes, but one must not give up; if one gives up at the first ball, one will never be able to go through a second."

"Yes; I told my daughter when we started that no matter what happened she must stay until the end."

The debate that followed was fruitful enough to carry them all through nicely to the pleasant goal of supper, at which they arrived well disposed for any conversion in favor of wealth; for a party supper is perhaps the one occasion where wealth can still hold its own against the claims of family, birth, and position.

The defeated ones, for there seemed to be some occult reason for so considering them, made their way through the throng in the hall to the great door, and beyond that through the street loafers that crowded the front steps, eagerly catching at any glimpses or snatches of sound of the inaccessible feast. In the dark silent streets every now and then one of Marron's crescendos would come running after them, as if to tug at them and coax them to return, reproaching them for at least a want of thrift in throwing away a gratuitous opportunity for pleasure, like refusing some toothsome delicacy on the silly excuse of want of appetite.

The street led, however, away from the sound of the piano: bar after bar, note after note, began to drop out of hearing, the hiatus of silence grew more and more continuous, longer and longer, until at last the great stillness overcame the stuttering, stumbling sounds, as great sleep finally overcomes a nodding man.

And so at last a stretch of street without, so far as eye could see or ear hear, any sign or sound of party-givers or party-goers, night everywhere filling it with night products—darkness, silence, sleep.

The garden gate stood open, just as they had left it when they went out, forgetting in their excitement to shut it.

The low, dim cottage was in hue and quietude a piece of the night itself.

All sleeping fast inside—the fast good sleep that comes after domestic excitement, burying well all plans, hopes, fears, and excitements under its depths, the sleep which one thinks God must make ever vaster and vaster, deeper and deeper, that it may rise well over the increasing accumulations of brain life.

The half-light, shining like a dim intelligence in the hall, made the usual mysteries out of the commonplaces there.

The party-goers tiptoed through them up the stairs to their chambers.

The young girl struck a match and lighted her gas. What confusion round about! The event that had come, had passed. The gloves, slippers, muslins, ribbons, necklace, hair-pins, fan, and the almost forgotten, but bought at the last moment, the new handkerchief; for of course there could have been no party without a suitable handkerchief. They all went to add to the débris and confusion on floor, chairs, and bureau. And, like an edifice falling down amidst all its carpentry and masonry, she fell on her bed.

She could hear her mother trying to keep her father awake long enough to hear the account of the party. All the rest of the family were asleep, still asleep, with anticipations of it. What feats of expectations, what feats of labor and patience and financiering, during the past ten days! What worlds and worlds of strangers! What heights of beauty and finery! What roulades and crescendos of Marron! What moments in the dancing-rooms! What—what hours in corners of parlors, with the mammas all talking!

She turned on her face to cry noiselessly.

A Quarrel with God

The time had come for the old Mademoiselle to die; Mademoiselle Herminie. And she was dying at Madame B——'s.

For all the guests, as they were politely called, there was something terrible in the thought of dying at Madame B——'s. To live there—yes; and Heaven alone knows the circumstances that constrained some of them into plotting and intriguing in order to get there to live. But to die there! Ah! we all want to die, at least, in the station to which we were born. The coffin and funeral of charity are bitter humiliation, even to the administered soul. And how they all shrank from it, the old ladies at Madame B——'s! It is one of the painful pictures of life, that of their sitting and waiting for the priest to come—or, as now, waiting for him to go; each soul of them trembling, as it were, over its own precipice. One should see them thus sitting—but the heart must be strong for that, and well moored to the great faith of religion.

Every one called it "chez Madame B——," "at Madame B——'s," and that is simply what it was. The institution, to give it technical definiteness, is accounted for in this manner. It arose, one may say, out of a necessity and an opportunity. The community one morning was shocked—no, not shocked, transfixed with horror—to learn that old Madame M—— had been discovered dead in her wretched little cabin of a home—dead of starvation. She had been dead three days when discovered; not in her bed, oh no! Starvation gives not the easeful death of that. She was not in her bed, but stretched on the floor, her poor skeleton hands outspread, grasping—perhaps for some phantom crust or crumb—her mouth open, distended, gaping wide. The sight of it!

Madame B—— was old, herself. "Is it a possible thing," she exclaimed when she heard of it, "that Aurore M—— could die, could so die, in her own city, amid her own people? But do you consider who Aurore M—— is?" she demanded; "the widow of a Confederate soldier, the mother of a Confederate soldier, the daughter, granddaughter, great-granddaughter of the best, the most aristocratic, the most honest of the city. Yes, in the veins of that old woman—before they were starved dry—coursed the blood of those to whom our city owes some of her proudest and most patriotic traditions. And to die thus! But that was it; she died thus, on that very account. For should she acknowledge that she was hungry? Should she go begging for bread? or asking the charity of money under the travesty of some fictitious employment? No! The best blood dies so; should die so. The other kind strikes and storms and destroys when hunger assails. Its wants must have its pensions, hospitals, homes, asylums, rostrums, organs, and, just Heavens! its platforms and political parties! Its sufferings and calamities are national affairs! . . . But no. . . ."

Madame B—— had not so very much of financial wealth herself, was not, in fact, more than a floor or two above the plane upon which Madame M—— had met her end. But, as she aptly quoted, "Tout calcul amoindrit l'âme." [3] She owned a valueless lot of unimproved ground, and she found, or invented in some way, the means to erect a building upon it.

The widows and children of roustabouts would have despised it. Had murderers and thieves been confined in it, philanthropic societies would have had emotions over it; the colored orphans of the gallows, as they are called, would have suffered in the exchange of their asylum for it. Madame B——, however, despite other deficiencies of knowledge, knew her world well. She felt, or maybe she did not feel at all, but did what she could with the means at her disposal, by building on her lot a row of chambers of the plainest and cheapest kind. Nothing more. No comforts, no curtains even. Each guest brought her own furniture, and if she had none, slept on the floor—as she wished, and as if she were at home.

Food was provided; a choice about that might result in the repetition of Madame M——'s scandal. There were coffee and bread in the morning; a good gumbo and rice, or a good soup with the *bouilli*[4] and vegetables, for dinner; in the evening, hominy, with hot milk and water. As you see, not enough to put one under obligations, nothing more than those necessities which ladies can offer and accept with honor.

To resume. It had come suddenly upon Mademoiselle Herminie, but death always seems to come suddenly—even when expected—like the slamming of a balancing door. Only yesterday she was about, and, as her companions said, more herself, more Mademoiselle Herminie, than ever. That is, more, at one moment, haughty, stiff, and reserved; at another, nervous, irritable, and cross, acrid, bitter, sarcastic, skeptical in speech, defiant in manner, shocking in impiety; more—in short and altogether—poverty's worst thorn in the establishment of Madame B——. But, as

3 *"Tout calcul amoindrit l'âme"* (Every calculation weakens the spirit) is not a well-known French proverb.

4 *Bouilli:* boiled beef.

they said, the fellow-guests, after resigning themselves to so much to please God, they could surely resign themselves to such an infliction as—Mademoiselle Herminie.

Florestine, the servant of the establishment, had found her ill when she took her her early cup of coffee. She had run instantly for the doctor, leaving word in passing the church door for the priest. The doctor came and went, evacuating the field before the only enemy and antagonist he possessed in the city. In truth, as he told Florestine, Mademoiselle Herminie had been an invalid for half a lifetime, and had been in a dying condition for over a year.

The priest, hastening to look after the interests of his principal in the case, could not arrive at so prompt a conclusion. He had been at the bedside all day, and it was now afternoon.

The old pensioners sitting together in the common or dining room made a brave effort at courage. Death! why, there was nothing in life they had been rendered so familiar, so intimate, with as Death. They knew the whole range of his powers of bereavement. He could wing his shafts in vain, for there were no more targets for him in their lives, in their loves. Had it been otherwise, they would not have been at Madame B——'s. But each one, fingering her prayer-beads in her lap, looked nervously into the others' faces; and, indeed, to the imaginative, each face must have appeared to the other like a mirror that by some neglect had been left uncovered at a funeral. There was the great consolation, however, that the end of no one in the dining-room could be like the end of Mademoiselle Herminie, for she had given up the practice of religion when, so to speak, the practice of misfortune had been put upon her; or, as Florestine expressed it succinctly, she had quarreled with God. Neither in church nor out of it would she recognize Him; and so long had been her practice of poverty and misfortune that she had become accustomed to the difference, and it was questioned now whether she ever thought of Him. It was a situation to appall even Death.

"Has she made no sign yet, Florestine?" some one would always ask whenever the servant would pass through the room.

"Not yet, Madame."

And then there would follow little spurts of talk about Mademoiselle Herminie. But the ladies were so deaf or spoke so inarticulately that their sentences fell isolated and extinct as to meaning, with the exception of a word every now and then which called forth misfit rejoinders.

"For a man to die so, one can imagine it; but for a woman!"

"Ah, yes! Men imagine that religion is only for women!"

"The rich and the prosperous might die so, but the miserable, the unfortunate . . ." pursued the first speaker.

"Poor soul!" ejaculated the oldest, and, as far as human judgment went, the most sorely tried of them all. That was all she had contributed to the conversation all day long—these pitying words, "Poor soul!"

And the others would at the words reiterate their theories about Mademoiselle Herminie, as they had been doing all day.

"She has suffered too much; that caused it."

"She had too much to bear; she had no chance."

"She revolted because she felt too much crushed."

"She holds God to account."

"But now she is dying—that changes all."

"She must make her submission to God."

"She should not let her life interfere with her death."

"Women expect too much of God."

"She felt that God had not given her a chance."

"A chance for what?" asked some one who heard.

"Happiness."

"Happiness! Blessed Virgin! At her age?"

"Well, what, when she was younger, she thought happiness."

"Ah!"

"But she was pious when she was young, and unhappy."

"And now—" A shudder ended the words.

"If she had suffered more, she might, perhaps, have been more at peace with God."

"If God had only sent her peace and resignation! that would have been the better way."

"But God is going to do as He pleases. She ought to know that," contributed Florestine. "God is the master."

"If she had had children to lose!"

"Or a husband!"

"Or a whole family—father, mother, sisters, brothers, at once!"

Each suggested her own misfortunes.

"But if she suffers more this way," suggested Florestine, "she must have had more to suffer."

"Does she suffer much, Florestine?" asked one who had caught only that idea.

"The doctor said she suffers more than she shows; that she has always suffered since she has been here, like—like a Pagan"—substituting her own term of comparison, and speaking in the loud voice she had trained herself to use towards the old ladies.

"It seems as if God might have spared her that!"

"Eh! When it comes to sparing—"

"If she had loved God more, she could have forgiven him more."

"Love! What did she know about love?"

"He could have taught her as he taught other women."

"No, he should have sent her resignation; resignation is the only thing for women in this world."

"Does she seem at ease in her mind, Florestine?"

"She does not seem anything, Madame; she is just so . . . and the priest, he is the same."

"But he should talk to her; he should try to touch her heart."

"He should awaken her early piety."

"He should make her hope again. Women can always hope at least."

"He should talk about her parents to her."

"And her infancy; her childhood."

"And her early life. . . . She could not reproach God then."

"He should tell her that what she suffers here will be paid back to her in happiness in heaven."

"He should tell her that she will forget it all there—that would be the best."

"And this life! What is this life!"

"He must not let her die before she makes her submission."

"A Jesuit father should have been sent for."

"Monseigneur himself should have been sent for."

"Florestine should have asked advice."

"She went for the nearest."

"So much depends upon the priest."

"How can he speak to her as he should? He knows nothing about her."

"If he knew all about her, he might be able to effect something."

"When one remembers how proud she is, and obstinate!"

"Oh, she is capable of talking to God just as she used to talk to us."

"But if this priest could once touch her heart, the rest would follow."

"Yes, that is it; he must touch her heart."

Florestine threw open all the shutters to let in all the light there was still left for that day. It was yet far from sunset; the afternoon was only begun; but she had lived so long with the old ladies that she felt with them a distrust, an uneasiness about the night.

This was the cheerful hour of the day, when she flung the windows open and new light flooded in; it was the hour for the hominy-and-milk and rice-and-milk supper, for the organ-grinder and noise of children in the street—so noisy they were, providentially; surely the gayest children in the world, the deafest ears could hear them. It was the kindly hour when life once again carried them on in its fullness of vitality, and they could feel the blissful obtuseness of children to the one more step forward they were making towards the verge of that which separated their good, old, known New Orleans from the unknown eternity and immortality beyond.

There had not been, properly speaking, any daylight in the sick-chamber since the physician had left it in the morning. The atmosphere in it was of a murky twilight until Florestine threw open the windows there also.

The priest sat at the bedside; still waiting for that sign of recognition of himself and his functions about which the ladies in the dining-room so eagerly questioned Florestine.

It seems hardly worth while to describe the kind and variety of misfortune that had gone into the making up of the unhappiness of Mademoiselle Herminie's life, and brought her to die in a pauper's retreat—no more worth while than to describe the pathological incidents that had brought about her physical destitution. The old women at Madame B——'s themselves recognized clearly enough that the recital of their misfortunes meant nothing to one another, or to themselves. Their misfortunes all seemed similar—there are, after all, only a limited number of misfortunes in the world; but each one recognized that, although apparently all had traveled a well-worn highroad, each had in reality marched alone, in a personal and private path, to Madame B——'s, . . . as, for the matter of that, they were also marching to death. It was of little import to them now whether the loss of all meant the loss of one or many, whether they had ached in a spot or in the whole body.

The priest also must have had some such thought, as he sat in patient watchfulness by the bed.

Such, however, was not Florestine's thought or attitude. The Master must be informed! This was the summary of the subject in her mind. A soul in her institution was not to be damned, any more than in old times a slave on her plantation was to be whipped, without some attempt on her part for mercy. The ladies in the dining-room were right; how could the priest do anything? He knew nothing about Mademoiselle Herminie. He was only a poor, humble, ignorant French priest—the servitor of one of the poorest and smallest churches in the city; only good enough for the souls of the Gascon milk and butcher people in his charge, and for the souls of negroes. He was as fitted for the ministration of Mademoiselle Herminie as the overseers of negroes in olden times were fitted for the supervision of the white owners. Such a priest might suppose that Mademoiselle Herminie was only a poor white woman dying impenitent in her misery at Madame B——'s.

Florestine stood behind his chair, upon which from time to time she laid an emphasizing hand; bending forward, she kept her eyes fixed upon Mademoiselle Herminie while she whispered in his ear the information upon which she and the old ladies relied for the salvation of a soul in its supreme moment of need. "God knows who she is, mon père; He knows her family well—from the grandfather down. They used to live in that big house on Orleans Street; you know, on the right hand as you go to the Cathedral. They were rich in that day! And everybody was glad to respect them, I guarantee you. The grandfather—the old Colonel—he was the big man in the State; they say the Governor himself used to be afraid of him. Oh! I remember him well. I used to see him at the head of the 'Bataillon d'Orléans' every January, on Jackson's Day, with gold on his hat, gold on his shoulders, gold on his front, and a big sword in his hand; he looked more like two men than one man; and he was not afraid of God on His throne, I tell you! And he had plantations, and negroes—more than he could count. You know how rich he was when I tell you there are masses said every month now at the Cathedral for his soul. Oh, he is safe enough in heaven by this time, depend upon it! And if she had money, she could have masses said for her soul too!

"And the father! He was still bigger! God could tell you that; God knows it all. God knows everything that goes on down here in this city! He could tell you about the father! Eh! His balls and his dinners, his fine cooking and his fine servants. His niggers were too fine to go with other niggers! They had no use for God; their master was God in their eyes. If she had some of that money now, she could have masses said; but she has no money, she must make her submission. God is the master: she must beg His pardon—and for what? Did she ever do anything? No! God in heaven knows she never did anything against Him. And what? For a few words, get a whipping! And who heard these words? Me—and

I swear to you I never opened my mouth about them. I am no tale-bearer. Nobody ever caught me carrying tales . . . And those poor old ladies sitting in the dining-room praying for her since this morning! Oh, mon père! If you saw them! So old, so poor—and with death always before them—so patient, so pious, so good, and never a word of complaint. They know what it is to be ladies! But God is right; the Master is always right; he owns his people, and he's right to do what he pleases with them. But the master does not know everything that passes on his plantation, and, mon père, if God saw what I see in this city, and if He knew what I know, He would not be hard on Mademoiselle Herminie; no, He would not be hard on her. Do you think if she had a family who had money, there would not be masses said for her too? Eh! He thinks it easy to lose everything—all your family, all your everything: mon père, He does not know. Why do you think I wait here day after day, year after year, without one cent of pay? No; I live off of scraps; I wear rags—why? Because I can't make a living, you think. You ask my people, you ask the people who know me! It is because my heart is so sorry for these ladies; it is because I can't sleep at night for thinking about them. God knows I would have to take my heart out of my body with my two hands and pitch it into a gutter before I could leave them in their misery to wait on themselves. Well, that is one thing! God will never be able to take their servant from them. I guarantee you that. I do not say this because I come from rich white people myself. No; my people were poor—even before the war; they lost everything, too; it is no new fashion, this misery. I know it from a long time back. I never lived in those fine houses on Royal, on Orleans, on St. Louis Street. No; and the negroes that lived in them, they would only spit my way. I never had fine tignons, and silk aprons, and gold earrings, and lace on my white fichu. No! God made poor people even before the war. And do not think, mon père, that I have done nothing for Mademoiselle Herminie: I have burned candles; I have made novenas; I have put images in her room when she did not know it; I have sewed scapularies on her clothes. I could show you now! Oh! she would be mad enough if she knew that! She would have been capable of putting me out of her room and slamming the door upon me. But that would make no difference with me, because I knew Mademoiselle Herminie was so alone. Listen, mon père: do you know what that is, to be left alone, but alone, alone, with nobody in this world to be your family? Well, God did that to Mademoiselle Herminie. Before the war I never saw that. There was always somebody left. And it is not with white people as with negroes. You cannot take away every one from negroes; there are always so many left; and, anyhow, they are all black together. And, then, they can always go to the white people. Who have the white people to go to? Listen! I could tell God on His throne, Himself: 'Why did you take everybody away from Mademoiselle Herminie, and then leave her alone? Why did you not send some one? Why did you not come yourself? That is how we do with children; we never leave them alone; we always send some one, or we go ourselves.' God knew her. He knew her family. He knew their characters. It was not right to make her alone, and then leave her alone. And you think, mon père, it was right for her to come here and not have even a relation to go to? Why could she not have a relation—just that little thing, a relation? You see those old ladies out there in the dining-room; you think they are alone, that they come here because they have no friends, no relations? Ha! I know, I watch, I listen, I find out all about them. Mon père, there is not one old lady out there but what has some relation to go to. Madame B—— knows that too. But, you see, the times are so hard, and the relations are poor, and there are big families . . . and the old ladies feel that they do not die, in fact, but live . . . and the little children have to do without . . . and so they come here. It may be different up-town in the American quarter, but that is the way we do down here. We are not rich like the Americans, but we have more heart. Mademoiselle Herminie, she had no one to love, to sacrifice herself for. Those old ladies out there, they look back, and they see what? . . . A husband; they have all been married; and old Madame M——, she has been married twice. Oh! some of the husbands were not worth counting. I know things about them . . . but, at any rate, they were husbands, and that is something; . . . and when they look back in their lives, they are always glad to see him there. Oh, I know them! And they talk to me about him, and they all thank God that they had him. . . . And the children! . . . Look at old Madame L——. 'Florestine,' she is always telling me, 'this is the anniversary of the birth of one of my children,' or 'the anniversary of the death of one of my children. . . . Thirteen children, Florestine, and all in the grave!' And she tells me all how they died. 'Madame,' I answer, 'you ought to thank God that you had thirteen children to lose; some have not had even one child to lose.' They are pious, those old ladies, and they submit to God; and you think they are better than Mademoiselle Herminie? No! They are no better! And their family is not so good. But God has been kinder to them than He has been to Mademoiselle Herminie; that is the truth, and the old ladies know it, and talk about it among themselves. Is there one among them would change her life for Mademoiselle Herminie's? No, not one, even if you paid them for it. In old days, mon père, it was the good master had the good negroes. That you may depend upon; I was there; I know it. How could Mademoiselle Herminie love God? Mon père, we sometimes love the devil because we think he loves us . . . better than God loves us. When Mademoiselle Herminie looks back in her life, what does she see, since her mother? . . . not even a negro. There is not an old lady out there that has not got a negro to come to her once a year to call her mistress and beg for something. Eh? You think that does not make them feel good? God did not leave Mademoiselle Herminie a baboon of a negro. . . . And she works; mon père, you must not think she does not work. She sews. You ask Madame B——. She knows. Mademoiselle Herminie, since she has been here, has sewed. She has not taken her board for nothing, I guarantee you."

The unquiet slumber of the patient showed signs of breaking. Florestine bent her head still lower, her whispered words came faster, her hand grasped the chair with all its strength. There were but a few moments more to work in. "Oh, mon père, listen: do you know how her mother died? . . . If I were to tell you, it would make you sick . . . you ask the doctor what she died of? . . . It was in the family . . . and Mademoiselle Herminie, she was young then—when it first came on. She nursed her. They would have killed a servant who told it . . . but it was told . . . the servants knew. . . . She nursed her one year after another—one year after another. Everything went from her—the old lady . . . her ears, her eyes. . . . She could not talk—she became foolish, foolish. Mademoiselle Herminie nursed her . . . still . . . The family went, the house went, the money went. . . . Mademoiselle Herminie nursed her still . . . and she worked for her. Oh, my God! mon père, do not make me tell you any more. . . . The grandfather, mon père, he was no saint. They had no peace with him; it was a secret . . . but I know all he did. No wonder they say masses for him! He needs them, mon père; he needs them. . . . And the father! . . . He was worse! . . . Mademoiselle Herminie, she knew it, she saw it, as well as her mother. . . . How God can create gentlemen so bad!

"Yes, she was cross, mon père; yes, she said things against God. . . . Yes, mon père, I will not deny it; I will confess it. . . . She did not do her duties in religion . . . she merits punishment, as the catechism says. But look at her, mon père—so old, so thin, so white—think what she suffered, think what she is suffering. And after all her misery in this world, after all she has gone through. It is respect for you that keeps me from telling you—but I could tell you, yes, I could tell you. Her mother was pious, her mother is up in heaven, and her mother did not suffer as Mademoiselle Herminie did. She did not have her mother die so! like a dog—yes, I say it, like a dog! And, think, this is all the life Mademoiselle Herminie had!

"I do not say, mon père, that God is not right, that He does not know best; He is bound to know best. And He knows that Mademoiselle Herminie did not do her duty to Him . . . and she was proud, and she was cross, and always in a bad temper . . . God knows that! She was not like the other old ladies who sit there day after day with the patience and resignation of angels. If you choose to call Mademoiselle Herminie a sinner, I will say yes. . . . I will not go against God's judgment. . . . I am only an ignorant negress . . . and I have been wicked myself . . . God knows I have! And if He knows it, what is the use of lying about anything? Mademoiselle Herminie . . ."

The whisper seemed to reach the bed; the patient's eyelids quivered; she was awaking. Florestine's whisper became still more intense; she laid her other strong hand on the chair. She had but an instant more. "Ah, mon père! You are good, you are patient. You know the poor wicked people . . . Mon père, that is why I went for you! I was afraid to go for the others! The meanest send for you, mon père—they are not afraid of you! . . . She is opening her eyes! . . . Say something to her, mon père! Do something! See how poor and thin and old she is! No! Do not look at her! Do not listen to her! She is out of her head! She has always been half crazy! She does not know what she is about! For God's sake, do not ask her! Think of your mother, mon père, think of her, and do your duty! . . . God will understand . . . God will understand . . ." There was time for no more.

Mademoiselle Herminie's eyes opened. The soft evening light filled the room, and through the open window came the pleasant evening sounds. It was the cheeriest hour at Madame B——'s, for it seemed to be the one hour that old hopes came back to the inmates not as disappointments and maledictions (the maledictions of old age are so often the hopes of youth!).

The priest gave no evidence of listening to Florestine. He kept his eyes fixed on the bed, his rugged face set in an expression of confident waiting. It was no first death-watch for him and no novel one.

Generally, after a long, hard life, when disease, tracking close upon poverty and misery, has overcome its final resistance; and pain, for the first time in years, is at last withdrawn, and the body lies calm waiting for death to take possession; generally, in the priest's experience—and his experience was his life—the eyes opening thus after an opiate rest were not eyes of recrimination, but eyes of peace and reconciliation. And if the childhood have been pious, it is as if the whole life but childhood were forgotten. Sometimes the aged lips babble childish sentences, and the worn soul takes its flight in an infantile respiration.

Sometimes the eyes open from the sleep or lethargy blank, blind to everybody, everything; and then there is only a sound needed—the voice of a child in the street, an evening bell.

Again, the eyes opening to the light falling across the bed, and to the sight of tender faces bending over; the sense of companionship, at last, after a long, solitary journey under a night sky from which all the stars have gone out, bring to the stiffening lips a smile of ineffable happiness, and long-forgotten words of gratitude.

Always the priest had found that it was the women who had been most sorely tried, those who have most to forgive, who forgive most easily. And his memory retained experience only with the sorely tried.

Or it may have been according to Florestine's reasoning and experience—and in her way she was as experienced as the priest, and she had often proved her reasoning in the old times—that the master sometimes would listen to an overheard explanation when he would not to a direct one; and one of her most successful devices as advocate for mercy when a fellow-slave was in peril of punishment was to tell his story, as she knew how to tell such stories, just inside the master's hearing. The old ladies in the dining-room had their theories, or experiences, too, about such cases.

At any rate, when Mademoiselle Herminie opened her eyes, she recognized the priest, performed her religious duties, and died at peace with the world or God—whichever she had been at war with.

Destiny

Imagine, if you please, that it is a balmy summer night, and that near an open window are seated, conversing, two old, two very old and intimate friends, M. Théodule Drouet and Mademoiselle Minerve O'Mouroy. They are seated near enough the window to see the night—that is, the heavens—but, according to good creole wisdom, not near enough to feel it—that is, the dampness.

The parlors are almost as dark as the night outside, the lights burning within their white globes as dimly as the furthest stars in the Milky Way.

And one must imagine that M. Théodule had asked for the particulars of an event which his absence from the city had prevented his knowing—the intimate particulars which intimate friends have a right to ask, in virtue of the lien and privilege of a long and carefully sustained affection. Mademoiselle was answering with the frankness which the same conditions and circumstances constrain—not that reasons were necessary to elicit frankness from her, for she was frank by nature and under all circumstances:

"I had gone to fulfil my yearly obligation of a visit to my old aunt O'Mouroy." She pronounced her name in French, Mou-roi. "And between you and me, my friend, if she were not ninety-five, and twenty years older than I, I would renounce the obligation. And just as I was preparing to say adieu, the devil sent me an attack of rheumatism. It was Aunt Mouroy's old cook, Adelma, who heard it in the market, that Théodora was very ill. I bounded from my bed when she told me. 'What! Théodora given up by her physician! Not twenty-four hours to live! I do not believe it! I do not believe a word of it! It is only one of your usual cancans picked up at market, gossiping when you should be attending to your business! And la grippe! What is it? Only a cold. People do not die of la grippe. Bah! You have no sense, Adelma. And a woman of your age not to know better!'

"I fell into a perfect rage with the old woman. She herself was excited.

" 'Would to God, mamzelle, that it should be as you say, but I ran there at once. They were all crying in the kitchen. Dr. Cambier himself had announced it to them; he himself had condemned their madam.'

"By this time, of course, I was out of bed, and out of my attack of rheumatism too, putting on my clothes, abusing Cambier for keeping me in bed with his abominable notions and misrepresentations, and berating myself for believing him.

"Ah, heavens! why had I allowed myself to be put to bed for two weeks—and that absurd idea of concealing it from her! What is anxiety in comparison to— My God! we mortals should never let a day pass without seeing one another. There is nothing so sure to happen as death!

"I got into the street, tying on my bonnet. A car was passing, but I suffered a hundred deaths before the mule reached St. Louis Street. Once upon the banquette, I made up for the slowness of the mule, I can tell you. As usual, the banquette was well sprinkled with groups of idle women and trifling servants, exchanging the news of the day—and it was Adelma's news—and they were all waiting to see the priest arrive—that pious crowd of St. Louis Street! You know we have ceased to contend with the police any longer about that street, and we are resigned to the fact that the patron saint of France names about as great a thoroughfare to hell as exists in the city. I opened the front door, and flew through the corridor to the kitchen. The servants and all their families were assembled there, just as Adelma had left them.

" 'Well, Placide?' I called out to Théodora's old factotum.

" 'Oh, Mamzelle Minerve! Mamzelle Minerve!' he answered, bursting into tears; and all, following his example, burst into tears, and 'Mamzelle Minerve! Mamzelle Minerve!'

"But I was very stern and indignant. 'What do you mean by not letting me know immediately?'

" 'Not let you know, Mamzelle Minerve! Not let you know! I sent you word day before yesterday. Before that she was so well she expressly forbade my sending you word, not to worry you.'

"Ah, these subterfuges between friends! But I pass that over.

" 'As soon as she got worse,' continued Placide, 'you were the first person I sent word to.'

" 'You did no such thing! I have just heard it from Adelma, who picked it up at market. A little more and I should not have heard it at all.'

" 'Before God, Mamzelle Minerve'—sobbed old Placide. 'But where is Lisabeth? Where is she? Let her tell you if I did not send her day before yesterday.'

"Lisabeth swore that she, having the toothache, had given the car fare and message to Fillette; and Fillette swore by all the saints in heaven that, as she could not go, she had given message and car fare to Italie;

and Italie, a good-for-nothing specimen, if ever there was one, confessed that she had forgotten the message and spent the car fare. Under ordinary circumstances Placide would have settled with Italie then and there. Now he could only wipe his eyes and whimper, 'Oh, Mamzelle Minerve! Mamzelle Minerve!' his chorus following him. I commanded them to make plenty of good strong coffee and drink it, and left them.

"Of course we, among the old, can expect only death; what else have we to expect? And Théodora and I were not sentimentalists over the prospect; but we were not sentimentalists over anything practical. And of course there is no longer anything new to be said or thought about death. By this time everything possible on that subject has been felt and suffered. The greatest poets even are now condemned to platitudes and commonplaces about it. But—at least it is always a new person that dies; and, I assure you, my friend, I seemed to think and feel about the death of Théodora what I had never felt or thought about death before. In the first place, as I passed from the kitchen—there was the old house, so respectable and so solid; built when there was so much more confidence in the stability of wealth and position than now—and the court-yard with its garden of shrubbery in tubs and pots, some of it older than I, and the handsome twisting staircase—I do not know why, but there was some quality in everything I saw to increase the originality of the event.

"The funeral seemed already to have commenced upstairs. You know what a mixture of friends and relations assembles on such occasions, and what a curious etiquette of whispers and eye-liftings they observe. And, as usual, it was which one should tell the greatest story about her intimacy with Théodora, and make greatest display of knowledge about her private affairs and—patati! patata! I have often asked myself in such emergencies why God could not have given women real brains instead of the imitation ones they have in their heads.

"Cambier seemed preparing to leave. You may imagine his surprise at seeing me. I believe confidently that at that very moment he was thinking of his morning visit to me.

"Théodora was sleeping. I sat down by the bed in the chair Cambier had just vacated. There was no use to question him. You know, his mania is to pretend to understand less about life and death the more he knows about it. There was nothing to do but to sit and wait.

"And if death appeared original to me in the garden and on the stairway, you may imagine how it appeared now. In fact, it seemed impossible that it was all to end—our future, so, now; after so short a time. I saw it as only yesterday, the day when, as it were, it commenced; our future —the day when I was taken by her father to her house to live, after my father was killed in his last duel—the duel that has passed into history; but all his duels were historical, for as an Irishman he would fight only Englishmen. I could feel the scratching of the black bombazine gown on my skin as it passed over my head when I was dressing for the funeral. Théodora's father was my father's best friend and my godfather, and I was confided to him—according to what seemed my father's invariable custom when preparing for such occasions. And it was a wise precaution too, for my father's estate amounted only to an Irishman's dreams—of fortune.

"There is no greater truth than that our childhood furnishes us our fatalities for life. My godfather therefore took his precautions well. I may say confidently that there was not a grain of earth in our childhood out of which a fatality could grow. My poor godfather! He was so wise, so grand, so imposing, so correct! I can truthfully say he inspired every sentiment except love. And Théodora resembled her father in a great many respects. She had his dignity, his reserve, his coldness, and his immaculate discretion. She resembled him in the essentials, just as I resembled my Irish father. The year after my father's death we left the city and lived entirely on the plantation. Oh, the dignity, the reserve, the seriousness, the implacable correctness, of our life there! and for studies, an unceasing *marmotage*[5] of grammar, catechism, French history, and etiquette. 'Théodora,' I used to say, 'your father is preparing us for a heaven presided over by Louis XIV. as God.'

"We should have petrified—I am sure we should have petrified had it not been for Bibi—Bélisaire Martin, my godfather's nephew. But you knew him. He was one, for example, who did not resemble Mr. Martin; on the contrary, I should say that Bibi was capable of inspiring no sentiment but love. He was an accomplished good-for-naught. My poor godfather disapproved of him in every way; but what could he do? To permit Bibi to live in the city was to invite a crevasse in his fortune. It is true, keeping him on the plantation was as damaging to his philosophy; but philosophy is acquired easier in this world than money, so Bibi was kept on the plantation. He did not like the arrangement any better than my uncle did. He called the plantation his Bastille, and said that living under the eye of his uncle was as comfortable as living under the eye of

5 *Marmotage:* a muttering or mumbling.

God. Oh, he had no religion; none whatever! He used to say that religion was the great discomfort of a pleasant world. Every now and then he would make little escapades to the city to pay his respects to the devil. But, after all, he was only twenty-five, and it was not given him to practise philosophy.

"As you may fancy, Théodora and I adored him; he made, as we say, our rain and sunshine for us. As he had nothing to do for himself but play the piano and study out problems in solitaire, he had abundance of time to bestow upon us. In fact, he did everything for us—our sums, our grammatical exercises, our résumés, our compositions. He even managed to secure our governess's book and teach us our dictation in advance. He showed us easy ways of reciting our lessons, so that the governess could not really tell whether we had studied them or not. It goes without saying that our governess was detestable, from an interesting point of view. Bibi taught us dance music, which was not at all in Papa Martin's programme, and taught us dances—such as ladies dance, not governesses. He told us stories about society: he could tell any kind of story he wanted, and knew the continuation of all the tales in the *Magasin des Enfants.* He knew our dolls better than we did ourselves; he named them for us, told us how to dress them, and related such things about them—such interesting and astonishing sentiments and relations as would have been incredible from any one but him. And then he could mimic the governess, and even Mr. Martin, deliciously.

"When we were twelve, and it was time for us to go to the convent and make our first communion, we regretted Bibi more than all the plantation put together. We more than regretted him. The truth is, we had become so dependent upon him for arithmetic, grammar, exercises, everything, that it struck terror to us, the idea of our ignorance without him—our naked ignorance. Even our catechism, how could we prepare for our first communion without his telling us how to remember this and that answer—by associating it with the most incongruous things? And I never could understand why it was we never had any difficulty in remembering the incongruous things, but only answers in the catechism. He promised everything he could think of to console and encourage us; but the only rainbow in our heavens was the assurance that he would visit us on the reception days, and would manage to assist us in our lessons in some way. As the convent was almost in sight of the plantation, this would have been quite feasible; but after two visits Bibi was forbidden the convent, after Heaven knows what adventure in the pious precincts. It was one of his favorite ideas that temptations were merely adventures for the adventurous.

"The life at the convent, although it was only four years, seems always the longest part of life to me. I suppose one never recovers from the impression of such a life. Even now, do you know, when I say my prayers at night, I do not say them as a wrinkled old woman wrapped in a shawl for fear of rheumatism, but as a slim young girl with long black plaits hanging down over an angelic white robe—and after that to sleep, the whole dormitory full of us, with our hands crossed over our breasts in case we died before daylight.

"Bibi, however, did not consider himself absolved from his promise by his adventure or misadventure. With him obstacles never failed to stimulate enterprise. My godfather had, of course, exacted that his own correspondence with us should be released from inspection. With such a man the sisters naturally felt they were securely warranted. They counted without reckoning Bibi. There never came to us a letter from my godfather in which Bibi did not manage to insert a communication from himself. Not that he wrote from himself; no, that did not suit his genius at all. He wrote from everybody and from everything imaginable but himself—from our dolls, pets, furniture; our desks, chairs, and pillows; from the rosevine on the gallery, the oak-tree in the yard that held our swing—in short, from the plantation in general, from the plantation in detail, all of which seemed to be following our studies, writing our compositions, doing everything we were doing, even to preparing for a first communion. We never answered; naturally we could not. When he had exhausted the novelty of every possible correspondent in his environment, he hit upon a device which pleased him so much that he continued it to the end—and it pleased us as much as it pleased him. This was writing letters to us from the page Gentil Galant and the chevalier Preux Vaillant. Ah, if you think those names did not interest us, or imagine that they were absurd to us, you do not know convent girls, and you underestimate Bibi's literary and poetical accomplishments. Gentil Galant wrote to Théodora, Preux Vaillant to me. Of course as personages there was no pretence as to their reality, which made them more interesting—for illusion then, with us, was our reality.

"And do not imagine otherwise than that they were perfectly discreet with us. They were models in that regard; my godfather himself could not surpass them. I may say that their mission was simply to assist us in our classes, and keep the fool's cap from our heads, for we were never able to retrieve those first years of not learning with our governess; and I may say that our whole career at the convent was devoted to concealing that we did not know what we were supposed to know. We were both of us absolutely without foundations. And our poor governess used to boast to my godfather about our foundations. Oh, I assure you, Gentil Galant and Preux Vaillant played a rôle in our lives! Gentil Galant was young, timid, hesitating, and bashful, of the kind that would have most influence upon Théodora. Preux Vaillant was a bluff, brusque, battle-scarred warrior, of whose kind I used to love to hear Bibi relate adventures. A man was never a hero to me at that time unless he was bold, bluff, rough-skinned, rough-mannered, swearing great oaths, doing impossible deeds. All that was what I adored. And Théodora liked none but gentle pages, with silken hose and curling locks, saintly morals and chivalrous manners, playing the lute and composing verses to some high-born lady, for whom he performed miracles of courage—until he died, young and fair and unhappy, with her name on his lips. As you see, we could never be rivals. Of course Preux Vaillant had an extraordinary past, and sometimes he incorporated his grammatical examples in examples of his prowess; and, to tell you the truth, the more extraordinary his past was, the better I liked it and the firmer I believed it, and I never thought of his grammatical examples. Gentil Galant seemed to hope for as extraordinary a future, which he loved to couch in rhetorical examples and poetical exercises. Oh, la! la! as we used to exclaim then. I do not know what Théodora's idea upon the subject was, because to obtain it would have been to confess my own; and we were too well reared for such confidences. But there was a young boy on the plantation—a young boy whose parents had died, and who lived with the overseer. We used to see him sometimes when we rode out into the fields with Mr. Martin. He was always so timid that he never raised his eyes to us, but stood blushing until we passed. He never did anything but pursue birds and insects. It seemed he had a passion for that. Well, in my idea, he assumed the rôle of Gentil Gallant. What if Théodora had suspected it! The protégé of the overseer! She would never have forgiven me. But I would not have had the idea except as an illusion, and I have always had a weakness for illusions. In fact, I can resist everything except an illusion. As for Preux Vaillant, I had arranged him also thoroughly in my mind. I figured to myself that he looked like the lion in our favorite book, *Les animaux peints par eux-mêmes;* and he lived—that was my most extraordinary illusion! Fancy? On our way to the village church we passed a kind of enclosure—that is the only way I can describe it—a fence that seemed to be pushed out into the road by a hedge, and a mass of shrubbery inside; acacia-trees, magnolias, and myrtles that were in fact woven together by wistaria and rose vines; and far, far inside one could see the roof of a house. I had never heard of any one living there. Heaven knows whether any one ever did live there; but no place on earth suited me so well for a residence for Preux Vaillant. And it suited him so well, my distinguished warrior in absolute retirement—limping slightly. I do not know why, but it was indispensable to me for him to limp slightly.

"It was of the utmost importance, and it was the great mystery of our lives, to destroy these epistolary aids to our education. And it seemed to be a point of honor to destroy them in the presence of one another. But I—oh, I never dreamed for an instant of destroying mine. When Théodora, after reading her letter, would tear it into shreds, and roll them into a ball to fling away, I would slip a piece of paper out of my pocket with which to imitate her admirable example. It was the great terror of my life and my secret of the confessional that she should discover the deception; and, in fact, it kept me preoccupied and absent-minded.

"And, despite all of Bibi's genius, we graduated ignominiously as to honors, failing even to obtain the contemptible prize of Christian conduct.

"Poor Bibi, we never saw him again. Just before we returned from the convent he made one of his escapades to the city. It was during an epidemic of cholera, which inspired him to give a dinner composed of all the forbidden articles of diet. And that was the end of him, and of most of his dinner party. Cambier escaped; but he was a physician, and, it is supposed, carried his antidotes in his pocket.

"I can best describe our life afterwards at the plantation by saying that I do not remember it any more than I remember a long sleep. The only event was going to church on Sunday, and the quarrel my godfather had with Poursine, the overseer, who ventured to adopt a new theory about mat-laying cane. Poursine and his whole family were summarily dismissed the plantation, including the young boy, whom we could see from time to time in the distance pursuing his insects.

"And society, in the city afterwards, was not interesting to us; we found it, on the contrary, stupid—stupid as our daily bread. There was such an utter absence of poets and heroes in it! Then my godfather died, and we have lived here in the city ever since. And that is all our adventure, I may say. Our life was filled full with what did not happen to us. I have often thought how stupid and commonplace it was to write novels about what happens to people; what does not happen to them is far more interesting and exciting.

"Of course, as long as my godfather lived, he managed everything for us. When he was dead, we tried to manage for one another, and so in conformity with my duty I used to preach common-sense to Thédora.

"Some women prefer going direct to novenas and candles, and even to the expense of sending to Europe for what is efficacious, to obtain what they desire. I, however, preferred reserving these means for cases of failure.

" 'Come, now, Thédora,' I would say, 'let us be frank and reasonable with one another. Tell me what it is you have in your head about this life of yours.'

" 'I have nothing in my head about life. That is, I have nothing in my head except what has been put there. I am not wise enough to invent ideas, as you know.'

" 'Thédora, how can you affect to be so silly? Do you wish me to ask you point-blank, like a washer-woman, what is the reason you do not get married?'

" 'My reason! But it is the same, doubtless, as your reason. Why do not you get married?'

" 'That is what you always do—instead of answering me reasonably, you try to exasperate me. But I will not follow your example. I will answer you reasonably. I will ask you, am I an heiress? Am I—not to flatter, but to speak the truth—am I beautiful? Have I, to use the polite metaphor, young men sighing at my feet? If you had not a *dot,* if you were not as you are, if you, in short, had not every opportunity, I should say nothing.'

" 'Ah! if I had no choice in the matter, of course there would be no choice.'

" 'The choice in the matter should not necessarily be your choice, but the choice of those who are wiser than you. Heavens! I should think you had learned that well enough from your father.'

"She would shrug her shoulders at this argument. 'I am going to do in life, Minerve, just what you do!'

"This would make my blood boil, but I would conceal the fact under the greatest coolness and patience.

" 'Well, then, you should start in life by being just like me. Am I a blonde? Have I the blue eyes and the light hair and the complexion of an angel? No; you know very well I am as dark as an Indian, with black eyes, black hair—in fact, ugly.'

" 'It would seem that you steal from my fence to mend your own!'

" 'If you mean anything by that, I do not understand it. And to return to our subject, I was only asking you for your idea.'

" 'Well, that is my idea!'

" 'But what is your idea? And what does it amount to? If that is your idea, for God's sake, abandon it! Go and get somebody else's idea!'

" 'If you will not allow me to have an idea of my own, perhaps you will permit me to say taste!'

" 'Taste, Théodora! Taste! As if it were a question of taking coffee with or without milk! That is unworthy of you, Théodora! What do you take me for, to answer in that way?'

" 'Well, my dear friend, I suppose the truth is, I have a feeling against —'

" 'A feeling! Oh, that is more senseless than ever. Tell me, I beg you to tell me, have you a feeling for the sun, the moon, the—the— Bah!'

" 'Perhaps it is my intelligence—that—forbids.'

" 'Your intelligence! Oh, la! la! You have no more intelligence than the great majority of women in this world. And if they—if they do it, why cannot you?'

" 'But the great majority of women, they can believe, they can trust—'

" 'Ah! believe! trust! I like that! You cannot believe, you cannot trust. You can trust your whole fortune to Davide!' And I presented her with a few items of M. Davide's biography.[6] 'And you believe Cambier about your very life—Cambier, who himself does not believe either in God or man. Do you believe a miracle has been performed to satisfy you about Davide and Cambier?'

" 'Nonsense!'

" 'How do you know what is nonsense? How can you tell? You, who the whole time you were at the convent could never, except by cheating, get beyond the twelve times twelve.'

" 'Well, if you will have it so, say it is a sentiment.'

" 'But I will not have it so; I will not say it is a sentiment! I will never say it is a sentiment! With women a sentiment is always good; it is never bad. When you say, a woman's sentiments, you say that which God

6 M. Davide's biography: probably Jean Baptiste David (1761–1841), French Roman Catholic missionary to the United States, whose devotional works were popular for a generation.

alone inspires a woman to feel. Oh, Théodora, you, who are a woman, how can you speak that way about a woman's sentiments?'

" 'After all, my dear Minerve, to come down to the fine point of it all, it is, as you know, in God's hands. If He desired me to— In fact, He rules us, and He makes us to act according to His designs.'

" 'Oh, Théodora! You cannot mean to assert that! You do not know what you are saying! You cannot mean that God made my poor father fight his duels; that He made your poor father act as he did to Poursine! Poor old Poursine, who had served him so long and faithfully, who would have laid down his life for him! Just because he had a theory which did not coincide with your father's, about mat-laying cane, he must be put off the plantation with ignominy—even his wife and children treated as if they were enemies!'

"This argument seemed always to strike Théodora, but she would never let me finish it—would always try to turn me aside, which was the very reason I would not allow myself to be turned aside. 'You remember, we did not acquiesce in that as in the will of God. On the contrary, Heaven knows how we exerted ourselves to prevent it. We knew it would break old Poursine's heart to leave the place, after he had lived there so long, and we said then it was not the will of God that injustice should be committed about differences in theories about mat-laying. No; it is God's will when the best happens; and if we want to conform to His will we must do the best.'

" 'But how do you know what is best? That is the difficulty.'

" 'I see no difficulty—I do not admit there is any difficulty. Bah! Women know very well what is best for them; but when their fathers are dead, and there is no one to enforce it, they pretend to be in doubt. You cannot deny, Théodora, if my godfather, your poor father, had lived, you would have been married by this time, firm and fast. It is because he is not here that you fabricate these delusions that you give me for arguments. You cannot deny it.' And she never attempted to deny it, for she knew that Mr. Martin had a way of interpreting God's will in the matter of our destiny that neither of us could resist.

" 'Well, put it that way if you choose—put it any way you like—what difference does it make now?'

" 'Théodora, quite simply and frankly, you are a fool.'

"This was the result every time I tried to argue with her, and I would determine never to speak to her again. I have no patience with a person who takes a false position and maintains it absolutely."

A comment from M. Théodule steered the monologue back into the home waters of practical information.

"All this time Cambier had apparently been thinking of something else. Returning, after an absence from the chamber, he communicated to me what he termed the business duty of the moment. He said he had written to you to come without loss of time, but that we had better provide against the emergency of your arriving too late. And he unfolded his recommendations and advice. You must confess, if men have real brains, they have only imitation hearts. Oh, that was not the first time the reflection came to me! My godfather produced and cultivated it in me all the time during my life with him, and the sentiment of his own death was sacrificed entirely to affairs. Indeed, it would not be an exaggeration to say that with men the voyage from life to death means no more than a business journey. God knows that on such occasions a man in his senses thinks more about the disposition of his money than of his soul. Of course I told Cambier to wait until you came; that you would arrange all; that, in fact, my godfather had expressly commanded us, on his death-bed, to do absolutely nothing in life without consulting you.

"Cambier insisted that I look in Théodora's desk and see if she had provided, like a business woman, for the disposition of her affairs. I refused as long as I could; for I am not a man, and business affairs are to me the affairs of least importance in life. I went to her desk. It was in our sixteenth year, on our return from the convent, that my godfather, with much ceremony, presented desks to us. He had ordered them from Paris. Mine was inlaid with a rose-colored design, Théodora's with blue. Théodora really loved blue so passionately that she had a prejudice against rose. We arranged our little papers in them exactly alike, and they are arranged so still. Old women, when left to themselves, do not change much, after all. You may be sure my godfather did not provide secret drawers in our desks, any more than he provided secrets in our lives, so I found great difficulty in disposing of my package of letters—my Bibi's Preux Vaillant correspondence—so that Théodora should not suspect their existence. How we invent mystery for ourselves when it does not exist! I assure you that concealment from Théodora was the charming mystery of my life—and, heavens! how frank we were with one another otherwise!

"Well, my friend, you will appreciate this—you know who know us all so well, who know us better than we do ourselves—you who know that my greatest pleasure in life is enjoying my own sagacity.

" 'A will,' I said to myself, 'is always hidden, secreted,'—and I put my hand in the secret place I had devised,—and I drew out—Bibi's Gentil Galant correspondence, and— At any rate, you arrived in time to arrange everything."

And, at any rate, as Mademoiselle Minerve would have expressed it, it was time to retire; the nine-o'clock bell was ringing. She arose stiffly, on account of her rheumatism.

M. Théodule had observed, in his long professional life, that those who apparently possessed least self-control exercised the most in critical moments, and that it was the most indiscreet women who exercised the most discretion in regard to important information. As his own discretion, like Cambier's ignorance about life and death, was a mania with him, he was somewhat dependent upon the indiscretions of others. And he had a mind that could not rest amid uncertain surmises. He remained in his seat until the half-hour struck. He then retired to the chamber that had been placed at his disposal ever since it had been necessary for him to journey from the country to the city to attend to the affairs of the family. Old Placide attended him. M. Théodule availed himself of him as he availed himself of every opportunity.

"Placide," he said, selecting a folded paper from a package taken from his pocket, "take this document to Mademoiselle Minerve."

He waited by the window, looking into the court-yard, with the garden of shrubbery in pots and tubs. On Placide's return he asked, without turning his head, "I hope you did not disturb Mademoiselle Minerve, Placide?"

"No, sir," answered the old negro; "she was sitting at her desk."

"Writing at this time of night!"

"No, sir; she was reading some old letters."

"Ah!" exclaimed M. Théodule, involuntarily, for all his discretion.

It was also one of the greatest pleasures of his life, the enjoyment of his own sagacity; and his sagacity was never more enjoyable to him than when experimenting for proofs of itself among the delicate processes which go into the making up of ladies' lives—or destinies, as they are called.

Making Progress

Walking rapidly along upon some quest of momentary importance that absorbed my thought and dulled observation, I was suddenly stopped by a crowd on the sidewalk in front of me: a compact, eager, curious crowd, not to be threaded, and using its elbows viciously against pushing. No wonder! A cart of the Little Sisters of the Poor stood backed up against the curbing, and four men were just in the act of pushing a stretcher into it. To see such a sight was well worth the while of a whole neighborhood of shopkeepers, for I was in the thickest shopkeeping quarter of the city. Practically speaking, there was very little to be seen: a slight form covered by a sheet, and the outline of a head on a low pillow. Every precaution had, as usual, been taken to ensure concealment, the only privacy possible. But as the stretcher slid into the wagon a murmur passed through the crowd, an involuntary shiver. The woman upon the stretcher slowly raised her head, opened her eyes, and gave a look upon the gazers. What a look! Woe! woe! woe!

The horses jerked forward; the head fell back; the cart rattled away.

I felt my elbow plucked, then grasped, and still looking after the cart, with the rest of the crowd, I was forcibly dragged into a doorway. It was my friend Madame Jacob, the second-hand dealer, who had hold of me, and I perceived now that it was her shop that had furnished the excitement to the street. It always seemed to be furnishing an excitement to the street. I never passed along there without noticing a turmoil: Madame Jacob putting her assistant, her nephew, out upon the banquette with cuffs and harder words, or hauling her husband in from a drinking-shop, or railing against a cautious customer, or assaulting the four corners of the heavens with voluble French, English, and German declamations upon some other misadventure. It was shrewdly suspected by some, and I believed it, that Madame Jacob used her noise and excitement as an auctioneer's drum, to call a crowd together, and so get at people. One could not help slacking one's pace to listen to her, nor, while one listened, glancing into her shop, and every glance of mine into that mysterious interior had, as I calculated it, cost me fifty cents. Others, of course, could get off cheaper, but they were not after bric-à-brac, or, to be more specific, old cut glass.

My eye hastily glanced around now, taking in the prospect of a bargain, as I was still pulled forward through the piled-up junk to a little recess behind the shop, the landing-place of the stairs, where I was thrust into a chair. Madame Jacob squatted on a low stool in the doorway, whence she could dominate her business and watch her nephew; and whenever she saw a customer edging away without buying anything, she would rush at the boy, box his ears, sell something, and come back to her stool, and her story, before the interruption was noticed.

Of course she wanted to tell me the story of the girl just carried away to the Little Sisters of the Poor: the young girl, she called her, although that gray-haired, ashen-faced head could by no means be called young, except in the sense of unmarried.

The story after all is not much, perhaps hardly worth writing down; but when it comes to that, what true stories are worth writing down? They are like natural flowers in comparison with the artificial—good only for the day, not for permanent show. The girl's name was Achard, Volsy Achard. When Madame Jacob first rented her shop, some thirty years before, the Achard family were living in the rooms above; they owned the building, rented the downstairs, and retained the upstairs—two rooms, a large one, and a small one adjoining. Madame Achard and Volsy slept in the large room. Paul, the boy, in the small one.

The family had been well-to-do shopkeepers in that very house, and in that very business. Madame Jacob intimated, for with a curious delicacy she would not say it outright, that Achard made his start with a sack over his back and a broom-handle with a crooked nail at the end of it. At any rate, when he died and Madame Achard became the head of the family, and sold his business and collected all his profits together, she found that she had enough to invest in two houses—that one and the one next to it —which she rented at, in a round sum, fifty dollars a month apiece. And so, as Madame Jacob said, we see them, rich enough for anybody, with the boy going to the public school, the little girl to the day school of the convent. The family could not have been any more comfortable anywhere, nor happier: close to the market, under the very spire of the Cathedral, and with the opera-house at the end of their foot, so to speak. The little daughter, Volsy, "was so good, so good; . . . and Paul, he was 'smart,' 'smart.' " There was no American in his school who was smarter than he—to quote Madame Jacob's own words. The mother adored her son; the daughter was devoted to the mother. When Paul left school, he said he would be a lawyer, that and nothing else.

Every day the boy would go to his law study, and every day Volsy and her mother would sit together and sew and talk, and watch the soup simmering on the furnace. They went a great deal to church, and Volsy had a particular devotion to the Infant Jesus: the mother with the Infant, or the Infant alone, was all she cared to have on her little altar, and her picture cards; never the Virgin alone, or any of the saints. Paul read law in the office of a low-born but very well known lawyer—one who had a great practice in the shopkeeping class.

When Paul was admitted to the bar, this same lawyer gave him a desk in his office. This was a great advance for Paul, in one way, although in another, as the young man was good-looking, well-mannered, spoke French and English, and was, in short, more than usually intelligent, he was not a bad investment of the sort that older lawyers are ever on the alert to make from among the younger ones. Many a young lawyer, so picked up, has been known in the course of time to carry an old patron on his shoulders and seat him on the bench of the Supreme Court for the reversion of his business, and marrying his daughter to boot. Going ahead means, necessarily, leaving behind, and Paul's advance caused the little family of three to change its rank. It did not, as of yore, march three abreast. . . . Paul stepped on in front; the two women came together after him.

Paul dressed better and better, and associating with lawyers and imitating them, he, in the course of a few years, was not to be distinguished from any gentleman among them. This was the radiant time of life for his mother and sister. They talked of nothing else but Paul, thought of nothing else, lived for nothing else, and in their gratitude to Heaven they devoted themselves more and more to the church, and spent more and more of their money in votive offerings—to ensure the continuance of favors, or patronage, as Madame Jacob put it. And according to Madame Jacob's superior judgment in such business, it is always well to wait awhile and be sure about your blessing before you go into excess of gratitude, for in her experience the greatest blessings, apparently, had turned out to be the most unmitigated curses, and one's prayers and money were thus thrown away.

As if in the course of nature, Paul, marching always farther and farther ahead, advanced beyond coming home to his dinner,—beyond going to church Sunday morning, beyond going to the opera Sunday night, beyond going to picnics in the spring, given by his mother's benevolent society, or the balls in winter, given by the society to which his defunct father had always belonged, beyond going on little excursions of summer evenings to music places, beyond passing even an evening at home,—beyond everything of the past, in fact, except taking the cup of coffee that his mother made for him in the morning and eating with it the roll fetched from the market for him by his sister.

But the farther he advanced the better he pleased the two women, and the more devoted they became to him, if that were possible. Volsy's first communion dress, white muslin, year after year had been taken out, enlarged, washed, ironed, and fluted. It lay the year through freshly done up, unworn, with the string of pearl beads she always wore with it, and the wreath of pink roses that Madame Jacob herself had presented when Volsy went to some extraordinary event of a ball somewhere. Her brother did not think of her; her mother did not think of her; she did not think of herself. All were too busy thinking of one person—Paul.

Then Paul advanced beyond his little room, and went to live in other quarters—advanced, in plain fact, out of the women's lives; but they, gazing into the place whence he disappeared, were still happy, and praised God all the more. He came at first every Sunday to see them, then every other Sunday, then once a month. They did not seem to mind his not coming—in truth, they did not mind it any more than they did the sun's not shining on a cloudy day. Serenely they awaited Paul's next advancement. It came, and even they had not expected so handsome an answer to their prayers. Paul announced that he was engaged to be married, and not to a nobody, but to the daughter of his patron. They—Madame Jacob, the mother, the sister—did not even know the old lawyer had a daughter! Judge what a miracle it was to them! . . . A young lady who lived in the rich American quarter of the city, who went into the fine society up there, and gave entertainments that the newspapers described. It was astounding! And then there was inaugurated in that upstairs room a boom of industry and enterprise and "making of economies," to furnish Paul's wedding-present. Table and bed linen, silken and lace coverlets, curtains, cut glass. The second-hand dealer did her part in ferreting out bargains—and indeed some of her triumphs in that line were well worth the pride she took in recounting them. And this, in Madame Jacob's opinion, was the greatest pleasure Paul ever gave his family in his life—the opportunity of complete devotion and self-sacrifice: they could have kept it up forever and never known otherwise but that they were in paradise.

Paul never brought his bride to see his family, never took his family to see his bride. The young lady went away, and the marriage took place in the North, so of course the mother and sister could not be at the wedding. When the young couple returned, it was arranged that Paul would be met by the mother and sister. Paul was to take them on a Sunday. It was a month after his return before Paul found the right Sunday. Then he came for them. Madame Jacob watched them depart, and counted the moments until they returned, when. . She did not recognize the mother! . . . Head up in the air, eyes shining, cheeks glowing, and tongue—talking at both ends. The fine house! The servant-man! The grand madame! Her elegant dress, and her elegant manners! Like a queen, yes, like a queen in the opera! . . .

In his mother's eyes, Paul had risen so high by his marriage that, as Madame Jacob said, he was to her like the picture of the Saviour in the transfiguration. Volsy had nothing to say; she went quietly up stairs.

Shortly after this there was another boom of energy and industry in the room upstairs, another furious making of economies. Laces and linens, piqués and flannels. Madame Achard shopped from morning till night; Volsy never left her seat at the window, but sewed and embroidered, sewed and embroidered, from daylight till dark, and sewed and embroidered on after that by lamp-light. Oh no! The mother's eyes were not good enough for this work. Volsy's even were not good enough, nor her hands, for Madame Jacob never heard the mother say now, as she used to, that Volsy had the eyes and hands to embroider for the saints in heaven,—and Madame Jacob seemed to hear everything that was said upstairs. Volsy grew tired and worn, but not the mother; she looked happier and happier. She lived not in a honey-moon, but in honey-moons.

When she became a grandmother she talked and laughed and boasted about Paul just the same as when she became a mother. She did not have to wait for Paul now, and she and Volsy raced up to the house, laden with their bundles, and you may imagine how well they were received, bringing so beautiful a present, the layette for a prince.

And now ensued another change in the marching order of the family. It was no longer abreast, no longer one close behind the other. Either Madame Achard stepped ahead or Volsy lagged behind, with a growing space between them; that was the way they went now. Volsy always had an excuse not to go to see her sister-in-law; Madame Achard always had an excuse to go and see her daughter-in-law. Volsy's excuses cost nothing, but her mother's—they cost not only money but work; always something new and pretty; a cap or a bib trimmed with real Valenciennes, a cloak with real Cluny, a silk-embroidered petticoat, dresses tucked to the waist, or hem-stitched in inch-wide insertings—all made by hand, by the hand of Volsy, working still from morning to night, and after. There was no time for cooking,—sometimes the soup simmered in the pot, but sometimes, too, the fire in the furnace went out, and staid out as long as Madame Achard did in the street. The coffee in the morning was often the only regular meal that Paul and his baby allowed them. And then Madame Jacob, who saw as much as she heard upstairs, observed that the soup meat in the pot began to diminish in size—from ten cents to five cents, from five cents to a quartee (half of five cents) bone, and the soup was saved over longer and longer. Nothing was spent for clothing, nothing for pleasure or comfort. What money did not go for the bare daily fare, went in presents to that baby, and after a while toys were added to clothing, not cheap, common toys, but toys such as the rich American children uptown played with.

Volsy was one of those persons that no one ever notices particularly. She was neither tall nor short, fat nor thin, fair nor dark, pretty nor ugly, sad nor gay. But after two years of her beautiful work Madame Jacob did notice her one day as she passed through the shop on her way from church. She was tall and thin, dark and sad, and Madame Jacob reflected to herself that girls become women, and women become old. And this reflection of hers made so great an impression upon Madame Jacob that she kept it not to herself, but repeated it to everybody she talked to in the shop for a week, and she repeated it to Madame Achard.

"Ay! ay! La! la! la!" . . . What a song she was singing! without a word of common-sense in it! Volsy! bah! bah! And then Madame Achard started off to talk about her grandson, showing his photograph.

Now we may believe it or not, Madame Jacob gives formal permission for the alternative—from that day the mother began to pout against her daughter, . . . to sigh, as Madame Jacob expressed it, and to raise her eyes to heaven against her. Why? Because Volsy did not love her nephew as she should. In vain the girl protested, in vain she worked harder than ever, in vain she volunteered special gifts of her own, in vain she carried them herself to the altar of her mother's divinity. The mother remained firm to her "tic," as the Jacob woman called it, and the "tic" changed her completely. In not a very long time she would not mention Paul, or his wife, or the baby, to the girl. She withdrew her confidence on this subject from her; she took to deceiving her about them. She let her do no more work for the baby; she hid its photograph from her; she made a secret of her visits uptown, slipping out of the house as if on an errand in the neighborhood, slipping in again with lips tight shut. But before she took the cars she always slipped into some shop or other and bought a present, which was as far as Madame Jacob's observations went, but the rest was easily inferred.

Volsy attempted an explanation once or twice, but the mother would lose her temper, raise her voice, and say things to the poor girl that were pitiful to the listener. There was no doubt the mother's feelings had changed absolutely, were turned, as the listener said, wrong side out.

Well, the girl changed too, naturally. No one would have said that she was the young girl who had worn the white muslin dress and pearl beads and pink flowers to balls, and laughed and danced there.

She seemed afraid of people; she never spoke to any one if she could avoid it. She never spoke at all, first.

At last, when one did not know what was going to happen next, Madame Achard fell ill with one of those little complaints that seem nothing at first, but which last until they kill.

And now, with Volsy nursing her, like an angel, with such tenderness and patience, and a strength that never gave out, and always so cheerful and bright, talking, laughing, singing ever—things from the opera that they used to like in old times—to amuse her, that flea-bitten mother's heart had to feel good again—and Volsy became her daughter again. But the old woman (to Madame Jacob any woman past fifty is old)—the old woman did not get strong; she got well—that is, she got out of bed, but always when she thought she would be able to go out she would fall sick again, and have to go to bed, and so she could not leave the house, and naturally could not go to the other house. And Volsy began to see that she was pining for the sight of her son and grandson. The son—oh, that she knew was impossible—a man in his position, you understand; for his position was now out of sight of his people; but the grandson, he was not old enough to remember; that was possible. So Volsy began to lay her plans. If she had not made plans before, it was not because she had not sense enough. She had just as much sense as her mother and her brother. Oh, she showed it now! She was shrewd! She bought presents too, but presents for the mother, not for the child. And every time she went to see her sister-in-law, and brought the child to see the grandmother, he took home with him a piece of silver, a crystal decanter, a piece of porcelain, a piece of old lace to make your mouth water. Madame Jacob knew, for she bought them all, of course, as Volsy left her mother but for the one purpose of fetching the child and taking him home again. The old lady did not know anything, except that the child came to see her, and that was enough to give her happiness; but she fretted after he was gone, because she could not go out and buy presents for him, and so Volsy saw herself obliged to provide her mother with pretty play-things, but of the expensive kind, for, as has been said, Madame Achard would have none other. And the iller she became and the more desperate her condition, the oftener would Volsy bring the child to her, to ease her. But it cost! It cost! And the doctors had to be paid too, and medicine bought, and fine wine. Volsy would not have had the money for it without borrowing.

One night, in the most unexpected manner, Madame Achard died. A messenger was sent for Paul. He came, and arranged for the funeral early the next morning from the church.

Volsy came back alone from the cemetery, and went up stairs without saying a word, to her room, which in her absence Madame Jacob herself had put in order. At three o'clock Madame Jacob went up stairs to take her some dinner. She was still sitting in the same chair, with her bonnet and gloves on. At nine o'clock she was still there. She would not eat; she would not talk; she seemed to be thinking, thinking. Madame Jacob, however, forced her to bed, in the little chamber, in Paul's old bed. The next morning she was up early and at work, and in a week she had accepted the new routine of life. Perhaps she had thought it out as the best way. When the first of the month came, Madame Jacob, before any other business, went up stairs and paid her rent, as she had done for over twenty years.

The money did not stay in Volsy's hand long enough to warm it. In that class, dealers do not send their bills delicately through the mail, they bring them, and stand and wait until they are paid. Some people, like Madame Jacob, when they have no money, or want to hold on to their money for a while, pay with their tongue. But Volsy, though she had little money, only her month's rent, had less tongue. She paid and paid, and borrowed to pay, borrowing from her very debtors to pay her debts—a transaction that only a tongue such as Madame Jacob possessed can properly qualify.

Before the month was out, Volsy asked Madame Jacob to find lodgers for the front room. She moved out into one of the little rooms on the gallery—the lodgings of the "*crasse,*" as madame described them. And in addition she did embroidery and sewing for pay. So she could look forward to facing the next first of the month like an honest woman. But there was no first of the month again for her, at least in regard to receiving rent. The mother's estate had to be settled. Madame Jacob had forgotten that—the opening and reading of the will.

When Volsy came back from her brother's office, the day of this ceremony, she motioned to Madame Jacob to follow her up stairs. In brief, and not to dwell upon a poor girl's pain and grief, the mother's will left a special legacy of a thousand dollars to the grandson, and the rest of what she possessed to be divided between her children. The rest of her possessions! "But, sacred Heaven!" exclaimed Madame Jacob. She had no more possessions! The papers signed at the time of the brother's marriage, signed by all three, mother, daughter, son—what were they but a mortgate on her property? Volsy knew it now, well enough! and the money for what? To give Paul to marry his rich wife on, to play the rich gentleman with. . . . And where did the old woman get the money to play the rich grandmother on? She borrowed it. As Volsy in her emergency had borrowed it. . . . For, said Madame Jacob, her voice hoarse and face red with the vehemence of her anger, "the rich love only the rich, as the poor old woman knew. They have no heart"; or, as madame put it more vigorously in French—they have no *entrailles.* "Money, money," rubbing her fingers together, "that is their heart, their soul, their body. May God choke them in purgatory with money!" Her temper was to conceal her emotion—any one could discern that. Well, what was there to say? Nothing by Volsy, much by Madame Jacob; and Madame Jacob found much that could be done by a lawyer. But Volsy, who had absolutely nothing, found nothing to do, except to try and make her living by sewing.

And now, just as before, when one was wondering what would happen next, Paul's father-in-law died, and so soon as his estate was settled and his fortune put into the possession of his daughter, Paul decided to go to Europe with wife and child. He was a rich lawyer now, and did not have to stay at home to look for business. He left in the spring. Volsy went to his office to say good-by. She did not cry then, but she cried when she came home, and Madame Jacob found her crying often after that.

When Volsy's fête came, on the 15th of August, Madame Jacob took up to her room a little present, such as she had always given, and Volsy had been delighted to receive, ever since she was a little girl—an image of the Virgin and Son, this time in porcelain, and much prettier than ever before, on account of the poor girl's troubles. But when Volsy saw it she could only shake her head, and tremble. Madame Jacob, to take her eyes away, looked around the room. What she had not noticed before, she saw now: there was not a Holy Mother and Child in the room; there was not even one on the altar! And Volsy had always been so pious! and the little Child had been her soul's devotion!

Madame Jacob crossed herself, as though washing her hands of the responsibility of that part of her narrative.

As the summer wore on, Volsy fell ill. She tried and tried to get well, to make her living, but impossible! She could not. And there was the doctor again for her, and the medicines. There was no other way. She herself sent for the Little Sisters of the Poor, . . . and Madame Jacob made a gesture to indicate what I had seen on the sidewalk.

The doctor had given her something to put her asleep, and keep her so as long as possible. The grating of the stretcher as it slid into the wagon had roused her. Perhaps she thought she was in her room, in bed, when she lifted herself up, . . . and then she saw; she knew all.

Madame Jacob's last words were, "Paul has made progress—that is, he has made money."

VII FROM *THE PLEASANT WAYS OF ST. MÉDARD*

FROM GRACE KING'S comments on *The Pleasant Ways of St. Médard* in a letter to Leonidas Payne (see p. 403), we learn that the story is closely based on the experience of the King family in the years that followed their return to New Orleans after the Civil War. The book is a novel, or it might be called a memoir thinly disguised as fiction. With its series of portraits of neighbors of the Talbot family loosely held together with action that resembles the course of everyday life, it is like a documentary study of how a patrician family, faithful to the Confederate cause, endures privations until a hopeful glimpse of the future can be seen. Their life is struggle, but the words "pleasant ways" suggest that the book is no tragedy. In contrast with the Talbots are the San Antonios, people who are without principle and who have grown rich on the war with complete indifference to any cause but their own enrichment.

The Pleasant Ways of St. Médard was first published by Henry Holt and Company, New York, 1916, and secondly by Macmillan, New York, 1927. The text of the chapters that follow is based on the first, 1916 edition. Of sixteen original chapters, six are here printed in their entirety; a seventh, "Mademoiselle Coralie," is complete except for about six pages at the beginning. In the text, the occasional use of ellipsis is authorial, indicating either a continuation of dialogue in the same manner, a breaking off of a sentence, or a brief pause.

A Journey into a Far Country

The Parish of St. Médard [1] used to be as far away from Canal Street, the center of life in New Orleans, as a slow moving mule could drag a car in an hour's time. It lay in the "faubourg Créole" the lower suburb of the city, the extremity that stretched down the Mississippi River. As cities progress upstream, not down, the other extremity was, ipso facto, as one may say, the American quarter. In it mules and cars traveled faster and distances were shorter than in the faubourg of the descendants of the old French and Spanish population. The limit of St. Médard, in truth the last street in the city, was held fixed by the buildings and grounds of the United States barracks whose tall fence ran in a straight line from the river to the end of the cleared land, almost to the woods in the distance, barring inflexibly any advance in that direction. Beyond the barracks stretched the open country; the rural and ecclesiastical domain of another saint, a region of farms and plantations.

On a bright May morning of 1865, the waiting St. Médard car on Canal Street was taking in its usual tale of passengers: Gascon gardeners and dairymen going home from the markets, soldiers on their way to the barracks, Creole residents of the quarter, and gentry belonging to the plantations along the river, when there entered it, comers, new to the driver and to his patrons; an American family, father, mother, and four small children followed by their negro servants, a man, his wife, and their three half-grown daughters carrying baskets and bundles innumerable, the awkward bundles and baskets of country people. Curious enough looking, doubtless, they were to the eyes observing them but not unique as specimens of their kind at that date. All over the city, every day, other cars might be seen receiving just such passengers to carry from one home to another, from one condition to another, nay, from one life to another, ferrying them in their jog-trot passages in truth, like so many barks of Charon from a past to a future.

The father, a tall, thin, erect, scholarly-looking man, singularly handsome of face, was dressed in black broadcloth which, with his clean-

1 St. Médard suggests the parish of St. Bernard, southeast of New Orleans. After the Civil War the King family lived within the city, near this parish.

shaven face, betokened at that time a gentleman of the profession. His wife, fair of hair and skin, was dressed in the grotesque and obsolete fashion of a half dozen years before. The children wore homespun and alligator hide shoes, the little girls, sunbonnets, the boys, or at least one of them, a palmetto straw hat, the other one was bareheaded. The negroes in their clean, coarse plantation clothes looked dazed and stupid; the woman, murmuring to herself all the time, without knowing it: "My God, my God!" All sat stiff and rigid, serious and half frightened.

The clouds of war had at last rolled by and the sun of peace was shining in full force again, but the city was still heavily garrisoned; companies of white and negro soldiers in bright blue uniforms were marching through the streets, orderlies with papers in their belts, dashing by on horseback, officers glittering with golden braid and buttons and epaulettes, strode the sidewalks, dominating the soberly clad civilians in a manner quite out of proportion to their numbers, bands of newly freed negroes, ragged and dirty, the marks of the soil still upon them, straggled along, leisurely impeding the way of other pedestrians as they gazed about them. Confederate soldiers, still in their shabby gray, were to be seen everywhere; gaunt, gray, hungry-looking animals, fiercely eying the smartly-dressed soldiery that had conquered them, and now owned their city.

The sharp eyes of the children, roving restlessly about and springing back in quick rebound from the sight of the soldiers, seemed to see nothing that pleased them, that is nothing they were accustomed to. Even their Mama was as strange to them as everything else in her unnatural costume. They might well ask themselves, looking askance at her, if she were the same Mama they knew on the plantation, who used to go around in a homespun dress and alligator shoes; the dress that they had watched growing as cotton in the fields, and had seen spun, woven, and dyed by their own negro women; the shoes, from an alligator that they had seen swimming in their own Bayou, and which Jerry, over there, had shot, skinned, and tanned the hide to make into shoes. A sunbonnet then covered the head that now wore the ugly bonnet trimmed with great pink roses and broad blue ribbons. And yet, how often, when the little girls had been ill and restless with fever on the plantation, had their Mama taken her city bonnet as she called it out of its careful wrappings and showed it to them as the greatest treat possible. It seemed beautiful to them then, and it always quieted them although it had no effect on the little boys and when she related to them how she had bought it at Florette's and what Florette had said and what Papa had said about it, it was the most interesting story, in truth she could tell them. The little boys never would listen to it but the little girls, even with the fever burning in their veins, could have listened forever to tales about Florette's wonderful shop and the beautiful things she sold. But now when they were on the very Canal Street that their Mama used to talk so winningly about, when their car was standing just in front of Florette's glamorous shop, they did not think of it nor did their Mama remind them of it! When the car started, children and servants gave a portentous start with it. The plantation! the plantation! the fields! the woods! the negro quarters! the sugar house! the stables! the blacksmith shop! the corn mill! the mules, cows, chickens! the Bayou! the Bayou! . . . The car seemed to wrench their hearts from it all. And from the steamboat, too, which during their five days' journey, they had learned to love and now regretted as passionately as the plantation. How proud they were to see it steaming up their Bayou and stop at their wharf! The greatest and grandest thing they had ever seen, greater and grander surely than anything in the world. How strange and small they felt upon it at first and oh! how curious it was to be nosing their way in and out of bayous and lakes, just missing a snag here or running into a bank there and nearly capsizing in a wind storm, one day in the middle of a lake when the captain cursed so loud that they understood why the crew called him Captain Devil. They could hear him and the mate kicking and cuffing the crew above the noise of the storm as their Mama held them around her in the cabin. The storm began by blowing off Billy's hat and he had been bareheaded ever since. When they got into the Mississippi, what a surprise that was! A hundred times larger it was than their own Bayou, the biggest stream, they had thought, in the world. And what great plantations on both banks! They did not know that there were such big plantations in the world. Their own plantation had been the biggest in the world to them before. It shrank suddenly to a sorrowfully small one, as small as their steamboat, alongside the great steamboats at the city wharf. They were almost ashamed of the Bayou Belle then and they whispered to one another: "Oh! I wish she were bigger."

The father paid no attention to soldiers, negroes, passengers, or anything else, so absorbed was he in what he was telling his wife. He had been in the city or according to the expression of the time, back from the war, two weeks; she had arrived that morning from a plantation, so remote and isolated in forest and swamp that news of the progress of the war, even, came to it only in slow, straggling, roundabout ways. She would not have known that it was over if her husband had not hurried to her from his camp with the news. Of what had happened in the city, of the home she had left there, she had heard nothing, since she had left it to its fate at the hand of a victorious enemy.

Her husband was telling her a strange story indeed, of his adventures since he had parted from her on the plantation, but she was not so much absorbed in it as he. Her blue eyes showed thoughts behind them other than the ones that lighted his dark eyes with heroic fire, and her wan delicate features grew more and more out of harmony with the full-blown, pink roses of the over-hanging bonnet brim. Yet she could from time to time cast a look and smile of encouragement to her children and servants and at some call of youth and spirit, raise her long fair neck as proudly as if it bore the august head of her husband instead of her own.

A skiff here, a pirogue there, by cart, horse, or mule, on foot for many a mile, he had made his way through a country given over to lawlessness, a people demoralized, swarming freed negroes, an insolent soldiery, ruin, wretchedness, and despair, no one knowing what to do or where to begin work again in the uncertainty of what the victorious government intended further as punishment for the defeated. But the city! The anticipatory laugh at what was to come revealed a different face from the one that wore habitually a mask of stern hauteur; a frank, pleasant, companionable face. His wife smiled in anticipation with him. "Such a lot of ruined, ragged, hungry lawyers and *ci-devant* fine gentlemen! Each one trying to raise a little money, hunting some one to lend enough to pay for a decent suit of clothes, a night's lodging, and a little food; and all being dodged or refused by the smug money-makers among the old friends who had shrewdly stayed at home. Every pocket was buttoned up at the sight of a poor Confederate; and every day new arrivals from the armies or prisons, all about naked or starving, and all clamorous for news and 'views' of the situation, and every man with a family somewhere to bring back. As I was walking along the street disconsolately, wondering what I should do next, whom should I meet but old Doctor Jahn, hobbling around just as he used to on his gouty feet.

" 'Hello!' he said, 'you're back, are you?'

" 'Yes,' I said, 'I'm back.'

" 'Well, what are you going to do?'

"I told him, first of all, to bring my family from the plantation, find a home for them, and then go to work to make a living and educate the children; that as far as I could see, we were ruined, but that I had made a fortune once out of my profession and I could do it again. He nodded, smiled, and tapped me on the breast in his way: 'The first thing of all, my dear fellow, is for you to get out of these God-forsaken clothes and buy yourself a Christian appearance. You know we are great on our Christianity and our appearance now.' So he pulled me along by my arm, to a desk in some office and wrote me a check for a hundred dollars and hurried off.

"I rushed to a shop before any one could borrow of me and bought these clothes. Egad! I was actually ashamed to pay for them; it looked suspicious for me to have so much money, and the price, twenty-five dollars, seemed tremendous. Then I went straight to the levee and hunted up our old friend, Captain Devlin. Fortunately, he was just in with his boat. I gave him fifty dollars and told him to go and fetch you all here. 'In old times,' he said, 'it used to be two hundred and fifty dollars and a sugar crop besides.' "

The car left the broad street with handsome houses behind it and entered a different district, that of the class that works for a living and lives for its work; the class of small houses and large families. Block after block of little cottages, hardly higher than the car itself, was passed; some of them no better than negro cabins on a plantation. Sometimes there would be a garden in front or at the side, and every now and then a cottage of brick and double-sized would be passed, protected from its surroundings by a high brick wall bristling on the top with broken glass; bananas, pomegranates, and crape myrtles stretching up above it. But this seemed a crest of prosperity; for blocks afterwards, the houses diminished in size and appearance, until a very hollow of poverty and squalor was reached. At short intervals, appeared a grocery, a drinking-shop, a bakery, at long ones, the church, school, or convent. On the low wooden steps of the little cottages sat women, sewing or nursing babies; around them on the sidewalk and in the gutters played their innumerable progenies of children, ranging in color, from the fairest skins, through all gradations of foreign complexions. The car went still slower through this quarter, for the streets, which had begun so handsome and broad at the beginning of the journey, grew ever narrower and more crooked. The driver was kept busy with his brakes and the plodding mule strained painfully over the accumulation of turns.

The husband, however, unconscious of street or gait, pursued his narrative:

"I thought it was then time to go to my office and see what had become of it. I knew that the building was still standing in its old place and that was about all I had been able to find out about it. I glanced at the names in the doorway; mine was no longer there. I marched upstairs. On my old door was a fine, bright, new sign. What do you think I read on it? 'Thomas Cook, Attorney and Counselor-at-Law.' "

"Tommy Cook? Little Tommy Cook?"

"Tommy Cook and no other.

"I opened the door and walked in. 'Well, Tommy,' I said, 'What are you doing here?'

"He looked up, arose, and without any surprise at seeing me, answered: 'Taking care of your office as you told me, Sir.'

"I looked around: 'How did you manage it?'

" 'I found a way, Sir.'

" 'You did, did you?'

" 'I stole it, Sir.'

"Well, that was literally what he did. He took down my name, put up his own. Who was to object, in all the stealing that was going on? And egad! he has business too."

"Tommy Cook! The little lame boy! Who used to brush your shoes and run your errands, and carry your law-books to court for you?"

"Well, he carried them for me this time, famously."

"But how can he be a lawyer without studying law?"

"I saw his license framed, hanging on the wall. And that was all I did see in the room different from the day I left it in his charge. The books were all there with the ledgers and papers in the bookcases, just as I left them.

" 'T'was the only way to save them, Sir,' he said, 'to steal them myself.'

"I sat down in my old seat and he stood, as he used to do, waiting for orders. I got all the news I wanted out of him and there is nothing on foot in the city that he does not know all about. I told him that the first thing we had to do was to find a house for you and the children . . ."

"You are sure," she said, interrupting him, hesitating and embarrassed, a flush mounting to her face: "You are sure, there is no hope still for our—our home." Her voice faltered. "I . . ."

He interrupted her. "Not the least in the world. As I told you this morning, it has gone with the rest."

He dismissed the subject, curtly, decisively, as he had done on the boat; but there was no dismissing it from her thoughts. She had not forgotten it an instant, since he had announced the fact to her. "I thought, maybe, that Tommy . . ."

"It was one of the first houses seized and confiscated," he interrupted her impatiently, and went on with what he was saying: "We looked for houses until I was tired out. Of course, with everybody coming back and wanting houses, no one I can tell you found the home he had left, if it was worth anything, for rents have gone up tremendously! The whole city seems to have been bought up by sharpers, who hold us in their hands, and squeeze us. At last Tommy found the place we are going to, for sixty dollars a month, and as prices go, it is a bargain."

She looked at the street they were going through. "I never was in this part of the city before, in my life."

"Nor I either until I came to look at the house. But we will find living cheap there. Tommy went all over the neighborhood; outside the barracks there is not an American family in it. The barracks is a great drawback, but that is the reason the house is cheap; otherwise it would have been seventy-five dollars a month instead of sixty. It is worth about twenty. But the soldiers are troublesome only on pay-day, when ladies and children have to keep out of the cars and off the street. I had a time getting the furniture; everybody was buying just what I was; beds, tables, chairs, and we had to pay for the commonest the price we used to pay for the handsomest. You will find it all in the house, with a stove and some groceries; about all I could think of. We shall have to live economically, and educate the children . . ." and so on and so on.

He unfolded the map of the future before her in the quiet determination of manner and terse language characteristic of him, as if it were a campaign to be fought again. She let her mind follow his with her characteristic docility, embracing his views, adopting his conclusions, conceding that the great future was his, the husband's, the man's affair; the little future of daily life, hers, the woman's, according to the traditions of conjugal life in which she had been raised. But with all her acquiescence of heart and mind, she had presentiments—they were all she ever had to oppose to his clear reasoning. Somewhat like her freed negro servants she was not sure of what she was riding into and she could have murmured with Milly: "My God! My God!" without knowing what she was calling on Him for.

As their hearts had been wrenched from the plantation where they had passed their lives, so was her heart wrenched from the home and the part of the city where she had passed her life, the only home she had ever known, to which, for four long years, she had been hoping to return, and for which her heart was now calling out with passionate longing.

What did Peace mean to her? What could it mean but to return to the past as she left it? The past! It had gone from her as if it had been a spoil of war. And as she saw it in her woman's way, her future, too, had been taken away from her as a spoil of war. She belonged to a period, a childhood, when parents of wealth secured the future of their children, as they called it. She was born into a secured future, so was her husband, so were their children. All of a sudden she was bereft of it. It had disappeared like a meteor from the sky. The prospect she had been looking at all her life was changed; another and a different one substituted. It was as if—for so also it came to her in her confused imagination—as if her husband, the man to whom she had been married for twelve years, that aristocratic gentleman with classic features and noble expression of countenance, should be divorced at a stroke from her; and a coarse, plain, common man substituted as her lord and master, the father of her children . . . and she had been no surer of her husband than she had been of her future.

About two-thirds of the route there was a station where passengers were transferred to an older, shabbier car, a stiffer mule and a rougher track. Three uptown cars were the regulated portion of the second car, and therefore it never started until well filled. Our family, being in the last car waited for, found but a poor accommodation of seats at their disposition and had to wedge themselves in wherever space could be procured by shoving. An old gentleman with a white beard, who looked like the picture of General Lee, was sitting at the end of the seats; he reached forward and lifted one of the little girls and placed her beside him. As soon as she was seated, she lifted the cover of a little basket on her arm and looking into it with a bright smile, whispered: "Kitty, Kitty."

"What's its name?" asked the old gentleman beside her.

"I just call her Kitty now, because she's a kitten, you know."

"But what will you call her when she's grown up?"

"Oh! I don't know, Kitty still, I reckon."

"But you wouldn't like to be called Baby, after you are grown up, would you?"

"Oh! Mama calls me that now, most of the time."

"Yes, but you have a name."

"Oh, yes! My name is Marian, but they call me Polly, because I talk so much. Even Papa calls me Polly. That's Dickey, I mean Richard, over there and that's Billy with his hat off. His name is William and he's got a dog tied to that string in his hand. Bob is his name, because he's got a bob tail. Papa told Billy not to bring Bob with him, so Billy has to keep him hid under Milly's dress. That's Cicely, leaning against Mama. She has chills and fever. . . ."

Catching her mother's eye and a warning shake of the head, she stopped abruptly, but in a moment after, peeping at her basket and calling, "Kitty," she began again; "I hate the city, don't you hate the city? I think the city's so funny, don't you? Everything looks funny in it. Mama looks so funny, and don't Papa look funny? Billy says if he was Papa, he'd be ashamed to go about in them clothes." She stopped short, frightened, and gave a quick look at her father. "I mean *those* clothes, I'm glad Papa didn't hear that, yes indeed," with a laugh. "He promised us that he would punish us next time we used *them* for *those*, like niggers, I mean negroes; and the next time Billy said it, he punished Billy. Billy don't say it no more now when Papa can hear him. And he makes us say saw instead of seen. I think it's funny to say saw for seen, don't you? But we don't say seen any more." . . .

Again the warning shake of the head stopped her for a moment.

"Them's Yankees over there. Ain't you glad you ain't a Yankee? They're so ugly, ain't they? I hate 'em. Don't you hate Yankees? Everybody hates Yankees, I reckon, except Yankees. We're going to live right by the Yankees, and Papa told us this mornin', before he took us off the boat, that he didn't want to hear no more such talk about hatin' Yankees and that we mustn't go about tellin' people how we hated 'em. That ladies and gentlemen didn't talk that way, and that we were ladies and gentlemen and he expected us to behave like ladies and gentlemen. But Billy says he's goin' to kill every one he sees when he's a man and so is Dickey——

"I would hate to be a Yankee wouldn't you?" she resumed when her mother took her eye from her. "I wouldn't be one, and havin' people prayin' for me."

"Praying for Yankees. Who prays for Yankees?" asked the old gentleman.

"Mama makes us pray for 'em because they're our enemies and she says we must forgive 'em too, and anyhow, the more we hate 'em the more we must pray for 'em. Pshaw! I'm glad I'm not an enemy to have people forgivin' me. Billy says he's goin' to train Bob to bark at 'em," and she laughed gleefully. "I would like to live on a steamboat, wouldn't you? But you ought to hear the Captain curse! Billy can curse just like him. Billy says he's goin' to be a steamboat captain when he's a man. But Dickey ain't. Dickey's goin' back to the plantation and I'm goin' with him. It's too funny in the city. Have you ever been on the Bayou Belle? I tell you we had a bully, I mean a nice, time on her." . . .

After the Station, the track ran over a rough country road with a deep ditch on each side, crossed by ragged-looking lanes. On the left, beyond the gardens, dairies and open fields, stretched the outline of the forest in the distance. To the right, the river could be seen by glimpses between the great groves of magnolia trees that surrounded the houses facing it. An exhilarating breeze blew fresh and strong from that direction. The children craned their necks to look at the Gascons toiling in their gardens; whole families, from the grandmother in her headkerchief, to little children, raking, hoeing, gathering vegetables and working the great long swinging poles over the wells.

Even the eyes of the negro servants brightened with intelligence at the familiar sight of it. Billy, who had made his way to the platform, could be heard excitedly imparting his sentiments about cows and gardening to the driver who seemed to welcome any distraction of his attention from the hard, dry, belabored back of his mule—no more sensitive to the whip than a painted wooden back would be.

The Gascons slipped off one by one as the car went along. The negroes left in a body at a path that led to a great brick ruin of a building—"the Settlement," they called it. At last, long after patience had come to an end, the journey came to its end also. The soldiers made a bolt for front and rear door; the other passengers waiting for them to pass. By the time the American family were out of the car with their baskets and bundles, the driver had taken his dram at the corner barroom; for this flower of civilization which had followed the track through the length of the city bloomed here also at the end of it.

"And now," said the father cheerily, "we must foot it awhile." The sidewalk consisted of a plank fastened upon the ground along which the party could advance only in single file. He took the lead; wife, children and servants tailing after him, he turning his head and calling out to them, his handsome face aglow with animation. He was never so animated and eager and never looked so handsome as when leading up to some hard pass, some breach of disappointment. The plank walk ran in front of a row of new, brightly painted little cottages, set so closely together that the lounging men and women on the steps could talk to one another, as if they were seated on a long bench. The women appeared only half dressed in their loose sacques and gowns and with their hair in disorder. The men were soldiers, but they seemed more abashed as the little procession passed in front of them than the women did.

Across the street was the high fence inclosing the barracks grounds. Soldiers were drilling inside; from the noise, the place seemed filled with them. Further on, towards the river, the officers' quarters could be seen through their surrounding groves of trees. Over it all, above trees and buildings, above everything but the blue sky, waved the United States flag.

The head of the little procession, turning sharply to the right, strode down the opening that served for a street. Its ruts and holes had been baked by the sun to stony hardness; but the little feet stumbled along over it, following the resolute tread in front without lagging or complaining. Children and negroes looked around them joyfully for they were in the country, the dear country again. The low-lying blue heavens overhead, flecked with white clouds, was the country sky; the bright, hot sun was the country sun they knew so well. The weeds growing rank and wild along the sides of the road, the droning bees, the mosquito hawks, darting hither and thither among the leaves and flowers, as well as the breeze that blew fitfully, just as it used to blow over the fields,—all that was the country, not the city. The sound of chickens, geese and ducks, the smell of manure; what a glad exchange this was for the long ride in the car!

Again they were wheeled abruptly, and led alongside an old, swaying fence, with an inside hedge of wild orange whose branches touched the heads of the taller ones among them. At a gate in this fence, stood a little bare-footed boy, who at sight of them, darted away, screaming at the top of his voice: "Madame Joachim! Madame Joachim!" And from the end of the street at once, a stout woman hurried forward, her wide *blouse volante*[2] of calico, flying out behind her, showing her fat feet in white stockings and carpet slippers. Wide as the *blouse volante* was, it fell only comfortably over the rotund parts of her body. Her well oiled curling black hair, drawn back tightly from her swarthy face, glistened in the sun, and her face, as far as it could be seen, wore a smile. She carried a great bunch of keys and after shaking hands all around selected the largest key—a ponderous iron one—unlocked the gate, threw it open, and stood

2 *Blouse volante*: a loose blouse.

aside for the family to enter their new home. The house also had suffered a revolution in fortune. Its paint hung upon it in rags, showing the naked wood beneath. The gallery was hidden by the vines that hung over it from the roof, the accumulated luxuriance of years; parterres and paths in the garden were grown together in a tangle of vines and shrubs. Over the outside of the rotting cistern, green moss followed the line of trickling water.

Madame Joachim, in spite of her size, lightly mounted the steps of the gallery ahead of the newcomers, and taking another monstrous key, unlocked the central one of a row of green batten windows, and with a smaller key, the glass door inside; and again, with a polite gesture, motioned the family to enter before her.

Without a word, they did so and stood in the dim interior while she went from room to room on either side, opening the glass windows and heavy green shutters. The clanging of the heavy iron hooks as she let them drop was the only sound heard until all were opened. The bright day illuminated a room at the back and two on each side. In each stood a small allotment of furniture.

"This," said Madame Joachim, waving her hand with pride to the glistening whitewashed walls and freshly black-painted mantelpiece, "this, as you see, is like new; the rest," with a shrug of the shoulders, "is according to nature."

She led the way out to the back gallery. Across a large yard, shaded with a fine wild cherry tree, stood a long, low cabin; the kitchen and servants' rooms. The fence here was lined with a row of old and gnarled fig trees. "St. Médard," said Madame Joachim, pointing to a small steeple that dominated the sky here, as the flag did in front. Descending the steps and crossing the yard, she opened the doors of the kitchen building, leaving each key carefully in its keyhole as she had done in the house.

The little group, instead of following her, remained on the gallery, silent and still; the husband, forgetting to be animated, the wife forgetting to look at his face, the children imitating her, looking ahead of them at nothing. The clear voice of a mocking bird in some near tree alone broke the silence. They were standing as she had left them when Madame, returning across the yard, reached the steps. There, springing forward, she exclaimed: "But that poor child has a chill!"

It was so. Cicely, the sickly one, was having a chill, *her* chill as the children called it. She and every one else had forgotten it in the excitement of the moment, but true to the day and hour as it had been for three months past, it had not forgotten her. The child was clinching her teeth and hands tight to keep them from shivering, but her poor little thin face was ashen, her lips blue and trembling.

Madame Joachim picked her up like a baby and with her soft swift walk carried her to the nearest bed, Cicely's face pressing into the great fat breast as into a soft pillow. When she was laid on the bed it was discovered she was crying; she who never cried, whom her Papa always called his Marshal Ney, because she was the bravest of the brave. The little family clustered around her in consternation; most of them feeling like crying too. It was as if this sorrow and disappointment were all of a sudden too much to bear. And whereas, on the plantation, the youngest child would have known what to do for a chill, now they stood as helpless as if they had never seen the miserable thing before.

It was Madame Joachim who hunted up sheets and spread them over the bare mattress, who undressed the child, and eased a pillow under her head. Then, slipping to the back gallery, and running her practised eye along the fence and selecting a certain hole, she called out in quick, sharp Creole patois: "Cribiche, my son, run fast, get some orange leaves and tell Joachim to make some tisane, as quick as he can, and you bring it; *Courri vite, mo di toi.*" [3]

When the tisane came, she gave it herself to Cicely, petting and comforting her, with the sweetest, softest voice in the world. "Never mind, never mind, bah! What is a chill! Everybody has chills! Now, one more cup, eh! There, there, see how good it tastes! By and by, you will take another cup, and you will sweat, and when you sweat, you know, you are most over it, and you will shut your eyes, and you will go to sleep, and when you wake, it will be all gone." She spoke in the soft singsong English of the Creole who has learned the language by ear. The little one obediently closed her eyes, and listening to the mocking bird, and hearing the cowbells and the faint droning of the insects outside, fell into the delusion that she was again on the plantation; delusions are the saving grace of chills.

Madame Joachim, with her finger on her lip, stepped softly out of the room, and, as she never forgot anything, went to the kitchen to see what was needed there. Milly and her daughters, having kicked off shoes and stockings and some of their stupidity with them, were moving about with something like a servant's activity. A fire had been made in the new

3 *Courri vite, mo di toi*: Run fast, I tell you.

stove, water put on to boil, but like all country cooks, when they do not know what else to do, Milly was proceeding to make biscuits.

"But your soup, my good woman," exclaimed Madame Joachim, amazed at such a want of sense, "put on your soup! don't you see the soup meat there on the table? And the loaf of bread? Get your rice ready to boil! parch your coffee!" She put on the soup pot herself, poured in water, added the soup meat and looked around. "Ah! The soup vegetables! Cribiche, my son!" she called out of the window, toward the fence, "Cribiche! run quick over there to Monsieur le Curé and ask him for some onion and some parsley and some carrot for the soup pot! Run quick, I see him in the garden now!"

Cribiche, evidently did not like this commission. It was one thing going to the blacksmith's who had nothing against him and another going to the priest. Joachim feared neither God nor devil, it is true, when he was angry, which he was not now, but the priest . . . Cribiche had his reasons for avoiding him. "But will you go when I tell you," impatiently called Madame Joachim looking out of the window, "or"—her threat was vague but effective. Cribiche at once crossed the street to the priest's garden where Père Philéas was hard at work, his cassock twisted up high around his waist.

Behind the church was the priest's habitation, for it could not be called a house; and behind the house was the vacant ground which he, by no better right than squatter sovereignty, had appropriated for his garden. He did not raise his head but remained bending over his weeds until Cribiche came up close to him, and he would not hear what he was saying until he came very close; then, like a loosened spring, he shot up in the air, seized Cribiche with his left hand, boxed him soundly with his right, and shook him until the boy's clothes cracked.

"Is this the way you pull up my weeds? Is this the way you come straight back when I tell you? Is this the way you think you can fool me?"

Rough as he was, Joachim with his trap was worse, this was all the consolation Cribiche had. He submitted without a struggle and without an answer, since both were useless. He saw, in truth, that he was himself in fault, he should not have come so near, too near to dodge or run; the next time, he swore to himself, he would know better.

When the priest heard the request, he at once went to work to comply with it, and generously, although it was only with parsley, onions, and carrots and a bit of thyme which Madame Joachim had forgotten to ask for. It is so pleasant to give that it is a wonder people do not more generally yield themselves up to this form of self-indulgence. As for poor old Père Philéas, he was a very sybarite about giving. His homely, honest face beamed as his knotted fingers pulled up carrots and onions and picked the parsley and thyme. And as he lost no occasion of advancing the merits of God with such a partisan of the devil as Cribiche, he spoke to him thus, before handing him the bouquet for the soup (who would ever suppose that only a moment before he had been cuffing and shaking him?):

"You see, my son, how good God is! He sends the friend to those who need one, and he sends the good deed to those who need that; to those who can bestow nothing else, good deeds, my child, are the picayunes of the poor. We are never too poor to give one of them even if we have not a cent in the pocket. The devil can always provide us with money, but it is only God who can provide us with a good deed. And even when one has money, one is always glad to have a friend as one is glad to have the moon of dark nights."

Cribiche showed as much appreciation for moral lectures as a snapping turtle for favors bestowed upon his back; and as a snapping turtle under a disagreeable ordeal advances his head out of his shell from time to time to peep with his little shrewd eyes and see if the way is clear, so did Cribiche peep from under his obstinate stolidity and dart his shrewd little glances around.

The priest accompanied him to the gate and held him by the shoulder, while he added affectionately and gently: "And now when you see the fruit of our labors, my son, are you not glad that you did even a small portion of the work here? See, we can give the vegetables needed for the soup of a neighbor—a stranger whom we do not know, who does not know us. Think! Yesterday, that old house was vacant, silent; today, it is filled with people; and just as we transplant a vegetable from one garden to another, the good God has transplanted our new neighbors here, to St. Médard, from whence, we know not, and the old house becomes an object of our good will and friendly services. And we will grow together, henceforth, like plants in the same plot. The difference, the difference, my child, always think of the difference between yesterday and today, . . . and fear and love God, for He alone accomplishes what we think we do in the way of good, as the devil alone accomplishes what is evil, and makes us evil. And be very careful that the devil does not put you up to some mischief to our new neighbors. If he tries to, put him behind you, or you will feel Joachim's strap. Ah! your friend, the devil, never saves you from that, you know. He can lead you into temptation but he cannot save you from the punishment . . . And do not forget to be in time to ring the Angelus."

But Cicely's chill proved to be not her chill, the one the family had grown accustomed to, that came and went like an easy tempered conqueror. A different and a savage enemy indeed, now invaded her little body. It would not loose its grasp upon her; and, when the fever came, it raged like a conflagration, consuming remedies as if they were tinder. When called, her face brightened in response and she strove to raise her head.

"Not yet, not yet, my child," coaxed the mother tenderly, bending over her, "stay in bed a little longer and then you can get up and dress and help us."

"Cicely loves to work," she explained to Madame Joachim. "She never complains and never gives up, and as soon as her fever is off she is as well as ever, eh, Cicely? . . . For three years she has had chills and fever. I may say she is never without them. Oh, yes! Sometimes we were able to break them and she would be free, but only for a little while. They always came back, they were sure to come back in the Summer. But never mind! it will soon be over for the day, eh, Cicely!" she added cheerily and turned to her work again. She had taken off her unnatural costume and wore her short homespun gown once more.

"Cribiche has never been sick in his life," answered Madame Joachim, following her around and working as busily as she. "We have not much sickness down here, a little fever sometimes, and sometimes chills and fever. Oh! if Doctor Botot had to live from his practice," dragging the physician into her conversation by the hair of his head, "he would not live down here. No! he would go uptown among the rich Americans. It is curious, how the rich are always sick. But Botot is a good doctor, why shouldn't I know it? When he comes to a sick one, the first thing he says is: 'Where is Madame Joachim? Send for Madame Joachim.' He lives on the levee in that fine house below the barracks. Oh! I guarantee, he lives with his mother-in-law, old Madame Séréno. She says she is poor, but don't you believe her; she is rich, very rich, as Doctor Botot knows. He married her daughter, *en secondes noces*. The first time he married the daughter of old Beaume, old 'Beaume tranquille,' we used to call him, the *pharmacien* on Enghien Street. Botot thought he had money, but he made a mistake, old Beaume did not collect his debts, or that is what they said," shrugging her shoulders; "anyhow he did not leave any money, and when Botot became a widower he married Mademoiselle Marie Séréno. She is the eldest daughter; Mademoiselle Amélie is the youngest. Mademoiselle Marie had not much sense; everybody thought she was going into the convent, that it was her vocation. Bah! it is well to say that when one wants an excuse. She is dead now, and the doctor is a widower, but not for long, I promise you. Some people believe that chills and fever won't fool you. Don't you believe that. Chills and fever always fool you if you don't cure them. Botot is a good doctor, but not as good a doctor as he thinks he is. It is always his worst cases that he cures; as he tells about them. When people die, he says nothing was the matter only they did not take his medicines. But he knows how to cure chills and fever. I have seen him cure them. He is called into the barracks sometimes and it is well for the sick that he is, for the doctor there looks as much like a doctor as Joachim like a priest. It is the season of the year to cure chills and fever."

"They generally go away in the Winter," said Mrs. Talbot.

"Go away! Yes! But, my God! They come back again; if you are there for them to come back to. Sometimes you are not there. To believe what Botot says, and to believe what you know, are cats of a different color. But if he says he can cure chills and fever, you can believe that. . . . You can see him pass here any time, going to church. He goes to church every day, he is very pious. Mademoiselle Marie married him on account of his piety. She also was very pious. You should see him praying in church! When he puts on his 'bon St. Joseph air, bon St. Joseph vas'!" . . .

"He is very rich," Madame Joachim resumed to break the silence, "that is in prospect. Mademoiselle Amélie it is, who will go into the convent. Oh, no! She will not get married . . . She will not meet a doctor as pious as she is. No, no, she will go into the convent, Botot will lead her there himself. And he will fasten the black veil on her, himself, if she wishes. You ask him if Madame Séréno is rich, he will shrug his shoulders. He will say: 'Who is rich after a war?' But listen to me, old Madame Séréno is rich; she did not lose a cent by the war, not even her niggers. Look at them, they are with her still. Lose her money! *Tra, la, la*, the geese in the street know better than that. Other people did but she did not. Not that the Yankees did not find out she was rich; they found out she was rich, just as Botot found out she was rich. Did she go to France? No. Did she hide and pretend she had gone? No. She sent for Louis, her man of affairs: 'Louis,' she said, 'see this paper, the Yankees have sent me to sign . . . they will come for it in three days.' Then she showed him some money, not paper money, but gold, *gold*, I tell you. 'You know, Louis, I could sign this paper; I could take this "*host*" ' ", Madame Joachim called it. " 'It is no sin to lie to robbers, but I don't want to be bothered. Here, take this paper and I give you the money; but, you understand me, eh? If I am bothered, I will sign the paper, I will take the host, and I will get absolution for it; but you'—Madame Séréno raised her finger, and shook it at Louis—'you will lose your place. I will give it to Simon. Simon is not a fool.' Simon, he was like the tooth-ache to Louis, and that is the way Madame Séréno did, and kept her money and property. God knows if it is true; but that is what I heard. I heard too that it was not Louis but an American, she sent for. But how did Louis make so much money then? Doctor Botot is a good doctor. His father was a good doctor for children. Only he was not a doctor but a leecher. They used to send for him and his leeches all over the city." And Madame Joachim with her fingers imitated how leeches were worked into a soft ball of clay. "I have bought leeches from him often, . . ." etc., etc. She talked on as unremittingly as she worked.

At last, the day, that in the morning lay like an unknown coast before the family, drew to a close, and evening began to enfold it. But the future that the father had planned, that the family was to enter upon at once, the very next day, had to be put off. At one time, it seemed indeed as if the family would enter it with one member missing. Cicely did not respond to her name; she was found to be, not asleep, but in a stupor; she could not be aroused. Cribiche had to be summoned from ringing the Angelus to run for the doctor.

Ah! Now it was seen that there was but one terror in life, only one; and it came from no earthly enemy . . . that there was but one loss that counted in the world . . . but one thing God could grant that was worth praying for!

The children would creep on tip-toe to the door and peep through at Cicely lying delirious, with half-opened eyes. "Is the fever going down, Mama?" they would whisper, and when she would shake her head, they would creep softly away, more and more frightened by the look on her face. They had seen her lose battles, armies, a fortune, a home, but they had never before seen her lose a child.

In her delirium, Cicely babbled about the plantation; laughing and laughing over her drolleries.

"Merciful God!" thought the mother sitting beside her. "What had she there to laugh over? Sick, sick, sick, all the time, hardly a day, never a week without fever . . . The doctor has no hope, I could see it . . . She has fought and fought, but her strength is exhausted. She has no chance! She is doomed! Too late! too late! . . . Perhaps a month ago! . . ." She would slip her hand under the sheet to feel the burning body, she would pass cooling cloths over face and hands . . . "Nothing but skin and bones" . . . How she yearned over the emaciated body! "Her poor little hands, her poor little hands like bird claws." She laid her cheek upon them and the tears gushed from her eyes—she who had boasted, that she never would or could give up hope for a child of hers!

Her heart rose up in passionate revolt and through her mind raced a mob of thoughts as senseless as Cicely's delirium.

"I thought, I thought, when the war was over, and peace came, when we could get back to our home and get a doctor, I thought we would then be safe. . . . Would to God we were back on the plantation! Would to God the war was still going on! Would to God I were still there, in that lonely, gloomy place all by myself; for there I could still hope, I had still something to look forward to . . . night after night watching and nursing my child . . . longing for daylight just to see her clearly again; but never losing courage . . . praying that God would work a miracle and send a doctor down the Bayou when I knew no doctor could come; running to the window to listen, sure that I heard a skiff and that it was bringing a doctor . . . hearing only the rippling of the water under the gunwales that sounded sometimes like the whining of a child in pain . . . God did not send a doctor, but he heard my prayers. He cured my child. He had to cure her, for we had no medicines to give her! There, her fever always went away at last!"

On the other side of the bed sat her husband; his face graver and sterner than ever.

"He should not have taken us to that fever-stricken place!" Her gentle thoughts, changed into furies by her grief, knew no bounds in their pitiless course. "He should not have kept us there! He knew it was a swamp! He knew it was unhealthy! He knew it, he knew it! Other men could send their families into healthy refuges. Other men could send them to Europe!"

To Europe! She had forgotten the scorn and contempt she once poured upon those patriots who preferred for their children the easy comfort of Europe to the heroic hardships of war; upon the poor-spirited women who could accept the despicable role of flying from danger and from their husbands, of abandoning their country fighting for its life, armies weltering in their blood on the battlefield!

"He said the war would not last! It would soon be over! And we would all be home again. Ah! he always imagines that what he thinks is going to happen! He thought it was our duty to stay and look after the negroes! He could think of them; he could not think of us! Duty! Duty! Duty is his God! And it costs us the life of our child! . . . She was always delicate and frail but the prettiest and brightest of them all! When she was born, I felt so happy! I never had thought that earth held such happiness as I felt then! . . . And when he came to me, he made me feel so proud! I would not have changed places with the greatest queen on earth!"

And now the little, bare, uncomfortable room in St. Médard changed to the great, luxurious, dimly lighted chamber, where in a lace curtained bed, she lay with Cicely at her side. She heard again the soft tread of her husband over the carpet, . . . was it his tread, or the beating of her heart she heard? She lifted her eyelids, he was there, he was there bending over her . . . Cicely had ceased her delirious babbling, a gentle calm had fallen over the room, the shaded candle in the corner made a soothing twilight. The long black hours passed, holding the suspensive balance even. The gray dawn came, the light of day fell over the bed. "Cicely! Cicely!" her father laid his hand on her cooling forehead and called her. The good little thing, who had never known what it was to be disobedient or hold back when she heard her father calling, was seen to strive to answer, but she could not. "Cicely! Cicely!" She heard him, she was wanted, she could not answer. Her heart strained and strained, her thin breast lifted, fell and lifted . . . at last a faint moan came through her lips and her eyes opened, she tried to smile.

"Doctor Botot! Doctor Botot," exclaimed Madame Joachim. "Did I not tell you that there was no better doctor in the city for fevers than Doctor Botot?"

"Madame Joachim," said the doctor later. "Well, if you want a good nurse, you send for Madame Joachim. Joachim," he added, "Joachim looks like a pirate, but if you ever want good Spanish wine, you send to Joachim."

Ah! the future could begin now whenever it chose. The land, that the day before lay like an unknown shore before them, they were in it now, and what a beautiful land it was!

The mother and all the children followed the doctor, as captives a deliverer, surrounding him as he stood on the front gallery, their faces aglow with gratitude and admiration. To a question the mother answered lightly, and pleasantly. "Oh! where we were living, on the plantation, it was so far from any doctor that we had to learn to doctor ourselves. It took a day to get to the nearest town, and of course a day to return, and then as likely as not, when our messenger got there, the doctor would be away, a day's journey off somewhere. But we had doctor's books and we followed their directions, that is so long as we had medicines, but we got entirely out of medicine." And here she laughed as at a humorous recollection. "When the quinine gave out we had to use willow bark tea. It was as bitter as quinine anyway and at first it seemed to do Cicely a great deal of good. And there was an old Indian woman doctor; the Indians were our nearest neighbors, they lived on a mound in the swamp. We sent for her to come every now and then. She brought her herbs with her, and sometimes they did Cicely a great deal of good too."

"Why did you not come to the city?" asked the doctor.

"To the city! But it was in the hands of the enemy!"

The doctor shrugged his shoulders. "And you were not in the hands of the enemy, eh? on the plantation?"

"It was the swamps all around that gave us chills and fever," she replied simply.

"You had the chills and fever there too?"

"Oh, yes! all of us had them, and sometimes," with a smile, "we all had them at the same time. My husband said, when we went there, that the enemy would never find us and they did not until last year . . . we were so far away, we could not get letters, we could not get newspapers . . ."

"But you could get the chills there," the doctor interrupted facetiously.

"Oh, yes!" with a decided affirmation of the head.

"And plenty of food?"

"Oh, no! at least not at the end. Food became very scarce then. And after the overflow, we had nothing but corn bread and some fat meat. All the cattle, you know, were drowned."

"You were overflowed?"

"Oh, yes! Twice, two years in succession. Once for six weeks. When our people cut Grand Levee, you know, to prevent the advance of the enemy, or their retreat, one or the other, I don't know which. All of our section of the country went under water then."

"Yes, yes."

"We had food up to that time. But one day, a gunboat passed, that is a steamboat with cannon and soldiers on it. We believe it must have got into our Bayou accidentally, for no one in that part of the country would have piloted them" . . .

"And after that you had no food?"

"No, the soldiers threw our meal and meat in the Bayou."

"And Cicely was sick then?"

"She had just had a hard chill; it was her day to have it." She paused and as the doctor said nothing, she continued: "We fished up some of the meat out of the Bayou as soon as their backs were turned but after a little while we could not eat it. The soaking in the water spoiled it. It was not very well cured anyway. We cured it ourselves but we did not have salt enough, salt was very scarce." . . .

The doctor was a handsome man and if nearly as old as his mother-in-law as Madame Joachim said, he did not show his age, unless Madame Séréno was in the neighborhood of forty-five. His short curling black hair and beard, his teeth and eyes were all favorable to his appearance; and if his dark complexion showed lines, they were still far from being wrinkles. He had a genial voice, his linen was fine, his broadcloth well made, his watchchain was massive with a great seal ring and a number of trinkets dangling from the loose end over his waistcoat.

"Well, keep her quiet," he admonished, "in bed" . . .

"That," interrupted the mother, hastily, "we will never be able to do. Even her father cannot make Cicely keep in bed after the fever and chill are over."

And all the children who were standing around listening, shook their heads and murmured their doubts about Cicely's staying in bed. "She must stay in bed now," ordered the doctor decisively. Turning around, he went back to Cicely in bed and repeated to her: "She must stay in bed now and when Monsieur le Chill comes again, he will find us in bed to receive him, eh, Cicely? and we will arrange it so that he will not come so often, and then he will not come at all. We know how to get rid of an importunate visitor, eh, Cicely?" He looked down upon her with what Madame Joachim called his "bon St. Joseph" air and Cicely gave in to it, as his wife had done, and his mother-in-law and sister-in-law, and his little patients at the convent gave in to it; all the nervous irritablity of her long, wearying illness, disappearing from her thin peaked, wan little face.

As he walked back to the gallery, his face for a moment looked somber.

"As my husband says," the mother apologized hastily, "it is the fortunes of war."

"There are no fortunes of war, Madame," he retorted sharply. "There are no fortunes of war for women and children. It is all misfortunes for them, they are the sufferers; and their war goes on after the peace, they will be still suffering for it, when the war is forgotten." He stopped abruptly but the children did not hear him, they had stayed with Cicely.

"Well, you will give her good food now and plenty of it." He told her what to get and where to buy it, the meat from this one, the bread from that one, the milk—"Get your milk from Madame San Antonio, yes, from Madame San Antonio, I will tell her about it."

"We must send them at once to school"—the mother pursued the important thought in her mind—"the boys to the public school, we think . . ."

"To the public school! No, no! you cannot send them to the public school now, the public schools are demoralized. The niggers go to our public schools now. No, no, you send them to my friend Badeau. Monsieur le Colonel Badeau, an old officer in the French army. He teaches well and he maintains discipline. His father was an officer under the great Napoleon, not the little one, and his son believes in the discipline of 'le petit Caporal.' You ask him about 'le petit Caporal' and you will hear some good stories. I will see Badeau, myself for you. The little girls will go to the convent, of course."

"Oh, no! We are Protestants, you know."

"But that makes no difference. Protestants can go to a convent as well as Catholics. A convent is the best place to educate little girls in and those ladies of the Ursulines . . ."

"Oh, I am sure they educate perfectly, but my husband thinks . . ."

"Oh, well! I understand," he now interrupted her, "then you must send them to Mademoiselle Mimi, Mademoiselle Mimi Pinseau, s-e-a-u; not Pinson, s-o-n; ha, ha, ha.

> " '*Mimi Pinson est une blonde,*
> *Une blonde que l'on connait,*' "

he quoted. "Mademoiselle Mimi is the teacher for you. She has a school, just there," pointing in the direction of the church. "You go to Mademoiselle Mimi, no, no, I will go to her myself and tell her to come to you."

He descended the steps of the gallery and walked down the garden path murmuring to himself:

"C'est l'étui d'une perle fine,
La robe de Mimi Pinson . . ."

"It Was A Famous Victory"

The bell of the little church roused Sunday betimes in St. Médard. No one, on that day at least, heard the trumpet at the barracks. A thin, clanging, jangling-voiced bell it was, and Cribiche rang it with no more sentiment than an overseer rings his bell on a plantation to call the negroes to their work. But to the ear that had been longing for a church bell for four years and had heard only the overseer's; to this ear, the bell of St. Médard, seemed in comparison with all other bells ever heard; even as the trumpet of an angel in comparison with the trumpet of the barracks.

From the earliest hour of the mass, one could hear the voices of those who were hurrying to get to the church and have their duty over and done for the day and for the week; gay pleasant voices, that made the pebbly Gascon French sound pretty. And if one peeped through the window, one could see the men, women, and children striding by in their clean Sunday clothes, hoofed, one might say in their Sunday shoes, for in sabots only do Gascon peasants walk lightly and at their ease.

For mass after mass the gay alarum jingled, until surely, only the dead of conscience as well as of ear could pretend to be deaf to it. Each ringing seemed to catch a different set of sinners or saints, the first netting the poorest and plainest, and each succeeding one ever more worthy game from a worldly point of view. The last one for high mass landing the fine people in carriages, or those who walked only the shortest of distances, the ladies, in trailing dresses, in the most delicate of shoes, planters' families from the lower coast, and the rich demoiselles San Antonio. These were the parishioners to whom Père Philéas addressed the sermons that he gleaned, it must be confessed, from the other classes of his congregation. He was not a brilliant priest, as priests go, but he knew as well as any Dominican who ever came from Paris to preach the Lenten sermons at the Cathedral that in order that those who have ears should hear, one must preach the sins of the poor to the rich and the sins of the rich to the poor. And so it was that the hard-working, the dairy, and gardening folk who rose at dawn to get to church for the first mass furnished the spiritual exhortation for the liesurely class, who reluctantly left easy beds to catch, as they called it, the last mass.

"Ah, God! I cannot thank Thee as I would here, but when I get home where I can go to church with all my children, then will I thank and praise Thee. Oh! Then will I fill the church with my thanksgiving and praise to Thee!" As Sunday after Sunday rolled by on the lonely plantation, this had been the poor mother's vow to herself as she strove with her inadequate words to express what was in her heart toward the One who was leading her through such a valley as, surely, she thought, no woman with four small children had ever been brought through safely before. Not a Sunday passed on the plantation that, after hearing their catechism and verses and hymns she did not remind the children of what the Sundays were at home, where there were churches and Sunday-schools.

When the lessons were over, and she and the children would start for their Sunday morning walk, the little girls would still cling to her and beg: "Please, Mama, tell us some more about your Sundays at home," while the boys, of course, took no interest in them but were always trying to slip away on their own adventures. The Sunday walk was always the same, along the road by the Bayou to the woods. She, herself, was always afraid of the woods. Her terror was, that in some incomprehensible way, she would wander in it out of sight of the Bayou and thus lose her clue to the direction of the home; or that one of the children in their frolics would run away, out of sight and hearing, and get lost. But she cunningly concealed her fears for she never allowed the children to suspect that she was afraid of anything; one of her husband's theories being that women were as brave as men. She therefore never went far into the woods; and she could always hold the children and their attention while she turned them homewards by telling them still more about anything she remembered, it made no difference what. She could tell an interesting story as well about one person as another and she could tell, not only her own stories but those her mother had told to her, which she had heard from her grandmother, stories that began, some of them, in the emigration of the Huguenots to this country, or the Revolutionary War, and all sorts of hair-breadth escapes of Continentals from Tories.

On the rare occasions, when the father was along, he would tell them hunting stories, for he had been a great hunter in his youth; and the walk with him as guide would go far into the woods to the *coulée,* a sluggish drain from the swamp whose glassy black water held no end of turtles and deadly moccasins. Even the youngest of the children had been taught not to fear these last, however, but to kill them boldly with a blow on the back of the head. In the Autumn, they would walk to a grove of persimmon trees, where, if there had been frost the night before, the ground would be covered with ripe fruit, both the large, full round pink persimmons, shaded with lilac, and the deep red ones that when dried in the sun tasted like prunes—the kind that, as the father related, the Indians dried and pounded and made nice bread or cake of. In his youth, out of which he could draw as many wonderful stories as Mama out of hers, he used to go hunting with the Indians, and often spent weeks with them in their villages, as many young men of his day preferred doing instead of traveling to civilized centers. From the Indians he learned all sorts of curious forest lore: the habits of trees, the tracks of animals, medicinal herbs, and subtle ways of telling the points of the compass by the bark of the trees; all of which he taught the children.

In the Spring, the walk would be to the sandy spot on the Bayou's bank where the alligators laid their eggs. He always knew the very Sunday when the sand would be marked by their tracks, and following the tracks find the spot where the eggs had been laid and covered.

Always on coming back from their Sunday walk they would go the rounds of the quarters, stopping first invariably at the cabin of old Aunt Patsy, the most venerable negro on the plantation. Her cabin stood apart from the others and she lived by herself: a silent, morose old woman, but after the master and mistress the most respected person on the place. Often when the mistress was surcharged with anxiety, she would go and talk with Aunt Patsy, and never came back without being eased, or without remarking how Aunt Patsy seemed to know everything about life. On Sundays she was always found ready to receive her visitors sitting in her low white oak chair covered with deer skin. She wore a cap, the only negress on the place who did so, a broad ruffled white cotton cap, tied under her chin. Very black she was; thin and wrinkled and with front teeth that stood out like tusks. On account of her age, she was exempt from work, but she was always busy, nevertheless, spinning the finest and best knitting cotton and doing the fastest and prettiest knitting. She had no relations, had never borne a child, and her husband had been dead so long that he had become merely a tradition on the place. A boy had been assigned to the duty of cutting wood and fetching water for her, and this was her only connection with her fellow slaves. When she died, her funeral was made a great event. And afterwards the negroes and the white children following their superstitions (as white children never fail to do) in passing her cabin always looked to see if she might not be still sitting there "anyhow" as they said.

The other negroes in the quarters would be sitting in front of their cabins; the babies, washed and dressed, lying in their mothers' or fathers' arms, their bright alert eyes, glancing around and their little hands grabbing at the flies in the air. The other children, in their clean *cotonnades,* with bare legs and feet well scrubbed, would be running around after the chickens—that is the happiest of them—the others would be wedged in the vise of a parent's knees, while their stubborn hair was being carded, divided and wrapped into stiff wisps with white knitting cotton. Here and there, stretched out in the sun the half-grown boys would be lying asleep, worn out with the exhaustion of having nothing to do.

After the greetings there would be talk of the weather, and the crops, and gossip about the animals. Sometimes a group of men would be gathered on Jerry's gallery "passing the time of day," as they called it, in discussion generally about the cause of things—such as the changes of the seasons, the revolution of the sun or God's ways. And when the master was along, he would step in and join them and answer their questions and make explanations; until all the other negro men would drift in too; and their wives following would sit around on the edge of the gallery to enjoy the entertainment, commenting freely, and guffawing aloud at the good retorts, as each man put his oar into the conversation whenever he got a chance. Meanwhile the mistress and the little girls would continue their walk to the house and the little boys make off with their black followers at their heels upon some adventure, that seemed to be innocent, but always turned out to be mischievous——

All this train of reminiscence was put in motion as the car jolted and rumbled along on the way to church. Still, the memories of the plantation forming the background of thought in the city, as the memories of the city had formed the background of thought on the plantation! Mrs. Talbot's face brightened with pride as well as love, at the sight, at last, of her church. The sacred edifice, which during the week seemed to sink into the ground completely lost from sight in the busy whirl of life, rose commandingly enough on Sunday when the shop windows were shut and barred and the merry-go-round of fashion-seekers turned off. Its only rival was the drinking shop on the corner. And blatant and brazen though this was on week days, it hung its head sadly enough in shame on Sundays, as if it knew then what it really was—not a drinking but a drunkard shop. How could it look otherwise with the fine old church casting its judgment day sentence upon it and with the stream of people passing under the granite portal, with that same judgment day in their minds?

With her children following her, the mother made her way quickly to her old pew, just as she had pictured to herself doing so often in the past. She could have gone to it blindfolded. A lady was in it who looked with haughty surprise at the intrusion and moved away to the end of the seat. She looked for the old books in the rack; they were no longer there. When the service began it recalled her to where she was; but over and over again she asked herself whether she were not still on the plantation, in the war and only dreaming she was in church, gazing at the window that as a child she had looked upon as a sign in the sky. . . .

But no, this was not her memory on the plantation! this was not what she saw there on Sunday, far far different from it! That was not her old minister's face and figure that ever since she could remember she had seen in the pulpit; whose voice had humanized the gospels and epistles to her. Looking around, she saw none of the starts of surprise and quick cordiality of eyes, that had made the charm of the plantation anticipation. She saw in the old places only drooping women, in mourning or shabby clothes, and no men that she knew. When the service was over, there was no hurrying forward with outstretched hands of welcome. Instead of that, the imperious lady in the pew showed unmistakable signs of impatience at her lingering and brushed past her with scant courtesy. And then she saw that the name on the pew had been changed, her father's and grandfather's name was no longer where it had been since the church was built. As in flight, she hurried out a side door and passed through the small churchyard which still, unlike the pew, held the name of her grandfather on a tablet. She did not linger to point it out to her children, and read the honorable inscription on it, as she had anticipated doing with pride on the plantation; but rushed out the gate to the car that took her away not so much from her past, as from the future of that past.

When the early Sunday dinner was over and a long afternoon lay before them, the family went out for the walk that always filled such afternoons on the plantation. The mistress, going first to give a direction to the servants, found Jerry and all his family sitting on their gallery, in their Sunday clothes, silent and dejected.

"Haven't you been out at all today, Jerry?" she asked.

"Yes, Mistress, I went out for a little while."

"We are going to walk on the levee to see the river, why don't you all go too and sit out there?"

"I have been there, Mistress."

"We've all done seen the river," added Matilda.

"But now you will see all the people passing."

"It's no use seeing people, Mistress, if you don't know them."

"Well, but talk to them and you will learn to know them."

Matilda shook her head gloomily.

"Isn't there any church somewhere tonight that you can go to?"

"I don't know, Mistress," answered Jerry indifferently.

"But you could ask some one."

"We don't know nobody to ask," Matilda retorted crossly.

"Oh! you may be sure there is a church somewhere hereabouts, that you can go to. Wherever there are darkies, there is a church, you know."

"Church ain't nothing, without you know the niggers in it."

The four girls sat around stolidly without a word.

"But Laura, Henrietta, Julia, and Maria would like to go out; take them to the levee."

"If it's good enough for Jerry and me here, it's good enough for them." Matilda looked at them with ill-temper.

They had evidently all been quarreling and there was nothing to do except leave them alone. But the Mistress's kind heart was smitten by their forlorn appearance.

"They are homesick for the plantation," she told her husband.

"And for some hard work," he answered. "I told Jerry he must find something to do. He is no more accustomed to idleness than I am. A good carpenter ought to be able to make good wages, and there can hardly be a better carpenter for plain work in the city. And he must put the girls to work, they ought to make at least their food and clothing."

"If they are made to work, they will work. Dennis has had them hoeing regularly with the field gang." Dennis was the negro foreman who replaced the white overseer when he went to the war. "And as soon as they were large enough to balance a bucket of water on their heads they carried water to the field hands."

"Well, there is plenty of work for them in the city; they will have to be taught, of course, but there is no reason why they cannot learn," the husband said in his decided tone. "Julia is stupid but she is steady; Henrietta is bright, she will learn easily; but she will turn into a rascal. . . ."

"Oh! do you think so?" This was said in the tone of the past days when masters and mistresses took upon themselves the failures of character in a slave. "What are you going to do about it?"

"I? I have nothing to do about it. That's Jerry's affair now."

"But what can Jerry do unless you are behind him?"

"Jerry comes of good stock and has been well brought up and he ought to know what to do by himself."

"Yes, but Jerry was trained by a master; if Jerry were a master. . . ." The levee rising in front, a tall green rampart, interrupted them. They climbed the wooden steps laid against the steep side and on the top, stopped to look at the river, not yet as habituated to it as were the other saunterers from the neighborhood, who, stretching their necks and laughing and talking to one another, noticed it no more than the public road inside the levee. The great yellow stream rolled majestically along; awful in its portent of power and fatefulness. Down the center of its swift current ran a glittering way, shot into the brilliancy of polished jewels, by the sun's rays. Dim and vague, like a foreign land, the opposite bank lay across the vast width of water.

As usual, the father strode on ahead, the captain. His wife followed next, now walking fast to keep up with him, now slow so as not to leave the children behind; her head ever-turning to look ahead, and then to look behind her; her feet tripping and stumbling in her uneven path and attention. The little path made a subservient detour around a plateau shaded with trees, where the officers of the barracks lounging on benches, were smoking and playing with their dogs. Behind them, facing the road, stood the heavy-looking red brick Spanish buildings of the barracks, with its towers, from whose loopholes protruded the grim muzzles of cannon. Sentries paced in front, squads of soldiers were marching around inside, booted and spurred cavalrymen were galloping up and away from the gateway—at whose posts horses bridled and saddled were hitched in readiness for an alarm. The river, itself, was not more fatefully portentous in its aspect. But out of sight, it quickly went out of mind and the "nature," as Madame Joachim called the country, that succeeded, was in no wise akin to it in mood. In truth, it seemed as merry and convivial to the eye as the spirits of the holiday-makers in the dusty road:

the bands of boys returning from hunting or fishing frolics; negro men and women in their gaudy Sunday finery and gaudy Sunday boisterousness; noisy Gascons with their noisy families packed in little rattling milk or vegetable carts; antique buggies and chaises, with their shabby-looking horses or mules, filled with voluble French chatterers; and every now and then, shining new traps behind spanking teams driven by gay young officers who looked neither to the right nor left—greeting no one, greeted by no one. Sprawling on the river-side of the levee and hidden from view, parties of white and negro soldiers were playing cards or throwing dice, or lying outstretched on the grass asleep or drunk.

Built so as to face the river and dominate it by their elegance, as the barracks did by its fierceness, stately mansions of the *ancien régime* succeeded—memorials of a day when the city's suburb of the *élite* was expected to grow down stream; and specimens of the elegant architecture that is based on the future stability of wealth—massive brick and stucco structures surrounded with balconies, upheld by pillars sturdy enough to support the roof of a church; with ceremonious avenues shaded by magnolias or cedars leading up to great gardens whose flower beds were disposed around fountains or white statuettes. And after these, unrolling in the bright sunlight like a panorama to the promenaders on the levee, came the plantations, the old and famous plantations as they used to be reckoned, whose musical French and Spanish names bespoke the colonial prestige of their owners. Hedges of wild orange, yucca or banana screened the fences, but every now and then the thick foliage was pierced by little belvederes; from whence the soft voices of women and the laughter of children—sitting within, to enjoy the view and breezes of the river,—would fall like songs of birds from cages upon the road below. Or out on the levee, itself, the families would be gathered in little pavilions, sitting in pleasant sociability, as the families of these plantations had been doing for generations, looking at the river and at the pleasant view also of their own possessions: mansion, quarters, sugarhouse, brick kiln, fields of sugar or corn, pastures studded with pecans, cherry trees, or oaks, smithies, warehouses,—some of the buildings and appurtenances as aged-looking and out-of-date as the great-grandmothers in their loose gowns, reclining in their rocking-chairs in the pavilions, gazing with the pensiveness of old age at the swift and sure current of the river.

At one place the stream had undermined its bank and swallowed up a huge horseshoe of land, taking levee and road with it. A new levee, whose fresh earth crumbled under the feet, had been thrown up around the breach; and a new road run, curving boldly into the privacy of a garden, or the symmetrical furrows of a field. A half-mile beyond, the river seemed to drop its booty of soil seized above, and was forming a new bank; the *batture,*[4] as it is called, could be seen shoaling up bare and glistening wet, far outside the levee.

"There!" the father stopped suddenly, and turning his back to the river, pointed with fine dramatic effect in the opposite direction, his face beaming with pleasure at the culmination of his carefully guarded surprise. "There it is! The field of the Battle of New Orleans! That is the monument!"

As he glanced down to see the effect, he could behold the glow from his face reflected in each little face looking up to him, as the glow of the sunset had been reflected in the surface of the river. And yet what could be more commonplace to these children than a battlefield? What else had they heard of for years but of winning and losing battles? Each one of the little band was surely qualified to say "Whatever my ignorance about other things, I at least know war." But now, it was as if they knew it not. Their eyes were gleaming and their little hearts beating as at the sight and sound of martial glory too great for earth to bear—the martial glory of poetry and history, not of plain every-day life! Breathless, they ran down the levee after their father, looking, as he looked, nowhere but in front, where rose the tall shaft that commemorated the famous victory. Faster and faster he strode, and they after him, until they reached the steps of the monument and climbing up, could look over the land roundabout; seeing only a bush here, a tree there, a house in the distance and still farther away the line of the forest. A bare, ugly, desolate scene enough, but not so to the little band——

"There were the British headquarters! There Jackson's! Along there ran the ramparts! In that swamp were the Kentuckians! There, next the river, the Baratarians! Away over there, hidden by the woods, the little bayou through which the British army came from the lake to the river! Across that field advanced Pakenham! Over there he fell! Up the levee came Lambert! Out there on the river was the Carolina firing hot shot and shell! Down the road we have been walking ran the reinforcements from New Orleans!" The fine old story sped on and on. . . . As he talked the little boys stretched themselves, taller and taller, and looked before them with the swaggering insolence of Baratarians looking at the En-

4 *Batture*: the alluvial land between a river at low-water stage and a levee.

glish, and the little girls' heads rose higher and stiffer and they curled their lips disdainfully at the foe, as ladies do in triumph.

On the other side of the monument, stood Polly's friend of the car, the old gentleman who looked like General Lee, listening rather wistfully. . . .

"The British marched up to the line of death as if they were on dress parade," the father continued his historical lesson, "and they died in their ranks as they marched. When the smoke lifted, and when the Americans saw them lying in regular lines on the field,—the brave red uniforms, and the dashing Tartans of the Highlanders,—a great sigh went down the line, a sigh of regret and admiration. . . ."

Polly's sharp eyes, roving around, had detected the old gentleman. Running to him, she caught his hand and drew him forward. The movement was so frank and hearty, that neither he nor the parents could resist it and at once they entered into cordial acquaintanceship with one another.

He was so tall and erect of figure, so noble of face, so soldierly in his bearing, that the civilian clothes he wore were a poor disguise. One knew at once, rather than guessed, that he had been an officer and had worn the gray, and that in short, he was one of the ruined and defeated Southerners.

"My father," he said, as he came forward, "was one of the Kentuckians."

"Was he?" exclaimed the mother enthusiastically. " 'A hunter of Kentucky.' " And with a smile and a toss of the head, she gave the refrain " 'Oh, the hunters of Kentucky.' [5] My grandfather sang the song at des-

5 "The Hunters of Kentucky" or "The Battle of New Orleans," is a ballad by Samuel Woodworth (1784–1842). First sung in 1826, it became a campaign song for the election of Andrew Jackson in 1828. Of eight stanzas the third and fourth are typical:

> I s'pose you've read it in the prints,
> How Pakenham attempted
> To make old Hickory Jackson wince,
> But soon his scheme repented;
> For we with rifles ready cock'd
> Thought such occasion lucky,
> As soon around the general flock'd
> The hunters of Kentucky,
>
> Oh, Kentucky, the hunters of Kentucky,
> The hunters of Kentucky.
>
> You've heard I s'pose how New-Orleans,
> Is famed for wealth and beauty—

sert on every anniversary of the battle. And my grandmother used to say that they were the handsomest men she ever saw," glancing involuntarily at the stranger, who in this regard was every inch a Kentuckian, "as they came marching down Royal Street, in their hunting shirts and coonskin caps with the tails hanging down behind."

"Sharpshooters every man of them," interjected her husband, "hitting a squirrel in the eye, on the top of the tallest tree." . . .

"She said," continued the wife, "that there were no men in the city to compare with them and all the young ladies fell in love with them and used to dream of them at night; rifles, hunting shirts and all. Oh, the women looked upon them as deliverers. You remember the motto of the British?" . . . She paused, and as no one answered went on: "My grandmother said the ladies all carried daggers in their belts, and as they sat together in each other's houses, scraping lint and making bandages, they would talk of what they would do in case of the British victory. And one day they became so excited that they sent a messenger to General Jackson, and he answered like the hero he was, 'The British will never enter the city except over my dead body.' " . . . And still no one took up the conversation, so she carried it a step farther: "My grandfather never approved of General Jackson's course after the battle, but she, my grandmother always defended him. She could never forgive my grandfather for not casting his vote for him for president, she vowed if she had had a hundred votes she would cast them all for him."

The stranger laughed heartily.

"After the battle, you know, the ladies all drove down to the field in their carriages carrying their lint and bandages, and refreshments for the wounded, . . . and they brought back the wounded British officers with them and took them in their homes and nursed them. My grandmother had one, a young boy not over eighteen, and so fair that he looked like an angel, she said. He was a gentleman of good family. But all the British officers were gentlemen, of course; and the young ladies lost their hearts

---

There's girls of every hue it seems,
    From snowy white to sooty.
So Pakenham he made his brags,
    If he in fight was lucky,
He'd have their girls and cotton bags,
    In spite of old Kentucky.
Oh, Kentucky, &c.

Sir Edward Pakenham was commander in chief of British forces at the battle of New Orleans.

to them, as they had done before to the Kentuckians. For years afterwards, Grandmama's prisoner used to write to her."

"Would you have liked them as well, if they had whipped you?" the stranger asked with a twinkle in his eye.

"Whipped us! They never could have done that! We would have burned the city! We would have fought from house to house! We would have retired to our swamps! No! We never would have surrendered the city." And then as the absurdity of these old hereditary boastings came to her in the light of the present, she stopped short and laughed merrily, "that is the way we used to talk."

They walked back slowly to the levee and mounted to the path on top just as a large vessel slowly steamed upstream. The children read out the name on the stern. It was from Liverpool.

The sun was sinking on the opposite side of the river amid clouds of gorgeous splendor. The vague green bank came now into clear vision with its plantation buildings, its groves, and its people walking like ants upon its levee. The rippling current and every eddy along the bank shone in unison with the sky or, indeed, as if another sun were burning under its depths. The great steamship passed into the circle of illumination and out of it, as the little group watched it from the levee.

"I should be ashamed to come here, if I was them, wouldn't you?" Polly's clear voice broke the solemn silence as she twitched the hand of the old gentleman, with free *camaraderie.*

"Ashamed? Why?"

"Because we whipped them so."

"Whipped them! Oh! You mean the British in the battle."

"Yes, we whipped them right here, where they have to pass by. I wouldn't like that, would you?"

"Perhaps they don't know it on the ship."

"Don't know it! I reckon everybody knows when they are whipped. I would hate to be whipped, wouldn't you?"

"I used to hate it when I was whipped."

"Oh! I don't mean that! I mean in battle. If I were a man I would never be whipped."

"What would you do if the other army were stronger."

"I don't care if it were stronger, I would whip it."

The path on top of the levee following the bending and curving banks produced the effect of a meandering sunset. Now it shone full opposite, now it glowed obliquely behind a distant forest, now the burning disk touched the ripples of the current straight ahead, and the British vessel seemed to be steering into it. Another turn and it had sunken halfway down behind the distant city, whose roofs, steeples, chimneys, and the masts of vessels, were transfigured into the semblance of a heavenly vision for a brief, a flitting moment. Further on the bank turned them out of sight of it all,—and shadows began to creep over the water,—and when next they saw the west, the sun had disappeared, and all its brilliant splendor with it. In the faint rose flush of twilight beamed the evening star . . . far away from the little church of St. Médard came the tinkling bell of the Angelus . . . the evening gun fired at the barracks.

Jerry

In the program for the future, it had been agreed between Jerry and his master that the two eldest girls should be hired out as servants as soon as possible and that Jerry should seek employment in his trade of carpenter. This, with Matilda's wages as cook and with their home provided, would insure not only comfort to the freed slaves but enable them to save something to meet the "emergencies," as they might be called, of their freedom: the illnesses, deaths, and disabling accidents that had been hitherto the master's portion.

As he had planned for his own life so Mr. Talbot planned for the negro's and did nothing by halves. He carefully explained to the negro that the principles that formed the basis of his dealings with other men and other men's dealings with him were the same truth, honesty, hard work, courage, patience, that he, Jerry, had possessed as a slave; and that all he had to do now to fulfil his duty to God and man was to continue living in the future as he had done in the past. A good slave was bound to make a good free man. His children were of an age to help him, which was a great advantage; Matilda was an honest, industrious woman; his trade was one in which he was sure to find employment. The master said he had never seen a good carpenter who was not well to do. Jerry listened as he always did to his master, devoutly raising his large intelligent eyes to him from time to time; his great hard hands lying heavily on his knees like hands of bronze. His thick, grizzled wool stood out in even height all over his head, increasing its size with fine effect; a short grizzled beard covered the lower part of his face, leaving his large lips bare. His expression was of perfect truth and honesty.

"I'll do my best, Master; I'll do my best," was the answer he made from time to time.

"You must not only do *your* best; you must see that your family does its best, too," with a slight laugh. "You know you are your own overseer and master now."

The negro did not smile at this. He had a face that seldom smiled; a serious, plodding face.

"It will seem strange at first being in the city; but you must not think about the city: your work will be the same in the city that it was in the country. Keep to your work and keep to yourself. The city is full of strange negroes who are up to all kinds of mischief; keep away from them. A lazy negro is a bad negro, as you know yourself. When you see a crowd of lazy negroes, herding together like sheep as they are doing in that old warehouse on the Levee, you may be sure they are doing no good to themselves or to any one else. Keep away from them and keep Matilda and your girls away from them. I cannot do anything to help you in this, you must do it all yourself."

"I'll do my best, Master."

"I'll give you a recommendation—that is a paper telling who you are and what you can do; guaranteeing you as the good, honest, industrious man you have proved yourself to be. Your character and your capability as a workman are your stock in trade; and I can tell you many a white man has made a fortune starting with less of that than you have. Show your paper when you ask for work. As I pass in the cars, I see some piled-up lumber on the Levee; there must be a lumber-yard there or a sawmill; I should think you could find work there. And show your recommendation when you apply for work for Henrietta and Julia. People naturally think that a good man has good daughters. Go over there to the barracks, perhaps some of the officers' families need servants. Take any wages they offer. Henrietta and Julia do not know much about housework but they can learn. You had better explain, Jerry, that they have never worked much about a house, and though they look rough and awkward, they will soon learn. You take them yourself, and hire them out and collect their wages—as they are both under age—just as I would have done once, if I were hiring you out."

"Yes, Master, I'll do my best."

The next morning the father and the two daughters, dressed in their best clothes as if they were going to church, started out on their momentous errand. Jerry had his recommendation in his pocket; but he carried it so well written on his face, that the paper could have been demanded only by a person very ignorant of negro physiognomy. It was not difficult to find situations for the strong, good-looking girls, ignorant and awkward as they were. Although the city was swarming with the disbanded negroes from ruined plantations and homes all over the State, wages were high; servants hard to get, and harder to hold. From the utmost luxuriance and extravagance of retinue, households had fallen to the barest necessities. Freedom from slavery meant freedom from work or it meant nothing to the negroes. Here and there an old man or woman would be seen toiling stolidly along in the old routine, although the door of their prison stood open before them. Inured to chains, perhaps more at their ease with them than without (even if the chains were forged of sentiment and affection as some of them seem to have been), they still remained in servitude when servitude grew harder and harder under the changed conditions—when, in truth, it became a slavery such as no former state of slavery could be compared with. But these were all old negroes. The young were foot-loose. There was nothing to bind them or to constrain them, neither past, present, nor future. They drank to their heart's content from the cup of their new liberty and gave themselves up to the delights of its intoxication. There was no master, overseer, or driver for them now by day; no patrol to demand passes of them by night. By night and by day they could go now where they pleased, as well as do as they pleased. No one now could force them to work, or keep them at work if they wished to quit. They could leave the baby crying in the cradle, the dinner cooking on the stove, the clothes in the washtub—nobody could prevent, nobody could punish them. That was the best of all, they were free henceforth from punishment! They even could be impudent with impunity now to the whites; to those sacred whites against whom to raise a hand was once a capital crime for a slave. They could have white people arrested now and taken before any provost marshal. And if the whites were not "loyal," as it was called, to the conquerors in the war, the negroes, merely because they were negroes—and so loyal—could gain any case against them, would in fact be believed before them. They could now curse white men, aye and even white women, to their faces, and if they were Southern white men and women be only laughed at for their insolence by the people in power. The negro soldiers could shove them out of their way in the cars, push and jostle, soldiering them as one may say, with their white officers standing by, indifferent, if not smiling at them. They, the negroes, had been freed and exalted—so their preachers preached to them—their owners conquered and abased. They, the negroes, were the victors; to them belonged the spoils and they were ready to claim them. Social equality was granted them; wherever a white man went a black man could go. Whatever a white man did a black man could do. There was nothing now but political equality to obtain, which, on account of their numbers and the disfranchisement of the whites, meant political superiority. And white men, from the victorious side's political party that had brought on and gained the war, were even now forming parties in the State, to gain this last triumph for them, and with it their vote.

There were old ladies still living in the city who, sitting in their quiet rooms, said that they knew all about revolutions: their mothers had related to them what had taken place in the French revolution. Whatever happened, these old ladies shook their heads and predicted something worse. They counseled prudence, submission, for they felt the cut of the guillotine still in their blood. There were other old ladies, too, who said they knew all about it: their mothers had fled from the insurrection of the slaves in Santo Domingo, and whatever happened they also predicted something worse, for they felt still in their blood what they could never relate to their children; what they only could describe as "God alone knew what followed" . . .

Jerry hired out both his daughters into service in the barracks and secured work for himself as carpenter.

At night, when the lessons were going on in the master's house, the negroes would be gathered around the flickering light of the fire on their hearthstone and they would turn together, as it were, the page of the day's experience. Not the pages filled with Latin declensions and Greek verbs, that puzzled and saddened the little minds over the way, but mirth-provoking pages to the negroes—for at first they experienced nothing but what they could laugh at; and they laughed at everything that differed from their plantation standard. And more than anything else, they laughed at their own race: "A city nigger was no nigger at all."

Sometimes the master, coming in to give an order, seeing them thus laughing, talking, and dozing together before their fire, would say wearily to himself: "*They* are as happy as ever they were."

But the two elder girls grew more and more like the city niggers that they at first despised and mocked; less like the country niggers they had been so proud to call themselves. Little by little they discarded their plantation garb: the *cotonnade* gown, heavy rawhide shoes, and headkerchiefs; and little by little assumed hats, calico dresses, and high heel boots. In three months they had traversed the stage from the one costume to the other. To their father these were dubious signs, but to Matilda they were glad tidings. She craved not for herself to go into the Canaan, the Land of Promise, that she heard was lying before all negroes for them to go in and take possession of. She counted upon remaining upon this side of Jordan with Jerry and her white people, in the *cotonnade* gown, headkerchief, and rawhide shoes of the days of her slavery. But she laughed ecstatically to herself over her work when she thought of her daughters in their new finery, as she would have laughed had she heard they wore the robes of salvation, the mystical finery of a negro's dreams during slavery. Salvation: That was the negro's hope in slavery—to save their souls and go to God. And as they were slaves, and black, and sinners as well, they indulged, not hopes, but certainties of salvation. The freed negroes soon learned not to worry themselves about salvation. What could heaven give above what they had been given and what was promised them?

The girls soon lost their places, but Jerry found others for them; and all went well as before except that they came home only once a week instead of every night. They lost the second places before their month ended, and Jerry found situations for the third time. . . .

After that he lost track of their engagements. They went in and out of their places without reference to him. They told their mother what they chose and she believed what they told her.

One day it came to Jerry, while he was planing a plank, to throw down his tool and go and see what his daughters were doing. He went off as he was, in his apron and shirt sleeves.

When he came home after dark Matilda saw that something had happened to him. He came in and sat down and held his head in his two hands and would not speak; as she had seen a negro man do on the plantation when he came home alone from a frolic that he had gone to with a companion. He said his mate had fallen out of the pirogue and drowned; but the plantation always thought he had thrown him out of the pirogue and drowned him. Matilda could think only of this, as she closed the doors and windows. But Jerry was worn out with hunger, fatigue, and sorrow; that was all. When she won him to talk to her, the tears rolled down his cheeks, and she knew he had not killed anyone.

He told her how it came to him, when he was working and not thinking of his girls at all, to go and hunt them up. A kind of voice came to him. He threw down his plane, left his work and went, as he was. That was all he knew at first. He walked and walked from place to place, until he got on their traces, and then he tracked them to where they were. They were not in any place . . . they had not been in a place for a month . . . they were at the "Settlement," with the negroes there, both of them. They had lied when they said they were working. They were not working . . . they were living with the negroes there—living like they lived . . . They had lied to Matilda and to him. . . .

"Did you see them?" she asked.

He had seen them; he had talked to them and he told Matilda what he had said to them, and what they had said to him, how they had answered him. . . .

When Matilda heard what they said and how they said it her fury stopped her mouth for an instant. Then when she began to talk she was beside herself with passion. She swore she would go to the "Settlement"; she would drag those "nigger girls" out; she would cut their vitals in two; she would stamp the life out of them; she would . . . All the old hideous plantation threats of an African's fury rolled from her hot tongue.

Jerry shook his head, saying nothing. But when, having talked herself to the point of action, she seized a knife and made a rush for the door, he caught her and held her. She now turned in her frenzy upon him; forgetting everything else. She fought him like a wild animal, tried to use her knife on him. Thin, supple, lithe as an eel, she was a match for him unless he used his full strength upon her. Again and again she almost got through the door. She had reached it, opened it, and was fighting in the crack of it, when at last Jerry, getting between her and the door, gave her a push that sent her to the other side of the room, where she fell against the bed.

"Go and call Master," he ordered his youngest girl Maria, who was cowering in a corner.

The master came and the mistress behind him. They had heard only Matilda's garbled accounts of the girls, and thought them still at work. Now they heard the truth as Jerry gave it. Wherever he went, tracking them from one place to the other, from their first situation in an officer's family in the barracks to their last one, he had found but one account of them—that they were lazy, impudent, and thievish. From her last place Henrietta had stolen a dress, and her employers were looking for her to have her arrested. He went finally to the "Settlement," and there found them. They told him they were not going to work any more; that they could make as much money as they wanted without working and that they were free, anyhow, to do as they pleased. When Jerry ordered them to come along with him they were impudent to him; they "sassed" him. When he threatened to whip them they laughed at him and gave him "the dare" to do it . . . they looked him straight in the face and dared him to touch them.

Matilda broke out again with her threats. Her master ordered her to be silent. He questioned her; she gave reluctant, surly but respectful answers.

"What do you want to do about it, Jerry?" he asked, turning to him.

"I want to fetch them back and punish them. Such conduct ought to be punished, Master, you know it ought to be punished."

"But you have tried that. They won't come back. How do you propose to make them come back?"

"If I find them," screamed Matilda, "so help me God, but I'll fetch 'em back! Let me once lay eyes on them, I'll . . ."

"And if you bring them back," the calm voice of her Master interrupted her, "how long do you think you will keep them here?"

"I'll keep 'em! Just let me get 'em here, I'll keep 'em!" and she began her threats again.

"Do as you please, Jerry," the master turned to him; "but," shaking his head, "I can tell you, it is too late now."

"But I must have my children back, Master," and Matilda began to cry. "I must have them back!"

"Don't cry, Mammy! don't cry!" called out the little girls, impulsively from the door where they were peeping in.

Their father sternly ordered them away.

"Master," said Jerry, "I can't let my children stay with thieves and rascals."

"Have you searched their things?"

"No, Sir."

"Go at once and search them."

"They ain't got no things to search, Master," whimpered Matilda. "They took all their things away with them."

She opened the pine chest in which they had brought their clothes from the plantation.

"Look in their bed. Look under the mattress." This was the traditional hiding-place of the negroes.

Jerry went into the next room with a light. They heard him turn the mattress up and give an exclamation. "Master, come here!" he called.

The turned-up mattress showed a slit and bulging moss. Jerry held in his hand a spool of thread, a handkerchief, a ribbon. He tore out more moss; a towel, a pair of scissors, a pair of stockings came out with it.

Matilda started forward, as mother and negro, to stay Jerry from further revelations.

"Matilda," asked her Master, "how much did you know of this?"

"Master! I'm no thief, you know I'm no thief! before God . . ."

"That's enough! Jerry, try to return what you can of these things. I suspect some of them came from the barracks. And go to that woman and pay for the dress. If you haven't the money, come to me and get it. And let Julia and Henrietta know that if I catch them about here, I will have them arrested and sent to jail."

Then the master and his wife left the room. Going across the yard, he said to her: "Jerry is honest, but Matilda knew they were stealing."

The negroes were never the same afterward. Matilda grew sulky and quarrelsome, Jerry silent and morose. Both suffered for the want of their children. On the plantation, during slavery, if Jerry had caught his daughters stealing, he would have whipped them and that would have ended the matter. He would have whipped them if they had been impudent or disrespectful to him. If they had refused to work they would have answered to the overseer. If Matilda had caught them acting badly, she would have whipped them. They had stolen, they had acted badly, they had been impudent and lazy, and they had received no punishment. Even the master did not talk of punishing them but of having them arrested and sent to jail. Jerry tried to study it out.

He plodded along in his work. He made good wages and brought them home and locked them in his chest. When Spring came he would go into the garden of an afternoon and work with his master and the two boys planting vegetables; peas, beans, okra, beets. . . . At night there was no more talking around the hearth. Matilda sat in the kitchen, smoking her pipe. He sat to himself, smoking his pipe and "studying" as he called it.

Out of his studying in the past had come great things for the plantation. He seemed to carry everything in his mind that he had ever seen, but he had to "study" to get anything out of it. His master used to go to him as to a book of reference. When the time came on the plantation that the people there had to weave their own cloth or go without clothing, his master said to him: "Jerry, do you remember that old loom that Aunt Patsy used to weave on? I can see her now," and he made the motion of flinging the shuttle and working the beam. "I can see the whole thing so distinctly that I believe we could make a loom together, you and I; you were playing around her as much as I in the old time."

Jerry answered in his cautious way: "I will study it out, Master, and see." He studied it out, knife in hand, whittling from soft cypress a little piece here, a little piece there; fitting them together; looking at them; pulling them apart; whittling again; fitting again; until he showed, at last, his model to his master, and then from it made a loom. How to warp the yarn—he studied that out too; and from experiment to experiment, failure after failure, he succeeded in creating from memory both loom and weaving, and all the cloth that was needed on the plantation was made there. He had studied out how to cure and smoke beef, how to dress leather, how to make shoes . . . He had even pieced together long hymns, from the fragments carried in his memory from childhood; hymns that all the negroes remembered but, as they said, could not recall. Anything that had taken place on the plantation since he had been there, give him time to study about, and he could report with perfect accuracy: the number of staves cut at such a time, the bushels of corn raised in such a field, where each certain mule had been bought and the long lists of the different shipments of sugar. He had even studied out how to pull teeth and to bleed people.

His great useful hands lay idle at his side; they could not whittle out the thoughts that lay in his head now, could not help him in studying out what was before him this time.

He would come to his master of an evening as he was sitting on the gallery, to put some of his questions to him.

"Master, what is it keeps white folks straight? They ain't got no overseer to whip them."

"They get their straightening when they are children if they have sensible parents," his master had answered, laughing. "I know what kept me straight and so do you."

"What keeps you straight now, Master?" he asked seriously.

"Myself," answered his master confidently.

"Master, why can't niggers keep themselves straight, without whipping, like white folks do?"

"The good ones do. You kept straight, you have never been whipped since you were a boy."

Jerry shook his head. "Master, if I had got my deserts, I would have been whipped many a time since I was a man."

The master laughed at his frankness and responded with the same: "So should I, Jerry, to tell you the truth."

"Master," persisted the negro, not to be put off: "If white folks needed whipping to keep them straight they would get the whipping if they had to whip one another for it—they would get it. But niggers ain't that way. Niggers won't keep each other straight, like white folks do. The white folks kept the niggers straight, the niggers don't do it for themselves. Master," looking him in the face, "how long would the niggers on the plantation have kept straight if you hadn't been there or the overseer? That plantation wouldn't have been a fit place for even niggers to live in, if the niggers had had to look out for the straightness of it, themselves. You know that, Master."

His master nodded his head and smoked in silence.

"But, Master, what puzzles me and what I can't study out, no matter how hard I try; if God wanted us niggers to be like white folks, why didn't he make us like white folks? He wants us to have white folks' natures, but he gives us nigger natures. If we go according to our natures, we are bad. We've got to go according to white folks' natures to be good, and when white folks are bad they go according to nigger natures."

As his master did not reply, perhaps for the best of reasons, Jerry continued:

"Master, over there, where we all come from, from . . . Africa . . . (even the best of negroes hate to pronounce the name) what sort of folks is the niggers there? They ain't got no white folks there. Well, what sort of niggers is they there?" He paused for an answer, which did not come. "I asked Marse Billy one day, and he told me they were savages. They go naked, they eat one another. And how we come here is: those niggers over there caught us like chickens and traded us off for rum, or for anything the traders gave them . . . That's how the white folks got us and brought us over here into slavery. Isn't that so, Master?"

"That's about it, Jerry."

"Master, did you ever hear of white folks selling their folks to niggers for slaves?"

"Oh! in old times, Jerry, there were all kinds of slavery. Don't you remember about the children of Israel and the Egyptians?"

Jerry shook his head dubiously.

"Well, now, Jerry," his master with cheerful voice questioned him in his turn: "how do you account for it that the negroes are so religious if they do not want to be good? You were all of you always singing hymns and praying and preaching and having revivals down in the quarters. It seemed to me then you were always wanting to be the best people on earth."

"It's the sinners that need praying for, Master, not the good," he answered with simplicity, and, rising from the step on which he had been seated he added—and now there was not a tinge of doubt in his voice, or misgiving in his mind—"God will forgive sinners; He says that, if they repent . . . if they repent. That's what makes us repent. Even the greatest white gentleman cannot go to Heaven unless he repents, you know that, Master; but the vilest sinner can, no matter what the color of his skin is. Old master taught us that; and he was right."

And lifting his head as if with reinforced strength and dignity, he walked back to his gallery.

What he had studied out, when the first talk of freedom turned his thoughts toward the great subject, had been thrown into confusion by the conduct of his daughters and the talk of the negroes about him. One of the answers he had received oftenest from his girls to his expostulations was: "I'm a nigger and I'm going to live like a nigger and I'm as good as white folks anyhow." The people at the Settlement repeated it, as they stood around jeering at him. His fellow workmen at the carpenter shop said the same thing. The black soldiers that he met in the cars said the same thing. Matilda would not mention the absent girls to him and when he talked about them she would not blame them. She, too, was beginning to think that there was a white wrong and a black wrong; a different code of morality for a different skin.

Jerry, in his trouble, would recur again and again to his old master, the father of the present one, a rigid Presbyterian, who enforced repentance and salvation upon his slaves with far more severity than he enforced work. "Ye shall be holy, for I am holy." There was no distinction allowed by him for color in that command and sinners found small mercy at his hands when delinquencies, like those of Jerry's daughters, came under his jurisdiction. And his slaves when they were submitting to chastisement were made to know that their master believed it was a question of their souls, of their salvation from eternal damnation.

Now, they could damn their souls as they pleased, there was no one to interfere or hinder. On the old plantation, besides being punished, they would have been prevented or hindered. They would have had no chance to be bad even if they had wanted to. And as they lived in the fear of their strict stern master, so he lived, as they knew, in the fear of God.

Looking up to the stars, which as he thought lighted the Heaven where the old gentleman had gone: "Old Master," whispered Jerry plaintively, "I wish you were here to look after your niggers. God don't look after your niggers as you used to."

At last, one dismal, one painful morning, when he came to make the fire in the house, he rapped at the chamber door of his master and mistress, and standing in the cold gray gloom he told them (the words sounding familiar from old association) that Matilda had run away, not from them, but from him; run away during the night while he slept, taking Maria with her; "run away, like a runaway nigger," he repeated in his humiliation.

In the blank emptiness and silence that succeeded to his family life he held on to his work and to his household tasks; to the fidelity to duty in which he had been raised; to the future that his master had planned for him, and that he knew God approved of. But he could not forget his wife and his children, although they could forget him.

He sat up evenings alone in his room, where at first they had been so happy laughing over the ways of "city niggers," wrestling with his nature, as he would have called the struggle, striving for the other nature, according to which negroes had to live to be good. He would hurry through the path to his work and back; never looking about him, never stopping, as if afraid he might see or meet some of them.

In vain! When Spring came, fresh, as it were to him, from the plantation, bringing the merry voices and laughter of the quarters, the cackling of chickens, barking of dogs, the brisk jingling of the harness of the mules as they trotted out to the field with their noisy riders sitting sideways upon their bare backs . . . above it all he heard the voice of Matilda calling to the girls, and the voices of the girls stepping out with their water-buckets balanced on their heads; little Maria sitting in her little chair that he had made for her. . . .

In vain! In vain! One morning—as bright a morning as Spring could bring—he threw down his tools as he had done once before, and started off almost running, hardly knowing what he was doing; but his feet brought him straight to where his mistress sat alone with her sewing. He told her—and as he talked his solid-looking tears rolled over his thick beard down to his blue shirt—he told her he had to go to them—to Matilda, and to his girls.

Her good, faithful Jerry! Her friend and servant who had stood by her during the war . . . many a time her only help! He alone of all the plantation knew the hard path she had been set to walk in, and how at times she shrank back in fear, how her feet trembled, and how her heart grew faint. She did not have to tell him. He knew, and she knew that he knew it all. She did not have to tell him. . . . Her tears ran too, straight from her heart to her eyes. Ah! That dreadful future! worse; worse than the war! This had not been in the plan; no more sorrow had been there, no more partings.

She told him he was right to go, for she knew that was what he yearned to hear; she told him to go to his wife and his daughters, that God would not abandon him—He saw it all; He would be over him wherever he was, at the Settlement or with his white people. . . . And they would all meet together some day, and be together and never, never part. So she talked as she used to do to the dying on the plantation, and it soothed him as it had always soothed them; and it soothed her too.

He had almost gone, when he returned, picked up her dress, and hid his face in it, sobbing: "Master, Mistress, Master, Mistress."

Later in the day he might have been seen, with his small bundle of clothes over his shoulder, walking up the road to the Settlement.

The San Antonios

Everybody in St. Médard knew that the San Antonios had begun their life, that is, of course, their wealth, in a barroom on the river front. But Madame Joachim remembered them even before that, when they kept an oyster-stand on the Levee itself and opened oysters and sold drinks to anybody who came along—dagoes, roustabouts, negroes—for it was at that time Joachim, himself, was running an oyster-lugger between Barataria and the city and gaining the appearance that made people think of a pirate whenever they saw him. The oyster-stand grew into a shop, and the shop into a saloon, where fine fresh Barataria oysters were sold, the best sharpener of the appetite for drink, as drink is the best sharpener of the appetite for oysters.

After this the classic road to Avernus[6] was not more easy than Tony's to fortune. At that time, Antonia, Maria, and Lisida were crawling around in the mud of the gutter in front of the saloon, "and that," said Madame Joachim, "was the beginning of the Demoiselles San Antonio."

The saloon-keeper cannot but grow rich, provided, of course, that he be as sober as his clients are drink-loving. His investment seems to return the surest of earth's profits. But as in other trades and with other staples, the demand must be fostered, the customer encouraged, the consumption stimulated. The weak beginner, the timid irresolute one in constant strife with his temptation, he to whom not having the price of a drink means the doing without, he must be tided over his failures of weakness, as cotton and sugar planters at times have to be tided over their failures of strength by their bankers. He has to be helped patiently along with credit until he is trained into a reliable client . . . until the week's earnings, the watch from the pocket, the wedding ring from the finger, the silver from the table, the market money from the wife, the hoard of a saving mother, the loans extorted by lying from friends, the purloinings from the till,—until the barkeeper sees it all coming in a safe and sure flow across the bar; until the once-timid speculator in intoxication at last ceases his struggle with his passion and comes to know no other will but its will; to have no other hope but to prolong its pleasure; until every drink taken becomes one more turn of the key winding up the automaton into the regular motion of so many steps away from the saloon, so many steps back; until Sobriety is the one dread left in the drunkard's mind; to keep it away his one preoccupation.

Sobriety, however, does come to him from time to time.

Any one can see the conscience-driven wretch, in some early hour of the morning, shivering in the hottest Summer, outside the door of the saloon. It is the only way remorse ever does come to the drinking shop. Then the bar-keeper gives more credit, unless he is a poor bar-keeper indeed. In this way he is necessarily a money-lender also, turning the cash

6 Avernus: a vaporous crater in ancient Italy, which the Romans regarded as the entrance to hell or hell itself.

from selling drinks into loans for buying them, adding golden links of interest to each end. The process is an endless chain; endless as the weakness and the cunning of man. And not in this way alone was money cast upon the waters to come back in its own good or evil time. It was known that Tony, after shaving the pockets of the poor man, shaved the notes of the rich; that when money was needed desperately, more than life—more than honor as sometimes happens—when money has to be procured, at no matter what cost, and the transaction covered up like murder, Tony was known vaguely to be the man for the deed; and stocks and bonds, title deeds and mortgages, family secrets and political influence, flowed into his coffers from this source. No one knew how much money he had, only that he always had it to lend.

"God knows," said Madame Joachim, "how the children got into the Ursuline convent."

But this was hardly so difficult a piece of knowledge as to warrant an appeal to the Supreme Authority. Any one who has seen the lugger landing and its drinking-shops and drinking-shoppers, and the gutters that serve as drains thereto; and seen at the same time, as one must see, the old Cathedral, hard by,—might, without divine omniscience, draw the inference necessary to connect little girls playing in the gutter with the pure retreat of the Ursuline convent. Particularly when, by one of those facts incomprehensible to logic-loving humanity, the little girls, who for very virtue's sake should have been ugly and repulsive, were on the contrary pretty and attractive—too pretty and attractive, despite their degrading condition, to escape the apostolic successors of those shrewd eyes that once before had discerned, *non Angli, sed Angeli*,[7] in white faces and nude bodies.

And the same eyes were shrewd enough perhaps to detect that no one has more money to spend on children or the church than the rich barkeeper, if he can be brought to do so. At any rate Maria, Antonia, and Lisida were taken from the gutter and sent to the convent, and once in charge of the sisters their parents showed little concern for them. So completely, indeed, did they become children of St. Ursula, so well were they dedicated in advance to her service, that in the expectations of the wise in such matters there was no more probability of their ever leaving the convent for the world than for children reared by the devil leaving the world for the convent.

7 *Non Angli, sed Angeli* (not Angles, but angels) are the well-known words of Pope Gregory the Great on seeing blond Anglians.

One child had died—a boy. Around him clung whatever of parental love Tony and his wife could feel. All that they did not know of the universe, all that they in their ignorance could not know, would have been easier for them to understand than the fact that the boy they wanted died, and that the girls they did not want lived. No priest or church, assuredly, would ever have gotten their boy from them. When he died their affections, like vines whose trestles have been destroyed, crept henceforward upon the ground.

Such people do not read newspapers. In fact the wife could not read. National questions were as much above their interest as the stars, which they never looked at. The fish in the deep sea were not more passive under the agitations of the storm overhead than the San Antonios to the muttered threats, finally breaking out, of the war between the North and the South. But, like the fish, in the absence of finer knowledge, they guided themselves by instinct. And although Tony knew only that in a fight the stronger beats the weaker, this was an immense superiority of knowledge over that possessed by the majority of the community in which he lived. When war was declared he said no more about it than the oyster in his hands; but he ceased to make personal loans, and turned his securities into gold. He bought Confederate money from the timid for gold, and sold it for gold to the confident; trading on the passion for patriotism as he had traded on the passion for drink. Running like a ferryboat from shore to shore, collecting fares before landing, he plied between hope and fear, working in the same secret and mysterious way that he made his loans, for he was never missed from his bar. While armies were being equipped, and companies raised, and men were going out from his very bar to die for their country—and some of his most drunken clients, those who were the most abject cowards in the morning about facing the world without a drink, did die for it heroically—Tony said nothing, but bought cotton. When the ships of the enemy made their appearance at the mouth of the river, and the price of cotton fell, like a dropping stone, he bought cotton. During the sharp but futile fight between the enemy's vessels and the forts that guarded the approaches to the city, when the young men were hastening away into the Confederacy, and the old ones stood in the streets listening to the guns and counting the minutes between them and ruin, Tony bought cotton, at lower and lower prices.

When the enemy's ships passed the forts and all that war could inflict hung in dread over the city, and when seeing itself doomed to capture it fell into the rage of despair that vents itself in wanton violence and destruction, Tony, shutting and bolting his barroom, left his wife inside and was seen by her no more for twenty-four hours. While the furious rabble rioted in drunken frenzy; while packs of wild negroes, screaming with delirious joy, rushed through the streets aimlessly like yelping dogs in the night; while stores of powder were being exploded, and millions of dollars of cotton and sugar burned; while warehouses and groceries were thrown open for pillage and whiskey and liquor ran in the gutters and stood in pools like water; while boats were being fired and sent down the current in flames, and the bank opposite the city seethed in one conflagration, from burning ships and shipyards; while the lurid clouds hung like another fire over the city, and the heavens turned to the blackness of pitch with smoke; while bells rang an unceasing alarm—Tony like a rat was slipping in and out of the hiding-place that he alone knew about; an old, empty, abandoned saloon whose batten doors and shutters were covered with the dust and cobwebs of years. But like most saloons it had a back entrance upon an alleyway that had been opened for the purpose of providing back entrances—exits they literally were—to the buildings, whose needs required at times means of quick and secret evasions. This was where Tony had stored his cotton—the building was packed with it. When the enemy's fleet anchored in front of the city and the despair of grief succeeded to the despair of rage; when in truth there was nothing left to be destroyed; when the enemy landed and marched through the streets—and had the cobblestones under their feet been human hearts the anguish they caused could not have been greater—then Tony returned to his saloon, unlocked the door, and began opening oysters again. When he left it the night before, he counted his dollars by tens of thousands, now he counted them by hundreds of thousands. The great battleships that brought disaster, death, havoc, and ruin to the city, with suspense and dread to last a half century longer, were, in sober truth to him, not battleships at all, but argosies of silver, masted with gold, rigged with silken sails, musical with thrilling flutes and with Cleopatras, aye! with Cleopatras had he wished them, greeting him from damask cushions.

At the Ursulines' convent Spring comes prettier than anywhere else in New Orleans; for she comes bringing not only flowers for the convent garden, but white dresses and blue ribbons for the convent girls; and the Easter lilies, themselves, might envy the young convent girls, as in the early light of a Sunday morning they wend their way, in their white dresses and blue ribbons and white veils, walking two by two, under the bright green trees, to the chapel. The lilies might have envied, and pitied, them too, as the young girls pitied the beautiful lilies on the eve of Easter, with the fate of the gardener's scissors hanging over them. The convent girls knew that the enemy's vessels, thirty or forty of them, were lying in the passes of the river; but they knew too that their city could never be taken, that their men could never be vanquished, that God was with them and they with God in the present war. The great tocsin of St. Patrick's, as all the church bells of the city, had been given to the Confederate Government, to be made into artillery. Cannon made of consecrated metal, shooting consecrated balls! The vision of it fired the young hearts with holy flames and made them wish that they might be the ones to serve that ordnance. Every little girl there who had a father, brother, uncle or cousin in the forts that guarded the river—and each one had some relative there or elsewhere in the army—held her head as high as if she were trying to reach her soaring heart with it, that virgin heart, higher up in the clouds than ever! The poor orphans, the charity scholars and half menials, were never pitied so compassionately as then; their hard fate and isolated lives in the community were never so sadly considered; their outcast lot, deprived of the glory and honor of defending their country, was apparent even to the convent slaves.

As for the sisters, never among the Ursulines of Louisiana could there be found a fear for Louisiana before the enemy. They too were happy enough in their gentle, pious way, except perhaps the Mother Superior, who must have been too old a denizen of the world of men or of God to have any more hopes or fears left in her heart. She must have cast them away, long ago, as grave-cloths of the soul.

They were happy enough at the convent, therefore, until the firing began at the forts. At the first shot, confidence was shaken; at the second, it vanished; at the third, the young girls gave a scream that brought the Mother Superior to them in haste. Louder and louder grew the bombardment, fiercer and fiercer the cannon. Sisters and scholars were hurried to the chapel. Once before in dire extremity of battle, when an overwhelming force threatened the city, when the British came to conquer and spoil it, the Sisters had prayed and God had heard them. General Jackson, himself, had come to the convent after the battle and assured them that their prayers and the favor of the Almighty had saved the city, not he and his handful of men. The convent could not have prayed more fervently then than now. Every shot that sounded, sped to Heaven with a prayer to avert its ball. "Oh, Thou, Our Lady of Prompt Succor, help but this time, once more! Remember, how first Thou guidedst us through the tempests of the ocean to this country! Remember, how when the conflagration raged in the city, threatening to consume us, Thou turnedst back the flames from the convent door! Remember, oh remember, how once before Thou gavest us the victory!" But God's face was turned away from them. Our Lady of Prompt Succor could not succor them this time.

The bombardment ceased, the event was decided, and still, when praying was all too late, they prayed with frightened lips, the rosary slipping through their icy, trembling fingers. That night they watched the lurid light spread over the city, flaming up, through the rolling smoke. The river itself seemed to be on fire. They could hear the explosions and at times the roar of the voice of the frenzied populace. At last word was brought them that the forts had been passed and that the ships were on their way to the city.

Throughout the night, white forms glided about the dormitories, from the beds to the windows. In the early gray of dawn, the time when watchers by the sick always look for death, the first gunboat slowly steamed by the convent. Fearful, fearful, fearful apparition! stopping the breath, freezing the blood. At sight of it, one little girl screamed in agony: "Papa, Papa!" and fell fainting. The rest could look no more. They ran back to their little beds again and laid their faces upon them and cried.

And the sisters! The nuns, the white veils and the black veils! Alas! the veils were rent asunder for that once and all the holy mystery of the hearts enshrined behind the pale impassive faces was revealed. They too had fathers, brothers, uncles, cousins, in the forts—for the Ursulines recruit their ranks, as the Confederate army did theirs, from the best families in Louisiana—and of what account are vows and renunciations when the woman's heart is pierced? Of what use are black veils or white veils, when the enemy advances over the corpses of her kin?

But the Demoiselles San Antonio looked on dry-eyed. They had no one in the contest to weep over. No cannon ball could render them more brotherless or kinless than they were. They winced not at the echoing boom, shrank not from the sight of the passing gunboats as their companions did. And well might these do so! As those vessels passed before the convent, family, friends, ease, comfort passed out of their lives; leaving behind, bereavement, desolation, poverty, wretchedness! The gaunt specter of war itself, flying over the convent roof, could not have sent down more directly upon their defenseless heads the thunderbolts of its dire tempest.

But not upon the Demoiselles San Antonio, whose father was creeping, like a rat, in and out among his cotton bales. Over their heads the golden cornucopia was turned and all the choicest Spring flowers of fortune showered down upon them; luxury, love, and enjoyment of their youth and beauty fell down upon them like the mystical roses upon Sainte Rose de Lima.[8] The moment of crucifixion for the others was their moment of transfiguration.

For one who has lived through the experience it is clear that the true fruits of conquest come not all at once in the moment of victory, but are a succession crop, yielding gratuitous reapings of profits to the one side as of pains and penalties to the other with unfailing regularity for many years afterward; as the true mortality of a battle is not the number of killed on the field but the resultant roll of the dead in the ensuing years. This could not be apparent at the time to the people of New Orleans, so unused to conquest, who it may be said, despite their vaunted love of fighting and military glory, knew not, as the event proved, what real war was.

It must have been the surprise of his life to Tony, "a heavenly surprise" he might have called it, to find that when he thought he was at the end he was only at the beginning of his harvest: that his gold and paper money speculations and his cotton buying were but the prelude of what was to follow. He had not dreamed of the wholesale confiscations of property all over the city, the auctioning off of buildings by the block, of houses and stores with their contents for a mere percentage of their value; the secret sales of trembling owners in fear of confiscation; the hidden cotton that still could be touched; the bargains from panic-stricken women, the endless reach of money-making, even beyond this, for any one, like him, who had no scruples about buying and none about compounding with the auctioneer who sold, the officer who seized, the soldier who guarded. San Antonio could compound with all officers, soldiers, white and black, camp-followers, and roughs from the purlieus of other cities. In a way, he knew well that, conquerors though they were, they were but men as the conquered had been, men who had the same taste for oysters and liquor. He bought in property of all kinds, spoiling

8 When St. Rose of Lima (1586–1617) was an infant, a rose was said to have hovered in the air above her and to have touched her.

the spoilers and looting the looters of their cotton, houses, silver, jewelry, velvets, furniture, libraries, pictures, pianos, carriages, horses, carpets, India shawls, diamonds, laces, the riflings of fine ladies' wardrobes, the treasures of baby layettes, for many a soldier came into possession of these so cheaply that anything he sold them for was a profit to him. Runaway slaves brought and sold to him what they had stolen and every runaway then was a thief. Successions of absent Confederates were opened and settled in ways so convenient to money-makers, that the corpse went to his tomb not more bereft of worldly goods than the absent heir was when he returned to his heritage. Money, money, money was cast out upon the streets as sugar and liquor had been when the city fell, for any one to pick up and enjoy who did not mind the filth on it.

From the convent windows, as one looked down the river over the roof of the convent chapel, could be seen the chimneys and the tops of the cedar and magnolia trees of what was known as the old Havel place. The old Havels had fled in a ship to Havana, in the first panic of the invasion, leaving behind what indeed they loved, only less than one another, their home: It was the prettiest one in the parish of St. Médard and no one in the Parish, even the most unworthy, could walk past it on the Levee, without feeling a covetous desire to possess it. The fence that surrounded it was of brick topped by an iron railing of delicate design which at regular intervals was upheld by brick pillars that supported vases, holding century plants. It was called the "Villa Bella." Its real name was "Isabella," the name of the bride for whom it had been built; but as the bride and her husband and the villa aged, the pretty name in gilded lettering over the gate had become rusted and dimmed and finally lost under the vine that had been planted in the bridal time, to encircle it with roses.

A broad brick walk, bordered with shrubbery, led to the house whose gallery was floored with white and black marble and instead of a balustrade had pedestals of marble holding vases of growing plants with vines hanging over the sides. In the center of the garden on one side was a fountain, on the other a sun dial with a setting of flowers in *parterres* encircling them. Under the magnolia and cedar trees, white plaster casts of nymphs and fawns seemed to be shrinking back in the shade cast by the heavy green branches overhead.

The old Havels had furnished their house as a young, romantic, bridal couple with taste and fortune would furnish a home for their love with fine lace and satin curtains, with rosewood and mahogany, bronze and marble statuettes, Sèvres and Palissy vases; with silver and cut glass candelabra and chandeliers; with pictures and with mirrors everywhere. No matter in which direction, at what angle they looked, the bride and her husband might, by lifting the eyes, see the reflection of their happiness and their luxury. The old Spaniard felt secure in his generosity as he had contributed money to the defense of the city against its invaders. When the invaders triumphed, therefore, the property was confiscated at once, sold at auction, and bought by Tony.

Thus the Demoiselles San Antonio were provided with a home just when they were leaving the convent and needed one. And it was one of the prettiest roses that fell to them from the gilded cornucopia. Heaven, by sending them the tenderest of parents, could hardly have benefited them so well as by sending them the sordid, selfish ones they had; who, to get rid of them, had gladly thrust them out of their drinking saloon home into the pure, holy atmosphere of the Ursuline convent and by never going to see them there had saved them from the shame that comparison with parents of other scholars would have produced.

But, the old villa? Old houses like old families never seem to fall in one clean drop from height to depth, they are always caught by some crag or bush growing on the side of the precipice and there kept gibbeted through their slow decay in no matter what ridiculous posture. The short, quick termination of destruction has no terror for the original owner in comparison with such a tragicomical ending. Had the Villa Bella, however, been closer to the center of the city's life, it might have been caught in a still more ridiculous position, for all its refined appearance and the tender sentiment of the old couple who in it had watched their young and rosy love grow old, bent, and wrinkled it is true, but yet remaining none the less love to them.

To their neighbors, particularly to Madame Joachim, the San Antonios were no better than masqueraders in the old villa; like the negroes who of *Mardi Gras* nights go to their balls dressed in the second-hand finery of the whites. There was not one among them who had not a jibe ready when opportunity offered for the slinging of one. "No wonder that his daughters were admitted to the Ursuline convent," sneered they. "No wonder they sing so well."

Ah, yes! They did sing well; their voices soaring like birds from a cage, out of the house, over the trees, to the public road so that passers-by could not refrain from stopping and listening to them. Even the young American officers from the barracks, sauntering along the Levee with their dogs of an evening, would stop, and had been heard to remark one to another: "How strange it is, one never hears such music from American *parvenues!* No matter how much money their fathers have they always seem to suffer from an extreme poverty of talent."

When one wanted to buy five cents' worth of milk or eggs or anything that Madame San Antonio had to sell—for different from Père Philéas, she gave nothing—one went not through the vine-festooned front portal, but through a distant backgate and ran for fear of the dogs through a path that led to the basement of the house, where Madame San Antonio would be found sitting before a table counting eggs or oranges, sorting pecans, plaiting garlic, straining vinegar or bottling *Merise*—as the Creoles call Cherry Bounce—dressed in the *cotonnade* skirt, calico sacque, and blue check apron of her barroom days; with a long black pocket tied by a tape around her waist; a perfect market woman.

"Madame San Antonio, *Maman dit comme ca, un picaillon de . . .*" and while she counted or measured, the little girls would stop and listen to the singing, milk-pitcher or basket in hand, forgetting everything, until like the trump of judgment came to them the thought that they must go. And Madame San Antonio? What was Faust, L'Africaine, Charles VI to her? (for they sang only airs from grand opera, the Demoiselles San Antonio). Madame San Antonio heard them not at all, but went on plunging her hands into this basket and that, this bucket and that, stopping only to blow her nose on her red and yellow cotton handkerchief. And San Antonio? When he came in from his business in the city and took his seat in the basement, his flannel cap pulled over his eyes, and a red handkerchief tied around his neck, he did not seem to hear his daughters any more than his wife did; any more than when he was in his barroom and they in their convent.

Three afternoons of the week Mademoiselle Mimi came to practise with the young ladies, and every morning came Madame Doucelet for her day's attendance upon them. This had been arranged by the superior of the convent when she had also advised that the Villa should be substituted for the barroom as a home, when it seemed good to her for the young ladies to leave the convent: their vocation not being that of St. Ursula.

Madame Doucelet was of the kind always to be found at the doors of convents and churches as other guides are to be found at the doors of museums—thin, wrinkled, sallow, somewhat bent, dressed in mourning, of good family, with a name that can serve as passport into society—one of those, in short, who seem in every generation to be reduced providentially to poverty in order to serve those who are as providentially elevated to wealth.

She was so shabby, in her old black bonnet and pointed black *cachemire* shawl pinned tight across her shoulders, and seemed so far removed from the brilliant world of fashion, that no one but that wisest of women —a superior of a convent—would have suspected her intrinsic merit as an initiator into the mysteries of the manners, dressing, and customs of good society; her vocation, in fine, in religious parlance, of a worldling.

"Religion and music," she thus explained herself to Mademoiselle Mimi, "what more can a woman want? Religion for the soul; music for the heart."

The Demoiselles San Antonio possessed these qualifications in perfection; that is if the practice of devotion be called religion, and singing music. As Maria was not so precocious as her younger sisters, and as Lisida was more precocious than her elders, the three went through the gentle curriculum of the convent abreast; and as they entered it together as babies, so they left it together, as young ladies. It may be said, that they were well educated; for whatever they could learn, the convent had taught them. They were drilled in good qualities, and knew all about them whether they possessed them or not: discretion, truthfulness, patience, industry, obedience, resignation, and the wholesome restraint of the feelings—or when this was not possible, that concealment of them which comes from the consciousness that they were always in sight or earshot of a sister, whether they saw her or not.

Of books, they knew what they studied in classes, or received as prizes; the pretty gilt and pink, blue or green volumes of pious histories authorized by the church as the proper reward for convent excellence. Of the world outside their schooling they knew only what the sisters told them, and they did not imagine aught else about it, for it was one of the qualities of convent education that the imagination (that cursed seed of damnation, planted by the subtlety of the serpent in the mind of woman in Paradise), since it could not be extirpated, was trained upwards in the harmless direction of Heaven. Their hearts, therefore, had been kept pure, as the saying is, their minds innocent. In short, the convent had done its best for them. It had taught them the only thing they could learn; had cultivated their one talent—music—and not in a niggardly way either, for when the limit of the convent standard and means had been reached, a professor of singing was procured from the city for them, the best professor there, and they were never excused from practising their piano.

Madame Doucelet's duty was to accompany the young ladies whenever they went out—never to let them go into the street without her had been the charge given her—and to teach them how to dress. Slipping in every morning, wrapped in her shawl, her reticule clasped tight against her breast, she took them into the city to the shops, showing them, what of course they had never seen before, the infinite devices and inventions for adorning and enhancing the interests of women in the world; that is their beauty. Showing them, what also they had never seen before, their own capital of beauty and how it could be profitably increased; by vigilance here, enterprise there. The poor idea of the nuns was that a woman's beauty was of her soul and that could only be increased by spiritual adornment.

Mademoiselle Mimi, when she took her position at the piano three times a week for the performance of her duty, could observe the progress Madame Doucelet was making in the fulfilment of hers: Maria's waist growing hebdomadally smaller, more corset-like, her complexion whiter; Antonia's slimness more sinuous and graceful; Lisida's fulness more engaging. The hair of each one had commenced to travel at once from the rigid uniformity of the convent coiffure, for what is hair or coiffure to the soul? Maria's long, thick plaits were wound around her classic head; Antonia's were unplaited and coiled loosely. Lisida's hair, which had been her sin almost at the convent, so unamanageable it was and curly and tangled—its reproach was turned into its beauty, for its disordered luxuriance was encouraged and even increased and it was carried to the top of her head and held there with a tall comb; black and brilliant over her black, brilliant eyes; soft and entrancing as her soft form. As soon as Madame Doucelet laid her small, faded eyes upon the youngest Demoiselle San Antonio, this transformation and other transformations sprang, as it were, before them.

And as their hair and their figures, so their complexions, hands, and finger nails. Madame Doucelet insisted upon long, polished, finger nails as authoritatively as the convent did on fasting and prayer. Long finger nails, she said, denoted a lady—that is, one who never worked with her hands—for, obviously, one could not work with long finger nails. Even the practising on the piano had to be sacrificed to them, for the lady with long finger nails cannot afford to break them on the piano keys.

As all these small sums of their capital were being rescued, as it were, from their uselessness, to be turned to profitable account, the convent dresses, which were indeed only dresses for a soul, not a body, were replaced by the apparel that fashion in truth seems to adopt for the purpose of revenging itself upon the soul for its servile treatment of the body.

Mademoiselle Mimi saw skirts grow longer, more flattering to the figure, waists more transparent, more open at the neck, sleeves more charitable to the eye of a lover of beautiful arms, heels higher. Earrings made their appearance, beads, chains. And as all this was observed by Mademoiselle Mimi, three times a week, she observed, too, that each sang better, according as she progressed upward in the teaching of Madame Doucelet. Sometimes, when as it seemed to her, the voice she was accompanying was making a triumphant, exultant escape from the body and all ties of the throat, to soar untrammeled through the greatest difficulties of *technique,* she would look up and find the eyes of the singer fastened on some mirror (as has already been said the Havels had multiplied mirrors in their pretty salon), where was the reflection of a beautiful, beautifully dressed young lady.

Ah! what were the poor nuns, with their feeble imagination of the angelic, to this revelation? What more rapturous gaze could the eyes of their pupils turn upon the pictures of the most immaculate saints?

Madame Doucelet, always in the corner, telling her prayer beads, would dart out every now and then, with her noiseless tread, like a spider out of its web, to put a footstool under Antonia's bronze slippers, to show off her foot; to thrust a bright cushion under Lisida's languid head and rumple her hair still a little more; to lift Maria's arm to the back of her chair and gently lay her shapely head, *en profile,* on her palm in the pose of a listening muse; fastening her ideas on to them, just as a spider fastens the ends of his threads to a leaf or twig, in making a trap. No woman could give more of herself to the work for which she was paid.

"Where, where?" Mademoiselle would ask herself, from the depths of her ugliness and ignorance, as her short, blunt fingers struck chords and ran trills; "where, in the name of piety, did she learn it all?"

But Mademoiselle Mimi, who could not sing for want of a voice, was she not apparently as badly equipped for her rôle as Madame Doucelet for hers?

The husband and wife would sit in the basement until the time came for them to go up the backstairs to the servant's room they had selected for their chamber. Here they would sit with shut door, forgetting themselves, and perhaps fancying they were again in their old chamber over the barroom, smelling of oysters, whiskey, and the foul emanations from the gutters. In a corner was the pine bed bought when the wedding ring, the marriage certificate of the ignorant, was bought; there stood also the wooden table with a pail and basin; a clothes chest and two short-legged chairs, as in the old chamber. The one addition to these old friends, the bridal accompaniments of the bed, was a safe with a combination lock. There had been no fireplace in their old room, nor was there one in this one. They would as soon have thought of warming their cow by a fire as themselves. When other folks made a fire in Winter, they tied a woolen scarf around their necks and over their heads; as when other folks drank their coffee out of china or delft cups, they drank theirs out of tin, stirring it with the handle of their iron forks or knives.

They would sit in their room, silent, inert, until the nine o'clock bell rang, when, together with a lighted candle, they would make the round of the pretty house that lay like a sleeping beauty under the spell of a curse. Ah! she would never awake, that beauty, nor find a deliverer to bear her away out of her doom!

They would go back to their room and sit there again, silent and still together—one might as well imagine the two magnolia trees in the garden caressing one another, as the husband the wife, or the wife the husband.

When the gray dawn was about coming on, when in old times the last drunkard would be put out of the barroom to the sidewalk, and they would be free, to fasten and bar their door and creep slowly on their tired feet to their room, to sleep off their day's work—not until then did their old methodical habits permit them to go to bed. They were hardly more silent and inscrutable in their sleep than when awake.

From *Mademoiselle Coralie*

Later on in the day, while the sun was marking off the radiant Autumn hours past the noon, and the quiet of St. Médard was disturbed only by the innocent noise of cattle and chickens, Mrs. Talbot stood under the fig trees of the garden, weeping in humiliation. There was no nook in the house where she could do so unseen. The fig leaves hung close around her; the place was like a cave; there was not light enough in it to see the creeping things on ground or branch, and the air was dull and heavy. But it was a good retreat. Instinctively, she had fled to it when she felt that the time had come when she could no longer restrain her tears, stifle her sobs. It had come to that. She had to weep like a child over what in truth could only be wept over; for there was nothing else to be done. And this thought made her tears and sobs come faster, more uncontrollably. She looked in her mind all around and about, far and near, on this side and on that; she could see nothing but darkness, desolation, degradation. And even while she wept more and more bitterly, giving up courage in hopeless despair, she would ask herself: "What can I do?" and exclaim: "I must do something! I must find something to do!"

In such moments, what has been done is much more present to the mind than what can be done. While the future seemed to shut the door in her face, the past brought forward, endlessly, needlessly, all that it could; going farther and farther back to heap an accumulation of memories that only made her tears flow all the faster. There was her childhood, her happy thoughtless childhood, her indulgent father who spent his money and good humor so generously; the tender grandmother who had replaced her mother. Then before she knew what love was, when she was only dreaming about it, her husband, descending like Jove out of a dazzling cloud, so great, so noble, so superior to all men! He, the supreme one, whom at the time she could not look at, could not talk to without trembling, he loved her! And then the life that followed: a bright life with a bright light shining upon it; even under the fig tree she saw and felt it again.

And then the war. That did not seem now a time of suffering at all. On the contrary, how easy were its struggles and hardships in comparison with what followed! What one suffered then, one suffered gladly, proudly. And afterward, when the family came to the city, the first days, how pleasant all that seemed! And now in detail and more minutely came the events of months, weeks, days, each one greater than years in the farther past. "Harry was right! Harry was right!" she cried to herself. "We are doomed! All has gone from us, even our old selves! What are we now? What friend would recognize us if we had such a thing as a friend left to recognize us? Friendship! We have not so much as a church nor a pastor to whom I could go and say:" —As a dream within a dream so in imagination within imagination, she saw herself speaking to a pastor such as the old pastor of her church had been, to whom the poor and suffering always went in their extremities of grief and suffering—"My husband is at the end of all his resources. He has tried everything. He cannot, in the conditions that exist, make money during the year to pay our house rent, let alone provide food and clothing for us. His old practice has left him, it is of no use to explain how; he will never get a new one. The times make that impossible. What he makes is from writing briefs for lawyers who do not know enough to write them for themselves. The children are being educated for nothing; we cannot pay for their schooling any longer. If it were not for the boys' fishing and hunting, I do not know what we would do for food. I do the cooking and washing. It is a miracle how I get a breakfast and dinner every day and a clean shirt for my husband. I brush and darn his coat and trousers every morning before day, so that he may not know how shabby they are. He dares not spend five cents on tobacco, he uses no carfare but walks every day to his office and back. He really has no office. He cannot pay the rent. He has, in truth, only a place in the office of his former office boy. He will soon have to sell his library which he has held to the last minute. Ah, if we could only prevent that! Great God!" she exclaimed, losing the thread of her imaginary address, "Great God! Prevent that! What will he do without his library? Has not his pride been cut enough already without that? Must he become a dependent upon Tommy Cook for his books too? He never complains, but I know what he suffers. He still pretends that it is all natural, that it will all come right in the end. He is always cheerful, he makes the boys study all the same, he still has the same confidence in his principles. Oh, God! make me suffer if Thou wilt, more and more, but spare him!" And as her love for her husband wrung her heart, she wrung her hands and moved her head wildly in the dim twilight under the trees, as if trying to see some way out of the darkness in her mind.

She had tried to help him in secret and private ways. She had gone one morning to see Benson, the millionaire now, whom as a porter she used to speak to out of mere kindness of heart. She went to see him as if he had been one of the most aristocratic, refined men in the city; went to his house, for, a lady going to a man's office, her husband would never have allowed. She thought it out in the car, what she would say to him and what he would say to her. He would naturally speak of her husband and then it would come to pass as she pictured it in her imagination. She could not go on with the humiliating memory of what she had expected. He had not mentioned her husband's name. He had pulled out his watch before she had more than time to speak and had dismissed her. He said he must go to his office.

And she had written to George Haight, written to him as she thought he would like to be written to according to the past; a letter of old friendship and kindly memories and frank humor over the present. Ah, she could have read between the lines of such a letter, had she received it! She in a rich home in New York impregnably strong in her wealth and he in despair. But she would not allow her imagination to follow this out either. Haight wrote as he talked; acted as he lived. He was not a gentleman as she had always maintained. God had not made him one, that was all. She despised him in her youth and she despised him now.

She had ventured to call on the wives of some of the men whom she and her husband used to know and go to the races with, and to the Boudreaux dinners[9] afterward—the wives of those who had been skilful enough to go up with the times and not down. Some of them fawned upon her and her husband obsequiously enough in the old days of prosperity. Ah! their wives now had put her well back in her place! The place of the wife of a poor man out of whom nothing can be made. A woman can be even meaner than a man!

"Where," she asked herself, "is the generosity to the poor and needy that he used to show, the delicacy, the tact in relieving want?"

At this thought, a whole landscape rose magically before her filled with the people her husband had been kind to in the past. And even now, when he was an object of kindness himself, was he not always finding out those in worse need than he? And if ever, by hook or crook, he gained a small sum of money! was there not always some one to whom a portion of it must go? Some one who even by hook or crook could not gain food for his children, some one always following him "to pick up the stalks of the herbs that he threw away," like the beggar in the Spanish verse.[10]

All these thoughts and memories did not take in her mind the time that it does to read them now. They came and went in a flash like the

9 "Boudreaux dinners" refers to Louis Boudro who was one of several celebrated chefs brought from Paris to Mandeville, across Lake Pontchartrain from New Orleans.

10 The beggar in the Spanish verse: a tale told by Rosaura in Act I of *La Vida es Sueño* by Calderón de la Barca. "They tell of a wise man who one day was so poor that he lived on herbs alone: 'Can there be anyone,' he said to himself, 'poorer and sadder than I?' And when he turned his face he found the answer, seeing that another wise man was picking up the leaves he had thrown away." Trans. Carmen de Zulueta.

thoughts of the drowning. Nervous and sentimental ladies might have spent a day in their beds over a single one of them, but she had only moments to spare, in any one of which she might be discovered, even under the fig tree. It was but a few moments, indeed, from the tears that had forced her to flee into privacy to the moment when she emerged from the tree, calm and composed, strong and determined, with a new project in her brain.

Coralie, the little governess, whom she had pitied and helped and consequently given her friendship to. After thinking that she had seen her in a confectionery, and finding she was mistaken, she had dropped her from her memory. She seemed to have no more need of her since she could be of no further use to her. But now, Coralie could be of use to the friend that had once served her. A ray of light seemed to fall across her mind! How foolish not to have thought of her before! Was her invalid father still alive? her dissipated brother still as much of a sorrow as ever? And was she as usual, still in dire want, needing everything?

How distinctly the figure of the little creole governess came before her, clad in her neat calico dress; the collar and cuffs scalloped in red, her curling, glossy, black hair, in a twist on top of her head, with the pretty fluffy *"accroche-cœurs"* on her temples, her rather small black eyes, always wide open and alert, her dark thin skin well dusted with rice powder, perfumed with the faint fragrance of Tonka beans, her yellow hands, with their long pointed finger nails, that were so useful in her embroidery. Where could any one have found a more gentle, docile, devoted dependent; one more grateful for kindness; more humble in her confession of need for it? Never without a pretty speech in her mouth, a compliment of some sort for somebody! She went about the house inaudibly, with her soft footstep; was never in the way but always within the sound of a question, a bidding. It was marvelous, in truth, to the patroness, how the dependent managed to fix herself so securely in her dependency in the short space of time at her disposal, and how, indeed, the patroness fell herself into a species of dependency upon her, the dependency of the generous upon the object of generosity.

Did she live in the same place? Somewhere, in a back street in a long row of little one-story houses, whose steps came down to the sidewalk, with heavy, green batten shutters. . . . She had gone there once or twice carrying some delicacy for the sick father. An apothecary shop, she remembered in an indistinct way, stood on the corner.

Coralie was the last person to whom she said good-bye when she left the city to go into the war as it was called. The details of the hurried departure (for she had been notified only in the morning that a steamboat would be ready that night to take her out of the United States lines) shot into her mind, with microscopic distinctness. Coralie at least did not lose her head, her hands did not tremble, as she folded and packed. She, herself, forgot everything whenever the bell rang or soldiers marched by in the street.

Armoires and drawers were left standing open, clothing was heaped in confusion on the floor, plates and dishes and silver were left on the dining-table, the sideboard glittered with its crystal, the buffet, with its silver coffee and tea service, and dishes . . . But Coralie was to put all away—she was to care for the carelessness of others. Surely, surely, she must have saved something for her patroness as Tommy Cook had saved for his patron! The silver forks and spoons—how easy to wrap them up and hide them in her trunk! The jewelry, left in the bureau—that little box, that had been so carefully tied up, containing the most precious pieces, to take away, and then forgotten at the last moment—each trinket in it, chain and locket, ring and bracelet resurrected suddenly in her memory as from the grave, perhaps some of it was saved! The officers who came to seize the house may have relented and relaxed in their vigilance.

It was not surprising that Coralie had not found her patroness. Who would have found her in St. Médard? She was waiting, yes, surely, she was waiting until word was sent to her and then—and then . . .

And so in spite of experience and of common sense, Mariana Talbot set out again fresh and buoyant on a new speculation of the imagination; investing in it all the remnant of hope still left in her heart. There was still something to do! Such an experiment as Mademoiselle Coralie, still to be tried!

. . . .

There is nothing mysterious in the ways of war. On the contrary it carries out its designs in the most open manner possible and by the simplest and most natural means, as we find out afterward—always afterward. One of the occupations of peace is to find this out; to see and handle the rude devices by which our undoing in war was accomplished. The surprises of war are indeed much surpassed by those of peace. As has been said, Mademoiselle Coralie received the last good-bye of her patroness, and when the family drove away from their home, of a dark, rainy night, she remained on the front steps, looking after the carriage as long as it was in sight. Then she went into the house, the sole mistress in charge, with what keys could be found in her hand (for housewives were careless in those days about locking up and a key once out of its hole was a key lost and a lock nullified).

The only directions given her, were to do the best she could when the emergency arrived, that is when the officer and soldiers came the next day to seize and take possession; for to leave the city, and join her husband in the Confederacy, instead of remaining and taking a proffered oath of allegiance to the United States, was construed into an act of enmity by the military authority in command.

Waiting for an emergency is a trial to the spirit as well as to the body when one is alone in a great empty house. The servants who had not wished to follow their mistress had been dismissed to their freedom; the only retainer left of the establishment was an old Irish scrubbing-woman, a supernumerary, and the erstwhile spurned and scoffed of the pampered slaves for her poverty. She was to remain and serve Mademoiselle Coralie and while also awaiting the emergency to prepare the house for it; for although housewives of that time were careless about keys, they were not about cleanliness.

Mademoiselle Coralie's trunk stood open in her room. She soon filled it and needed another one to hold all that was given her in the last moments when in the hurried packing there had been a constant discarding of articles and: "Coralie, this ought to be useful to you, Coralie, you had better take that." Ladies *en route* to a war and with the limited amount of luggage allowed by a foe carry only the new and the strong, the serviceable; not lace-trimmed *sacques* nor fragile *déshabillés,* light evening dresses, embroidered petticoats, *fichus,* sashes, hats, feathers, artificial flowers, the follies, fripperies, and extravagances of many a day's amusement in a pretty shop. They were all as welcome to Mademoiselle Coralie, as the bonbons her mouth had been watering for from infancy. And with what zeal can a woman long for pretty clothing? It can become a passion with her, like drinking to those of the opposite sex.

The old Irish woman saw her in the solitude of her room before her mirror, trying on hats and veils, laces, and dresses, when from moment to moment, as she knew, the summons might come that announced the arrival of the emergency. But all over the city, the emergency was knocking at the doors of houses, hastening in one direction and perforce lagging in another. Mademoiselle Coralie had ample time to sip at her own beauty in the glass as she tried on each new seasoning of it. And when she had a pause in that pleasure she sought and found the other trunk needed to hold her recent acquisitions. She chose the largest one that offered, and thence perhaps came the divergence in her life, for there was space left in her new trunk after packing what she rightfully owned and she sought to fill this space—with what?

If one had a great houseful to choose from, what would one select? When one saw, all about, everything one wanted, and remembered the poor, bare rooms awaiting one at the other end of the city and knew that the emergency was on its way that would put an end to choice? In truth, before she had half made her selection she needed another trunk, and having begun to collect what she needed she could not stop. The house was deserted, and in a few hours, minutes perhaps, she would no longer have option or opportunity in the matter. It became a race between her and the emergency, a race for possession. Can it be believed that it took only the time from nightfall, when the family departed, until daylight for Mademoiselle Coralie to be on the street engaging a cart to remove her trunks? She found it as one can generally find a chance to do wrong, no farther than the street corner. Carts were always waiting in sight of every corner then for surreptitious removals. High prices were charged but high prices were paid for such services. Mademoiselle Coralie was accommodated to perfection in man and cart. The former was shrewd, the latter covered; only a half word was necessary to explain the urgency of secrecy and prudence.

About midday the house was formally seized by the military authorities. Mademoiselle Coralie was at her post. She received the officers and transferred the keys to them; her personal trunk was duly examined and she was dismissed.

On reaching home, did not the little governess regret, in looking back upon her night's work, that she had not taken more? What were the blankets, the bed linen, the table linen she had, to those she left behind?—the wines, the liquers? Perhaps, had she known the ease with which the transaction could be accomplished, her poor old Pleyel piano would have been replaced by a grand one. Why leave velvet rugs behind when there was only matting at home? She could have provided herself with books and pictures; and she was fond of both. But if to Mademoiselle Coralie, who could compare what she took with what she left, the covered wagon brought little; to her invalid father, and invalid (from bad habits) brother it was much, far more than they had ever hoped to possess, and they adapted themselves to it as naturally as heirs to a rightful legacy.

The curtains were hung, table covers spread, *bibelots* disposed of, china and glass awarded to the empty sideboard, and Mademoiselle Coralie lost little time in donning some of her new toilettes; the dainty dressing *sacque* over the long, full, trailing half-worn *moiré antique* skirt, or the slightly *chiffoné foulard* (bunches of pink roses on blue and salmon stripes over a white ground) or the pretty silk gauze; white with pale pin-dots of green and sprigs of red roses.

All this, however, turned out to be but a means to an end, not the end in itself. There could be but one end in Mademoiselle Coralie's mind as in the mind of every young woman like her and it is needless to say what that end is, so well is it known, so well was it known even to the *garçons* of the confectioneries where she munched cakes and candies with the officers of the United States army.

Men strive no harder for wealth and fame, old women for immortality, than such young women to get married. Everything else in life is subservient and conduces to that one end, and it may be said that they never cease to work for it, even when they are past it.

Mademoiselle Coralie, having been born in the condition to which so many of her sisters had been reduced by a hard turning of fortune, had naught to catch a husband with but art and good luck, notoriously poor servitors of the poor. Always her sorest envy of the rich had been that they could get married *"quand même"* as she expressed it; no matter who or what they were. And for such benefits as she and those like her expected from marriage, to be married to no matter what or whom, to be married *"quand même"* sufficed. What a luxury in her eyes, would have been the decried *mariage de convenance!* What an announcement, as of the Heavenly Father Himself, the: "I will that you become the wife of so and so. Come! No prayers! No tears! Prepare for your wedding!" Ah, only in novels do poor girls find such royal chances in their path! In truth, Mademoiselle Coralie's poverty was so great and her matrimonial chance so meager that they would have warranted any tyrannical interference of this sort. Thus, her plunder was the fulcrum she needed, only that! Would not Archimedes have stolen one if he could not have gotten it any other way?

Had Mademoiselle Coralie been engendered in the bosom of Napoleon Bonaparte's army she could not have known more about conquerors. Yet, perhaps, it may only have been her five minutes' interview with the young officer who received the keys from her that revealed to her that it rested with no one but herself to change her lot from being governess of children to governess of men. She very soon traveled up from that young officer to the supreme peak of military state and authority and became *gratissima* in all military social gatherings; and before her borrowed plumes had received their second wearing out, she was fledged in feathers of her own growing. Handsome as they were, she wore them well. To the manor acquired, as women have proved for ages, passes just as well in demeanor as to the manor born.

In the course of a year, Mademoiselle Coralie's treasures became her own as much as a kidnapped child would have been. They served her pleasure and furthered her plans. They were shown and cited to substantiate circumstantially the history she had adopted for the satisfaction of her conquerors and herself—a history as current in New Orleans as the little song *"Au clair de la lune"*—of flight from San Domingo, escape from massacre, faithful slaves, etc., etc., etc., and the ensuing, long, patiently-borne straitened circumstances of the *ancien régime* colonial . . . a romance that was new to her audience, who believed and admired it and her for it. Her little *bibelots* of china, silver, and crystal, the bits of antique coral and tortoiseshell, the real lace, and the few precious relics of old jewelry . . . they were her witnesses; she and they, only, knowing the truth.

When she saw her old benefactress in the confectionery, she acted (as we know) on the flash of the moment with presence of mind. She decided promptly what to do furthermore. She kept her drunken brother on guard at the window of the little house with a well-taught story. But nothing came of the recognition in the confectionery, and the times were such that she could not but grow confident in her immunity. She ripened in it.

Then came the day that, sitting at the window, whose shutters were turned to command that view of the street that the passersby were denied of the interior of the house (this precaution was almost a necessity, living as she did with visitors to be admitted and visitors to be turned away plausibly)—sitting at her crack of observation, her quick eyes, trained to be always on the alert, caught sight of a lady, pausing irresolute before the apothecary shop at the corner; hesitating whether to go in and inquire, or hazard a trial inquiry first. The trial was decided upon; and with confident sureness and a wistful smile of anticipation she approached the little house whose wooden steps came down on the pavement, whose shutters were heavy green, as she remembered from the past. The invalid brother it was who answered the knock, he to whom she used to bring wine and delicacies. His drunken, loud voice demanding her business, would have been enough to convince the inquirer of her mistake, to have sent her off in terror; but that was not enough for the sagacious Mademoiselle Coralie. The inquirer was made to ask her questions in order that she might be told that the people had moved away long ago, and nobody in the neighborhood knew where they had gone to.

What did the little governess feel when she heard that gentle voice on the outside of her door? The sweet sorrowful voice, almost breaking from regret and disappointment? When she saw the thin, graceful figure, so well known in old days, in a shabby dress move slowly away, on tired feet? When the kindest friend she was ever to know in this world was turned away with a lie?

Could the benefactress of old have looked into that room she would have seen Mademoiselle Coralie shrinking from her voice as from the voice of a monster listening to the passing away of her footsteps, as to passing away from her of a dragon or ogre.

At the Villa Bella

On such long Summer afternoons the young San Antonio ladies were at their happiest. The roses in their garden were not fonder of warmth and brightness than they; nor did the roses make a richer show of beauty and color than they nor a sweeter dispensation of fragrance—when the time came for them to emerge from their chambers, in their thin, trailing white organdie dresses; all ruffles and lace, breathing the subtile scent of French perfumes around them (Madame Doucelet herself was subtile to extreme about perfumes; the discretion of one as she called it—the indiscretion of another).

Even Madame Doucelet, who strained her eyes to discover defects in the young ladies in order that she might have the pleasure of something to correct, even she, could find no fault with them, externally. As she saw it only original flaws remained; the mistakes of their Creator, who, Madame Doucelet was forced to confess—despite her carefully acquired piety—made more failures than successes in the production of perfect female beauty. The hair, the complexion, the neck and the arms, so naïvely exposed under the thin muslin; the waist, the hands, the feet; the walking, the standing, the sitting; God alone, who knew the truth, would have taken them for the daughters of Tony, the barkeeper, and of the market-woman, downstairs, in her short *cotonnade* skirt and loose *sacque,* sorting onions and garlic.

And, never did the Demoiselles San Antonio sing so well, so near the complete beauty of their voices, as on these long, Summer afternoons, in their fine thin dresses, with their throats bare and free, looking at their reflection in the glass, and listening to their notes, soaring as has been said like escaping birds through the open windows into the soft, fragrant atmosphere outside; to listening admirers on the Levee.

"Love, love, always love," Mademoiselle Mimi would exclaim to herself, wearied of the everlasting amorous refrain of the words and timing her measure to the vocalization above her: "Love, love, always love! *Mon Dieu,* how monotonous!"

She herself was not at her best on these warm afternoons. The perspiration rolled from her red face, and the cadenzas, runs, arpeggios, and trills grew more and more slippery under her moist fingers. The toilettes of expectation, as she called them, suited well the theme of the singing, that seemed to be always seeking, seeking something, until the something was found, and the doctor came into the room.

Madame Doucelet must have noticed it too; but not philosophically as Mademoiselle Mimi did. There was no philosophy in the mind of Madame Doucelet; no theories, no generalizations, no reasoning, no deductions. They were not necessary to such an expert as she. What she saw she saw with her eyes and not with her mind, as Mademoiselle Mimi did; and she had good eyes for seeing a long way off. From the beginning of her official duties, she had seen, with the same eyes that saw a car coming, the equivalent of what was now before her; saw it clearly. She wondered how long it would be before the young ladies themselves saw it. But, as she kept telling herself in private, to ease her restrained feelings, they were stupid in the extreme; stupid for all their beauty and singing.

Mademoiselle Mimi knew when the doctor entered the room, for she felt then as if her accompaniment were the reins of race horses, so hard did the fresh, gushing, thrilling voices pull against it, bounding ahead in all the grace and strength of youth and joyousness through variations, *roulades,* trills, as if they were nothing. Each one at times rising on her toes and throwing her head back so that the pearly notes might be seen throbbing in the pearly throat; each one going back to her seat afterward, and extending foot or curving arm as Madame Doucelet had prescribed; or leaning back in their chairs,—the accomplishment that Lisida possessed to such perfection of charm that her soft hair would always seem to be almost falling from the tall comb to curl and glisten on the bright yellow cushion behind her; the hair that grew so prettily around face and neck.

Past forty, neither tall nor handsome, and with a face of the most ordinary type (but such prosaic indices of personality were the last things noticed or thought of, in the emotion that the doctor knew how to produce; the emotion, as it seemed to the observant Mademoiselle Mimi, that came from the sensation of being called by something unseen, unknown; and of following, following, that call in a charm of mystery and glamor)—it did not need even the presence of the doctor to produce this effect. Long before he made his appearance, the effect began to be felt. Mademoiselle Mimi saw it approaching, with the hour, with the minute; with the sound of the step, the opening of the door; seeing at the same time, each one of the three young ladies recede as it were, further and further back into herself; farther and farther and farther away from her sisters; away from even the consciousness of their presence—each one separately and alone in her own way to follow the call that each one thought she alone heard; following it, out, beyond—personality, self, into forgetfulness of them, of everything, save that she was following something unseen; but felt, moving ahead of her, calling, calling, so that one could not help following when once she had heard it and begun to follow it. This was the effect the doctor knew how to produce upon the young ladies.

All the while, he would be walking leisurely up the Levee toward the Villa Bella. As he approached it, he would look at the fine old iron fence with its interlaced design and brick pillars holding their vases of century plants on high. As he passed up the broad walk, his quick, shrewd, black eyes glanced at the handsome old garden, on each side, with its *parterres* and fountains and palms; and at the white statuettes that appeared as if they were fleeing from pursuit into the dark shadows of the magnolia trees. And as he mounted the steps of the balcony with its pedestals and vases of growing plants, and walked over the black and white marble pavement, his eyes grew ever larger and softer with their gratification at so much that they liked to look upon.

He did not stop to ring the bell; but with the *bonhomie* natural to him in the home of little girls he had known all their lives, in the convent; he entered without ceremony among them as their old doctor; and as such was familiar, almost paternal with them: calling them *"ma jolie brune,"* or *"ma gentille blonde,"* or tapping *"ma petite Lisida,"* on the cheek as he used to do to all the pretty young girls at the convent; throwing himself into one of the great low satin *fauteuils,* leaning his head back to enjoy the music; asking for the *"Air de sommeil"* from l'Africaine, or the Jewel Song from Faust, *"Ah! s'il me voyait ainsi,"* or the *"Ah! Dieu, si j'étais coquette"* from the Huguenots, or the *"Rosine aria"* from the *"Barbier,"* that Lisida sang so deliciously, almost like Patti, he said,—or any other compliment that came to him; for it was all the same to him what they sang. Notwithstanding her educational formula for young ladies, one might as well suspect Madame Doucelet as the doctor of caring for music.

Never forgetting herself an instant, she was always on the alert to fetch a fan, or a glass of *sirop* and water; open or close a window; advance a footstool, or a pillow, as this one or that one of the young ladies needed the attention to accentuate something in attitude or expression that Madame Doucelet thought complimentary. It must indeed have been a pleasure to her to note the efficiency of her delicate training upon the doctor; to note it as she did, with her sharp little eyes peering from the dim veil she managed at certain moments to throw over them.

The eyes of the doctor too, would peep out from under his closed lids, now at the foot, now at the arm, now at the hair! And now, as if at last he could not resist the temptation any longer, he would rise and go from one to the other, Maria, Antonia, Lisida, to make the most insignificant of remarks to her—in the manner of a man who has his way with women.

Mademoiselle Mimi played not more skilfully on the piano than he on the instrument he best liked to practise on. But Mademoiselle Mimi knew nothing of her art in comparison with what he knew of his. No one, without turning one's back on her, could forget Mademoiselle Mimi in her music, as she sat at the piano; but no one remembered the doctor in his performance, although he was before one's eyes.

"Love, love," thought Mademoiselle Mimi playing away. "Love, always love! Do they never get tired of singing of love?" and while meditating thus as usual upon music and love, people and life, she thought she heard—for in truth she did not listen to the singing after the doctor came in, no fear of false notes or measures then—she thought she heard something like an animal crying; but nobody else heard it and she went on playing, until she heard the sound again: something like an animal, but calling.

"It is poor old Aglone," she said to herself. "He is dead; Mr. Talbot is dead." And in a flash she saw it all before her; the little girls with her father in the backyard; the end of life in the front room. "Aglone has come for me; that is her poor old voice, calling from the back, instead of ringing the bell in front, which she won't do, because she despises the rich dagoes."

By this time, she had risen from the piano, seized her gloves and portfolio, and was hurrying out of the salon, making a sign to the doctor, who, quick as she at an inference, followed. They hurried through the hall and down the steps, the back ones, hearing the cries still clearer.

"That stupid Aglone!" exclaimed Mademoiselle Mimi impatiently, this time aloud. The doctor who had no thought of this kind to mislead him arrived before her at the truth. He pushed by her and ran down the steps and found the San Antonio woman trying to give an alarm; to call assistance to her husband who was lying on the brick pavement of the basement.

She had seen him leave the car and watched him as he walked across the open pasture land, into which the evening sun was slanting its rays; still as hot as at midday. But when had Tony ever noticed the sun or its heat? His wife saw he did not walk straight and that he staggered every now and then. She wondered at it, for Tony, whose business it was to make men drunk, did not himself drink. He was too good a barkeeper, as we have seen, for that. He staggered forward, as far as the brick pavement, and there fell like a log and lay unconscious, breathing heavily.

His wife was rubbing his hands, calling to him and crying aloud; the cries of an animal, more than of a woman who has given birth to daughters with beautiful voices. Her daughters, hearing her cries, at last, ran frightened into one of the corners of the salon and crouched down, shutting their eyes and stopping their ears.

Madame Doucelet hastened downstairs, and after one glance at the prostrate body ran for the priest.

By the time the doctor was ready to go to his fever patient, the priest had expedited the departing soul, the heavy breathing had ceased, and Tony lay on his wife's long table in a clean blue shirt with a crucifix on his breast and candles burning at his head.

Ah, Death that, like a skeleton with finger on lip, had been moving so stealthily around the cottage of the Americans, put on a different aspect when he visited the Villa Bella!

When Tony was out on the hot Levee, chaffering with oystermen about his September supply, Death had him then, and could have taken him; but he played with him, like a cat with a mouse; letting him out of his grasp to catch him again. When Tony took the car to go home, and sank into a corner seat; drunken—as the driver and the passengers thought him—Death was watching him all the time, opening and shutting his hand over him. Death let him reach his gate, which the driver of the car had to open for him and help him to get through, watched him staggering toward the house, let him reach the threshold, but there the play closed. Death caught him and this time held him. As the doctor and the priest walked away together from the Villa Bella, the doctor began gently to speak of the San Antonios. Père Philéas, evidently, never imagined before who and what they were; that is, what great wealth they possessed and what good Catholics they were and all else that the doctor unfolded about them with the agile hand of a surgeon at the operating table—the probable and possible consequences to St. Médard of the union of this great wealth with the great faith.

"Tony," proceeded the doctor, from his initial base, "made money, we shall not ask how; he is not accountable to us now. He accumulated a fortune; we ask ourselves wherefore—seeing that as for himself and his wife, for poor, hard-working people they were born and poor, hard-working people they lived."

The doctor shook his head reflectively and improvised (at least the priest thought he improvised) further along.

"He made money and he stored it in one bank and another, and in that safe in his and his wife's room; that safe which her eyes never forgot, not for a moment did she lose sight of. Of course, you do not know it, but that is the reason that she never left the house; never left the place where she could sit and watch the room the safe was in. She is sitting by her husband's body now; but she sits so as to keep watch on that safe. In banks and in that safe he stored it," the doctor reverted to the beginning of his sentence, for he was as neat in his oratory as in his bandaging. "More in the safe than in the banks, for good reasons, doubtless. It is a mistake to suppose that he was only the vulgar common *dago* he appeared to be. No, he was what we call a financier; in truth, *mon Père,* a great financier; and as a priest guards the mysteries of his faith, so the financier guards the mysteries of his wealth. All wealth, like all religions, has its mysteries, its inexplicable . . . But we see now, you see it too, *mon Père*"—the doctor paused significantly. "The daughters in the convent carefully preserved in their piety and innocence . . ." (but the doctor did not dwell upon the convent; for it has always been notorious in St. Médard that the church and the convent cast, at the best, only cross-eyed looks at one another) . . . "storing good intentions while their father stored wealth. And now; just as they reach the perfection of their piety, and the full bloom of their youth and sentiments—ah, when it comes to sentiments, it is only the young who are bold and strong and daring. A young girl can put the strongest man to shame when it comes to expressing sentiments. Yes, the young dare anything that the heart bids, they do not know what prudence, what caution means . . ."

Père Philéas, as he strained his mind to follow intelligently so many flights and so many tracks at once, could not but thank God in his heart, that while he was attending to Tony's soul, and only to that; so wise and sure a ministrant was at hand to think of what seemed in truth of so much more importance—of the wealth that the soul had been obliged to leave; the wealth, which the doctor gave him to infer had been accumulated in a mysterious way for the eventual profiting, so at least the priest construed it, of the church in St. Médard; the poor little church of poor little St. Médard and not of the rich convent of the rich Ursulines as might have been expected.

"What they need now, the San Antonios," the doctor turned in the path and faced the priest impressively, "what they need now, mon Père, after the consolations of the church, is a good lawyer, an honest one. Think of it, money in banks all over the city,—and that safe full of securities, bonds, stocks, banknotes, who knows? Gold and jewels, too, perhaps—and that old woman—she is not really old, she and Tony were both younger than people thought—that old woman who cannot read or write, who never talks, who hardly knows her daughters; while they do not know her at all. I do not know if there is a will. I expect not. Such people do not make wills. (The doctor's sentences grew laconic as he approached the nucleus around which he had been revolving.) If there is no will, you know the public administrator will put his hands to it! and you know who the public administrator is! A negro! And if he were only a negro, no more than that! But in addition there is a politician, a white carpet-bagger, behind the negro; that is what the public administrator is; negro, carpet-bagger; carpet-bagger, negro; that is what our government is from governor down. Negro in front; carpet-bagger behind. Carpet-bagger in front; negro behind. Whew!" the doctor blew out his breath as if that was what he feared Tony's fortune would amount to in the hands of the public administrator.

"A good lawyer could arrange it all . . ."

"A good lawyer," continued the doctor. "A good lawyer! But Madame San Antonio! will she ever think of such a thing? Never. She will sit watching her safe; selling her picayune worth of milk; and onions . . . and . . . Ah, if she had only a good lawyer? A lawyer like our friend over there," he nodded toward the sick room.

"But," began Père Philéas again, with pardonable curiosity. "But . . ."

"A good American lawyer, an American lawyer could manage it, an honest one with a reputation. You know he has a great reputation up-town—our friend over there—one to make a public administrator afraid." The doctor, too astute not to foresee the question and evade it, paid no attention to the attempted interruption.

"She must be protected—the widow—in her rights, and the daughters in their heritage," pursued the doctor, scratching his head reflectively. "What Tony left belongs to them—the fortune he made in spite of the question of how he made it. Money, mon Père, as you of the church know, is like running water, it purifies itself in its course."

"But," the priest eagerly availed himself of the opening afforded by the pause, "if . . ."

"He could manage it; he could save that fortune and put it in the good course, as we may say. It is not the good course the public administrator will put it in, of that we may be sure. And our friend, here . . ." They were close to the gate; he thought a moment, and then went on briskly: "Another lawyer, even one with a great reputation, might do—but there is always danger with lawyers! Even with those of the best reputation at the bar." (Which showed that he knew lawyers at least as well as lawyers knew doctors.) "They have a way of managing a rich succession, of settling them, as the kings of France used to settle an inconvenient personage, by shutting him up in the Bastille and keeping him there until he died. Eh, mon Père?" (He gave an interrogatory end to his phrase in deference to Père Philéas's knowledge of the kings of France.) "The lawyer, he only shuts up the succession in court until he eats it up with his costs, and his fees, and a little borrowed here, and loaned there, at ten, twenty, fifty per cent. profit—not to the estate, oh, no! to their own pocket. . . .

Ah, mon Père, you know this world and you know the other; but you do not know lawyers. But," taking the priest's arm genially, "there are good lawyers to be found if one takes the trouble to look for them. St. Médard has one here—one would say he has brought one here—for the purpose, his purpose—why should we not say it? . . . and a good lawyer could arrange it all as easily as you could a case of disquieted conscience."

Poor Père Philéas! What case of conscience had he ever arranged? From all that he had ever seen of a conscience disquieted or otherwise among his flock, he might affirm that Gascons were born without them. He could frighten them with hell; yes, if that could be called arranging cases of conscience.

They were now at the gate of the cottage and at the end of their conversation. "When you are praying for Tony, Father, pray to St. Médard for his family, that they may not fall into the hands of the wrong lawyer. . . . Good-bye then to their money, and," he reiterated, "their pious intentions."

The good Père Philéas—who was docile enough in listening to advice and accepting assistance in behalf of his parish, and who was not one to shut his eyes to any light held out to him whereby the affairs of St. Médard might be bettered—was not so simple, however, as to be put off any longer when he had an important question to ask; one all the more important since he saw what great results the answer included. Firmly, therefore, he opened his mouth to put his question for the third time. The wily doctor, however, again eluded him for the third time, by anticipating his direct words: "What can one say? As long as there is life, well, there is life . . . a fever?" he shrugged his shoulders. "It kills or it goes away, there is no other alternative." He could not hazard anything more definite, not willing, like the good doctor he was, to run the risk of having his judgment reversed by the event. "Nevertheless," deftly mingling his science with piety: "we doctors must always hope, mon Père, as you good priests must pray, no matter what we fear. Our hopes are our prayers, is not that so?"

After this, he entered the sick room as has been described, himself to pass the night on watch.

"What has happened? But what has happened?" The question gathered slowly in Madame Joachim's mind from a thousand minute sources; imperceptible ones to any mind but one who depends on observation for knowledge. "What has happened?" she repeated continually to herself during the night as she watched the doctor, watching his patient. She could not have explained, to herself, the reasons that formed such a question, any more than she could have explained the reasons of the formation of the clouds that passed over the sky.

But why should she bother herself with explanations? She did not need them as, to quote her own words, she knew what she knew, for the doctor no more carried a face for people to read, than the sky, one for people to understand. So, as the night went on, she asked herself, whenever she looked at him, not "Has anything happened?" but "What has happened?" Finally, as one tired of walking in a dark tunnel, she chose her moment, and softly leaving the room on her fat feet, she went to Cribiche on the gallery.

"My son," she whispered, shaking her head significantly: "Go find out what has happened. Something has happened, run quick and bring me the answer."

The longer Cribiche tarried on his errand the better satisfied she was.

When he returned with his report, she took him to the far end of the gallery. He was breathless with running, and beside himself with amazement, excitement, and exultation at what he had discovered.

"Eh, Madame Joachim! It is Tony! But it is Tony who is dead!"

He closed his eyes and folded his hands on his breast to show how Tony looked; as he told of the crucifix, the clean shirt, the candles; Madame Tony on one side, Madame Doucelet on the other, praying. He had seen it all. "Dead! He is dead! Madame Joachim! Eh, but St. Médard has sense," winking in the dark at her and laughing. "St. Médard knows what he is about! He has sense; he jerked Tony up! And Tony was fooled! Tony was fooled this time!" He laughed and jeered: "Blow, San Antonio! Blow! Blow, San Antonio! Blow," mimicking the prayer of the Italian luggermen to their patron saint when their luggers are becalmed.

"A . . . h H . . . a!" was all that Madame Joachim answered. When she went back to the sick room, she had emerged from her tunnel and was in the clear light of day.

"Lisida, Maria, Antonia, which shall it be? Maria, Antonia, Lisida?" She knew now what the doctor was thinking about, what had made her sure that something had happened.

Madame Doucelet put her young ladies to bed and stayed with them until they went to sleep because they were afraid to be left alone. They did not keep her long, and when she left the room, she left it until the time for the chapel bell of the convent to ring in the morning. Convent girls know how to sleep soundly.

Then, Madame Doucelet went downstairs with her prayer beads. She could pray a night through by a corpse, as easily as her young ladies could sleep upstairs. Her poverty had made many things easy to her; had taught her to be useful to others, in many ways; in superintending funerals and mourning, as well as shopping, and the training of young ladies. And now, she could pray by this corpse almost happily, animated with the perfect faith that makes prayer a satisfaction, that sees clearly as through a glass, that what is prayed for is sure to arrive. Now, she could look ahead as far as she cared to the point where she expected to find—what she never for a moment of the day forgot; what she was ever seeking, ever, without intermission, no matter what she appeared to be doing; what, it had been her vocation to seek, as she would have phrased it, through her long life of poverty—money; the money that would free her henceforth to do nothing but her pleasure, that is—live undisturbed by word or torment in her little room in St. Anthony's alley (where she could almost touch the Cathedral from her window)—go to church and pray. There was nothing now ahead of her to prevent her seeing that point clearly; nothing at all. The abject wife and mother, sitting on the other side of the corpse, too stupid in her grief and bewilderment even to weep; she was nothing to Madame Doucelet, no obstacle in the way of anything she saw ahead of her or the young ladies. The young ladies, far from being an obstacle, were to be her means to the end—the goal in view.

The prayer beads ran faster and faster through her fingers; the prayers, faster and faster through her lips, as she thought of all that was ahead of her and the young ladies—her means to her end. The doctor, himself, was not more absorbed in his meditation than she in hers.

The Turning of the Road

When daylight came into the sick room, and the shaded lamp was extinguished, and the windows were thrown wide open, the patient opened his eyes and followed the doctor going the rounds of his inspection. His lips were too weak to speak, but not his eyes.

"Sonnez clairons, tambours battez!" The loud voice of the commander called his officers to his side. "What did I tell you? He has gone! Our enemy has gone! Ha! We held out too long for him! No, he will not come back! His ultimatum was 'You go or I go'! and we bluffed him! He has gone!"

How prosaic the scene! The shabby little room with its cheap furniture; the disordered bed; the ugly details of illness; the worn, tired wife; Madame Joachim in her rumpled *blouse volante;* the doctor, despite his good qualities as doctor, so loud of voice, so offensive of manner; the children's towzled heads peeping through the door; all so commonplace. But no stage however heroic, no circumstances however resplendent, no personages however exalted, no language ever invented by dramatist, could have produced a moment of greater effect than the one in the little room, among the poor accessories of St. Médard. To one of the personages, Heaven itself could not have opened a more beautiful, radiant vision than what she saw then. And what did she see? Only an ugly little dirt road of a future opening out again before her, twisting its way along, with all its ruts and weeds, its ugliness and roughness; but in it she, the wife, and all the family, trudging along hopefully after their head.

"Ha, ha, ha, ha!" laughed the doctor, over the joke that was to come. "The fever will not be ready for another case soon, I warrant you, but you? Ha, ha, ha!"

They stood around the bed, sipping the cups of black coffee that old Aglone herself brought them. She had sat up all night too, in the kitchen, in case (that responsibility of the cook in the hour of danger) they needed black coffee during the night. Were the doctor the believer he wished the devout to take him for, he must have believed that the Lady of Lourdes, or St. Médard, both being beholden to him, had placed Tommy Cook there on the gallery, in the early morning light, for their own grateful purposes.

And Tommy, after his long night on the gallery, looking at the brilliant August stars above him, and pondering over life and death and the even graver question of people making a living; when he saw the rich succession falling down so close to his patron's hand, like a planet as it were out of the clear heavens; he might have believed something equally as probable, could he have believed in anything but his patron's principles and his own sharpness. This sharpness—as he decided even while the doctor was speaking to him, as he spoke the evening before to the priest—the sharpness must be called into service at once (as it had been called into service to save the library during the war) before Tony's death was known through the papers to a whole bar of greedy lawyers—a rich succession makes even the richest lawyer greedy. After the sharpness had secured the succession, it could wait until the principles were well enough to proceed upon it.

A good succession! That was a prize worth capturing! And not many of that kind sailed the sea of litigation. Such a succession as Tony's would indeed furnish a living to any lawyer, for any number of years, until, at least—and that was all Tommy cared for—the State was restored to her *status quo,* and his patron to his.

The name of Talbot seemed to brighten out again on the office sign as he thought of it, and the faces of the inquiring lawyer friends grow dim. As he and the doctor walked along together, the doctor seemed to be treading on air, so elated was he. And he was not vague as when talking to the priest, but as man to man, clear and to the point. No lawyer could have made himself clearer as he told off the points that rose before his mind: the ignorant widow who would necessarily be always in tutelage to her legal adviser whom in the end she would follow as blindly as she had followed Tony, the daughters as ignorant for all their education as the mother, completely in the hands of an unscrupulous sharper (so he diagnosed the case of Madame Doucelet) who he was confident had already planned to stir up trouble, very likely had a lawyer already engaged for the purpose—and so they came to the house from whose doorpost a long black crape was floating in the breeze.

In the presence of death, what an intruder Time seems to be? Who then pays any regard to him or to his paltry trade of minutes? He is treated, indeed, then, no better than a peddler, singing *"Rabais! Rabais!"* So short a while from daylight! And yet, Tommy found what looked like mid-day at the Villa Bella. Servants were sweeping, Madame Doucelet was throwing open the windows of the salon, and directing the pinning of sheets over the mirrors and the pictures, and the arranging of the chairs. She surely was a woman of inexhaustible enterprise and activity in funeral emergencies. Tony, she had decided, must be brought up into the handsome drawing-room that he had entered so seldom in life, and he must have a funeral that befitted, not his past but the future of his daughters; and no one knew better than Madame Doucelet what that future required in the way of the conventional. Madame Doucelet had, herself, bargained with the undertaker for a handsome coffin with silver handles and silver candelabra to stand around it holding wax candles.

Tony, in short, was to lie like some rich respectable merchant amid the pretty furniture, ornaments, laces, and frescoes, that the old Spaniards had gathered together for their own life and death; a symbol himself, indeed, among symbols!

When the young ladies heard that the coffin was to be brought upstairs and put there just over the hall from their chamber, they were more frightened than ever. They wanted to run out of the house, they frantically pleaded with Madame Doucelet to let them go to the convent for the day, or just for the funeral. They caught hold of her dress and held on to it (strong young women as they were) when she wanted to leave them. Ah, yes! They were frightened enough then to forget even their looking-glasses. When Madame Doucelet did leave them—for she was going over her opportunity with a microscope as it were—they buried their heads in their pillows and stopped their ears to keep from hearing what was going on. There is no power on earth that would have induced them to look out of the windows or doors, so afraid they were of seeing the coffin brought in.

Madame San Antonio was still in her same place, sitting by her husband, almost as dead-looking as he; too stunned still even to replace the flickering candles in the sockets of the candlesticks. The doctor, himself, did it when he came in. But she was not so stupid, and ignorant, as she seemed to be; as the clever people about her thought her to be. She had lived with Tony too long to be that, at least about business. She had been saving and holding on to money too long to forget it, even now. Indeed, she would have sold five cents of milk or eggs that very morning if any one had come to buy.

Tony had been forced to learn much about the law and therefore was not inexperienced in lawyers. How could he be? The law being to the barkeeper what the devil is to the righteous. The path of his money-making had been little more than one long dodging of it; one continuous flight from the pursuing jaws ever seeking to devour him. Many a time—driven to bay by the legal *condottiere* sent by the city against him—he had been forced (though all unknowing in his ignorance) to adopt the distinguished expedient of famous illicit money-getters of picturesque past ages: to subsidize those forces sent against him—the lawyers. He found that he could always afford to pay them more than their clients could. Whatever Tony knew, his wife knew, silent as he was. Wives of such husbands gain their knowledge, as parasites do their growth, from the tree they live on.

Tommy had little trouble with her. He felt with her none of the embarrassment that intimidated him with a lady; lifted by long inheritance of refinement, far, far above his standing ground in human nature. He could talk to her as he could have talked to his mother.

The priest? The doctor? Could St. Médard himself have opened the old woman's safe any easier than he did? Or have confided more trustfully to him the handling of the papers whereby the precious succession was to be secured from the hands of one who would not put it in the good way?

It has been explained that the one grief of the barkeeper and his wife was the loss of a son, whose life was a trellis upon which they were training their affection and ambition to climb, and how, in their despair at his death, they let their affection and ambition grovel henceforward on the ground; and how in their ignorance, they could never understand why the son whom they loved, and wanted, should be taken from them; and how the daughters they did not want should live. One cannot speak surely about a father; but a mother—even though she spend her life groveling on the earth alongside of a husband—when she loses a son that she loves she loses him not from her heart; his life is never dissevered from the life that conceived him. From year to year she follows his growth, from birthday to birthday counts his age; and her best dream is that she is still carrying him in her arms, suckling him at her breast. And when in after life she meets one of the age the son might be; who talks to her mayhap in the voice he might have had; who takes her hand, her onion-smelling hand, as he might have done; in her loneliness, with only three fine daughters upstairs . . . (But all this is, it must be, conjectural) . . . In sober truth, all that can be said by one who knows only the outside of a woman's or a mother's heart is that as easily as the undertaker's men lifted the corpse and laid it in the coffin, so was the corpse's succession lifted by Tommy and laid where no other lawyer but his patron could get it; and well out of the reach of the public administrator.

And by the time that Tony's hearse had accomplished its slow journey to the Louisa Street Cemetery, Tommy had towed his prize safely to the office and anchored it in the armoire of litigation. And Tony, who had laid up treasures nowhere but on earth, entered the other world as great a pauper as he had entered this one.

"And now," said Tommy succinctly to himself, as he sat in the office, waiting for the appearance of the kind inquirers of his patron's health, "now, the country *is* safe."

VIII HISTORY

FEW WOMEN of the nineteenth century were so devoted to the study of history as Grace King. As novelist and story-writer she was always conscious that her role was that of realist and social historian rather than author of romances. As historian she saw herself as a scholar who tried to earn the respect of other professionals while she attracted laymen to the vitality of history.

The two selections that follow illustrate one of the great interests of Grace King's life—the early history of New Orleans and the Louisiana Territory. They record events of importance in the history of the city and the nation: the Louisiana Purchase and the battle of New Orleans. In writing of these events Miss King produced an effect very different from that of her fiction. Her stories are almost invariably feminine: they concern women usually and are told from the point of view of women. But it would be difficult to divine the female mind behind her spirited accounts of historical events. She presents them with the immediacy of contemporary journalism; she intends to give the reader the sense of her presence at the event as observer. She is usually more interested in the visual events of history than their more abstract motivation. In her account of the battle of New Orleans, "The Glorious Eighth of January," she assumes the power of an omniscient narrator, moving with the agility of Tolstoy on the battlefields of *War and Peace.* With complete familiarity with her terrain she passes with ease from the events within the city of New Orleans to the positions of the various units preparing for the battle. Her dramatization makes judicious use of sensory appeals, but there is no question of her historical authenticity.

The following are the copy-texts on which the selections are based: "The Old Cabildo of New Orleans," *Harper's Magazine*, CII (January, 1901), 283–87; "The Glorious Eighth of January," Chapter XII in *New Orleans, the Place and the People* (New York, 1895), 211–51.

The Old Cabildo of New Orleans

It will be one hundred years, come December 20, 1903, since the old Cabildo held within its walls that great event of its history, the official ceremony of the transfer of Louisiana by France to the United States.

The new Cabildo, it was then, fresh from the munificent hand of Don Andres Almonaster, the Alférez Real.[1] The great stone stairway, easy and majestic of ascent, now blackened and hollowed by a century's footfalls, was then clean and smooth; the noble front, now worn and weather-stained, was then virginal in its beauty! A goodly domicile it was held to be, and indeed it was, for the Very Illustrious Cabildo, and no mean-looking Capitol for that domain, superb though it was, that twice in its council-chamber was signed away to different powers, like a dower to a grasping spouse. Twenty days before the eventful December date the French had taken possession of the city and official possession of the territory. They had raised their flag in the Place d'Armes, where the Spanish colors had waved, as the populace were wont to believe, in secure and proud dominion of the earth and sky of Louisiana; they had bowed out of the Cabildo its whole "Illustrious" company of councillors—Alcaldes, Alguacils, Regidores, Escribanos, the Contador, the Alférez Real, the Gobernador;[2] had closed the huge tome of the Spanish Register, the ponderous plodding chronicle of municipal deliberations and decisions for thirty-seven years past—proceedings they could hardly be called—and they had opened a new volume in the name and language and under the date of the French Republic.

Between one volume and the other, as we see them before us, stretches the whole extent of the French Revolution—the whole space of difference between imperial Spain and republican France. The last page of one tome marks the crawling progress of the city; the first page of the other the colossal stride of a Power through the world—his Catholic Majesty and Napoleon Bonaparte.

1 Don Andres Almonaster y Roxas was "Alférez Real" or royal standard-bearer, a lifetime honor with privileges to sit at meetings of the council board.

2 *Alcaldes:* justices of the peace; *alguacils:* constables; *egidores:* prefects; *escribanos:* notaries; the *contador:* the accountant; the *gobernador:* the governor.

The Supreme Court of the State of Louisiana holds its sessions to-day in the room where the Very Illustrious Cabildo held theirs—in the room where the two Transfers took place. Busts of former Chief Justices on high pedestals around the tribune, and, thick hung along the walls, portraits of eminent jurists who have passed away, suggest, with some solemnity, a watch and guard that is more than metaphorical—they represent, and represent well, that American domination into whose keeping Bonaparte ceded the great territory—the territory which he predicted would affirm forever the power of the United States, and give England a rival that sooner or later would lower her pride.

The 20th of December fell upon a Tuesday in 1803, a day that dawned with such radiance, and in such contrast with the dull, dark Wednesday upon which the French took possession, that the new proprietors, the Americans, claimed it as a particular compliment from Heaven to their flag—and so demeaned themselves. As they did not know that bright and beautiful days are the common coin of the climate, the Americans might have been pardoned their bragging and strutting; but they were not pardoned; on the contrary, their conduct and language were considered so unmannerly by the polite Creoles that deductions unfavorable even to the Constitution of the United States were drawn from them; and although the chronicles of the time do not mention the fact, no doubt more than one Creole gentleman, and all the Creole ladies, remarked, with ill-concealed disdain, that if old Don Andres could have foreseen what ceremony his stately edifice was called upon to subserve, only five years after his death, he would have lifted not a finger towards repairing the ruin and desolation of the fire sent by God to punish the city for its sins, as the priests accounted for it, on Good-Friday, 1784. Indeed, if, lying over there under the altar of the Cathedral (which he had also built and presented to the city at the same time of affliction)—if, lying over there in his coffin, he could even now dream what was going on outside, no matter whether the prayers for the repose of his soul were said, as compounded for with the Church, every Saturday afternoon at the ringing of the Angelus, was there a prayer in the Church that could ease him of his spite?

The crowd began gathering along the route of the procession, Chartres Street and the Place d'Armes,[3] betimes: not that this means more than

3 Chartres Street still exists; the Place d'Armes, in front of the Cabildo and the Cathedral, is now Jackson Square.

the idlest curiosity and wanton excitement, for all the city rose by daylight in that day, and the city all lay within easy stone's-throw of the Cabildo, securely within the Ramparts raised by the careful government to guard against the political accidents that befell so many promising governments in that revolutionary period; tumblings of children out of bed at night—to speak as the Spaniards did. Every household within the Ramparts could be, and in fact was, timed by the Cathedral, timed both for here and for hereafter. Outside the Ramparts it was different. There lay the Faubourg St. Marie, the American quarter, that rough, rude, boisterous, riotous, irrepressible settlement of flatboat men from the Ohio and upper Mississippi, with their congeners from all over the Western country, who, with their wild talk about rights of deposit and ownership of the mouth of the Mississippi, had kept the Spanish Governor in a constant state of preparation for attack, and the President of the United States in a state of preparation for their filibustering capture of the city from Spain, or a no less filibustering capture of the West by Spain from the United States. It was the Faubourg St. Marie, the American settlement, that handful of squatters, that, in truth, forced the hand of Jefferson, and making the cession of New Orleans the critical political necessity of the hour, had secured it.

At nine o'clock the militia began to arrive and form in the Place d'Armes. The Colonial Prefect, Citizen Pierre Clément Laussat, stood upon the central balcony of the Cabildo to look at them. Robin, the genial historian and traveller, was in New Orleans at the time, and he relates that upon that eventful morning he accompanied Laussat to the Cabildo and stood upon the balcony with him. From that spot then, as from the roof of the building to-day, the eye could sweep unobstructed up and down the river and take in the crescent curve of the bank and all its magnificent possibilities of harborage. Across the Place d'Armes, at the government landing, and along the levee to the right and the left, lay a full complement of vessels loading and unloading. Where the vessels could not be seen, there rose their masts, decked for the day in gala bunting. On each side of the Place d'Armes ran Don Andres' handsome row of buildings, two-storied, with iron-balustraded balconies and high, pointed, red-tiled Spanish roofs—the choice location of the city for trade, on the ground-floor, for residence above. Along the line of the levee could be seen the roof-trees, thick and close, of the warehouses and counting-houses and shops—wholesale and retail—the growth of healthy, vigorous trade. And the Cabildo itself was hardly handsomer than some of the residences about it—hôtels, as they were rightly called, of the wealthy citizens, with their *portes cochères,* courtyards, pigeon-houses, cellars, arching doorways, and marble mantels brought from Italy, and furniture imported from wherever in Europe it was made most luxuriously.

Robin writes that, pending the arrival of the American commissioner, Laussat and he walked up and down the balcony, conversing upon the event about to take place, their eyes, we dare say, losing naught to be seen; gathering in the city not only in general, but also in detail: the motley composition of the crowd, the gallant bearing of the gentlemen militia, the gayly dressed ladies on the balconies surrounding the square, the radiant blue and white sky overhead, and under the sky, so close to it as almost to seem, what it was so often described to be in the fulsome eulogy of the day, a heavenly meteor, the Tricolor, waving proudly, gracefully, beautifully, serenely, at home. It is easier for pride to abandon a territory than to lower a flag, as Laussat felt keenly that day. He knew what Bonaparte only pretended to know—the value of what France was giving away. Robin discreetly does not publish their conversation; but Laussat did not conceal his sentiments in his despatches. "The Americans," he wrote, "have given fifteen millions of dollars for Louisiana; they would have given fifty millions rather than not possess it. . . . In a few years the country as far as the Rio Brazos [4] will be in a state of cultivation. New Orleans will then have a population of from thirty to fifty thousand souls, and the country will produce sugar enough to supply America and part of Europe. . . . What a magnificent New France have we lost! . . . The people are naturally gentle, though touchy, proud, and brave. They have seen themselves rejected for the second time from the bosom of their mother-country. . . . Their interpretation of the cession, and their comments on it, show too clearly the extreme bitterness of their discontent. . . . Nevertheless, they have become tolerably well disposed towards passing under the new government. . . . There are advantages in the Constitution of the United States of which it will be impossible to prevent them from experiencing the benefit. . . . And being once freed from her colonial fetters, it would be unnatural to suppose that Louisiana would ever willingly resume them. . . ."

At half past eleven o'clock was heard the impatiently awaited cannon-

4 Rio Brazos is in eastern Texas, west of present-day Houston.

shot that announced the marching of the Americans from their camp above the city. Another shot announced their entrance into the city through the Tchoupitoulas Gate. Then came from the forts a salute of twenty-four guns. As twelve o'clock was ringing, the Americans filed in front of the Cabildo; Governor Claiborne and General Wilkinson, the American commissioners,[5] riding side by side, followed by (the enumeration makes it appear small now, but in the vista of time and under the glowing light of tradition it was indeed a grand procession) fourteen dragoons in red uniforms, four pieces of artillery served by forty cannoneers, two companies of infantry, one of carabineers, with an escort of grenadiers from the city's militia.

The Americans aligned themselves in the square opposite the French soldiers. The American commissioners, dismounting, ascended the Cabildo stairs and entered the great council-chamber, where the Colonial Prefect awaited them, surrounded by his staff and all the dignitaries of the city, civil, military, and ecclesiastical, by Spanish officers, and by all the notable citizens of the place. Laussat led the way to a chair of state with a smaller and lower chair on each side. He took the seat of honor; Claiborne placed himself on the right, Wilkinson on the left. The secretaries of the commission stood in front.

The ceremony was opened by the French commissioner, who in a few words stated the object of the assembly. The Treaty of Cession was then read by the secretaries, in English and in French. Laussat read aloud his credentials, those empowering him to receive the colony from the Spanish authorities, and those directing him to transfer the territory to the agents commissioned by the United States to receive it, after which Governor Claiborne read aloud the credentials empowering him to receive the territory from the agent appointed by the French government to deliver it. Thereupon Laussat made the formal announcement that he put the United States in possession of the lands, countries, and dependencies of Louisiana in conformity with the articles of the treaty, under the same limits and conditions as he had received them by the Treaty of St. Ildefonso.[6] Taking the keys of the city, he presented them to the American commissioner, and turning to the assemblage in front of him, pro-

5 William Charles Coles Claiborne (1775–1817) was governor of the territory of Orleans (1804–12) and of the state of Louisiana until 1816. James Wilkinson (1757–1825) was governor of Louisiana territory (1805–1806).

6 Treaty of San Ildefonso (1800), by which Louisiana was secretly returned by Spain to France.

nounced these words: "I declare, in virtue of the powers with which I am invested, and the commission with which I am charged by the First Consul, that all citizens and inhabitants of Louisiana are from this moment relieved from their oath of fidelity to the French Republic." He then changed places with the American commissioner.

Governor Claiborne, on taking his seat, offered the people his congratulations on the event which, he said, had irrevocably fixed their political existence, and no longer left it open to the caprices of chance, assuring them that the United States would receive them as brethren, and that they would be protected in the enjoyment of their liberty, property, and religion; that their commerce would be favored, their agriculture encouraged. The secretaries then read aloud the procès-verbal of the transfer, in French and in English. After these papers were signed and sealed by the commissioners, and reciprocally interchanged, the ceremony was declared over, and there was a movement of the audience towards the front of the building.

The commissioners walked out upon the central balcony and stood together. Their appearance was the signal for the lowering of the French flag. Slowly, trembling, fluttering, it descended. The flag of the United States as slowly ascended. When the two came together, midway of the staff, they paused a moment, mingling their colors and their folds. A cannon-shot broke the silence, and it was followed by a hoarse roar from guns all over the city—from the forts, from the ships, from the pieces in the square; the soldiers fired their muskets, the men shouted and tossed their hats, the women on the balconies waved their handkerchiefs—whether saluting the flag going down or the flag going up is not certain; but certain it is the flag that went up and the flag that went down, each went up and went down in the heart of every onlooker.

A French officer standing at the foot of the standard received the Tricolor in his arms, and with all its folds around him, silently strode away with it. Men fell in, one by one, behind him as at a funeral procession; the American soldiers presented arms as they passed; the citizens in the street uncovered before them and made way for them.

The United States banner, despite all efforts to relieve it, hung for a moment embarrassed from the peak of the staff, and an anxious quiet fell over the Americans as they gazed upwards at it; but by degrees the great folds slowly unwound, caught the breeze, and like a flower burst open against the sky. Then such shouts arose from the Americans; they tossed their hats so wildly, and their fifes and drums played their best so loudly, that that moment at least was theirs.

The Colonial Prefect in a few gracious words presented his successor to the people, and the American Governor, the first American Governor of the Territory, made what may be truly called an inaugural address. "Louisianians, my fellow-citizens. . . ." His language was unintelligible to all but a few, as unintelligible as the government he praised and proposed to inaugurate. The Cabildo itself was not more unresponsive to the patriotic eloquence flowing from its balcony than was the crowd upon whom it flowed. But a hundred years have made a difference. As for the eloquence that has followed Claiborne's from the Cabildo, did words wear away marble like footsteps, the outside of that old building would be more worn than its stairway; did language flow not merely in metaphor, its old walls would be furrowed and rilled like mountain-sides by torrent streams.

Since 1803 time has passed lightly over the stolid building, lightly over the old quarter. As in other cities, the worst ravages have been caused not by time but by the architects; and as in other cities, the architects called their operations a renaissance. It was not time that changed the front of the Cathedral, that replaced the pointed Spanish roofs of the Cabildo with French mansards, and tricked out the old buildings of Don Andres' row in the furbelows of a new régime. It was not time that cut up the fine old martial square into parterres for flowers, and Schilinger-paved[7] the gravel walks—the pleasant evening promenade of so many generations of saunterers. Nor can we reproach time with the long low railroad warehouse that shuts out the view of the river from Cathedral and Cabildo—a view that they owned, we might say, by right divine.

The old quarter was "reborn" between 1830 and 1850; and reborn, it was fondly hoped and proclaimed, American; which then, as now, meant enterprising, progressive, rich. It was a strenuous effort on the part of the artistic French and Spanish Creoles; and a praiseworthy effort, a real step towards progress, it was considered by the appreciative Americans, who applauded and encouraged, and we may say practised, the renaissance incessantly then, as they still do in their own peculiar domain—the American quarter of the city, as it is called by the Creoles;—practising every imaginable step architecturally away from the original taste and

7 Schilinger-paved probably means "asphalt-paved."

temperament of the city, and towards what they, rightfully or wrongfully, call Northern ideals. But as the young Creoles of to-day anglicize their names and forswear their language to Americanize themselves with no better result than to accentuate their ineradicable foreign charm, so the "slang" and brusque manners imposed upon the Creole quarter by the well-meaning architects bring only into higher relief the vestiges that remain there of foreign ideals—the massive dignity of proportion, the noble lines, the graceful archings, the winsome coquetry of balcony and windowseat, the fragile elegance of hand-wrought iron-work.

In view of the approaching centennial anniversary of the cession of Louisiana, the Louisiana Historical Society is proposing that a fitting way of celebrating the great historical event by city and State would be to provide for the preservation of the fine old building in which the actual transfer took place; to maintain it as a perpetual memorial of the 20th of December, 1803, by transforming it into and endowing it as a historical museum, where could be stored and treasured such mementos of the past as it is pleasurable, and needful too, for a wise country to carry into the future.

The Cabildo, pensioned off and cared for, would be the State's veteran, living to all time, an immortal old Granther in his arm-chair telling his stories, over and over again, unwearily to the children clustering about his knee.

The Glorious Eighth of January

In the early summer of 1814, the reverberating news of the fall of Napoleon Bonaparte, and of his abdication at Fontainebleau, shook the city to its foundations; and the first instinctive impulse of the people was a passionate outbreak of love to the mother country. The city became French as it had not been since the days of Ulloa.[8] Popular feeling frenzied and raved in talk. In the family, in the coffee-houses, in the new exchanges, the refugees from every nation and every political party, the new Americans and the ancient Louisianians, as they were called, assembled in

8 Antonio de Ulloa (1716–95) was sent to New Orleans in 1766 as governor of Louisiana after the cession of the territory by France to Spain. He left after an uprising in 1768.

their different coteries, to throw, very much as they do now, their tempers, prejudices, and passions into political opinions.

There was no doubt that victorious England, her hands at last liberated, would give the United States a demonstration more characteristic of her military ability than she had exhibited up to this time in the war between them. The report came that, as a condition of peace with France, England would demand the retrocession of Louisiana to Spain, who had indignantly protested at Napoleon's sharp sale of it to the United States; and, trailing after this report, came from Spanish officers in Havana and Pensacola, to friends in Louisiana, and even from the governor of Pensacola, and from the Spanish minister in Washington, expressions of belief that Spain would take up arms to repossess herself of her former colony.

Hardly had this been digested colloquially, when tidings arrived of the presence of British ships in the Gulf, and the landing of British regulars at Pensacola and Apalachicola, where, with the passive, if not active, assistance of the Spanish authorities, they were rallying the Indians, enlisting and uniforming them into companies. Then came Lafitte's communications from Barataria.

It must be acknowledged, if ever there were dreams to give a city pause, New Orleans had them then and there. Even now one is chary of publishing all the national weaknesses that, in this crucial moment, the city's examination of conscience revealed. There were no friends of England in the community, but there were many and ardent ones of Spain, and as for the French Creoles, the United States had been at best, in their eyes, but a churlish and grudging stepmother to Louisiana, apparently intent only on getting back the worth of her money paid for the colony. And besides, the government at Washington, with its Capitol burnt and its neighbourhood ravaged by a force not one-fourth as large as the one preparing against New Orleans, offered anything but an inspiring example. And there was slavery. The English, by a mere proclamation of emancipation, could array inside the State against the whites an equal number of blacks and produce a situation from which the stoutest hearts recoiled in dismay. The neighbouring South was too weak in population and resources to count upon for any appreciable help. There was only the one hope, but it was a good one, in the West, the brawny, indomitable West! So long as the Mississippi flowed through its great valley to the Gulf, New Orleans felt confident that the West would never leave her without a companion in arms to fight against foreign subjugation.

The federal government stationed four companies of regulars in the city, ordered out the full quota of the militia of the State, one thousand men, to be held in readiness, put Commodore Patterson in charge of the naval defences, and appointed Major-General Andrew Jackson to take command in the threatened section. After that, it washed its hands of the whole affair.

In September the British opened their campaign, as the military *quidnuncs* in the city had predicted they would, by an attack upon Fort Bowyer,[9] which, if taken, would give them command of Mobile Bay, a solid position on the Gulf, and an invaluable basis of operation against New Orleans. But the new general-commandant, who, so far from being a military *quidnunc,* had only the military training of rough and tumble, hand-to-hand fighting with Indians, forestalled the design of the British with all the prescience of the most practised tactician. He threw a handful of men into Fort Bowyer, one hundred and thirty, with twenty pieces of cannon, and these held it against the four British ships, with their ninety guns and the six hundred marines, and regulars, and two hundred Indians that came against it. The elated Jackson sent the news of this success from Mobile with two ringing proclamations to the Louisianians, one to the white and one to the free coloured population, treating his foes with fine and most inspiring contempt:—

"The base, perfidious Britons have attempted to invade your country. They had the temerity to attack Fort Bowyer with their incongruous horde of Indians, negroes, and assassins; they seem to have forgotten that this fort was defended by free men," etc., etc. After which, to give the Spaniards a lesson in the laws of neutrality, he attacked and took Pensacola.

It was on the morning of the 2nd of December, 1814, as our preferred chronicler of this period, Alexander Walker, relates that General Jackson and escort trotted their horses up the road that leads from Spanish Fort to the city. On arriving at the junction of Canal Carondelet[10] and Bayou St. John, the party dismounted before an old Spanish villa, the residence of one of the prominent bachelor citizens of the day, where, in the marble-paved hall, breakfast had been prepared for them; a breakfast such as luxury then could command from Creole markets and cooks, for a

9 Fort Bowyer, original name of Fort Morgan, on a neck of land at the entrance of Mobile Bay.

10 Canal Carondelet was perhaps the first artificial waterway constructed in the territory of Louisiana. It was built to connect New Orleans with Lake Pontchartrain through Bayou St. John in 1794.

guest whom one wished to honour. But, the story goes, the guest of honour partook, and that sparingly, only of hominy. This reached a certain limit of endurance. At a whisper from a servant, the host excused himself, left the table and passed into the antechamber. He was accosted by his fair friend and neighbour, who had volunteered her assistance for the occasion.

"Ah, my friend, how could you play such a trick upon me? You asked me to prepare your house to receive a great general. I did so. And I prepared a splendid breakfast. And now! I find that my labour is all thrown away upon an old 'Kaintuck' flatboatman, instead of a great general with plumes, epaulettes, long sword, and moustache."

Indeed, to female eyes, trained upon a Galvez, a Carondelet, a Casa Calvo, Andrew Jackson must have represented indeed a very unsatisfactory commandant-general. His dress, a small leathern cap, a short blue Spanish cloak, frayed trousers, worn and rusty high-top boots, was deficient; and, even for a flatboatman, threadbare. But his personality, to equitable female eyes, should have been impressive, if not pleasing: a tall, gaunt, inflexibly erect figure; a face sallow, it is true, and seamed and wrinkled with the burden of heavy thought, but expressing to the full the stern decision and restless energy which seemed the very soul of the man; heavy brows shaded his fierce, bright eyes, and iron-grey hair bristled thick over his head.

From the villa the party trotted up the Bayou road to its intersection with the city, where stood a famous landmark in old times, the residence of General Daniel Clarke, a great American in the business and political world of the time. Here carriages awaited them and a formal delegation of welcome, all the notabilities, civil and military, the city afforded, headed by Governor Claiborne and the mayor of the city, a group which, measured by after achievements, could not be considered inconsiderable either in number or character.

General Jackson, who talked as he fought, by nature, and had as much use for fine words as for fine clothes, answered the stately eloquence addressed him, briefly and to the point. He had come to protect the city, and he would drive the enemy into the sea or perish in the attempt. It was the eloquence for the people and the time. As an interpreter repeated the words in French, they passed from lip to lip, rousing all the energy they conveyed. They sped with Jackson's carriage, into the city, where heroism has ever been most infectious, and the crowd that ran after him through the streets, to see him alight, and to cheer the flag unfurled from his headquarters on Royal street, expressed not so much the conviction that the saviour of the city was there in that house, as that the saviour of the city was there, in every man's soul.

That evening the "Kaintuck" flatboatman was again subjected to the ordeal of woman's eyes. A dinner party of the most fashionable society had already assembled at a prominent and distinguished house, when the host announced to his wife that he had invited General Jackson to join them. She, as related by a descendant, did what she could under the trying circumstances, and so well prepared her guests for the unexpected addition to their party, that the ladies kept their eyes fixed upon the door, with the liveliest curiosity, expecting to see it admit nothing less than some wild man of the woods, some curious specimen of American Indian, in uniform. When it opened and General Jackson entered, grave, self-possessed, martial, urbane, their astonishment was not to be gauged. When the dinner was over and he had taken his leave, the ladies all exclaimed, with one impulse, to the hostess: "Is this your red Indian! Is this your wild man of the woods! He is a prince."

From now on the city was transformed into a martial camp. Every man capable of bearing arms was mustered into service. All the French *émigrés* in the community volunteered in the ranks, only too eager for another chance at the English. Prisoners in the Calaboose were released and armed. To the old original fine company of freemen of colour, another was added, formed of coloured refugees from St. Domingo, men who had sided with the whites in the revolution there. Lafitte, notwithstanding the breaking up and looting of his establishment at Barataria, made good his offer to the State, by gathering his Baratarians from the Calaboose and their hiding places, and organizing them into two companies under the command of Dominique You[11] and Beluche. From the parishes came hastily gathered volunteers, in companies and singly. The African slaves, catching the infection, laboured with might and main upon the fortifications ordered by Jackson, and even the domestic servants, it is recorded, burnished their masters' arms and prepared ammunition, with the ardour of patriots. The old men were formed into a home guard and given the patrol of the city. Martial law was proclaimed. The reinforcements from the neighbouring territories arrived: a fine troop of horse from Mississippi, under the gallant Hinds; and Coffee,[12]

11 Dominique You was Jean Lafitte's ablest and most famous lieutenant.

12 General John Coffee was a friend of Jackson and commander of a force of Tennessee militiamen.

with his ever-to-be-remembered brigade of "Dirty Shirts," who after a march of eight hundred miles answered Jackson's message to hasten, by covering in two days the one hundred and fifty miles from Baton Rouge to New Orleans. At the levee, barges and flatboats landed the militia of Tennessee, under Carroll.[13]

On the 10th of December, eight days after Jackson's arrival in the city, the British fleet entered Lake Borgne. In the harbour of Ship Island, in the pass between it and Cat Island, out to Chandeleur Islands, as far as the spyglass could carry, the eye of the look-out saw, and saw British sails. Never before had so august a visitation honoured these distant waters. The very names of the ships and of their commanders were enough to create a panic. The Tonnant, the heroic Tonnant, of eighty guns, captured from the French at the battle of the Nile, with Vice-Admiral Sir Alexander Cochrane and Rear-Admiral Codrington; the Royal Oak, seventy-four guns, Rear-Admiral Malcolm; the Ramilies, under Sir Thomas Hardy, Nelson's friend; the Norge, the Bedford, the Asia, all seventy-four gunners; the Armide, Sir Thomas Trowbridge; the Sea Horse, Sir James Alexander Gordon, fresh from the banks of the Potomac,—there were fifty sail, in all carrying over a thousand guns, commanded by the *élite* of the British navy, steered by West Indian pilots, followed by a smaller fleet of transports, sloops, and schooners. It seemed only proper that with such ships and such an army as the ships carried, a full and complete list of civil officers should be sent out, to conduct the government of the country to be annexed to His Majesty's Dominions,—revenue collectors, printers, clerks, with printing presses and office paraphernalia. Merchant ships accompanied the squadron to carry home the spoils; and even many ladies, wives of the officers, came along to share in the glory and pleasure of the expedition. "I expect at this moment," remarked Lord Castlereagh, in Paris, almost at the exact date, "that most of the large sea-port towns of America are laid in ashes, that we are in possession of New Orleans, and have command of all the rivers of the Mississippi Valley and the Lakes, and that the Americans are now little better than prisoners in their own country."

The city must indeed have appeared practically defenceless to any foe minded to take it. There was no fortification, properly speaking, at the Balise.[14] Fort St. Philip, on the river, below the city, was small, out of re-

13 General William Carroll (1788–1844) was a friend of Jackson and later governor of Tennessee (1829–41).

14 The Balise was a harbor station near the mouth of the Mississippi, 107 miles south of New Orleans.

pair, badly equipped and poorly munitioned. Back of the city there was pretty, picturesque, Spanish Fort, a military bauble; a hasty battery had been thrown up where Bayou Chef Menteur joins Bayou Gentilly, and further out, on the Rigolets, was the little mud fort of Petites Coquilles (now Fort Pike). As every bayou from lake to river was, in high water, a high road to the city, these had been closed and rafted by order of the government, and, by the same token, Bayou Manchac has remained closed ever since.

Vice-Admiral Cochrane promptly commenced his programme. Forty-five launches and barges, armed with carronades and manned by a thousand soldiers and sailors, were sent to clear the lakes of the American flag.

What the Americans called their fleet on the lakes consisted of six small gunboats, carrying thirty-five guns, commanded by Lieutenant T. ap Catesby Jones.[15] These had been sent by Commodore Patterson to observe the English fleet, and prevent, if possible, the landing of their troops. If pressed by a superior force, they were to fall back through the Rigolets, upon Fort Petites Coquilles. In obeying his orders, Jones in vain tried to beat through the Rigolets, with the current against him; his boats were carried into the narrow channel between Malheureux Island and Point Clear, where they stuck in the mud. Jones anchored therefore in as close line as he could across the channel, and after a spirited address to his force of one hundred and eighty-two men, awaited the attack.

It was about ten o'clock of a beautiful December morning. The early fog lifted to show the British halting for breakfast, gay, careless, and light-hearted as if on a picnic party. The surface of the lake was without a ripple, the blue heavens without a cloud. At a signal the advance was resumed. On the flotilla came in the beautiful order and in the perfect line and time with which the sturdy English oarsmen had pulled it through the thirty-six miles without pause or break, from Ship Island, each boat with its glittering brass carronade at its prow, its serried files of scarlet uniforms and dazzling crest of bayonets, and the six oars on each side, flashing in and out of the water.

The American boats lay silent, quiet, apparently lifeless. Then, a flash, a roar, and a shot went crashing through the scarlet line. With an answer

15 Thomas ap Catesby Jones (1789–1858) was a young naval officer who would later gain fame for an unauthorized capture of Monterey, Calif. (1842).

from their carronades, the British barges leaped forward, and clinched with the gunboats. It was musket to musket, pistol to pistol, cutlass to cutlass, man to man, with shouts and cries, taunts and imprecations, and the steady roar throughout of the American cannon, cutting with deadly aim into the open British barges, capsizing, sinking them; the water spotting with struggling red uniforms.

Two of the American boats were captured, and their guns turned against the others, and the British barges closing in, the American crews one by one were beaten below their own decks and overpowered. By half-past twelve the British flag waved triumphant over Lake Borgne.

The British troops were forwarded in transports from the fleet to the Ile des Pois, near the mouth of Pearl River, a bare little island and a desolate camp, where, with no tents, the men were drenched with dew, and chilled with frosts during the night, and, during the day, parched with the sun; many died from it. From some fisherman it was learned that about fifty miles west of Ile aux Pois there was a bayou that had not been closed and was not defended and which was navigable by barges for twelve miles, where it joined a canal, leading to a plantation on the river, a few miles below the city. To test the accuracy of the information, Sir Alexander Cochrane despatched a boat under charge of the Hon. Captain Spencer, son of the Earl of Spencer, to reconnoitre the route. Arrived at the Spanish fishermen's village on the banks of Bayou Bienvenu, the young captain and a companion, disguising themselves in the blue shirts and tarpaulins of fishermen, paddled in a pirogue through the bayou and canal (Villeré's), walked to the Mississippi, took a drink of its waters, surveyed the country, interviewed some negroes; and returned with the report that the route was not only practicable, but easy.

Sixteen hundred men and two cannon were embarked immediately for the bayou. The sky was dark and lowering; heavy rains fell during the whole day; the fires of charcoal, which could be kept burning in daylight, were extinguished at night; and the sharp frost cramped the soldiers into numbness. A detail sent in advance on a reconnoissance surprised and captured four pickets, who were held at the mouth of the bayou until the flotilla came up to it. One of the prisoners, a Creole gentleman, was presented to Sir Alexander Cochrane, the British commander, a rough-looking, white-haired old gentleman, dressed in plain and much worn clothing, and to General Keane, a tall, youthful, black-whiskered man in military undress. Their shrewd cross-questioning extracted from the Creole only the false statement that Jackson's forces in the city amounted to twelve thousand men, and that he had stationed four thousand at English Turn. As the untruth had been preconcerted, it was confirmed by the other prisoners, and believed by the British officers.

At dawn the barges entered the bayou. The English sailors, standing to their oars, pushed their heavy loads through the tortuous shallow water. By nine o'clock the detachment was safe on shore. "The place," writes the English authority, an officer during the campaign, "was as wild as it is possible to imagine. Gaze where we might, nothing could be seen except a huge marsh covered with tall reeds. The marsh became gradually less and less continuous, being intersected by wide spots of firm ground; the reeds gave place by degrees to wood, and the wood to enclosed fields."

The troops landed, formed into columns, and, pushing after the guides and engineers, began their march. The advance was slow and toilsome enough to such novices in swamping. But cypresses, palmettoes, cane brakes, vines, and mire were at last worried through, the sun began to brighten the ground, and the front ranks quickening their step, broke joyfully into an open field, near the expected canal. Beyond a distant orange grove, the buildings of the Villeré plantation could be seen. Advancing rapidly along the side of the canal, and under cover of the orange grove, a company gained the buildings, and, spreading out, surrounded them. The surprise was absolute. Major Villeré and his brother, sitting on the front gallery of their residence, jumped from their chairs at the sight of redcoats before them; their rush to the other side of the house only showed them that they were bagged.

Secured in one of his own apartments, under guard of British soldiers, the young Creole officer found in his reflections the spur to a desperate attempt to save himself and his race from a suspicion of disloyalty to the United States, which, under the circumstances, might easily be directed against them by the Americans. Springing suddenly through his guards, and leaping from a window, he made a rush for the high fence that enclosed the yard, throwing down the soldiers in his way. He cleared the fence at a bound and ran across the open field that separated him from the forest. A shower of musket balls fell around him. "Catch or kill him!" was shouted behind him. But the light, agile Creole, with the Creole hunter's training from infancy, was more than a match for his pursuers in such a race as that. He gained the woods, a swamp, while they were crossing the field, spreading out as they ran to shut him in. He sprang over the boggy earth, into the swamp, until his feet, sinking deeper and deeper, clogged, and stuck. The Britons were gaining; had reached the swamp. He could hear them panting and blowing, and the orders which made his capture inevitable. There was but one chance; he sprang up a cypress tree, and strove for the thick moss and branches overhead. Half-way up, he heard a whimpering below. It was the voice of his dog, his favourite setter, whining, fawning, and looking up to him with all the pathos of brute fidelity. There was no choice; it was her life or his, and with his, perhaps the surprise and capture of the city. Dropping to the earth, he seized a billet of wood, and aimed one blow between the setter's devoted eyes; with the tears in his own eyes, he used to relate. To throw the body to one side, snatch some brush over it, spring to the tree again, was the work of an instant. As he drew the moss around his crouching figure, and stilled his hard breathing, the British floundered past. When they abandoned their useless search, he slid from his covert, pushed through the swamp to the next plantation, and carried the alarm at full speed to the city.

The British troops moved up the road along the levee, to the upper line of the plantation, and took their position in three columns. Headquarters were established in the Villeré residence, in the yard of which a small battery was thrown up. They were eight miles from the city and separated from it by fifteen plantations, large and small. By pushing forward, General Keane in two hours could have reached the city, and the battle of New Orleans would have taken place then and there, and most probably a different decision would have been wrested from victory. The British officers strongly urged this bold line of action, but Keane believing the statement that General Jackson had an army of about fifteen thousand in New Orleans, a force double his own, feared being cut off from the fleet. He therefore concluded to delay his advance until the other divisions came up. This was on the twenty-third day of December.

"Gentlemen," said Jackson to his aids and secretaries, at half-past one o'clock, when Villeré had finished his report, "the British are below; we must fight them to-night."

He issued his orders summoning his small force from their various posts. Plauche's battalion was two miles away, at Bayou St. John, Coffee five miles off, at Avart's, the coloured battalion, at Gentilly. They were commanded to proceed immediately to Montreuil's plantation below the city, where they would be joined by the regulars. Commodore Patterson was directed to get the gunboat "Carolina" under way. As the Cathedral clock was striking three, from every quarter of the city troops were seen coming at a quickstep through the streets, each company with its own vernacular music, Yankee Doodle, La Marseillaise, Le Chant du Depart. The ladies and children crowded the balconies and windows to wave handkerchiefs and applaud; the old men stood upon the banquettes waving their hats and with more sorrow in eyes and heart over their impotence than age had ever yet wrung from them.

Jackson, on horseback, with the regulars drawn up at his right, waited at the gate of Fort St. Charles to review the troops as they passed. The artillery were already below, in possession of the road. The first to march down after them were Beale's rifles, or, as New Orleans calls them, Beale's famous rifles, in their blue hunting shirts and citizens' hats, their long bores over their shoulders, sharp-shooters and picked shots every one of them, all young, active, intelligent volunteers, from the best in the professional and business circles, asking but one favour, the post of danger. At a hand gallop, and with a cloud of dust, came Hinds's dragoons, delighting General Jackson by their gallant, dare-devil bearing. After them Jackson's companion in arms, the great Coffee, trotted at the head of his mounted gun-men, with their long hair and unshaved faces, in dingy woolen hunting shirts, copperas dyed trousers, coonskin caps, and leather belts stuck with hunting knives and tomahawks. "Forward at a gallop!" was Coffee's order, after a word with General Jackson, and so they disappeared. Through a side street marched a gay, varied mass of colour, men all of a size, but some mere boys in age, with the handsome, regular features, flashing eyes and unmistakable martial bearing of the French. "Ah! Here come the brave Creoles," cries Jackson, and Plauche's battalion, which had come in on a run from Bayou St. John, stepped gallantly by.

And after these, under their white commander, defiled the Freemen of colour, and then passed down the road a band of a hundred Choctaw Indians in their war paint; last of all, the Regulars. Jackson still waited until a small dark schooner left the opposite bank of the river and slowly moved down the current. This was the "Carolina," under Commodore Patterson. Then Jackson clapped spurs to his horse, and, followed by his aids, galloped after his army.

The veteran corps took the patrol of the now deserted streets. The ladies retired from balcony and window, with their brave smiles and fluttering handkerchiefs, and, hastening to their respective posts, assembled in coteries to prepare lint and bandages, and cut and sew, for many of their defenders and Jackson's warriors had landed on the levee in a ragged if not destitute condition. Before Jackson left Fort St. Charles, a message had been sent to him from one of these coteries, asking what they were to do in case the city was attacked. "Say to the ladies," he replied, "not to be uneasy. No British soldier shall ever enter the city as an enemy, unless over my dead body."

As the rumoured war-cry of the British was "Beauty and Booty," many of the ladies, besides thimbles and needles, had provided themselves with small daggers, which they wore in their belts.

Here it is the custom of local pride to pause and enumerate the foes set in array against the men hastening down the levee road.

First, always, there was that model regiment, the Ninety-third Highlanders, in their bright tartans and kilts, men chosen for stature and strength, whose broad breasts, wide shoulders, and stalwart figures, widened their ranks into a formidable appearance. The Prince of Orange and his staff had journeyed from London to Plymouth to review them before they embarked. Then there were six companies of the Ninety-fifth Rifles; the famous Rifle Brigade of the Peninsular Campaign; the Fourteenth Regiment, the Duchess of York's Light Dragoons; two West Indian regiments, with artillery, rocket brigade, sapper and engineer corps —in all, four thousand three hundred men, under command of Major-General John Keane, a young officer whose past reputation for daring and gallantry has been proudly kept bright by the traditions of his New Orleans foes. To these were added General Ross's three thousand men, fresh from their brilliant Baltimore and Washington raid. Choice troops they were, the gallant and distinguished Fourth, or King's Own, the Forty-fourth, East Essex Foot, the Eighty-fifth, Buck Volunteers, commanded by one of the most brilliant officers in the British service, Col. William Thornton; the twenty-first Royal, North British Fusileers,—with the exception of the Black Regiments and the Highlanders, all tried veterans, who had fought with Wellington through his Peninsular campaign from the beginning to his triumphant entry into France.

Only the first boat loads, eighteen hundred men, were in Villeré's field on the afternoon of the twenty-third. They lay around their bivouac fires, about two hundred yards from the levee, enjoying their rest and the digestion of the bountiful supper of fresh meat, poultry, milk, eggs, and delicacies, which had been added to their rations by a prompt raid on the neighbouring plantations. General Keane and Colonel Thornton paced the gallery of the Villeré house, glancing at each turn towards the wood, for the sight of the coming of the next division of the army.

The only hostile demonstration during the afternoon had been the firing of the outpost upon a reconnoitering squad of dragoons and a bold dash down the road of a detachment of Hinds's horsemen, who, after a cool, impudent survey of the British camp, had galloped away again under a volley from the Rifles.

Darkness gathered over the scene. The sentinels were doubled, and officers walked their rounds in watchful anxiety. About seven o'clock some of them observed a boat stealing slowly down the river. From her careless approach, they thought she must be one of their own cruisers which had passed the forts below and was returning from a reconoissance of the river. She answered neither hail nor musket shot, but steered steadily on, veering in close ashore until her broadside was abreast of the camp. Then her anchor was let loose, and a loud voice was heard: "Give them this, for the honour of America." A flash lighted the dark hulk, and a tornado of grape and musket shot swept the levee and field. It was the "Carolina" and Commodore Patterson; volley after volley followed with deadly rapidity and precision; the sudden and terrible havoc threw the camp into blind disorder. The men ran wildly to and fro, seeking shelter until Thornton ordered them to get under cover of the levee. There, according to the British version, they lay for an hour. The night was so black that not an object could be distinguished at the distance of a yard. The bivouac fires, beat about by the enemy's shot, burned red and dull in the deserted camp.

A straggling fire of musketry in the direction of the pickets gave warning of a closer struggle. It paused a few moments, then a fearful yell, and the whole heavens seemed ablaze with musketry. The British thought themselves surrounded. Two regiments flew to support the pickets, another, forming in close column, stole to the rear of the encampment and remained there as a reserve. After that, all order, all discipline, were lost. Each officer, as he succeeded in collecting twenty or thirty men about him, plunged into the American ranks, and began the fight that Pakenham reported as: "A more extraordinary conflict has, perhaps, never occurred, absolutely hand to hand, both officers and men."

Jackson had marshaled his men along the line of a plantation canal (the Rodriguez Canal), about two miles from the British. He himself led the attack on their left. Coffee, with the Tennesseeans, Hinds's dragoons, and Beale's rifles, skirting along the edge of the swamp, made the assault on their right. The broadside from the "Carolina" was the signal to start. It was on the right that the fiercest fighting was done. Coffee ordered his men to be sure of their aim, to fire at a short distance, and not to lose a shot. Trained to the rifle from childhood, the Tennesseeans could fire faster and more surely than any mere soldier could ever hope to do. Wherever they heard the sharp crack of a British rifle, they advanced, and the British were as eager to meet them. The short rifle of the English service proved also no match for the long bore of the Western hunters. When they came to close quarters, neither side having bayonets, they clubbed their guns to the ruin of many a fine weapon. But the canny Tennesseeans rather than risk their rifles, their own property, used for close quarters their long knives and tomahawks, whose skilful handling they had learned from the Indians.

The second division of British troops, coming up the Bayou, heard the firing, and, pressing forward with all speed, arrived in time to reinforce their right; but the superiority in numbers which this gave them was more than offset by the guns of the "Carolina," which maintained their fire during the action, and long after it was over.

A heavy fog, as in Homeric times, obscuring the field and the combatants, put an end to the struggle. Jackson withdrew his men to Rodriguez Canal, the British fell back to their camp.

A number of prisoners were made on both sides. Among the Americans taken were a handful of New Orleans' most prominent citizens, who were sent to the fleet at Ship Island. The most distinguished prisoner made by the Americans was Major Mitchell, of the Ninety-fifth Rifles, and to his intense chagrin he was forced to yield his sword, not to regulars, but to Coffee's uncourtly Tennesseeans. It was this feeling that dictated his answer to Jackson's courteous message requesting that he would make known any requisite for his comfort; "Return my compliments to General Jackson, and say that as my baggage will reach me in a few days I shall be able to dispense with his polite attentions." The chronicler of the anecdote aptly adds, that had the major persisted in this rash determination, he would never have been in a condition to partake of the hospitalities which were lavished upon him during his detention in New Orleans and Natchez, where the prisoners were sent. On his way to Natchez he became the guest at a plantation famed for its elegance and luxury. At the supper table he met the daughter of the house, a young Creole girl as charming and accomplished as she was beautiful. Speaking French fluently, he was soon engaged in a lively conversation with her.

She mentioned with enthusiasm a party of Tennesseeans entertained by her father a few days before. Still smarting from his capture, the major could not refrain from saying: "Mademoiselle, I am astonished that one so refined could find pleasure in the society of such rude barbarians." "Major," she replied with glowing face, "I had rather be the wife of one of those hardy, coarsely clad men who have marched two thousand miles to fight for the honour of their country, than wear a coronet."

To return to the battlefield. The Rodriguez Canal, with its enbankment, formed a pretty good line of fortifications in itself. Jackson, without the loss of an hour's time, sent to the city for spades and picks, and set his army to work deepening the canal and strengthening the embankment. For the latter, any material within reach was used, timber, fence-rails, bales of cotton (which is the origin of the myth that he fought behind ramparts of cotton bales). His men, most of them handling a spade for the first and last time in their lives, dug as they had fought a few hours before, every stroke aimed to tell.

General Jackson established his headquarters in the residence of the Macarty plantation, within two hundred yards of his entrenchments.

The British passed a miserable night. Not until the last fire was extinguished, and the fog completely veiled the field, did the "Carolina" cease her firing and move to the other side of the river. The men, shivering on the damp ground, exposed to the cold, moist atmosphere, with now none but their scant, half-spoiled rations, were depressed and discouraged, and the officers were more anxious and uncertain than ever, and more completely in error as to the force opposed to them. From the intrepidity and boldness of the Americans, they imagined that at least five thousand had been in the field that night. Other observations strengthened this misapprehension; each volunteer company, with its different uniform, represented to military minds so many different regiments, a tenfold multiplication of the Americans. Besides, in the din of commands, cries, and answers, as much French was heard as English. The truth began to dawn upon the British, that, much as the Creoles hated the Americans, they were not going to allow a foreign invader to occupy a land which they considered theirs by right of original discovery, occupation, and development, whatever might be the flag or form of government over them.

The dawning of the twenty-fourth disclosed in the river another vessel, the "Louisiana," in position near the "Carolina," and all day the camp lay helpless under their united cannonading. A gloomier Christmastide, as our genial chronicler Walker puts it, could hardly be imagined for the sons of Merrie England. Had it been in the day of the cable, they would have known that their hardships and bloodshed were over, that at that very date, the twenty-fourth of December, the peace that terminated the war between the two contending countries was being signed in Ghent. The unexpected arrival, however, on Christmas day, of the new commander-in-chief, Sir Edward Pakenham, accompanied by a distinguished staff, sent through the hearts of the British a thrill of their wonted all-conquering confidence, and the glad cheers of welcome that greeted Sir Edward from his old companions in arms and veterans of the Peninsula rang over into the American camp.

Well might Jackson's men, as they heard it, bend with more dogged determination over their spades and picks. Sir Edward Pakenham was too well known in a place so heavily populated from Europe as New Orleans was, not to make the thrill of joy in his own army a thrill of apprehension in an opposing one. It is perhaps from this thrill of apprehension, at that moment in their breasts, that dates the pride of the people of New Orleans in Pakenham, and the affectionate tribute of homage which they always interrupt their account of the glorious eighth to pay to him.

The son of the Earl of Longford, he came from a family which had been ennobled for its military qualities. From his lieutenancy he had won every grade by some perilous service, and generally at the cost of a wound; few officers, even of that hard-fighting day, had encountered so many perils and hardships, and had so many wounds to show for them. He had fought side by side, with Wellington (who was his brother-in-law) through the Peninsular War; he headed the storming party at Badajoz; actually the second man to mount one of the ladders; and as brigadier of the Old Fighting Third, under Picton, in the absence by illness of his chief, he led the charge at Salamanca, which gained the victory for England and won him his knighthood. An earldom and the governorship of Louisiana, it is said, had been promised him as the reward of his American expedition, an expedition which the government had at first seriously contemplated confiding to no less a leader than the Iron Duke himself.

Sir Edward's practised eye soon took in the difficulties and embarrassments of the British position. His council of war was prolonged far into the night, and among the anxiously waiting subalterns outside the rumour was whispered that their chief was so dissatisfied after receiving Keane's full report that he had but little hope of success, and that he even thought of withdrawing the army and making a fresh attempt in another quarter. But the sturdy veteran Sir Alexander Cochrane, would hear of no such word as fail. "If the army," he said, "shrinks from the task, I will fetch the sailors and marines from the fleet, and with them storm the American lines and march to the city. The soldiers can then," he added, "bring up the baggage."

The result of the council was the decision, first, to silence the "Carolina" and "Louisiana," then to carry the American lines by storm. All the large cannon that could be spared were ordered from the fleet, and by the night of the twenty-sixth a powerful battery was planted on the levee. The next morning it opened fire on the vessels, which answered with broadsides; a furious cannonading ensued. Pakenham, standing in full view on the levee, cheered his artillerists. Jackson, from the dormer window of the Macarty mansion, kept his telescope riveted on his boats. The bank of the river above and below the American camp was lined with spectators watching with breathless interest the tempest of cannon balls, bursting shells, hot shot, and rockets pouring from levee and gunboats. In half an hour the "Carolina" was struck, took fire, and blew up. The British gave three loud cheers. The "Louisiana" strained every nerve to get out of reach of the terrible battery now directed full upon her, but with wind and current against her she seemed destined to the fate of the "Carolina," when her officers bethought them of towing, and so moved her slowly up stream. As she dropped her anchors opposite the American camp, her crew gave three loud cheers, in defiant answer to the British. That evening the British army, in two columns, under Keane and Gibbs, moved forward, the former by the levee road, the latter under cover of the woods, to within six hundred yards of the American lines, where they encamped for the night. But there was little sleep or rest for them. The American riflemen, with individual enterprise, bushwhacked them without intercession, driving in their outposts and picking off picket after picket, a mode of warfare that the English, fresh from Continental etiquette, indignantly branded as barbarous.

Jackson, with his telescope, had seen from the Macarty house the line of Pakenham's action, and set to work to resist it, giving his aids a busy night's work. He strengthened his battery on the levee, added a battery to command the road, reinforced his infantry, and cut the levee so that the rising river would flood the road. The Mississippi proved recreant, however, and fell, instead of rising, and the road remained undamaged.

The American force now consisted of four thousand men and twenty pieces of artillery, not counting the always formidable guns of the "Louisiana," commanding the situation from her vantage ground of the river. The British columns held eight thousand men.

The morning was clear and frosty; the sun, breaking through the mists, shone with irradiating splendour. The British ranks advanced briskly in a new elation of spirits after yesterday's success. Keane marched his column as near the levee as possible, and under screen of the buildings of the two plantations, Bienvenu's and Chalmette's, intervening between him and the American line; Gibbs hugged the woods on the right. The Ninety-fifth extended across the field, in skirmishing order, meeting Keane's men on their right. Pakenham, with his staff and a guard composed of the 14th Dragoons, rode in the centre of the line so as to command a view of both columns. Just as Keane's column passed the Bienvenu buildings, the Chalmette buildings were blown up, and then the general saw, through his glasses, the mouths of Jackson's large cannon completely covering his column, and these guns, as our authority states, were manned as guns are not often manned on land. Around one of the twenty-four pounders stood a band of red-shirted, bewhiskered, desperate-looking men, begrimed with smoke and mud; they were the Baratarians, who had answered Jackson's orders by running in all the way from their fort on Bayou St. John that morning. The other battery was in charge of the practised crew of the destroyed "Carolina." Preceded by a shower of rockets, and covered by the fire from their artillery in front and their battery on the levee, the British army advanced, solid, cool, steady, beautiful in the rhythm of their step and the glitter of their uniforms and equipments, moving as if on dress parade,—to the Americans a display of the beauty and majesty of power such as they had never seen.

The great guns of the Baratarians and of the crew of the "Carolina" and those of the "Louisiana" flashed forth almost simultaneously, and all struck full in the scarlet ranks. The havoc was terrible. For a time Keane held his men firm in a vain display of valour, under the pitiless destructive fire, no shot or bullet missing its aim or falling short. Then the Americans saw the heaving columns change to a thin red streak, which disappeared from view as under the wand of an enchanter, the men dropping into the ditches, burying head and shoulders in the rushes on the banks. Pakenham's face grew dark and gloomy at the sight. Never before, it is said, had a British soldier in his presence quailed before an enemy or sought cover from a fire.

Gibbs had fared no better. He who had led the storming party against

Fort Cornelius, who had scaled the parapets of Badajoz and the walls of St. Sebastian, could not but despise the low levee and the narrow ditch of the American fortifications; but after one ineffectual dash at the enemy's lines, his men could be brought to accomplish nothing, remaining inactive in the shelter of the woods until ordered to retire. As the American batteries continued to sweep the field, the British troops could be withdrawn only by breaking into small squads and so escaping to the rear. Sir Thomas Trowbridge, dashing forward with a squad of seamen to the dismounted guns, succeeded, with incredible exertion, in tying ropes to them and drawing them off.

The British army remained on the Bienvenu plantation. Pakenham and his staff rode back to their headquarters at Villeré's. Another council of war was called. Pakenham's depression was now quite evident, but the stout-hearted Cochrane again stood indomitably firm. He showed that their failure thus far was due to the superiority of the American artillery. They must supply this deficiency by bringing more large guns from the fleet, and equip a battery strong enough to cope with the few old guns of the Americans. It was suggested that the Americans were intrenched. "So must we be," he replied promptly. It was determined, therefore, to treat the American lines as regular fortifications, by erecting batteries against them, and so attempting to silence their guns. Three days were consumed in the herculean labour of bringing the necessary guns from the fleet. While the British were thus employed, Commodore Patterson constructed a battery on the opposite side of the river, equipped it with cannon from the "Louisiana" and manned it by an impressment of every nautical-looking character to be found in the sailor boarding-houses of New Orleans, gathering together as motley a corps as ever fought under one flag, natives of all countries except Great Britain, speaking every language except that of their commander.

On the night of the thirty-first, one-half of the British army marched silently to within about four hundred yards of Jackson's line, where they stacked their arms and went to work with spades and picks under the superintendence of Sir John Burgoyne. The night was dark; silence was rigidly enforced; officers joined in the work. Before the dawn of New Year, 1815, there faced the American lines three solid *demilunes,* at nearly equal distances apart, armed with thirty pieces of heavy ordnance, furnished with ammunition for six hours, and served by picked gunners of the fleet, veterans of Nelson and Collingwood. As soon as their work was completed, the British infantry fell back to the rear and awaited anxiously the beginning of operations, ready to take advantage of the expected breach in the American works. The sailors and artillerists stood with lighted matches behind their redoubts. A heavy fog hung over the field, so that neither army could see twenty yards ahead. In the American camp, a grand parade had been ordered. At an early hour the troops were astir, in holiday cleanliness and neatness. The different bands sounded their bravest strains; the various standards of the regiments and companies fluttered gaily in the breeze. The British had one glance at it, as the fog rolled up, and then their cannon crashed through the scene. For a moment the American camp trembled, and there was confusion, not of panic, but of men rushing to their assigned posts. By the time the British smoke cleared every man was in his place, and as the British batteries came into view their answer was ready for them. Jackson strode down the line, stopping at each battery, waving his cap as the men cheered him.

During the fierce cannonade the cotton bales in the American breastworks caught fire, and there was a moment of serious peril to that part of the line, but they were dragged out and cast into the trench. The English were no happier in their use of hogsheads of sugar in their redoubts, the cannon balls perforating them easily and demolishing them.

In an hour and a half the British fire began to slacken, and as the smoke lifted it was seen that their entrenchments were beaten in, the guns exposed, and the gunners badly thinned. Not long after their batteries were completely silenced and their parapets levelled with the plain. The British battery on the levee had, with their hot shot, kept the "Louisiana" at a distance, but now the Americans turning their attention to it, that battery was reduced to the same condition as the redoubts.

The English army again retired, baffled, and during the night, such of their guns as had not been destroyed were removed. The soldiers did not conceal their discouragement. For two whole days and nights there had been no rest in camp, except for those that were cool enough to sleep in a shower of cannon balls. From the general down to the meanest sentinel, all had suffered in the severe strain of fatigue. They saw that they were greatly overmatched in artillery, their provisions were scant and coarse, they had, properly speaking, no rest at night, and sickness was beginning to appear.

Sir Edward had one more plan, one worthy of his bold character. It was to storm the American lines on both sides of the river, beginning with the right bank, which would enable the British to turn the conquered batteries on Jackson's lines, and drive him from his position and cut him off from the city.

By the 7th of January, with another heroic exertion, Villeré's Canal was prolonged two miles to the river, and the barges to transport the troops to the other bank carried through. During the delay a reinforcement arrived, two fine regiments, Pakenham's own, the Seventh Fusileers, and the Forty-third, under Major-General John Lambert, also one of Wellington's apprentices. Pakenham divided his army, now ten thousand strong, into three brigades, under command respectively of Generals Lambert, Gibbs, and Keane. His plan of attack was simple. Colonel Thornton, with fourteen hundred men, was to cross the river during the night of the seventh and steal upon and carry the American line before day. At a signal to be given by him, Gibbs was to storm the American left, whilst General Keane should threaten their right; Lambert held the reserve.

Jackson steadied himself for what he understood to be the last round in the encounter. He also had received a reinforcement. A few days before, the long expected drafted militia of Kentucky, twenty-two hundred men, arrived, but arrived in a condition that made them a questionable addition to his strength. Hurried from their homes without supplies, they had travelled fifteen hundred miles without demur, under the impression that the government would plentifully furnish and equip them in New Orleans. Only about a third were armed, with old muskets, and nearly all of them were in want of clothing. The poor fellows had to hold their tattered garments together to hide their nakedness as they marched through the streets. The government of course did nothing. The citizens, acutely moved, raised a sum of sixteen thousand dollars and expended it for blankets and woolens. The latter were distributed among the ladies, and by them, in a few days, made into comfortable garments for their needy defenders.

The American force now amounted to about four thousand men on the left bank of the river. One division of it, the right, was commanded by General Ross, the other by General Coffee, whose line extended so far in the swamp that his men stood in the water during the day and at night slept on floating logs made fast to trees; every man "half a horse and half an alligator," as the song says. The artillery and the fortifications had been carefully strengthened and repaired. Another line of defence had been prepared a mile and a half in the rear, where were stationed all who were not well armed or were regarded as not able-bodied.

A third line, for another stand in case of defeat, still nearer the city, was being vigorously worked upon.

Owing to the caving of the banks of the canal, Thornton could get only enough boats launched in the river to carry seven hundred of his men across: these the current of the Mississippi bore a mile and a half below the landing-place selected, and it was daylight before they reached there.

Gibbs and Keane marched their divisions to within sight of the dark line of the American breastworks, and waited impatiently for the signal of Thornton's guns. Not a sound could be heard from him. In fact he had not yet landed his men. Although sensible that concert of action with the troops on the right bank had failed, and that his movement was hopelessly crippled, Pakenham, obstinate, gallant, and reckless, would, nevertheless, not rescind his first orders. When the morning mists lifted, his columns were in motion across the field.

Gibbs was leading his division coolly and steadily through the grapeshot pouring upon it, when it began to be whispered among the men that the Forty-fourth, who were detailed for the duty, had not brought the ladders and fascines. Pakenham riding to the front and finding it was true, ordered Colonel Mullen and the delinquent regiment back for them. In the confusion and delay, with his brave men falling all around him, the indignant Gibbs exclaimed furiously: "Let me live until to-morrow, and I'll hang him to the highest tree in that swamp!" Rather than stand exposed to the terrible fire, he ordered his men forward. "On they went," says Walker (who got his description from eye-witnesses), "in solid, compact order, the men hurrahing and the rocketers covering their front with a blaze of combustibles. The American batteries played upon them with awful effect, cutting great lanes through the column from front to rear, opening huge gaps in their flanks. . . . Still the column advanced without pause or recoil, steadily; then all the batteries in the American line, including Patterson's marine battery on the right bank, joined in hurling a tornado of iron missiles into that serried scarlet column, which shook and oscillated as if tossed on an angry sea. 'Stand to your guns!' cried Jackson, 'don't waste your ammunition, see that every shot tells,' and again, 'Give it to them, boys! Let us finish the business today.' "

On the summit of the parapet stood the corps of Tennessee sharpshooters, with their rifles sighted, and behind them, two lines of Kentuckians to take their places so soon as they had fired. The redcoats were now within two hundred yards of the ditch. "Fire! Fire!" Carroll's order rang through the lines. It was obeyed, not hurriedly, not excitedly, not confusedly, but calmly and deliberately, the men calculating the range of their guns. Not a shot was thrown away. Nor was it one or several discharges, followed by pauses and interruptions; it was continuous, the men firing, falling back and advancing, with mechanical precision. The British column began to melt away under it like snow before a torrent; but Gibbs still led it on, and the gallant Peninsula officers, throwing themselves in front, incited and aroused their men by every appeal and by the most brilliant examples of courage. "Where are the Forty-fourth," called the men, "with the fascines and ladders? When we get to the ditch we cannot scale the lines!" "Here come the Forty-fourth!" shouted Gibbs, "Here come the Forty-fourth!" There came, at least, a detachment of the Forty-fourth, with Pakenham himself at the head, rallying and inspiring them, invoking their heroism in the past, reminding them of their glory in Egypt and elsewhere, calling them his countrymen, leading them forward, until they breasted the storm of bullets with the rest of the column. At this moment Pakenham's arm was struck by one ball, his horse killed by another. He mounted the small black Creole pony of his aid, and pressed forward. But the column had now reached the physical limit of daring. Most of the officers were cut down; there were not enough left to command. The column broke. Some rushed forward to the ditch; the rest fell back to the swamp. There they rallied, reformed, and throwing off their knapsacks advanced again, and again were beaten back; their colonel scaling the breastworks and falling dead inside the lines.

Keane, judging the moment had come for him to act, now wheeled his line into column and pushed forward with the Ninety-third in front. The gallant, stalwart Highlanders, with their heavy, solid, massive front of a hundred men, their muskets glittering in the morning sun, their tartans waving in the air, strode across the field and into the hell of bullets and cannon balls. "Hurrah! brave Highlanders!" Pakenham cried to them, waving his cap in his left hand. Fired by their intrepidity, the remnant of Gibbs's brigade once more came up to the charge, with Pakenham on the left and Gibbs on the right.

A shot from one of the American big guns crashed into them, killing and wounding all around. Pakenham's horse fell; he rolled into the arms of an officer who sprang forward to receive him; a grape-shot had passed through his thigh; another ball struck him in the groin. He was borne to the rear, and in a few moments breathed his last under an oak. The bent and twisted, venerable old tree still stands, Pakenham's oak, it is called.

Gibbs, desperately wounded, lingered in agony until the next day. Keane was carried bleeding off the field. There were no field officers now left to command or rally. Major Wilkinson however,—we like to remember his name,—shouting to his men to follow, passed the ditch, climbed up the breastworks, and was raising his head and shoulders over the parapet, when a dozen guns pointed against him riddled him with bullets. His mutilated body was carried through the American lines, followed by murmurs of sympathy and regret from the Tennesseeans and Kentuckians. "Bear up, my dear fellow, you are too brave to die," bade a kind-hearted Kentucky major. "I thank you from my heart," faintly murmured the young officer; "it is all over with me. You can render me a favour. It is to communicate to my commander that I fell on your parapet, and died like a soldier and true Englishman."

The British troops at last broke, disorganized, each regiment leaving two-thirds dead or wounded on the field. The Ninety-third, which had gone into the charge nine hundred men strong, mustered after the retreat one hundred and thirty-nine. The fight had lasted twenty-five minutes.

Hearing of the death of Pakenham and the wounding of Gibbs and Keane, General Lambert advanced with the reserve. Just before he received his last wound, Pakenham had ordered one of his staff to call up the reserve, but as the bugler was about to sound the advance, his arm was struck with a ball and his bugle fell to the ground. The order, therefore, was never given, and the reserve marched up only to cover the retreat of the two other brigades.

At eight o'clock the firing ceased from the American lines, and Jackson, with his staff, slowly walked along his fortifications, stopping at each command to make a short address. As he passed, the bands struck up "Hail Columbia," and the line of men, turning to face him, burst into loud hurrahs.

But the cries of exultation died away into exclamations of pity and horror as the smoke ascended from the field. A thin, fine red line in the distance, discovered by glasses, indicated the position of General Lambert and the reserve. Upon the field, save the crawling, agonizing wounded, not a living foe was to be seen. From the American ditch, one could have walked a quarter of a mile on the killed and disabled. The course of the column could be distinctly traced by the broad red line of uniforms upon the ground. They fell in their tracks, in some places whole platoons together. Dressed in their gay uniforms, cleanly shaved and attired for the promised victory, there was not, as Walker says, a private among the slain whose aspect did not present more of the pomp and circumstance of war than any of the commanders of their victors.

About noon, a British officer, with a trumpeter and a soldier bearing a white flag, approached the camp, bearing a written proposition for an armistice to bury the dead. It was signed "Lambert." General Jackson returned it, with a message that the signer of the letter had forgotten to designate his authority and rank, which was necessary before any negotiations could be entered into. The flag of truce retired to the British lines, and soon returned with the full signature, "John Lambert, Commander-in-Chief of the British forces."

On the right bank of the river it was the British who were victorious. The Americans, yielding to panic, fled disgracefully, as people with shame relate to this day. It was on this side of the river that the British acquired the small flag which hangs among the trophies of the Peninsular War, in Whitehall, with the inscription: "Taken at the battle of New Orleans, January 8, 1815."

The bodies of the officers were first delivered. Some of them were buried that night in Villeré's garden by torch-light; the rest were hastily interred in the rear of Bienvenu's plantation; the remains of Gibbs and Pakenham were conveyed to England. Of the six thousand men who made the attack on Jackson's lines, the British report a loss of nineteen hundred and twenty-nine. The American estimates increase this to two thousand six hundred. The Americans had eight men killed and thirteen wounded.

The prisoners and wounded were sent to the city. Some of the little boys of the time, now in their nineties, who watched the slow, sad cortege, tell of their childish pity and sympathy for them, and their admiration for the great, tall, handsome prisoners, in their fine uniforms.

The citizens pressed forward to tender their aid for the wounded. The hospitals being crowded, private houses were thrown open, and the quadroon nurses, the noted quadroon nurses of the city, offered their services and gave their best skill and care at the bedside of the English sufferers.

As soon as the armistice expired, the American batteries resumed their firing. Colonel Thornton with his men recrossed the river during the night of the eighth. From the ninth to the eighteenth a small squadron of the British fleet made an ineffectual attempt to pass Fort St. Philip. Had it timed its action better with Pakenham's, his defeat might at least have cost his enemies dearer.

On the 18th of January took place the exchange of prisoners, and New Orleans received again her sorely missed citizens. Although their detention from the stirring scenes of the camp formed in their lives one of the unforgivable offences of destiny, their courteous, kindly, pleasant treatment by the British naval officers was one of the reminiscences which gilded the memories of the period.

Sir John Lambert's retreat was the ablest measure of the British campaign. To retire in boats was impracticable; there were not boats enough, and it was not safe to divide the army. A road was therefore opened, along the bank of the bayou, across the prairie to the lake, a severe and difficult task that occupied nine days. All the wounded, except those who could not be removed, the field artillery and stores, were placed in barges and conveyed to the fleet, the ship guns were spiked, and on the night of the eighteenth the army was stealthily and quietly formed into column. The camp-fires were lighted as usual, the sentinels posted, each one provided with a stuffed dummy to put in his stead when the time came for him to join the march in the rear of the column. They marched all night, reaching the shores of Lake Borgne at break of day.

Early in the morning of the nineteenth, rumours of the retreat of the English began to circulate in the American camp. Officers and men collected in groups on the parapet to survey the British camp. It presented pretty much the same appearance as usual, with its huts, flags, and sentinels. General Jackson, looking through his telescope from Macarty's window, could not convince himself that the enemy had gone. At last General Humbert, one of Napoleon's veterans, was called upon for his opinion. He took a look through the telescope, and immediately exclaimed: "They are gone!" When asked the reason for his belief, he pointed to a crow flying very near one of the sentinels.

While a reconnoitering party was being formed, a flag of truce approached. It brought a courteous letter from General Lambert, announcing the departure of the British army, and soliciting the kind attentions of General Jackson to the sick and wounded, whom he was compelled to leave behind. The circumstances of these wounded men being made known in the city, a number of ladies drove immediately down the coast in their carriages with articles for their comfort.

The British fleet left the Gulf shores on the 17th of March. When it reached England, it received the news that Napoleon had escaped and that Europe was up again in arms. Most of the troops were at once re-embarked for Belgium, to join Wellington's army. General Lambert, knighted for gallantry at New Orleans, distinguished himself at Waterloo.

A handsome tablet in St. Paul's Cathedral, London, commemorates Pakenham's gallant life and heroic death.

Walker relates that the Duke of Wellington, after the battle of New Orleans, always cherished a great admiration for General Jackson, and when introduced to American visitors never failed to inquire after his health.

IX BIOGRAPHY

GRACE KING'S accomplishment in biography, closely allied to her historical writing, is an indication of her versatility. In addition to her books on Bienville and De Soto she wrote many brief sketches, of which three in this section are of women she met in Paris during her first stay there, 1891–1892. Madame Blanc and the Baronne Blaze de Bury became two of her closest friends at the time. Apparently she met the Comtesse Tascher de la Pagerie only once, but that was enough to provide her with material for the profile of the elderly aristocrat. The late volume *Creole Families of New Orleans* (1921) contains a series of brief lives of local importance. "Bernard de Marigny" is perhaps the most interesting of these because the man epitomized the Creole aristocracy of the early nineteenth century.

"Mark Twain, First Impression" was written June 4, 1887, shortly after Grace King had met Clemens, while she was a guest of the Charles Dudley Warners in Hartford. "Mark Twain, Second Impression" was probably written in the fall of 1888, after she arrived to be a guest of the Clemenses in Hartford. Both sketches are from a manuscript notebook in the Grace King Papers, Department of Archives and Manuscripts, Louisiana State University, Baton Rouge. The greater part of the first and all of the second were published in Robert Bush, "Grace King and Mark Twain," *American Literature*, XLIV (March, 1972), 38–40. They are reprinted here with permission of the editor. The texts of the profiles of the three women are based on the following copy-texts: "Madame la Baronne Blaze de Bury," *Harper's Bazar*, XXVI (September 16, 1893), 758; "Madame la Comtesse Tascher de la Pagerie," *Harper's Bazar*, XXVI (September 30, 1893), 807; "Theo. Bentzon—Madame Th. Blanc," *Harper's Bazar*, XXIX (August 8, 1896), 666–67.

Mark Twain: First Impression, Hartford, June 4, 1887 [*from* Notebook, 1886–1901]

"Mark Twain" is a disappointment to the eyes until he begins to talk; then his features explain themselves. The head is not so heavy as massive, the eyes not stupid but introspective—his air and manner, not so much the vulgar carelessness of the ignorant—but the unconscious carelessness of the preoccupied. He is a man of genius—the material not so very rare and unique as inexhaustible in richness. His wit runs to fat—his humor is fleshy—coarse-grained—but solid and generally wholesome, where the mind has not been too much pampered with delicacies of intellect. He said that in a hundred years from now America would be leading the world—in art, letters, science, and politics. Our population would be so great that we would be the market—the customers of the world's intellectual commerce. We therefore would set the fashions, regulate the taste—would have an opinion to express, an opinion that would have a cash value, as we would have the money with which to back it. Opinion is the authoritative expression of the supreme court of art, morals, science. His reasoning followed naturally from the premise and sounded irrefutable—but across it all—there was felt the want of spiritual provision in his argument. Money, or pay in his opinion would call out the best work every where—and money would be the highest reward. He did not consider those who working for a higher aim would disdain the prompt paying American market. He seems to have made a slave of his soul—& condemned it to trudge along with him as he shakes his cap & bells—clipped the wings—and put out the eyes—making it a physical impossibility to see the world above. He said he had made a note of a recent thought. Taking out his "Calepin" he read it. "Could we endure a French Saviour?"— Fancy a Frenchman saying "Come unto me all ye who are weary & heavy laden"—or an Irishman—Englishman or German. No, our Jew was the best after all." Speaking of his home (which is beautiful) He spoke of the change in the fashion of hard-wood furnishings. It all seemed to represent a fashion to him, nothing more.

Mark Twain: Second Impression

The train I was on reached Hartford after dark. I got off, and soon saw the grey head of Mr Clemens under his slouch hat—rushing to the further end, passing coach after coach, in his hasty scrutiny, leaving me farther and farther behind. I took after him—and fortunately succeeded in arresting his attention before he turned off disgusted into the station house. His welcome was warm and sincere. There is a good fellowship in his manner that is most pleasant. He is an easy man to get along with socially, in his own house, and with his own family. He is quick to catch your idea—and nice to it, after he catches it. He does not impose his opinions, at least on me he did not—and he listens—at least to me—with attention. His spirits rise easily—his fun is never asleep—at a wink it is alert. When he talks—there is something delightfully unpremeditated in the way he brings in his stories; good or bad, appropriate or inappropriate, egotistical or otherwise. He is not an egotist—but he is always, at any party, the entertainer, I might say, the entertainment. He does not [mow?] from books, but from his own life, his absurd, grotesque Mark Twain mind—takes what the eye brings to it—and turns out fun. His fun is so personal; it is autobiographical. He cannot conceal—his frankness is startling. He simply doesn't care; he cannot stop to apologise or explain, and beg you not to consider him egotistical. And the absence of this uneasiness about the opinion of others, is perhaps the pleasantest trait in his intercourse, for it puts you also at your ease. If you do anything absurd or philistinish—or mean and stingy—he will notice it—and no doubt tell it on you some day when your character is being discussed. But he does not pick at your words, or test your sincerity or get shocked at a breach of etiquette—or sniff a lèse moralité—in you. He takes you at the moment for what you want to be taken. If you make an impression there is a sum-total of your character in his mind somewhere. He treats ladies generally as if they were nice clever boys—like himself. If they need his advice or protection—he treats them as if they were nice, good sort of sisters—without any sentiment, or exaggeration of his services. I should say that Mark Twain had a beautiful heart—a rough, country-beauty of a heart—awkward, shy—and [heavily?] strong. It is grotesque, at times when it might be graceful. It has never been to dancing school. It may be rough—as country beauties have rough hands—but it is a heart—"brut"—as the French say—original in its essence and strength. He has the great mind of a great humorist—not the great mind of a great philosopher or moralist. He is not critical—nor picturesque. If he were he would be a great novelist. He ought to be a great realistic novelist—but he is not. I cannot suspect such a mind as he has of limitations. I would rather accuse it of underdevelopment. On the side of reverence there is lacking—and in the region of poetry—there are chords missing. History does not enter willingly into it. He has to face her in [word missing]—Strength always inspires him. He admires Ingersoll.[1] He loves to see Ingersoll knock down his opponents. And yet—there is no man in the world further removed from the coarse athleticism, of Ingersoll. His family is refinement itself—his domestic horizon is bounded on all sides by religion—and sentiment.

Madame la Baronne Blaze de Bury

It is on the "other side" of the Seine, as we of the Quartier de l'Europe call it, 20 Rue Oudinot, close under the dome of the Invalides. The great gilt superstructure dominates, and, even as he who rests in the coffin it canopies might have done, oppresses in its domination the whole vast neighborhood—the Champ de Mars, the Chambre des Députés, and all the noble array of public buildings and private dwellings which mark the footsteps of newer and ever newer Paris away from the consecrated relics of dead history treasured in the old hospital of Louis XIV.

Colossal wooden doors swing heavily open at the ring of the bell, and one crosses the portal with the rare sense nowadays of really crossing a barrier, a defence of inner from outer life. The quiet secluded court-yard seems, indeed, the portico of a domestic sanctuary; its quietude and se-

1 Robert Green Ingersoll (1833–99), the popular agnostic lecturer and author.

clusion are, in truth, its only beauty. And yet it seemed picturesque enough that first day, with driftings of snow in the corners and crevices of the rough granite pavement, with the pump muffled from the weather, and a few bleak branches from some hidden tree striking across the low gray sky, and a new acquaintance, perhaps friend—at any rate, a new personality in one's existence—just over the crossing of it.

What one hears about a notability goes for very little, after all, after one sees the individual. One's reading, even, prepares one meagrely for the reality. With a notability, with a genius, as with one's seamstress, the beginning of knowledge lies in the application of those primitive tests of eyes and ears, as facile to the infant as to the graybeard—the ingathering of those thousand little indices by the heart upon which the brute as well as higher animals depend for authority to like or not like.

Although the huge wooden portals are exclusive, they are not perhaps as inclusive as they might be. In Paris one hears much about Madame de Bury. What one can hear really depends upon the time and patience at one's disposal. Tales grandiose beyond credibility in their proportions, with repartees, anecdotes, *on-dits,* all sorts of fragmentary hearsays, the disintegrated mosaic bits of who knows how many and what treasures of conversations and encounters.

On her general reception days, Saturdays after four o'clock, Madame la Baronne sits by the corner of her fireside, which, if it be winter, blazes and warms with that fascinating brilliancy of a real Parisian fire, confectioned with Parisian art from wood and "briquets." The warmth and brilliancy of the hearth are not more genial, however, than the welcome one receives—that true Parisian welcome, which, if it be like the fire, a confection of Parisian art, is no whit less but rather more perfect than the best nature achieves elsewhere.

One always glances at room and furniture nowadays, one cannot help it, shops and things having so far made good their claims upon a careless public for equal recognition with the individual. But all that is observable here is large rooms, abundant pictures, and handsome furniture, which are so far under subjection to the individual that they take tone and presence from her, and, dignified, reserved, discreet servitors that they are, permit you only to infer the part they have played, the scenes they have witnessed, in the history of this house life, and also in the political history of Europe. Nothing of the furnishment belongs to to-day except in the smaller reception-room, where madame receives, the tables and stands loaded with files of newspapers and the latest periodicals.

The visitor who wishes to enjoy the salon should be as well provided, for the conversation comes hot from the presses of public action and thought. The conversers—an Italian count just from Rome, a Belgian diplomatist arrived but that morning on a mission, the leader of the new spiritualistic movement, the great French preacher and writer Wagner, a young theologue from Scotland, with women coming and going, women interesting, interested, representing important husbands or important personalities of their own. If the conversation, with its breadth and height of interest and freedom of speech, astonishes and charms an outsider, the elegance of diction, the choice of language, the irreproachable tone, give to that charm and astonishment a gilding which tips it with perfection—frankly the discouraging perfection of the stage of the Comédie Française.

If one is given to aberrations of thought, despite the honest protestations of eyes and ears, one cannot forbear wondering and theorizing about Madame la Baronne, as she sits by the fireside thus, a point of pilgrimage for so many different representatives, an oracle for so many different questions, the recipient of so much genuine admiration. Physically a large woman—a typal woman—the kind with which we stamp coins and conventionalize in marble; a rare head in proportion and intellectual fulness; eyes that have a way, quite their own, of catching yours and flashing conviction into them; a mouth, that if you did not describe it as formed for supreme eloquence, you must describe it as formed for supreme beauty.

Why do we not speak of Madame de Bury's attractions in that past tense which inevitably commemorates the charms of women over the Rubicon of middle age? We do not know. It is perhaps because we are speaking of Madame de Bury, and that thus to be spoken of is one of her distinctions.

To have aberrations of thought about her in her salon, to wonder, which really means to question, about her to her face, to go again and again to see her, as one goes again and again to an elusive problem, and when one could not go to see her to hold those delightful and thoroughly French postal conversations with her—all this does not betoken a mind quiescent before the facts of her existence—her *raison d'être.* And so by degrees the history of Madame de Bury came to join itself on in time, the necessary addendum to that first visit on that cold February afternoon to 20 Rue Oudinot. She is not French, but Scotch; and, as Rose Stuart, commenced her career of celebrity at but short distance from the cradle.

She is said to have been a strange child, in some respects a kind of Anna Schuman, with such lively exhibitions of force of character, strength of will, and moral determination as to merit the philosopher Victor Cousin's[2] dictum of her: "She was a man of action from her birth." But men of action, even when they belong to the opposite sex, must await the pleasure of time and opportunity. She, however, did no supine awaiting. The field of literature was there, and unfenced, as usual, for any wayfarer or trespasser. She entered it in pinafores, so to speak, with a treatise on the Latin passive verbs, written at twelve—one year later than Madame de Staël's first production. At sixteen she made a double début and reaped a double triumph by her publication in the course of the same week, of a fifty-page article on the drama of Molière in the *Edinburgh Review*, and an essay almost as long on Dickens in the *Revue des Deux Mondes*. Both articles attracted encouraging attention from their respective audiences, and merely from a linguistic point of view are achievements of most remarkable distinction. Then followed her marriage with the Baron Blaze de Bury, the well-known *littérateur* and contributor to the *Revue des Deux Mondes*, and one of the leading idealists of France. Her eldest child was born when she was but a little past eighteen.

As she would express it, from thought launched into words, she passed into the period of thought launched into action, and began to do what she imagined to do.

She was scarcely over twenty when the Franco-Austrian war and the Austro-Hungarian troubles stirred her intensest enthusiasm for the race whose old-fashioned chivalry she knew, and whose misfortunes she bewailed from her heart's core. She bewailed them too sincerely to bewail them idly. A woman, perhaps, could only have imagined to do the impossible, and a woman only could have achieved it as she did. Financial aid was needful then to Austria. The English markets refused to admit the so-called "occult values" of the "despotic Austria" of the radicals, the "abomination of obscurantism" of prejudiced public opinion. She wrote to London; she went to Austria. Fired by what Shelley calls "the unselfish passion of things," she was, it is said, irresistible in her youth, beauty, strength; arguing, reasoning, expostulating, predicting, with that

2 Victor Cousin (1792–1867) was in his time the chief authority in France on matters of philosophy and education. For Anna Schuman, Clara Schumann, the musician and wife of Robert Schumann, may be intended.

keen political foresight of hers, which is still so remarkable. Bankers listened, members of the House of Commons paid attention, aristocratic influences rallied around her, ministers grew respectful; Benedek,[3] then in the pride of his popularity, surnamed her "the vital principal" (das belebende Princip); the Emperor became and remained her firm friend throughout and against all opposition. And the Anglo-Austrian Bank was established, the principle of the conversion of the currency consented to, and the modification of the tariff in the direction of freedom of trade admitted—all on the basis of an English alliance, to be recognized, at all events, as the strongest of future political hopes. It was what the *Times* called "the English era in Vienna."

Perhaps from this success germinated her next idea or effort, for both words mean the same to her, of bringing Europe and the United States financially together. An interesting diplomatic correspondence, in which figure President Grant, General Dix, Mr. Washburne, the French financial statesman M. Pinard, and Mr. Hitt,[4] and Madame de Bury, ensued, and was the only result, save the linking of Madame de Bury in friendship and even intimacy with some of our most distinguished public men.

After what she calls (when she does not term it more harshly) the catastrophe of the empire in France, Madame de Bury and her husband (her high-minded husband, she would say) stood, as they always had through life, the inflexible champions of public right, manifested by the will and voice of the whole nation, and, the Bonaparte disgrace wiped out, worked their utmost to further the cause of French freedom, moral progress, and mental improvement.

Four years ago M. de Bury died, but his wife's work still goes on, one may say, more fearlessly and dauntlessly than ever. She is now one of the inspirers, leaders, and to the world at large the most important worker in the new spiritualistic movement in France. And if the movement become, as it should, one for a world and not for a nation, it will be no less owing to her. In the front ranks of the "Young School," the so-called "Psychic School," formed by the youth of France, a kind of Holy Alliance for the Right against aggressive Wrong (an association, it is said,

3 Ludwig von Benedek (1804–81) was an Austrian general who distinguished himself at the battle of Solferino.

4 John Adams Dix (1798–1879), statesman and railroad executive, was U.S. minister to France (1866–69). Elihu Benjamin Washburne (1816–87) was Grant's minister to France (1869–77). Robert Roberts Hitt (1834–1906) served as secretary of the U.S. legation at Paris (1874–81).

counting several hundred thousand), she stands shoulder to shoulder with Desjardins, De Vogüé, Wagner, Lavisse, and de Beaurepaire,[5] doing man's work, and a young vigorous man's work, in the effort to stem the tide of impurity which from literature and art streams a damning, blighting flood over the actual vital principle of French life, the youth of France. She can no more tolerate modern French realistic literature and art than she can tolerate incarnate sin.

Of the long current of antecedent writings it is said that a collection of them has been formed in England and France—twenty-five or thirty stout volumes filled with papers on every subject, in every known form of publication; papers all of importance in their day, all struck hot from some generous enthusiasm or high-minded resentment. All anonymous, for until two years ago she published nothing over her own name. She says of herself, "I have neither imagination nor talent, but I see, and only reproduce what I have seen"; and she should add, "foreseen," for she possesses the woman's gift of intuition to a marvellous degree—a gift which her masculine judgment regulates to, humanly speaking, perfect accuracy of aim. Lamartine was wont to say of her, "Her judgment is infallible"; and Montalembert,[6] it is related, never tired of repeating, "Always rest on her opinion of coming events and men's capacities, for she never errs." Naturally around such a woman anecdotes coruscate, and the pleasantest of all anecdotes, those that commemorate great friendships. No woman of modern times has had greater friendships with prominent men, and for women it is charming to read their tributes to her. Lawrence Oliphant, after his last visit to Paris, wrote to Kinglake[7] of her: "Well, I've seen our inspirer again! She is an immortal from high Olympus! Just precisely what she was when we scoured Europe together in quest of incidents of knight-errantry. Yes, all she was, only ten times more attractive, because there is so much more radiance. . . . Hech, sirs! But she is aye a compelling creature!" Kinglake's own appreciation of

5 Paul Desjardins (1859–1940), professor and critic, was the founder of *L'Union pour l'action morale*; Vicomte Melchior de Vogüé (1850–1910), novelist and critic, was known for his studies of Russian literature in *Le Roman russe* (1886); Charles Wagner (1852–1918), Alsatian Protestant minister, was author of *La Vie simple* (1895); Ernest Lavisse (1842–1922) was editor and part author of *Histoire de France* (1900–11, 1920–22); Quesnay de Beaurepaire (1838–1923), was a novelist and *procureur général* of France.

6 Charles-Forbes-René, comte de Montalembert (1810–70), was a historian and leader of the militant Catholics during the Second Empire.

7 Lawrence Oliphant (1829–88), British religious mystic, traveler, and author; Alexander William Kinglake (1809–91), historian of the Crimean War, author of *The Invasion of the Crimea* (1863–87).

her was given some years before: "Of all the men or women I ever knew in public life, on one alone, perhaps, could unalterable reliance and faith unlimited be placed. Nothing on earth could in any way modify Rose de Bury. Nor time nor circumstance could touch her. We used to call her Rosa Ferox at one time—her true name will always be, amongst us, Rosa Victrix." "A man, a woman, and a lion," the same friend once described her to Lord Beaconsfield.

It has been said of her—it has been said of every celebrity—that she can only be described by her friends; but she objects: "No, I can best stand by what my enemies say of me." And she is probably not wrong, for she has never been an acrimonious, evil-speaking writer or talker, and has always been generously fair to her opponents. Mazzini, one of them, paid her the following tribute in a letter to a friend (Mr. George Cooke,[8] the friend also of Carlyle): "I am busy over my 'Byron,' but want the advice of Madame de Bury, who knows him better than any of those who ever really saw him. Find out if she will let me write to her. . . . I know our violent political discussions, know well how she has fought me, but she is such a noble enemy, better to be trusted than a dozen ordinary friends. I want her ideas on Byron. She is always just, and besides that she sees. . . . *'C'est une royauté'.*" Unfortunately, before the letter which Madame de Bury gladly undertook to write for him could reach him he had died, and she who had been one of his most untiring foes has never ceased speaking of him as the grandest of Italian patriots out of the classical ages.

She possesses, in truth, the characteristics that attach men to women collaborators. She is enthusiastic, optimistic, altruistic. She embraces a cause with the whole-hearted devotion of a woman who loves, and she works for it as only women do work for a cause, sacrificing with enthusiastic zeal self, family, home. Self-sacrifice, in fact, has become a kind of fetich with her. "I am powerless for myself," she says, "but I am certain of succeeding if I work for others; once working for another, or others, I feel myself invincible. I clutch my victory, which, under these circumstances, has never failed me." There is "light" in her. When she speaks it radiates from her face. One feels illumined in listening to her. But the great, the perhaps true, bond between her friends and herself is trust—mutual trust. In all of her intercourse with public men, in all of her writing, thinking, acting, with and for them, there have been no stories or

8 George Wingrove Cooke (1814–65), British lawyer and author.

revelations of betrayals, treasons, indiscretions. The two friendships of which she seems to speak with most pride are the one with William Kinglake, author of the *Invasion of the Crimea*, in the past, and with the celebrated French magistrate M. de Beaurepaire, whose patriotic handling of the anarchist cases has just culminated a brilliant series of juridical services to his country. His famous dictum, *"Le mal c'est le mal, voilà la loi de Dieu,"* she has adopted, and it bids fair to become the device of the new school. Her appearance? The general verdict is, she looks and has always looked what she is. Her age? Oh! (Who can accuse her of being a masculine woman?) No one will ever know it, for, as she was born in Scotland, it is unnoted, and her friends say she will never betray her secret, for to preserve the mystery is so easy.

Her *intimes,* however, gaze upon her with wonder, and speak of "la radiante jeunesse" as of some miracle.

Madame la Comtesse Tascher de la Pagerie

A dinner party in the Faubourg St. Honoré was the opportunity of making her acquaintance—a small dinner party of eight, one of the hospitable inspirations (the Parisian hostess entertains, however, only by inspiration) which reveal the true place and worth in the civilized world of the thing most of us know only in the ideal called society.

How the very *salon* lent itself to its purpose—everything in it willing and fitting, nothing in it contrary or self-assertive! One felt it a prelude—such a prelude as the rare musician, as well as finished woman of the world, its mistress, Madame F. de V.,[9] knows so well the value of in music as well as society. Perhaps, of all women, a musician should know best the technique of society; and that brilliant technique of a French musician, through which personality glistens and glitters like a jewelled bottom, knows best the truest rendition of a social function—social sonatas; symphonies they should be. It is a pity that there is not in Paris a conservatory of manners as well as of music, a school of heart as well as

9 Madame Foulon de Vaulx: See *Memories of a Southern Woman of Letters*, 151–54.

of art, to which foreigners might have access; for, despite the smile, if not the sneer, of the not-French, it is its heart quality that differentiates Parisian if not all French society from that of the rest of the world. But a Parisian would say that accomplishments of the heart are not to be educed, but lived, and living proves that loving has more variations and applications than foreigners—so much the worse for them—seem to be aware of.

And the quality of Madame F. de V.'s little dinner party was precisely this heart, this loving quality, the absence of which is so conspicuous, so drearily conspicuous, in the common eating and drinking around that archmisnomer of a festal board. One's welcome dated from the valet who opened the door, and by the time one's wraps were disposed of one's mind was in harmony with surroundings and surrounders. It is so easy to know one another, and so pleasant, when one does not have to perambulate drawing-rooms in the clumsy buskins of an archaic conventionality, hiding our insignificant, it may be, but true individuality under stifling and wearily burdensome bushel masks! It is a curious fact that in the best French society individuals, acting in their own true characters, seem to feel all the exhilarating freedom and spontaneity of intelligence that in other parts of the world is exhibited only under disguise in the gay incognito of a masked ball.

The *mauvais quart d'heure* before dinner being a fault—rather a crime—of the hostess, we had none. The Comtesse made her appearance when under other circumstances it might have been about to commence, and what minutes were allowed to elapse before dining, to show that we were not assembled entirely in the interests of food, were skilfully utilized by the hostess to bring about an appetitive prologue of conversation, during which the always momentous opening of the dining-room doors was accomplished unperceived. As naturally now as during the old days at the court of Napoleon III., the Comtesse Tascher de la Pagerie is the centre of attraction in whatever society she finds herself. Still gay, still brilliant, and more interesting than she could ever have been in the old court days, it would be hard in Europe, hard even in Paris, to find a contestant rival in attractiveness. Unfortunately her name spoils the surprise attendant upon her description, and reveals prematurely the historical *dénouement* of her life. There are women in life who, like the fine gold-work of the ancient, represent as no other data do the taste and luxury of a past age, things of a different beauty, delicacy, and originality from our own, which most of us long for and try to imitate, sending our goldsmiths in despair to brood over cases in museums, and which we but barbarously imitate at the best—as if the efflorescence of one period were possible in another—the efflorescence, that is, of women and art!

There is such a quaintness of design and expression, such an exquisiteness of form, such a finish of detail, in the Countess, such a spurning of filigree and fastenings of dainty rolettes over the solid and stable character of her, that, inestimable piece of workmanship that she is, she might justly by an art-loving committee be placed on a cushion all to herself in a glass case of some museum; and the label upon it might fitly be, "A court jewel of the Second Empire."

The Second Empire. How far past it is already! Not so far, it is true, as the dynasty of the Pharaohs, but in our fast-marching century as dead and gone. Its little belongings and ornaments have already become antique bric-à-brac, its men and women relics; legend has already begun its incrustations upon the history of it, and its history is assuming more and more the ominous aspect of a didactic legacy, a lesson, a tragedy. A brilliant little empire it was. Or rather, a brilliant representation of one. Irving[10] himself could not have put up a better. A very long memory is not needed to recall the newspaper tributes to its success; and of its spectators and auditors, who tell of the triumphs of the *dramatis personae,* they are still almost as plentiful among us as those of the first performances of Wagner.

The men of the Second Empire, they seem to have sunk into a common grave with their chief. All that is not a reproach seems silence and obscurity around them and their names. Not so the women. The cup of sorrow, on the contrary, contains a drop of immortality for women, and it is not too much to say of them that there are but few who after disaster do not live for the betterment of the worldly reputation of the cause for which they suffered—even for so poor a cause as the Second Empire. And of that gay bevy of court ladies who a sparse quarter of a century ago were dazzling the world with their extravagances of pleasure and toilette, showering such brilliancy of beauty and wit over the dark background of the *coup d'état,* until it was almost forgotten if not forgiven in their presence even by diplomatists—of these fascinating caryatides of an enigmatical structure there are, indeed, but few of the many who remain among us who have not contributed by their bearing to securing a commutation of public opinion from that Lynch-law process of judg-

10 Sir Henry Irving (1838–1905), the noted English actor.

ment passed at the time of disaster upon them, their Empire, and Emperor. They are witnesses whom history herself must consult before handing in her verdict.

The Comtesse Stéphanie Tascher de la Pagerie is now about seventy-eight; she looks about sixty. Of medium height; slight frail figure; a pale, delicate, refined face, with no or very slight marks of age; fine eyes; and chestnut hair turning and only turning gray; dressed in a "changeable" light silk with full skirts that look as if they could not get over the habit of "hoops," with the traditional old lace at sleeves and neck; hair combed in *bandeaux,* under a handsome black lace cap—she is the typical "lady" of half a century ago, preserved in the freshness that one sees occasionally in Europe in the old families, but in fashion-ridden America to be found only in family portraits or frontispieces of "keepsakes." Her manners belong to her type—manners that are almost archaic now, when it appears somewhat impossible to contain a great flow of intelligence within the prescribed boundaries of etiquette, and to be original without infractions of harmony. The Countess is madame only in virtue of her title of Canoness in some Bavarian chapter; an old maid, as one may say, without the consciousness of being one. Her mother was heiress of the small German principality of Lien, over which her ancestors had reigned for generations. It followed the usual fate of small principalities at that time—it was annexed to the empire—and the heiress of it also, eventually, by her marriage with the Comte Tascher de la Pagerie, the nephew of the Empress Josephine.

Upon the accession of Napoleon III. So notable a member of his mother's family could not but be honored. He was transplanted to Paris, with his family of four daughters and one son, was installed in residence at the palace of the Louvre, placed in court upon the princely footing of imperial relations. The old count was made "Grand maître de la maison" to Eugénie. In addition to his maternal title of Duc d'Alberg, the son was made Duke of France. All the daughters, with the exception of Stéphanie, were married.

Stéphanie, then in the full maturity of person and mind, remained attached to the court, of which, with the Princess of Metternich, she was the life and the charm, particularly distinguished among all by her intellectual qualities, her wit, humor, *à propos,* and presence of mind. The Emperor and the Empress, it is said, adored her. But she was known even then to be something more than the successful court lady. A witness or a participant in the various phases through which the Second Empire rose to absolute power and sunk to defeat and disgrace; cousin, friend, and acquaintance of all the principals connected therein; knowing much and divining more from her woman's wit and intuitions, and restless under the accumulations of information, impressions, judgments, and apprehensions—she was known to keep on hand that woman's resource, a journal, the intimate chronicle of men, women, and events about her—matter not to be talked of, but not to be forgotten. Such a journal passes inevitably from its original position of means, to end. It has assumed in the Countess's life more and more the importance of a life work; its service has imparted to her character a literary bearing, striking from the outset to even a careless observer, and it obtrudes into every turn of her conversation.

Speaking of the Emperor, for whom she has a profound affection, defending him with the warmth of a generous woman, eager to clear, to explain, the misunderstood, giving reasons (and good ones), names of persons, dates, circumstances, with convincing frankness and boldness, she invariably concludes or breaks off a sentence abruptly with "But wait until you read my 'Souvenirs'; it is all explained; it will all come out there." And this is indeed the termination of all conversation upon subjects pertaining to questions connected with the Second Empire: "You will see I have put all that in my 'Souvenirs.' "[11]

There is very little trace of her French or creole lineage in her face, but it is redolent in her conversation and manners. Her mind, with its firm historical philosophy and unshrinking facing of unpleasant truths, its resignations and revolts, seems, at different times, all German, all French, all creole.

The fall of the Empire, which disrupted her life and sent her forth from her palace home, never, her friends say, caused a moment of weakness or discouragement. She left the Louvre with all her wonted energy, courage, and dignity not a whit diminished, saddened only by the fate of her cousin Napoleon.

The namesake and goddaughter of the late Grand-Duchess Stéphanie of Baden (who died in her arms), she passes every autumn with the reigning Grand-Duke and his wife, the daughter of old Emperor William of Germany. In this court opportunity is given for the historical continuity of her experiences, and if the journal be not further fed and prolonged from this source, the "Souvenirs" will doubtless show from contact with

11 Stéphanie, comtesse Tascher de la Pagerie (1814–1905), published her *Souvenirs* in 1894.

it the needful corrections and verifications, which time alone cannot be relied upon to bring about. She passes her summers at Sugernsee,[12] near Munich, her winters in Paris, Rue des Écuries d'Artois, No. 47, latterly very much occupied with the preparation of her journal for publication as "Souvenirs," for the motives of discretion which have hitherto withheld her appear at last to have ceded to motives of affection and loyalty to Napoleon III., and the desire, while still alive, to give him the benefit of her testimony. An evening with her speeds all too soon, the hours overrun too quickly, and adieux become a renunciation instead of the release one is accustomed to.

And the dinner! The dinner's encomium was its effacement; it was so perfect that it passed unnoticed.

Theo. Bentzon—Madame Th. Blanc

Personal impressions are almost too private to be made public. Outside of one's religious convictions there is nothing so personally private as personal impressions. They are really confessions. Are not one's admirations one's aspirations? Fault-finding, fault-feeling? And in chronicling one's impression perhaps it would be safer and wiser to plead all the extenuating circumstances which usually accompany a confession.

In life it seems to be becoming harder and harder for a woman to attain the full bloom of her natural development. There is so much "strain of the stuff" and "warping past the aim." Every day seems to be adding so much more to the inevitable and unavoidable compromises between her best instincts and her duties, her ambitions and her necessities, that more and more she is getting to look at her highest accomplishments as mere excuses in default of an ideal of a still higher; and outside praise of her is burdened with "riders" in the shape of palliations.

Rarely and more rarely one meets a woman in whom one can recognize the untrammelled, simple, full development of her type; the easy and harmonious equilibrium of all the innumerable qualities of mind and

12 Sugernsee: Probably Tegernsee is intended here.

heart that go to the making up of the woman into the intellectual woman—a woman at one with her destiny, who looks upon life with the clear eyes of intelligence and faith, and whose heart casts upon the future no shadowy blurs from the past. This last is the *rara avis* of a woman's qualifications; for a woman is more truly made up of her past than a man. In truth, she may be said to be the accident or the miracle of her past.

Among women, without any subdistinctions of literary or otherwise, Madame Blanc is a cadence—once heard, never to be forgotten.

Let it be kept in mind that this is an impression. One lodges in Paris as one dresses—with consummate taste and discretion. To a true Parisian one's *appartement* can no more be at fault than one's bonnet. When the door closes upon one in the *salon* of Theo. Bentzon one feels the pleasantest sense of intellectual isolation and harborage. Indeed, in the great overwrought, intense Paris this tiny retreat reminds one of a quiet thought in a superexcited brain. All the doors are concealed by rugs, but the window-glass is free and clear to the sky, and when there is a sun it shines into the *salon* as if that was its special mission for the day. And on a reception day, Monday, it might scarcely find a pleasanter mission. The *salon* itself, to begin with, is so—congenial. To call it pretty (which it nevertheless is) is to misconceive it—as it would be a misapprehension of the mistress to specify her physical charm, although it is none the less apparent. When one's attention is called to it, there are interesting photographs scattered around, and what bric-à-brac there is, is fine and suggestive. One does notice immediately a beautiful portrait on the wall, the portrait of Theo. Bentzon when she made her début into what we are pleased to magnify as the *world* of literature. An habitué of the *salon* loves to sit in a position from which one can discreetly vary gazing at the original with gazing at the copy. The Titian-colored tresses of the former have become, it is true, almost white, and the eyes and mouth are still halfway behind on that journey the experiences of which have flavored the expression of the latter; but from the forecast of the canvas to the lived-out reality of the present there is such a symmetrical advance that one knows not which to admire the more, the sure eye of the artist that saw so unerringly the fruition ahead and expressed it in his picture, or the simple directness of the model progressing thus faultlessly to the fruition predicted—her life attaching with a straight cord the present to the past.

In a few words the life is as follows:

Theo. Bentzon was Thérèse de Solms. The pseudonym comes from her mother, who, as it testifies, was of Danish origin. The young girl was reared and educated at home in the country, under the direct supervision of her mother, seconded by an English governess of inestimable worth. Travels in Italy and Germany, where she met a varied and interesting society, continued the auspicious development of her character and talents. The second marriage of her mother, with an officer of the court of Napoleon III., opened the new and still more brilliant world of the empire to her. Her novels testify the perfectness of her novitiate; her knowledge of the provincial, Parisian, imperial, and republican social life, as shown in them, could not be more complete.

Although always possessed by the passion to write, it is doubtful if her youthful shrinking from the publicity of print would not always have kept her manuscript a secret of the desk had it not been for the propulsion of reverses of fortune. The pseudonym furnished complete disguise, and for a long time most of the circle of her friends ignored that Theo. Bentzon was in reality Thérèse Blanc, as she had become. These first publications, her work from twenty to thirty, are not collected in volumes. Many of them won the golden meed of approbation from George Sand, the sacred fountain-head of encouragement to the literary neophyte of the time. It is to George Sand, to M. Caro, the eminent professor of philosophy, and to Mr. Milsand,[13] more recently known as the friend of Browning, that the young writer owes the evolution of her mental development from uncertainty and hesitation to its present delightful self-poise. But she enjoyed other and rarely fructifying influences. Although living in a state of comparative retirement, she had come into more or less intimate contact with all the distinguished writers of the time. The charm of her literary style as well as the charm of her personality evidence this, and color the suave fineness of her conversation.

Her first distinct literary success was "Un Divorce" (A Divorce), in the *Journal des Débats*, 1871. This opened the doors of the *Revue des Deux Mondes* to a short but very remarkable story, "La Vocation de Louise" (The Vocation of Louise). Then followed, in the *Revue des Deux Mondes*, the *Journal des Débats*, and sometimes in the *Revue Bleue*, a long series of some twenty novels, of which the principal ones are: "Une Vie Manquée" (A Missed Life) "Georgette," "L'Obstacle" (The Obstacle), "La Petite Perle" (The Little Pearl), "Tony," "Un Remords," (Remorse),

13 Elme Marie Caro (1826–87), French philosopher of the school of Victor Cousin; Joseph Milsand, whose friendship for Robert Browning began in 1851, after he had written enthusiastically on the poet's religious philosophy.

"Constance," (the last three crowned by the French Academy), "Le Veuvage d'Aline" (The Widowhood of Aline), "Le Mariage de Jacques" (The Marriage of Jacques), "Tentée" (Tempted), "Le Retour" (The Return), and "L'Emancipée" (Emancipated); also, for young girls, "Tetta," the history of a creole, and "Les Souvenirs d'une Fille Laide" (The Souvenirs of an Ugly Girl). *Jacqueline,* one of Theo. Bentzon's latest stories, is also perhaps one of her best, and the best of its type in modern French literature. The elegant edition, with matchless illustrations by Lyod, is well known in all artistic and literary circles of the Old and New World. It was during this steady driving period of her imagination that Theo. Bentzon took upon herself the important literary function of keeping the readers of the *Revue des Deux Mondes* in current intelligence and communication with the pictorial work in the English and American guild of letters. Her admirable criticisms, adaptations, and translations are unique of their kind. Her refined and pure literary treatment of her subjects, her sympathy, her fair and even balances of judgment, differentiate her method from similar foreign work of various quarters; and although at times she has excited the susceptibilities of the English, her articles form a most notable and encouraging advance towards that ideal of the intellectual of all countries, literary solidarity. And while her compatriots are learning to call as their own the names and works of the writers across the Channel and across the ocean, young writers, more and more, turn to measure themselves by the gauge of Theo. Bentzon's past and present articles, and more and more aspire to an introduction through her to the fastidious and exclusive French court of letters.

Of her novels one can hardly speak the praise one wishes without sounding like an echo, so much have they found favor from press and public. And it is a recommendation to the press and public that this is so. In the whole range of French novels there is none in which figure so little what the rest of the world is pleased to call the "French sins." Madame de Bury, writing, as she always did, for purity in literature, does not fail to note this in an article in the *National Review* of April, 1889, entitled, "Some Sound French Novels." In an age of so much pseudo-scientific work by French fictionists upon women, it is most refreshing to turn to a woman's instinctive and natural knowledge of herself and her sex, and read not the lucubrations of an artificially sensitized brain, nor the imaginations of an artificially heated heart, but the forceful, simple, natural expositions of a genuinely feminine nature. It is more than refreshing; it is good. There is so much that might be written in this connection on

'Tony, for example, or *Jacqueline.* But it is not the place or time to discuss them or theorize; only, in order to define their place and the place of their author in modern French literature, let them be read in connection with and in contrast to other novels of the day and place, signed by men or women, it matters not which. In this country Theo. Bentzon will be best known in the future through her incomparable volume of the *Conditions of Women in the United States,* a series of articles written as the result of a visit to the Columbian Fair and of extensive travels on this continent. No such careful and judicious treatment of one of the most complex phases of our civilization has ever appeared in literature. Madame Blanc herself acknowledges but one interesting item in her personal history—the perfect unanimity which always existed between herself and her mother. It was indeed admirable! They were never separated, until death came between them some years ago. At that quaint Hôtel Sinon, in Barbizon, there is, among its heterogeneous and picturesque collection of artists, littérateurs, and dogs, one boarder that attracts universal attention and sentiment. It is Musette, the handsome, superannuated gray cat —the pensioner of Theo. Bentzon—the old pet and companion of her mother, and the last object her dying fingers caressed.

It is said in Paris by authorities on the subject that the particular and brilliant distinction of Theo. Bentzon's *salon* is its high-bred avoidance of "blue-stockingism," and all that suggests it, however remotely, and that for its influence it has never had the affirmation of wealth. One meets in it only the best—that is all. And as for conversation—that delicate fragile flower that blooms from the meeting of sympathetic minds—can any other *salon* in Paris vie with the cullings from this one? The circle seems always complete, the current of thought always on, and the tongue not only dutiful but graceful in the rare enclosure. When the portière sweeps aside, one forgets to shudder over the interruption, as in other parts of the world. There are no interruptions possible, no intrusions—only additional completeness, additional satisfaction. But we are verging upon indiscretion! . . .

Bernard de Marigny

It was the third child of Philippe Bernard Xavier de Marigny de Mandeville, who represented the family during the last century; and who is the hero *par excellence* of New Orleans' social traditions; who, we may say, was to the Marigny family what the final bouquet is to a pyrotechnical display. He, more than any of his family or men of his time, is responsible for what we call to-day the Creole type; originating the standard of fine living and generous spending, of lordly pleasure and haughty indifference to the cost; the standard which he maintained so brilliantly for a half century, until, even to-day, one receives, as an accepted fact, that not to be fond of good eating and drinking, of card playing and pretty ladies; not to be a *fin gourmet,* not to be sensitive about honor, and to possess courage beyond all need of proof is, in sober truth, if such a truth can be called sober—not to be a Creole.

It was a standard that required the greatest fortune Louisiana could produce to maintain it. It ravaged the great wealth of Marigny himself, and ruined many and many of the old families who tried to follow in his aristocratic footprints and who arrived at poverty as Bernard did but without the prestige that distinguished him to the end. The handsome furniture, cut glass, porcelain, jewelry—the real lace, and delicate bric-a-brac of all kinds that have delighted the eye for decades past in the antique shops of New Orleans, are indubitably remnants of the wreckage of the fortunes that went to pieces in the wake of the Marigny standard of living. And as in the course of two centuries the Marigny family intermarried only with the best families in the place, and, as we shall see, all of the old families bear one or two of the Marigny names as the proudest fruit of their genealogical trees—the name has come to be in the city's estimation as sure a guarantee of social prestige as it is of artistic beauty and genuine value when attached to mere objects of domestic use.

Elegant of manners, polished of tongue, fearless of opinions, Bernard was the kind of man that shone in conversation, particularly at the banquet table, sowing repartees and witticisms that have sprouted ever since in the memory or imagination of his fellow citizens, until they have attained a growth and luxuriance of bloom out of all proportion to our powers of belief to-day. And it is always repeated with apparent conviction that the best and greatest number have been lost—as seems always to be the fate of good stories. Those who were born too late to know him have always regretted the lost opportunity of meeting in person a hero who would have graced the Court of Louis XIV—or at least the pages of Alexandre Dumas.

Upon Pierre Philippe's death, his kinsman, De Lino de Chalmette, assumed the management of his vast estates and the guardianship of the fifteen-year-old Bernard. The latter charge proved not a light one for the staid and prudent godfather. The youth, indulged and spoiled, reared, according to local gossip, like some rich nobleman's son, had from childhood known no other authority but that of his own will and pleasure. Precociously wild and extravagant, with unlimited wealth now at his command, more was feared than hoped from his future.

De Lino had recourse to the time-honored expedient, ever adopted by troubled guardians, of a change of environment. He sent his ward to Pensacola, and placed him there under the care of the great millionaire merchant, Panton, of the historical firm of Panton and Leslie, whose commercial transactions at the time amounted to a virtual monopoly of the Indian and European trade of the southern portions of America. The young Creole, however, was given such a handsome allowance of money and liberty by his tutor, and he made such good use of it for his own pleasure, that he soon scandalized the austere Scotchman and Protestant, Panton, who returned him after a short experience to New Orleans.

But Chalmette had still another resource whereby he hoped to make a staid business man of his charge. He sent him to England, and placed him under the care of Mr. Leslie, the resident partner of the firm in London. Two anxious letters* on the subject by Chalmette have survived in a mass of Panton family correspondence.

He writes frankly to Mr. Forbes, a member of the firm, who apparently had intervened in the affair:

> The friends who have informed you unfavorably about the young man, have not misled you. He has been guilty of irregularities of conduct, errors caused rather by his youth than by

* Obtained through the courtesy of Héloise Crozet, a descendant of Mr. Panton [Grace King's note].

> corruption of heart. Besides, at the time he was under the guidance of a most respectable father, but one full of weak indulgence toward him which contributed not a little to his ill conduct. I have made him understand your fears about introducing him. He feels them sensibly. But his expressions and his increase in age, his promises to me, and his good conduct since the death of his father, are strong reasons for me to hope that he will become one day, an agreeable and intelligent member of society.

Some days later he writes:

> I am writing to Mr. Leslie acquainting him with the character of the young man. I am giving him full power to place him in the college or seminary he selects as the most proper. I also leave to his will all that pertains to his clothing and small expenses. In fact, I make over to him all the authority I have as his tutor, approving in advance whatever measures he may adopt in regard to him. I tell Mr. Leslie also, that if the 1200 gourdes (dollars) that I have settled as Bernard's pension for the first year, do not suffice, I pray him to supply the deficit, and so to advise me that I may return his advances.

He explains:

> According to what information I have been able to gather from different persons here as to the expenditures necessary to obtain a good education, lodging, food and small pleasures for a young man in Louisiana or London, I am assured that twelve hundred dollars will suffice to procure comfortable ease. He must keep within it the first year at least . . . Bernard knows all this and seems disposed to fulfill my desires.
>
> De Lino, April 29th, 1808.

Later he thought of increasing the allowance to two thousand dollars, whenever Mr. Leslie assured him that the young man was making good use of the money, for it would be dangerous for him to possess large means in a city which offered so much temptation as London.

Introduced into the best society by Mr. Leslie, who himself was connected with old and aristocratic families of Scotland and England, even with the Gordons then shining in the luster of their luminary, Lord Byron, Bernard de Marigny gained in London much in the way of the

English polish of manners of the time. He gained also the fine fluent use of good English that distinguished him through life, although his accent remained amusingly bad. (In social life and with his family, he spoke only French.) Of business methods, however, he learned naught that was profitable. In short, he made so many visits to Paris, spent money so lavishly on his pleasures, and his pleasures increased so alarmingly in moral and financial cost, that his alarmed tutor recalled him in 1803 to the bosom of his family.

His portrait at this time represents him with the clean-shaven, handsome face of the full-blooded young Englishman of the day, dressed with the foppery of a dashing young fellow; his eyes, large and handsome, bespeaking intellect; his handsome mouth and full lips showing the devotion to the good things of life which he always professed, to which indeed he showed a lifelong fidelity. His figure was symmetry itself; he was about five feet ten inches tall and admirably proportioned.

Gayarré, his cousin, gives this glimpse of him:

> One day as our family, seated on the front piazza, was enjoying the balmy atmosphere of a bright May morning, there came on a visit from New Orleans, M. de Boré's favorite nephew, whose name was Bernard de Marigny. He was one of the most brilliant and wealthiest young men of the epoch. He drove in a dashing way up to the house in an elegant equipage drawn by two fiery horses. Full of the buoyancy of youth, he jumped out of his carriage and ran up the broad steps of the brick perron that ascended to the piazza. As he reached the top of it, he said, with a sort of familiarity, "Bonjour, mon oncle, bonjour! "

Marigny was at this time eighteen, and master of himself and of his fortune. A most favorable occasion for the employment of both was at hand. Louisiana was to be transferred back to France. M. de Laussat was sent to New Orleans, with the title of Colonial Prefect, to represent France and receive the province from the Spanish Commissioners. He brought a letter of introduction to Bernard Marigny from Delfau de Pontalba, who suggested to his young kinsman to tender the use of his house to the French Commissioner. This advice was at once acted on; and de Laussat, his wife—"a woman of remarkable beauty and wit," as Marigny describes her, two young daughters, his staff of four officers and his secretary were all entertained in this great house on the levee, in which Philippe de Marigny had entertained the Royal Princes.[14]

Bernard proved the equal of his father in bounteous hospitality, and surpassed him in the brilliancy of the fêtes given in honor of his guests. He himself was tendered a seat at Laussat's table as well as entrée to his salon, and he became one of the intimates of the circle.

He participated in Laussat's anxiety over the delay of General Victor's[15] arrival with the army to take military possession for France, and was a witness of his extreme disappointment when he received the order to cede the province with as brief delay as possible to the Commissioners of the United States. The courier who brought the dispatch was a dashing young French officer named Landais who, charged to avoid the usual route and conveyance from Washington, rode at full speed through the Indian territory to New Orleans.

Preparations were at once begun for the ceremony of the cession and the fêtes and entertainments to celebrate the event were renewed and prolonged. Salcedo, the Spanish Governor, who was old and infirm, wished to defer the ceremony until he had heard from his government, but Casacalvo, the Commissioner sent by Spain to assist him, "a man of no ability," says Marigny, was anxious to return to his family and interests in Cuba, and hastened the preparations.

At both ceremonies of cession, Marigny, at Laussat's request, acted as his aide-de-camp; but ardently American in sympathy, as soon as Louisiana was given over to Claiborne, he volunteered on the staff of General Wilkinson.[16] He remained in active service until 1808 when, on account of the fatal illness of his wife, he sent in his resignation. Her death, he says, "closing the political career that might have been his." Nevertheless, with confident intrepidity, he afterward entered into politics, embracing the principles of the Democratic Party, of which he remained a faithful partisan through life. At the time of his death, it was said that for fifty years no Democratic mass meeting was held to be complete that was

14 In 1798 Bernard's father was host to the three sons of Philippe Égalité: the duc d'Orléans (later King Louis Philippe), the duc de Montpensier, and the comte de Beaujolais.

15 General Victor (1766?–1841), duke of Belluno, marshal of France, was governor of Louisiana briefly in 1802.

16 For a detailed account of the Louisiana Purchase, see *New Orleans, the Place and the People* (New York, 1895), 107–54. General James Wilkinson (1757–1825) when governor of Louisiana territory, conspired with Aaron Burr in his plan to "liberate" Mexico from Spain and make Louisiana an independent republic. Wilkinson later betrayed Burr by denouncing the plan to President Jefferson.

not presided over by Bernard Marigny. In 1804 he married Mary Ann Jones, daughter of Evan Jones, a wealthy Pennsylvanian, for a time American Consul in New Orleans, and of Marie Verret, of a fine old Creole family.

Mary Ann Jones died in Philadelphia, June 4th, 1808; her body was transferred to New Orleans, August 4th, 1808. She was interred in a new sepulchre, built by her husband, in a corner of the garden on his plantation, the lot and tomb having been previously blessed by the reverend Father Antonio de Sedella.

By this union were born two children:

Gustave Adolphe, born in 1808, was killed in a duel and left no issue.

Prosper François de Marigny, who died in Natchez in 1836. He married his cousin, Marie Celeste d'Estrehan. (His widow remarried Mr. Alexander Grailhe, a barrister.)

They left two children:

Gustave Philippe, who married Elmina Bienvenu; and Marie Odile, married Alphonse Miltenberger.

About 1809 or 1810, he remarried Anne Mathilde Morales, daughter of Don Ventura Morales, former Spanish Intendant and Royal Contador, unenviably known to history for his intrigues against the American Domination, until Governor Claiborne forced his retirement from the city and States.

His courtship of Anna Mathilde Morales is thus related by one who heard the original account of it:

> Arriving in Pensacola, Marigny went to a ball where his attention was soon attracted to the most beautiful woman in it. He expressed his admiration and asked her name. His informant thought proper to warn him: "You will meet trouble." "That's what I like!" answered Marigny lightly, and at once engaged the young lady to dance, and made himself agreeable to her the rest of the evening, to the exclusion of her other admirers.
>
> The next morning he received seven challenges. "I cannot fight all at once," he answered, "but I will meet one every morning before breakfast, until all are satisfied." His first opponent fell with a sword thrust through the body. The other six professed themselves satisfied and made their apologies: "We see that you are a man of courage and honor." Marigny obtained without further opposition the hand of the beautiful young lady.

Morales was reputed to have hogsheads filled with gold in his house; the hogsheads, as described, were found in his house—but they were not filled with gold!

In 1810 Marigny was elected to the Legislature. In 1812 he was elected a member of the first Constitutional Convention of Louisiana and, although the youngest of its members, he took no small part in framing the Constitution that ruled Louisiana for thirty-three years. He always fought frankly and squarely on the side of the Louisianians and against the increasingly aggressive partisanship of the Americans.

In this first Convention took place the historic effort by the Americans to change the name of the State to Jefferson. It was a proposition warranted to inflame the Creoles to the point of frenzy, and it did so. Marigny relates that one of the members, Louis de Blanc de St. Denis, declared that "if such a proposition had any chance of success, he would arm himself with a barrel of powder and blow up the Convention!"

In 1811, at what is still considered the most important marriage ceremony that ever took place in the city, when the Baron de Pontalba (the son of Marigny's godfather) was married to Micaela Almonaster, daughter of the Spanish Alférez Real, the historic benefactor of New Orleans, Marigny, acting as the representative of Marshal Ney, the distinguished friend of the Pontalbas, gave the bride away.

A few years later de Pontalba proposed a more personal connection between his friend and the great Marshal. Among the papers found on Ney at the time of his arrest, was the following letter written by de Pontalba to Marigny:

> PARIS, 11th July, 1815.
>
> You know, my dear Cousin, the attachment that my son and I have felt for a long time for M. Maréchal Ney, Prince de la Moscou. Circumstances are sending him to New Orleans. He has chosen that part of the world from what I have told him of the liberty that one enjoys there and of the kindly and hospitable character of its inhabitants.
>
> Among them I have distinguished you, my friend, and it is to you that I am sending him, being confident that you will render him all the services in your power. See about an establishment for him according to the desires that he will communicate to you. Be assured that I will be much more grateful to you for anything you can do for him than if you did it for myself. You

will be the first person he will see on arriving. I have insisted he shall land at your home, because I know he will find there a good welcome and full liberty.

When you know him you will see that he is the most modest and simple of men. If he sees that his presence is causing you any embarrassment or expense on his account, he will leave you to go to a tavern. Receive him then with the greatest simplicity; act as if he were not in your home. He will arrive in the sickly time in the city. I wish that you would obtain his consent to pass this time in the country. I am very certain that you will make the strongest insistence upon this, but I am afraid he will resist, if in a few days he sees that his presence is leading you into extraordinary expenses, as happened when upon my recommendation you received M. de Laussat so splendidly.

In the meantime, my friend, and after he has become acquainted with the place, you will see about procuring for him a house, in the country near the city; I need not tell you how to go about this. I know you well and am very certain you will know how to meet all his desires. St. Avid will second you with all his power. You will not have forgotten that it was you who were charged by M. le Maréchal to represent him on the occasion of the marriage of my son . . .

PONTALBA.

Archives Nationales.
Procédure de M. le Maréchal Ney.
de la premiére Div. Militre

In another letter to his nephew St. Avid, Pontalba writes: "I pray you my dear nephew to join Marigny in rendering to Maréchal Ney, Prince de la Moscou, all the services that you can." Five months after these letters were written the Marshal was executed.

At this time, 1814–1815, Marigny was acting as Chairman of the Committee of Defense, charged by the Legislature to place the entire resources of the State at the disposition of General Jackson. He was one of the party of distinguished citizens who assembled to meet and welcome the General at his landing place on the Bayou St. Jean. Marigny thought that he should have had the honor of entertaining the great soldier during his stay in New Orleans. "My name," he writes rather bitterly, "was not unknown to him; he had very recently been the guest of my father-in-law, M. Morales (in Pensacola), who made known to me the desire of the General to stay with me, and it would have been infinitely agreeable to receive him. . . ."

But a more pushing aspirant usurped what it almost seems was the right of a Marigny. Jackson arrived at Bayou St. Jean and the Mayor made his speech of welcome. It is worth while repeating what Marigny writes further about the reception: "The rain was pouring down; all present were wet, muddy and uncomfortable; but the Mayor (given to singing madrigals to persons in power) assured the General that the sun is never shining more brilliantly than when you are among us!"

At the Battle of New Orleans, Marigny distinguished himself by his courage and activity. It is noteworthy that the glorious victory was reaped on the fields of the plantation of his Uncle de Lino de Chalmette.* In 1824 he supported General Jackson for President not only with his usual fiery eloquence, but also, perhaps more effectively, with force of arms. He was an ardent duelist and an expert with sword and pistol, and he has been credited with fifteen or more encounters.

His two duels in later years with Mr. Grailhe, the distinguished barrister, live with amusing distinctness in the memory of old friends of Marigny to-day. Grailhe married the widow of Marigny's son and made too free with her property. Bernard, the ever ready champion of the ladies, challenged him, and in the duel that followed shot or thrust Grailhe through the body, giving him a wound that resulted in a bend forward which made him walk, in local parlance, "doubled up." At his second duel with Grailhe, provoked by the same cause, Bernard told his seconds nonchalantly: "This time I shall try to straighten him." He shot or thrust him, in truth, in exactly the same place as before; and Grailhe did lose his bend forward, but gained a bend backward that made him even more conspicuous than before!

In 1825, when General Lafayette came to the United States and accepted the invitation of the people of Louisiana to visit their State, Marigny was selected to make the speech of welcome in French, and his family was the only private one that was visited by the General during the visit. Marigny says that he knew Lafayette well in France in 1822–1823, and that the General thanked him for having suggested that he visit the United States.

* Bernard Marigny's "Reflections sur la Campagne du Général André Jackson en Louisiane," New Orleans, 1848, is the best account we have of the preparations made to meet the enemy before the battle; and of the ensuing episode.—Library of Louisiana Historical Society [Grace King's note].

In 1827, when General Jackson paid his memorable social visit to New Orleans, accompanied by Mrs. Jackson, General Carroll and his wife, and General Houston, they all stayed with Bernard Marigny, who, as he says "was able to give them some pretty entertainments."

His second marriage not proving a happy one, he passed more and more of his time at his father's old summer home of Fontainebleau, on the northern shore of Lake Pontchartrain, not for the sake of the seclusion and quiet it offered after the excitement of American politics and financial speculations, but for the greater liberty it granted for the enjoyment of his favorite pleasures—the table and convivial intercourses with friends. Here it is that his standards of both enjoyments attained a height of perfection that has resulted in his gastronomic apotheosis in Louisiana's traditions and romance.

A more favorable spot for the pleasing of an epicure can hardly be imagined; a beautiful lake ever rippling under gentle breezes, or scintillating at the hour of dinner with the glitter of the setting sun; a white beach shaded by magnificent oaks, draped with hangings of moss; luxuriant flowers disposed like jewels on the green sward; hedges of Cherokee roses; vines of wild honeysuckle; the illimitable pine forest behind, fragrant and balmy, traversed by slow-meandering bayous; the forests teeming with game, the bayous and lake with fish. For service he had a retinue of accomplished, devoted slaves and a luxurious city was within easy reach to draw upon for wine. What could a crowned head ask for more?

He entertained at Fontainebleau with the exquisite generosity all his own, that allows no self-questionings save such as concern the comfort and pleasure of the guests. A paradise for an epicure and for Bernard de Marigny! It is not surprising that pleasure-loving friends from New Orleans flocked to Fontainebleau as pilgrims to a shrine; and with more confident assurance of the results than pious pilgrims ever enjoy.

There they found *grassets* that fed on magnolia berries; turkeys fattened on pecans; papabotes and snipe kept until they ripened and fell from their hangings; terrapin from his own pens; soft-shell crabs from the beach; oysters fresh from his own reefs; green trout and perch from the bayous; sheepheads and croakers from the lake; pompano, red fish, snappers from the Gulf; vegetables from his own garden; cress from his own sparkling forest spring; fruit from his orchard; eggs, chickens, capons from his own fowl yard. These, with sherry, madeira, champagne, and liqueurs, were the crude elements of repasts that he combined into ménus that Brillat-Savarin[17] would have been glad to have composed.

It is not surprising that the little town of Mandeville is as redolent of good cooking as some other little towns elsewhere are of religion and piety, for Fontainebleau had begotten the most beautiful, most charming, picturesque little lake shore town without doubt in the United States. The weary citizen of New Orleans can still find there seclusion, cool breezes, green shade of century-old oaks draped with moss, a lovely view, and liberty of enjoyment, in the good cooking as not the least of its attractions.

The boon of this unique and precious little town, the State, or rather the city, owes to Bernard de Marigny.

He it was who, during the early years of the century, conceived the idea of purchasing land along the lake shore and forest adjoining Fontainebleau until sufficient had been acquired for his purpose. He was inspired to make a town as poets are inspired to make a poem. He gave himself over, as a poet should, to his muse, and she, as a muse should, confided herself to him. Nature and art lent themselves kindly to the enterprise. Streets were made, trees were planted, lots were placed on sale, with an eye fixed rather to avoid undesirable additions to the community, than to secure financial profits. Public buildings were provided for, bridges built, a church and a market hall duly erected. Above all, a town government was instituted that eliminated, as far as mere human supervision could, the corrupting influence of American elections. In short, such as the little French town is to-day refined, elegant, yet simple—it left Bernard de Marigny's hand in 1830.

His congenial friend John Davis, an émigré from St. Domingo, and known to all as the famous impresario of what is always called the "celebrated Orleans Theatre," was associated with him in the Mandeville enterprise which included the employment of a steamboat to make the daily trip from New Orleans to Mandeville. Davis is also thanked (at Mandeville) for bringing thither the renowned cook, Louis Boudro, from Paris (with the other artists, lyric and dramatic, engaged for his theatre). Other celebrated chefs followed Boudro in the course of years and by way of insuring the perpetuity of the town's culinary celebrity, they became in time the hotel keepers of Mandeville.

Marigny's continual financial extravagance, however, and the depreci-

17 Anthelme Brillat-Savarin (1755–1826) was a French lawyer and gastronomist, known for his witty book on food, *La Physiologie du Goût* (1825).

ation of his city property, produced their inevitable results. The clouds that later darkened his life began to gather, but it is to this period of his life that belongs the most famous adventure in it—the one that is always remembered first in New Orleans when his name is mentioned.

In 1830, when his own fortunes were ebbing, those of his father's old guest and friend, the Duke of Orleans, reached their flux with his ascension to the throne of France as King Louis Philippe I. He promptly showed his recollection of past favors by sending to his New Orleans friend, de Marigny, with whom he had kept up a faithful correspondence, the conventional French royal token of appreciation—a beautiful dinner service of silver, each article bearing a portrait of the royal family. In a cordial letter (which is still in existence) the King invited Bernard to pay him a visit. This was not to be declined and Marigny, with his young son, called "Mandeville," went forthwith to Paris and to the Tuilleries. They were received in the palace with open arms according to their highest expectations. They were presented to the Royal family and given seats at the family table. In fact, the Creole hospitality of yore was returned with Creole cordiality. Bernard, after six months of the King's hospitality and court life, made his reappearance in New Orleans, perhaps with the satirical smile that usually accompanies the narrative as told by his friends. The King had returned to the son every obligation he owed to Philippe de Marigny, save the one debt of honor—the princely sum of money that had been loaned to him![18]

But with paternal friendship, he offered to provide for the future of young Mandeville by placing him, for military education, in the Academy of St. Cyr, which assured him an officer's rank in the French Army. The offer was accepted. Mandeville was sent to the Academy and in a few years gained his rank as lieutenant in a cavalry corps of the élite. All should have gone well with him but, according to the chronicler,* who seems to speak from personal knowledge, the young Creole, accustomed to the activity and rough exercises of hunting and fishing in Louisiana, soon tired of the monotonous military life in France during a peace, ruffled only by an acrimonious feeling against the American Republic which expressed itself in uncomplimentary remarks in public places. He became involved in a duel on this account, which necessitated his retirement from the army and his return to his own country where he was re-

18 In 1798 the elder Marigny had lent money to the royal princes who visited him in Louisiana.

* Castellano's "New Orleans as It Was" [Grace King's note].

ceived with acclamation as a hero. With the exception of his father he was the handsomest man in the city; the most gallant "beau" in society. A perfect cavalier, he had brought with him from France the beautiful charger presented to him by the King, upon which he was fond of displaying himself. His father, who prided himself also on his horsemanship, was wont to look upon his son's equestrian feats with a cold eye. One day, after a brilliant exhibition by Mandeville, Bernard remarked coldly that he could do the same.

Mandeville instantly dismounted and, with a low bow, handed the reins to his father with a courtly "Montez, mon père." No sooner said than done.

But Bernard had not seated himself in the saddle before the horse promptly threw him to the ground.

Bernard never forgave his son the "trick," as he considered it.

Mandeville married Sophronia, daughter of Governor Claiborne. He entered the Confederate Army as Colonel of the Tenth Louisiana Volunteers and served in Virginia. The Confederate Government, however, recognizing his high military fitness, assigned him South to organize a force of cavalry.

He survived his father and, through a long life of poverty, maintained an unimpeachable reputation as a man of courage and honor.

This adventure or experiment over, Marigny fared on through middle age, as he had through youth, shrugging his shoulders at ill fortune and not troubling his digestion about what might betide him or those who came after him. His separation from his wife became permanent; his daughters married; his sons, smaller than he, went their smaller way.

Marigny was re-elected to the House or Senate successively until 1838. The truth of what he said of himself in a political pamphlet, printed in Paris as early as 1822, has never been contested, and is borne out by the rest of his political career:

> Ten years of my life have been sacrificed to public affairs; and no one doubts that this has cost me considerable expenditures. These expenditures I have borne, for I have never solicited or obtained a lucrative office. I have contributed my efforts that my compatriots should not be entirely dispossessed of their language, their customs, their laws. I possessed an immense fortune, whereas now it barely amounts to the value of one of the four inheritances that I successively received; and I think I may claim

> that the use I made of them has always been honorable, by my household standards as well as by the assistance I have been able to give to the needy; to the poor mother of an indigent family, and to unfortunate strangers. Have they not always found me willing to tender a helping hand? *

The allusion to his waning fortune is to be explained by other reasons than those mentioned. The natural antagonism between the American and Louisianian citizens of New Orleans developed into the fierce rivalry of business competition between the American quarter (the Faubourg St. Mary) and the Creole quarter (the Faubourg Marigny); between the "uptown" and the "downtown" ideal of progressiveness. It was a purely financial struggle. Marigny, as the most prominent among the Creoles and the largest landowner in the city, was the natural leader of the Creoles; but he and they, with their antiquated principles, were as children before the keen-witted Americans—trained to perfection in the skilled manipulation of municipal patronage for private profit.

In the fight New Orleans was rent into three distinct parts or municipalities, each one with its own Board of Aldermen, but all under one Mayor and Council. Marigny protested with might and main against this rendition of Solomon's judgment. What he foresaw, happened; the Faubourg St. Mary became, as he called it, "the spoiled child of the Mayor and Council, the object of their tender affection," and grew with amazing rapidity into the beauty and prosperity of an enterprising American city, pulsing with Western blood and energy; while the Faubourg Marigny, motionless and inert, still lay, like a sleepy bayou, on its own outskirts.

The motive power of the development in the American quarter was supplied by the genius of two men, great in the history of New Orleans: an American, Samuel Jarvis Peters, and an Englishman, James H. Caldwell. They introduced gas and waterworks, paved the streets and built hotels in the American city, and improved its quays along which the flatboats from the West, gorged with produce, tied up three deep to unload their rich cargoes into vast warehouses.†

We are told by an American narrator that Peters, who lived in the

* This statement is borne out in every particular by Bernard Marigny's constituents. He was, according to their belief, the most generous and charitable, as well as honorable of men [Grace King's note].

† "Autobiography of Samuel Jarvis Peters," by George C. H. Kernion. Publications of Louisiana Historical Society. Vol. VII, 1913–14 [Grace King's note].

vieux carré with his auxiliary and co-worker, Caldwell, had originally selected the Creole Faubourg as the field for their civic improvements, but it happened that the old Faubourg was virtually owned by that proud Creole princeling, Bernard de Marigny. Being informed of the plans to beautify his domains by the building of a first-class hotel, a large theatre and the laying out of handsome paved streets as well as warehouses, cotton-presses, gas and waterwork plants, etc., to make it a commercial and social center, Monsieur de Marigny finally consented to dispose of his vast estates for a fabulous price. The act of sale was finally drawn up, but when purchasers and vendor met on the appointed day in the notary's office to sign the deed of transfer, Madame de Marigny failed to put in an appearance, and as her signature was necessary, on account of certain rights she possessed in the property about to be sold, the deal could not be consummated without her. Trembling with rage at this unexpected and, as he believed, premeditated disappointment, Mr. Peters, after soundly berating Monsieur de Marigny for his breach of agreement, finally exclaimed: "I shall live, by God, to see the day when rank grass shall choke up the gutters of your old 'Faubourg'!" His prophecy was, unfortunately, ultimately fulfilled.

Marigny's rapier did not leap from its scabbard, as might have been expected; for in another version of the affair that comes down to us, he had upon reflection decided, with characteristic arrogance and obstinacy, to build up his own Faubourg himself, and make a Creole city of it that would outshine forever the American one. He would suffer no usurpation of American "genius" in his own municipality, and thus the refusal of his wife to sign the deed gave color to Peters' suspicion that it was a ruse of Marigny's own invention. A suit filed shortly afterwards, however, by his wife for the restitution of her paraphernal rights, exonerates him from the suspicion of bad faith, and gives as the reason why Madame de Marigny did not sign the deed that she wished to protect her own rights.

Marigny made an attempt to fulfil his ambitious schemes. The great Marigny property was cut into streets to which he himself gave the pretty names Poet, Love, Good Children, Port, Moreau, Piety (but the original of this was a friend, Piété), Enghien, Craps (from the game of cards to which he was addicted), Bagatelle, Désiré. The pretty names are all that survive of his scheme; which his evil fortunes, and not his will, prevented his carrying to a success.

The losing of this golden opportunity brought him almost to the verge of unpopularity with his fellow Creoles. Although he had served his party well and had been sent to the State Legislature in 1817, acting there as President of the Senate, he was, unfortunately, not elected when he was nominated as candidate for the position of Governor of the State. "A Creole for Governor!" had been his slogan in every gubernatorial contest. He claimed that it was owing to him that Villeré was elected to succeed Claiborne, and added with caustic wit, when Robertson succeeded Villeré, "He will be succeeded by Mr. Johnson" (as he was) "and Virginia will be exhausted before another Louisianian is made Governor in his country."

His last public service to Louisiana was in the Constitutional Convention of 1845, when, as he says, he defended the great Democratic principles of universal suffrage and free public education, and when also, he made his speech in defense of Pierre Soulé, that contains the ever-memorable rebuke to Judah P. Benjamin[19] which sounded the death knell of American exclusiveness in Louisiana. No politician has since then re-opened the question that Marigny settled forever.

> "Sir," he addressed Mr. Benjamin, "contrary to all parliamentary usage you call upon the other distinguished member from New Orleans, Mr. Soulé, and ask him, 'Sir, suppose you had been placed at the head of an army to meet in deadly combat your own countrymen. Could you, would you have done so?' Sir, I tell you that you have inflicted upon him an unjust provocation; and I give you distinctly to understand that I take up the glove in his behalf; and Sir, I trust that you will not complain of my not being a native of the country, since I descend from those ancient warriors who conquered the country, and here represent six generations of Louisianians.
>
> "Fortunately for me, all your fine quotations are lost upon me. I never read any of those works which are supposed to make a logical man. But, Mr. President, I am one of those who, looking at things as they are, feel myself able to meet the emergency of the hour, and to accord my political acts to the political needs of my country. But, Sir, I ask you by what right do you expect to disfranchise in 1845 those who have rights guaranteed

19 Judah Philip Benjamin (1811–84) was a prominent New Orleans lawyer in 1845 and delegate to the Constitutional Convention before he became U.S. senator and later a Confederate cabinet officer.

> them in 1812? Sir, I tell you, I, Bernard Marigny, tell you that you are, after all, nothing but the servant of the people—nothing more, nothing less; presume upon your authority, and they will soon bring you to a just appreciation of their power over you, and it would not at all surprise me, if they were to obstinately persist at the very next election in selecting a Governor from the very men whom you are now so anxious to exclude. The laws of the country recognize no distinction between one class of citizens and another. Is there any principle of free government, any principle of republicanism, to sanction such a pretension? They say that a naturalized citizen is not to be entrusted with the power we confer upon our Governor. What, Sir, is the power of that Governor, compared with the power we are administering now?" *

W. H. Sparks, who served with Marigny in the Legislature, says that his wit and satire were his most dreaded weapons, and ridicule was his forte. Mr. Sparks gives the following incident: "At the end of the heated debate on the question of cutting New Orleans into three municipalities, during which Marigny had exerted himself to the utmost to protect the city and himself against the disaster, as he saw it, Marigny was observed passing around among his friends a squib containing the following lines: 'Sparks and Thomas Green Davidson, Rascals by nature and profession.' "

A day or two later Sparks read to a group of his friends his quite sufficient retort. It begins: "Dear Marigny," but concludes with:

> "A warmer heart or weaker head,
> On earth, I own, I never met.
> . . . .
> And on your tomb inscribed shall be
> . . . .
> In letters of your favorite brass
> 'Here lies, O Lord! we grieve to see
> A man in form, in head an ass!' "

Marigny heard the reading, arched his brows and, without speaking, retired. An hour later he came to Sparks and said: "Suppose you write no more poetry? I shall stop. You can call me a villain, a knave, a great

* *De Bow's Review*, 1846 [Grace King's note].

rascal, every great man has had that said about him. Mr. Clay, Mr. Webster, General Jackson, all have been called so. You can say that; but I tell you, Sir, I do not like to be called an ass!"

"He was the aggressor," continued Sparks, "and though offended, was too chivalrous to quarrel. He had fought nineteen duels and I did not want to quarrel either." *

The last remnants of the great riches that Marigny inherited were lost by him. In scriptural language, his fortune took wings and flew away, as fortunes always do; unless, as Marigny says of certain rich men of his day who kept their wealth, "they were born dead, since they never knew how to live."

When he was nearing seventy years of age, he wrote in self-defense against the sneering accusation of poverty and printed a pamphlet for private circulation:† "To my fellow citizens: The calumnies," he says, "of which I have been the object for some time, the epithet of 'old fogy,' thrown at me by certain individuals, force me to give to the public the following facts."

He enumerates his services to the State in a very modest and moderate vein, and then follows his private explanation; a story of financial loss and failure, only too well known in Louisiana; a road to failure well trodden by sugar planters in the past.

> "Certain persons," he writes, "have often asked the question: 'How did Mr. Marigny lose the fortune he possessed, of five or six hundred thousand dollars?' The answer to the question is as easy to make as to understand—it disappeared under the influence of events and circumstances which I could not control. In 1839, Messrs." (he names five gentlemen) "undertook the estimation of the value of my possessions, an estimation I judged necessary at the time of my departure for France. The amount of my fortune was fixed by these gentlemen at nine hundred and fifteen thousand dollars. My debts then amounted to three hundred and twenty thousand dollars, two hundred and eighty thousand of which represented a debt to the Citizens Bank. I rallied my resources and asked for longer terms from my creditors, for I thought I could re-establish my fortune. I had a sugar plan-

* "The Memories of Fifty Years."—W. H. SPARKS, 1870 [Grace King's note].

† "Bernard Marigny à ses Concitoyens." New Orleans, 1853. Pamphlet in T. P. Thompson Collection [Grace King's note].

tation and a brickyard, but to develop the sugar plantation I needed to construct buildings, dig canals, provide equipments, and put in necessary machinery. To meet such great expenses, crops were needed. They failed in consequence of a crevasse in 1850, followed by another in 1851. That is not all: bricks fell to their lowest price" (he owned a large brickyard which he worked with his slaves,) "and the price of sugar* was reduced from two and a half to three cents the pound.

"On this the Citizens Bank announced to me that if I did not decide to sell the plantation, they would seize it. I was, therefore, forced to sell at a very moderate price. The Citizens Bank, naturally took possession of all the products of the sugar house and of the brickyard.

"Calculating upon a fine crop in 1851, which I could have made if it had not been for the crevasse, counting also upon an office (that of Mortgage and Conveyance), whose commission did not expire until February 10th, 1855, I had contracted a debt of eight thousand dollars in order to put my sugar house in a condition to work profitably. But my hope was disappointed.

"In 1851 the crops failed. There remains to me, therefore, today only my office, which, as I have explained, expires in 1855. I have still a few slaves, but their value is partly covered by the (paraphernal) rights of Madame de Marigny, and the returns from their hire pays the taxes and expenses of her house. As for my other property, it barely covers what is owing to the Citizens Bank."

The site of the great Marigny canal on Champs Elysées, which in colonial days had fed a sawmill that poured gold into Pierre Philippe's coffers, was bought by the Pontchartrain Railroad. Fontainebleau went from Marigny and all his land in Mandeville, with the exception of one small house, which still enjoys local fame as the last residence of the whilom Lord of all Mandeville, to which he would still come from New Orleans seeking recreation and refreshment.

Estrangement from his wife was followed by estrangement from his

* A cause of the financial distress in Louisiana was the tariff which had depreciated the value of American sugar in proportion as the duty had been reduced on the foreign article. In 1837, one hundred and thirty-six sugar plantations were given up; numerous bankruptcies followed. Lands could no longer be sold; fortunes based on them fell even more suddenly than they had risen.—*Annals of Louisiana* [Grace King's note].

children and grandchildren; the friends of his convivial days declined with his fortunes. He retired to an apartment in one of the houses which he could still claim as his own (Frenchman Street, near Royal, still standing), a plain three-story brick building kept by a colored housekeeper. And here, in sight of the great mansion of Pierre Philippe de Marigny, his father, where he was born, and where took place the great and stately entertainments that made the name of Marigny famous in the past, in two rooms furnished with remnants of his old furniture, the portraits of his ancestors on the wall; on the sideboard, the silver service presented by Louis Philippe, afterwards sold to the mint by weight, he passed his days like some old sailing vessel, its stormy voyages over, safe in the harbor. In this seclusion he penned his pamphlet, "Bernard Marigny a ses Concitoyens," in 1853. It concludes with the lines: "Nearly seventy years old, with no fortune whatever, I ignore the destiny that awaits me. However painful it may be, I will support it with calm and resignation."

In a postscript he adds: "Believing it to be my duty, before descending into the tomb, to make known the results of more than forty years of minute research into the history of my country, I announce to my readers that I am at present writing a work, already well advanced toward completion. Its title will be 'Reflections upon the History of Louisiana, under France, Spain and the American Government.' "

The work did not advance beyond a sketch, which was published in pamphlet form in 1854. It bears the following dedication:

> To the Honorable Members of the General Assembly of Louisiana.
>
> Gentlemen:
>
> Unforseen vicissitudes having deprived me of a considerable fortune, I have been compelled to abandon the political career which had been to me peculiarly attractive. Consigned to an office (mortgage and conveyance) where my duties require my presence, I have devoted a few hours of my leisure to a work which, I trust, will at least show my attachment to my native land of Louisiana, as well as my devotion to the United States of America. This work is dedicated to the General Assembly of Louisiana. Be pleased, gentlemen, to accept it as a humble pledge of my patriotism.
>
> I remain with respect,
> your obt. servt.,
> BERNARD MARIGNY.

It closes with words that cannot fail to touch the hearts of a Louisianian, or indeed of any lover of a "good sport" of the old-fashioned kind.

> "Having nearly attained the age of seventy, having lost my fortune and independence, it is an arduous task which I undertake. Reader, I solicit in advance your indulgence in view of the motives which renovate my strength and make me almost forget my troubles. I venture to hope that Providence will aid me, and that my moral energies will not be wanting. I also hope, my beloved countrymen, that you will say at some future day: 'We have read the work of old Bernard Marigny—we have recognized therein his patriotism.' To noble hearts the native land is ever dear!"

This tender commitment of his work to posterity stays the hand of a Louisiana critic, which would not if it could dissect it coldly, any more than it would use the scalpel upon the body of an ancestor.

A prettier historical legacy than "old Bernard Marigny's" to his countrymen has rarely been made. Well may Alcée Fortier[20] declare that it was received with almost filial respect.*

Beginning with the Treaty of Aix-la-Chapelle, 1748, he explains, in his shrewd personal way, the causes of the American Revolution, and the subsequent political evolution of the United States, its growth in power and in moral influence. He urges the annexation of Cuba, for reasons contained in his statistical study of the island. Strange to say, as Fortier remarks, although writing only seven years before the Civil War, for all his political wisdom, he did not foresee the bloody chasm that lay across the path of his country. He was confident, he says, that the compromise of 1850 had allayed the passions of the United States.

In his relation of Louisiana history, he "drank of the brook in his way," and he passes the refreshing draught on to his readers. The faded documents in the archives of the Louisiana Historical Society, that historical students study to-day, he knew practically in their living form. From Bienville to Aubry, from Ulloa to the old and infirm Salcedo and Casacalvo, "the man of no ability," he knew every man of importance, either from his own personal intercourse with them, or as they lived in the memory of his father or of his father's father.

20 Alcée Fortier (1856–1914) was professor of French, Tulane University, and historian of Louisiana.

* Louisiana Studies. 1894 [Grace King's note].

The preliminaries of the cession of Louisiana was fresh in the minds of men whom he knew in France and New Orleans. He was a familiar of Laussat; Lafayette was an old friend, and so were Jackson and Henry Clay and Sam Houston.

Marigny relates among other personal reminiscences, a conversation held with Louis Philippe in 1837, when the King, addressing him as "mon cher Bernard," asked his opinion about the political condition of Texas, and whether the new republic would be able to withstand the army of Mexico. Marigny responded that the King, who had traveled all through the United States and knew its power and population, was well able to answer his own question; but he gave his reasons for believing in the future of Texas as a member of the Union. The King listened attentively and observed to him: "What you say is very reasonable." The Republic of Texas was shortly afterwards recognized.

"Louis Philippe," comments Marigny, "was a wise and enlightened King. I have seen but few men who entertained a greater admiration for our institutions and high opinion of the American people. Louis was really a man, under the garb of royalty; he was a republican King."

The Louisiana Assembly passed a vote accepting his historical sketch, and ordered one thousand copies printed; five hundred in English and five hundred in French, for which M. de Marigny was to be paid one dollar apiece.

Marigny lost his office in 1855, and thenceforth lived on the crumbs of his former possessions, selling here and there small pieces of property that had lain, as it were, unnoticed at his feet. Having lost all, he had nothing more to lose in the Civil War. In his humble home he escaped the rude hand of the Military Governor of the city that fell so heavily upon his descendants, and the descendants of his friends and the relatives about him. He has left no record of himself during these hard years of the war, nor of the harder ones of reconstruction that followed the war. The breaking up of old ties; the inroad of strange men and strange measures; the wrecking of old estates and of hopes, old and new, left him apparently, for once in his life, speechless.

He passed his evenings in the congenial circle of the family of the son of his old friend, Governor Claiborne, where he devoted himself, as he had devoted himself through life, to the ladies; amusing them with his good stories, his wit and his puns. Occasionally he recited for them, in the fine manner learned in France from Talma,[21] in his youthful days, al-

21 François Joseph Talma (1763–1826) was the greatest French tragedian of his time.

ways choosing some beautiful lady to address as queen. Never sad, never complaining, ever the polished, courteous, dignified old French nobleman of the old régime, who for all his gay wit and persiflage was never known to speak lightly of religion, or its sacred practices. He dressed as simply as any citizen of moderate means, but he always wore broad silver buckles on his shoes.

The handsome residence of the Clairbornes faced Washington Square, the ground which Marigny had presented to the city; its lower boundary was the Champs Elysées, named so fancifully by him in the days when his ideas were fanciful and poetical.

After his evening visit, accompanied always by the young son of the Claiborne family (now Judge Charles F. Claiborne), he would skirt Washington Square and cross the Champs Elysées and wend his way a block further on to his home on Frenchman Street, talking to his youthful friend of his old days and sowing many a good story in the fertile, appreciative mind. Always lively and interesting, he never let fall, however, a word or hint relating to his writings or to any serious preoccupation.

Of a morning or afternoon, he loved to saunter up Royal, Chartres, or Bourbon Streets, which held the houses so full of gayety and pleasure to him in the past, and which must have lain in his memory, like some fine opera; with beautiful scenery, gallant actions, charming actresses, lovely figurines, fascinating dancers.

In old days he always rode in a carriage, now he went on foot, sometimes essaying an omnibus. It is related that he never found an omnibus driver who would accept fare from him. "No! No! M. de Marigny, not from you!"

In passing a house, if he heard a piece of music beautifully played on the piano inside (one heard such playing then oftener than to-day) he would stop and listen. Music held him in bondage in old age as in youth. Then, mounting the little wooden steps, he would knock on the door or ring. When the servant opened the door: "Say it is M. de Marigny." He would enter without ceremony and sit in a chair, making a sign to the pianist to continue, which she was glad to do. M. de Marigny! Whom would any woman rather play to?

Men would stop on the streets to look at him; "old Bernard Marigny!" a relic of Colonial Days, walking the streets, at ninety! Handsome, active, erect, with intellect clear and vigorous, manners courtly; the hero who, in current parlance, could throw away thirty thousand dollars on a bagatelle, but who would never consent to bring a lawsuit against a fellow citizen.

So, on the 4th of February, 1868, in his usual gayety and friendliness, on his daily promenade, greeting those who saluted him with kindly cordiality, his foot tripped on the pavement. He stumbled and fell heavily, striking his head. Death ensued almost instantly.

His body was conveyed to his apartment on Frenchman Street and there, in the habiliments for the grave, Bernard de Marigny was laid underneath the portraits of his family and his royal friends. "It was impossible," writes the reporter who chronicled the event for a daily paper, "to gaze unmoved upon the aged form, the last of the Creole landed aristocracy, the representative of the strength, the follies and wealth of a passed generation, one who knew how to dispose of a great fortune with contemptuous indifference."

In cold, inclement weather, next day, the funeral took place. An extended line of carriages headed the long and imposing procession which, passing Washington Square, slowly proceeded up Royal Street. It stopped not at the Cathedral, as expected, but went out to the old St. Louis Cemetery to which the tomb of his first wife had been transferred.

People on the sidewalk looked with solemnity upon the hearse that carried him who for seventy-five years had represented without a rival the life, gayety, wit, polish, refinement and luxuriance of society; who, for all his wealth in youth, died poor yet left behind him nothing to put a stain upon his proud escutcheon!

He once wrote an epitaph to be placed on his tomb and confided it to a friend, but when the time came to use it, the friend could not find it. He could only remember that it was well written and characterized by originality, simplicity and wit; not ostentatious nor self-flattering. The epitaph was never found, nor the other valuable relics and papers left by him.

His will, dated July 8th, 1865, contained the following requests:

> I ask that my body shall be placed in the tomb of my first wife, in the old cemetery facing the Carondelet basin; that a tomb with two compartments be made there of brick, plastered with cement.
>
> My grandson, Gustave de Marigny, is the head of my family, being the son of Prosper de Marigny, by my first marriage with Maria Jones. My testamentary executor will remit to him my

family portraits, the engravings representing the Orleans family, all my family papers, the letters of my ancestors, and correspondence, particularly with the Duke of Orleans, who became King Louis Philippe, and the letters of that King.

By his union with Mathilde Morales, Marigny had five children:

*(1) Antoine James (known as "Mandeville" Marigny; born 1811, died 1890. He married Miss Sophronia Claiborne, daughter of William Charles Cole Claiborne, first American Governor of Louisiana. She died in 1890. The three children born to them died without issue.

(2) Rosa de Marigny; born 1813, married to M. de Sentmanat, of Mexican fame. They had three daughters; one married Nelvil Soulé, son of Pierre Soulé; the other married Allain Eustis (descendants living in Europe); and the third married Philippe Villeré, no issue. Rosa de Marigny remarried, in 1832, Enould de Livaudais; no issue by this marriage.

(3) Angela de Marigny; born 1817, married Mr. F. Peschier, Swiss consul in New Orleans. They had several children; one of the daughters married Leon Joubert de Villemarest of New Orleans.

(4) Armand de Marigny.

(5) Mathilde de Marigny; born 1820, married Albin Michel de Grilleaud, son of the French consul of that name in Louisiana. Descendants are living in Europe, where they still enjoy the highest social preëminence.

By the death of Prosper de Marigny, great-grandson of Bernard de Marigny and Mary Jones, his first wife, in Mandeville, 1910, the name of Marigny became extinct in Louisiana, where it had held sway for over two hundred years.

* Biographical and Genealogical Notes concerning the family of Philippe de Mandeville, Ecuyer Sieur de Marigny, 1709–1910. J. W. Cruzat. *Louisiana Historical Society Publications*, Vol. V [Grace King's note].

X LETTERS AND NOTEBOOK SELECTIONS

WITH NO LITTLE IRONY Grace King wrote her sister on the subject of Judge Gayarré's letters: "The Judge is distressed to death at the illness of Paul [Hamilton] Hayne. It would be a pity for the Judge to outlive even his biographer, and I fear this will be the case. After all the beautiful letters he has written to Hayne too, expressly to be published after his death." [1] The comment reflects her typical private criticism of her family's most important friend, and it also reflects her own notion of the function of letters. To her they were for the graceful communication of ideas and emotions. To write a letter with the consciousness that it was to achieve some sort of immortality as an individual literary work was a foolhardy sign of pompousness. Grace King's letters are rarely self-conscious. She wrote them constantly throughout life until her handwriting in old age became almost illegible. She made constant use of the dash, which conveys the spirit of her letters: she thought and jotted down her ideas as they came and as she might have spoken them. Sometimes the style is awkward, but more usually it is quite graceful. Charles Dudley Warner praised her for her letters because for him they reflected so well her personality, her kindness, her pride, her irritability, her dignity. She wrote with candor and sincerity whether she was quarreling with editors of the *Yale Review* for cutting her article or

1 Grace King to May McDowell, May 28, 1886, in Grace King Papers.

advising the Clemenses to return to Hartford after the death of Susy. She was well aware of the importance of keeping letters and spoke of "my archives," by which she meant the King family papers, which are today the property of her heirs and are now preserved at the Department of Archives and Manuscripts, Louisiana State University, Baton Rouge. Letters published below are from that collection except for the following: to Olivia L. Clemens (one letter) and Mark Twain (one letter) in the Bancroft Library, University of California, Berkeley; to Edwin Anderson Alderman (one letter) in Alderman Library, University of Virginia; to Warrington Dawson (five Letters) in William R. Perkins Library, Duke University; to John R. Ficklen (two letters) in the Louis Round Wilson Library, University of North Carolina; to Robert Underwood Johnson (one letter), Manuscripts Division, New York Public Library; to Fred Lewis Pattee (one letter) in the library, the Pennsylvania State University; to Edward Garnett (two letters) and Leonidas Warren Payne (one letter) in Academic Center Library, University of Texas, Austin; and to George W. Cable (one letter) in Howard-Tilton Library, Tulane University.

To Charles Dudley Warner

Oct. 18, 1885

You needn't fling your being a Yankee and Abolitionist at me; if you can stand it, I can. That's one of the things that makes you so fascinating—the contradiction of the least Yankee of persons coming from the most Yankee of places. Indeed, my kind friend, when I think of the trials, humiliation, and suffering—the, in short, anguish of body and mind involved in the honorable bearing of the title of Southerner I thank God that you can honorably be on the successful side. When I contrast your position now, with what it would be as a Southerner, I don't believe I would mind if [fragment].

To Charles Dudley Warner

Nov. 22, 1885

The only vocation I feel, is the desire to show you that a Southerner and a white person is not ashamed to acknowledge a dependence on negroes —nor to proclaim the love that exists between the two races, a love, which in the end will destroy all differences in color; or rather—I had better say—that the love is the only thing which can do it. . . .

To her sister, May King McDowell, after Grace King's final visit to the New Orleans Exposition

New Orleans, May 31, 1885

Mrs Howe[2] presided, as a matter of course. She presided at everything—& has done it so long that her air, manner, smile & language are actually threadbare, from constant use. It is a pleasure to know that if she presides in the next world—which she will do, if she has a chance, that she will be regenerated & renewed. Maud [3] read a speech, which I did not like at all—it was so extremely personal—& egotistic; while her language & manner were not up to a High School performance. She made much of

2 Julia Ward Howe (1819–1910).

3 Maud Howe was the daughter of Julia Ward Howe.

her present—the trouble she had suffered, & the sacrifices she had made in coming here; among them the abandoning a novel, half way through. Preston Johnston's[4] answer was a ludicrous effort on his part to come down to the occasion. He tried to be very grateful for the volumes of *women's* books,—complimented books & women['s] work in general, vague, terms—& then by a happy thought finished up by an eulogium of Mrs Howe & her accomplished daughter. Mrs Howe responded—& then Maj Burke[5] presented her with a basket of flowers—& a ton of "taffy." This was highly appreciated by the audience who knew perfectly well the warfare that has been going on between them for months. In her thanks for the flowers, Mrs H informed us of very much that she thought & knew,—& gave us a peep at Boston & the position the women occupied there. . . .

To Olivia L. Clemens

My dear Friend.

What pleasure your letter gave me! I was in the parlors putting flowers in vases and plants in windows, trying to enliven the place for a festivity in the evening—a kind of reception to my brother's fellow Judges—and his fiancée[6]—to whom he had made up his mind to get married all of a sudden. Maman was upstairs, grieving over the prospect of losing her eldest son (overlooking the conventional gain of another daughter, which she protests she doesn't care about), Nan, my sister crawling through a slow convalescence after a fever. Your letter came—the only one by the mail, and it invigorated me immediately. I carried it around in my heart all day, the feeling that you would care to have me spend some time with you—in your family—under your house roof—to talk about books, life, and a little of our experiences. I felt it more, the letter coming as it did, when life had given me a new and not altogether joyful experience.

Whether I can get away or not in the Autumn is a doubt which I confess afflicts me sorely. I need the change a thousand times, and I want it, a million—that is just the proportion, the pleasure I would derive from it, swells and broadens when I think of it until I think it is all a pleasure, and I am selfish and pleasure seeking alone in contemplating it. Mr Warner (and Susy too) have written, urging me to come. I did not care to

4 Colonel William Preston Johnston (1831–99) was president of Tulane University (1880–99).

5 "Major" Edward A. Burke was director-general of the Cotton Centennial Exposition. He was also the principal inspiration behind it.

6 Frederick D. King married Eleanor Moise Levy in 1888.

monopolise their room as I did last year so it was decided for me to pass a short while with them—and then go to the inn, where I would be in hailing distance if they wanted me. To substitute your home for the inn would be a delightful prospect. But to avoid any complications caused by my uncertainty, you must not hold room for me. I know the exigencies of your hospitable heart. Until the 1st of September, I cannot say whether I can go or not. Then I shall, D V. make some plans.

I have not read Cabot's Emerson—only read about it. I admire Emerson; but to tell you the truth he is too excellent for me. Besides he makes goodness and success almost undistinguishable to me. He converts my brain, but he does not touch my heart. He makes it so *sensible* to be good. It is a kind of a profitable investment. It is more profitable to be high principled. I feel that, but I like to lose sight of it. I want it to be disinterested—from the heart. I read Emerson's axioms and really think at times that I live in an Emerson altitude—but the least grievance drops me right down—philosophy doesn't seem to prop me up at all. Browning can—Mr Clemens converted me to Browning and this summer he has helped me amazingly, bless his fat, fleshy, pudgy face!

"To see a good in evil and a hope in ill success" [7]—is what I for one must strenuously strive for, I who live amid so much evil, and am confronted by so much ill success. I have been writing very assiduously. You know what that means; happiness as long as the work lasts, misery the moment it is out of one's hands. I would pray for self-confidence if I did not think that resignation were a better state for the writing mind to be in. It is an immense relief to be patted on the head by the "Post" [8] when one expects a fool's-cap. I wish I did not so much feel that I had simply escaped punishment.

My brother was married yesterday—today it is raining in torrents. Last night there was not much sleeping done by any of us; I am groping sleepily after my ideas. I write such beautiful letters in my mind! I wish you could have received not one, but the dozen I wrote to you since last Friday. I am sure you would have enjoyed them. I quite enjoyed them myself. My heart expresses itself exquisitely to me; it is such an appreciative little heart, so full of gratitude for kindness, so afraid that its love will not hold out, to the end of a life where there are so many good people.

I owe Clara a letter—a nice letter to repay her's—and I owe Susy for the intentions to write. Give my love to them both. Jean will soon be

7 From Robert Browning's *Paracelsus*, V, 11. 893–94.

8 The New York *Evening Post* praised *Monsieur Motte* for its style and dialogue, August 4, 1888, p. 8.

large enough to remember transient faces too, when she must have her message. Remember me to Mr Clemens—the dutiful salute of a subaltern to a brigadier general. I am sorry that I did not have the pleasure of meeting your mother, but I venture to send her, as we say here—"Mes amitiés."— Believe me dear Mrs Clemens, Sincerely and Cordially Your friend

Grace King

23 Rampart St. South
New Orleans
Aug: 15th 1888

To Mark Twain

My dear Mr Clemens.

If your Express Co. is animated by the same spirit as our's, you will in the course of a week receive a package which starts the same day as this note.[9] The package contains a "carrot" of tobacco. Now for the history of the tobacco.

It is not supposed to be the common ordinary weed that grows for the vile populace (whatever you may discover it to be.) It is tobacco of pedigree, strictly private and exclusive grown by an amateur on Cane River in Nachitoches Parish.

The Amateur sends it to my brother Branch as a high favor and distinguished compliment. My brother, who smokes only cigarettes and mild cigars, looking around for some one to pass favor and compliment on to, remembered my describing you smoking a pipe. He asks me therefore to send it to you from him, the gentleman; in fact a general send from the country to "Mark Twain."

I have told you the best I know of the tobacco; but I know also, that whiskey and tobacco are made (by the devil I candidly believe) specially to order for each constitution—and this may not be your brand.

One merit, you see it has, it can easily be given away. You know you must cut it with a sharp knife and rub it fine, thumb on palm; but you haven't got the kind of thumb or palm. I have seen them, they grow down here on the darkies.

Sincerely your's
Grace King

Sept. 5th 1888

9 For Mark Twain's acknowledgment of her gift, see King, *Memories of a Southern Woman of Letters*, 203.

To her mother, Mrs. William Woodson King

Paris. Sunday 28 February
[1892]

Dear Mimi

I think I had better conclude Nan's letter to you instead of writing to May as I intended. You can forward to her after you have read and so she will be kept au courant, which is all that is necessary. Nan says, she has given you an introduction to the de Bury's—so I can take you right along through our visit yesterday. Madame Blanc[10] wrote that she would meet us there at 5 oc. The hotel is 20 Rue Oudinot near the Invalides. We thought we would have time to finish our inspection of the Musée des Invalides, before going there—but we had to take two cars, & they took such a circuitous route that it was 4½ before we arrived at the Invalides, a half hour after the Musée closed. We whiled away the time by wandering around in that very ugly part of Paris—whose only ornament is the gilt dome over Napoleon's tomb—wondering why they could not have put the tomb somewhere else—than there which is no better than Dryades St. It was pretty cold and bleak, & by 5 we were [illegible word] there ready to ring at 20 Rue Oudinot. We were directed by the Concierge, au fond—a gauche—3*eme* étage. The Apartement, like Madame Blanc's is across a big square old fashioned courtyard—& the narrow, dark stairs, are worse than our's. We rang—a valet, in rather shabby attire opened the door—and lead [*sic*] us through the dining room, a salon, very much filled with bric-a-brac, pictures, & shabby furniture—into another salon still more filled, & with still shabbier furniture; where the Baronne sat in the corner near a wasting fire. She received us very pleasantly. Mme Blanc had not arrived—but that made no difference. We took seats, & she began to "converse" which is her profession—& we began to look around, taking mental notes—which seems to be our's. I do not believe anywhere but in France, such a woman could have a showing—but here—in the city of beauty & pleasure, she simply reigns. Fancy—she is very tall, with large limbs—never wore a corset in her life—her face—which must have been handsome, is horribly marked by the small pox. She wears a wig. She was dressed in a black skirt & grey jacket, [2 illegible words] a red silk belt—pretty vivid—& the shoes she had on looked like those Nan & I keep to dust the room in. I suppose she

10 For Grace King's friendship with Madame Blanc and the Baronne Blaze de Bury, see Introduction, p. 19.

is about fifty. And she talks and talks with the voice and determination of a Tartar. And with all the persistency of a woman. Her forte seems to be politics—& to hear her you would suppose she was in the secrets of all the cabinets of Europe. She is a Scotch woman by the way & speaks French correctly & fluently but with a terrible accent. The great man of the century, to her, is Leo XIII & his last Encyclical, the greatest piece of statesmanship. Bismarck is her intimate friend—& Andrew White.[11] She is in correspondence with Thomas Nelson Page—& this gives only a faint idea of her versatility in the matter of friendship—it is only a little sample that she threw out. She really seems intimate with everybody who has ever written a book or made a speech, in America or Europe. But what Madame Blanc especially wanted me to know her for, was to talk about Desjardins—(also M. de Bury's intimate) and his great new spiritual movement in France, upon which Mme B wants me to write an article. But it was a case of leading a horse to water & trying to make him drink. We kept bringing the Conversationalist to Desjardins but she would keep wandering off again to the Pope's Enclyclical. The valet brought in the tea—& while the Baronne was preparing it—Mme B whispered—"She is very intimate with D—— but she likes to keep him to herself. I shall arrange it so you can meet him." Mme B is, to me, by far, the more interesting woman, although Mme de Bury may be the greater thinker. She complimented me very much on M. Motte—& said she thought she could get it translated into French, & published in one of the magazines here—which of course would be a great advantage to me. Mme de Bury as delighted to hear that Nan & I had read Desjardin's book,[12] & that we were in the "movement"—which is nothing more than the stand we took for morality & religion, in politics in the Lottery Fight. The TD. called us sentimentalists.[13] We are called here Idealists—or spiritualists. After Mme Blanc left—a very pretty intelligent young woman came in. She also is in the Movement. There had been a great deal of talk about the "Pasteur Wagner" [14]—and Nan seized an opportunity to slip a whisper athwart Mme de B's monologue, to ask who the Pasteur Wagner

11 Andrew Dickson White (1832–1918), American diplomat and educator, was the first president of Cornell University (1867–85) and was minister to Russia (1892–94).

12 Paul Desjardins (1859–1940) had published *Esquisses et impressions* (1888) and *Le Devoir present* (1892). The latter is a pamphlet containing the seminal ideas of the Union for Moral Action.

13 The New Orleans *Times-Democrat* supported the controversial state lottery; Grace King opposed it.

14 For Grace King's friendship with Charles Wagner, see Introduction, p. 20.

was. We were informed that he was the "pasteur d'une église protestante, près de la Bastile [*sic*]—" & that he was one of the leaders of the new movement towards the re-religionising of the French people. We literally had to drag ourselves away from the charming circle. Mme de B making us promise to return often. We raced to the train—& had to "hoist" ourselves, long trains, velvet hats & all to the Imperial to get home—cold & biting as the air was—and as it was, we did not get home until dinner was half through. As you may imagine, our going into this high literary circle, creates a profound impression in the house.

This morning, one duty was clear. We must hunt up the Pasteur Wagner. We started off immediately after our tea & bread & butter, one youthful and admiring neighbor accompanying us. We thought it was the beautiful old church near the Bastile—(Henry IV) which had been converted into a temple. So we went directly there. And it was a curious sight. Everything pertaining to Romania had been done away with, & a flourishing Sunday School was in full progress—in the bare, Protestantized space. After listening a while to their hymns—& finding out that Wagner's church was somewhere's else—we started again in search. And it was a search. It was not a church at all but a mission hall—down an alley way in the Rue des Arquebusiers—an old very dirty & most disreputable St. But not so the congregation. I never saw a more intelligent lot of men & women who sat as if entranced under the sermon of Wagner. And Wagner was most worth going to hear. Nan, the Russian & I, sat simply electrified. Such a strong, startling original version of Christianity! I shall get the man's book & send it home. Just to give an idea what the man & his mission is. We were very late for breakfast—but we didn't mind that, we were so exalted. After making Desjardin's acquaintance, I think I shall try for Wagner. This to me is the cream of being in Paris—The intellectual life. . . .

Notebooks Selections

Sept. 22, 1901

Mr. Préot[15] is passing away from the earth today;—my good friend is breathing his last—he may at this moment be not of the living. He was

15 George C. Préot was friend and literary advisor to Grace King. She dedicated *Tales of a Time and Place* to him.

the truest, and the most unselfish friend I ever had. I can never have another like him. . . .

I am thankful that I had a long pleasant conversation with him sometime in June. I was going to Tulane to a Committee meeting of the Historical Society. He joined me on Canal St.—He told me that I had grown so much pleasanter—more aggreeable—that I used to be so nervous—striving—never seemed at peace—unhappy. I told him, that I was happier, since I had got rid of all my hopes—and had my future behind me—that I strive no more—for there was nothing new that could give me the pleasure. I sought this—and he became rather sad too. He said my last story was too sad—he asked me why I did not write gayer stories—more cheerful. I told him I could only write of life as I knew it—but that I thought that story extremely amusing ("Making Progress"). He thought it was the best one that I had written.

He was the only one who ever helped me in my writing. He was the first one who thought I could write. I remember how much pleased he was with my "Heroines of Fiction" that I read at the Pangnostics—and how he came around to persuade me to publish it—and to go regularly into writing. . . .

Monday 23d Mr. Préot died this morning at 800. And so the world feels empty of friends, to me. The comparison with him—the others were not friends—he alone was unselfish and disinterested. Nan & I went up there about 1200 carrying a large bunch of white flowers—I hope they will put near him.—I keep going over the pleasant times we have had together—the Coquelin supper—the seeing La Vie de Boheme—& that evening that he found places for us to see Lohengrin—and the many pleasant evenings—when he came to see us. . . .

To Edwin Anderson Alderman

February 11, 1903

My dear Dr. Alderman,[16]

Your letter has made me think a great deal. I am not at all prepared to answer your questions. It seems to me as if you had asked me my candid opinion about my mother and father.—And I know too well the sneering

16 Edwin Anderson Alderman (1861–1931) was president successively of the University of North Carolina (1896–1900), Tulane University (1900–1904), and the University of Virginia (1904–31).

smile that comes to the lips of people when a Southerner allows himself or herself to make any claims about the South. I mean to the lips of people that are wiser, better, stronger than I. It is only with intellectual intimates that I venture now, to talk upon the subject;—although, I fancy that you think I go around gushing out my sentiments about the South that was—and the South that might be.

I ought not to mind however—that is—I ought to have the strength of mind to stand up for my convictions even before those who call them prejudices.

I think that the Country owes it to the South that we have a standard of easy and luxurious living; that the millionaires of to-day are glad to follow. Every home, club house—I may say every association for refined social life is modeled on ideals furnished by the South—just as surely as we model our financial associations on ideals furnished by the North. But these ideals of generosity, hospitality, chivalry—are never invented out of hand, as you know—they are the flowers of a past life that have born fruit in individuals. I believe today that if Southern blood etc. could be drawn away from the nation; it would drain away with it such a mass of individuality that we would see only business corporations and associations left.

The Southern man has begotten in the country a confidence in self as self, independent of any extraneous acquisitions. He stands for self against theories. I would venture to say that "I" and "We" are used a hundred times in the South—to once in the North. It is their own self esteem that makes Southerners careless of appearance. They would spend a million on any or every extravagance—but not a cent for the reputation of being wealthy. When a Southerner says that one man is just as good as another or that a man is worth only what he accomplishes in life, you may begin to suspect him. He is tolerant of his own sins—and the sins of others—openly. He cannot play the hypocrite.

The Southerners are usually so confident of themselves—so buoyant with hope—so sure of their ability to meet whatever God sends, that I cannot understand their present position of alms-begging. They are wont to give, but not to ask charity. I feel that this phase in their character invalidates the worth of all I have said in praise of them. And this it is that has prevented my writing to you. I have been trying to think out an argument that could harmonise the Southerner as he is with my ideal of him. I am afraid it is only an ideal. I am afraid that Mr. Dillard,[17] for instance,

17 James Hardy Dillard (1856–1940), for whom Dillard University at New Orleans was named, was dedicated to the advancement of Negro education in the South.

comes nearer the truth about Southerners than I do—in his explanation of his Carnegie mission.

I should say that Washington, Jefferson, Marshall, Lee, Lanier and Poe are very typical Southerners, but Vance, Ben Hill, Lamar, Wade Hampton, Tillman[18] are typical also, as well as Clay, Randolph, Calhoun, Andrew Jackson,—and so many others.

Would it sound too aphoristic to say that if it were not for the South—the term gentleman and lady would fall out of our vocabulary, which would contain only man and woman—or that the South has prevented us from being a nation of Yankees, that the South stands out for the heroic against the successful?

I have always thought that a nice study could be made out of the "ideals" in fiction and poetry represented by North and South. The fictional hero is the ideal one.

Sincerely Your's
Grace King

To Warrington Dawson

1749 Coliseum Place
22 January 1905

My dear Mr. Dawson—[19]

On receipt of your letter I wanted to send an answer by the next mail—telling you what pleasure your news gave me. But my letter has been delayed by one little obstacle, then another. I can tell you truthfully however, that not a day has passed since your letter came that I did not feel some moment of pleasure in thinking of your first work. A first work is always a success in its way—when it is written by the author predestined to bring it forth. I have confidence in The Hadleighs. It will be published—if not by McClure or Harper—then by some one else. And when

18 Zebulon Baird Vance (1830–94), Civil War governor of North Carolina and later U.S. senator; Benjamin Harvey Hill (1823–82), Confederate States senator from Georgia, later U.S. congressman and senator; Mirabeau Buonaparte Lamar (1798–1859), editor, soldier, statesman, diplomat, poet, and second president of Texas; Wade Hampton (1818–1902), the Confederate general; Benjamin Ryan Tillman (1847–1918), governor of South Carolina and later U.S. senator.

19 Francis Warrington Dawson (the younger) (1878–1962), Charleston-born journalist and novelist, was United Press correspondent in Paris after 1900. Among his distinguished friends were Joseph Conrad and Theodore Roosevelt.

it is out—you will find that there is one just behind it that pushed it out —as the adult teeth push out the pretty milk ones. You see you must write—(novels)—I mean. You owe it to yourself—which means you owe it to your father and your mother—and all the good ancestral blood that flows in these veins. You owe it to Charleston—poor Charleston—and you owe it to the South. The now voiceless South. The South must *write* itself to the front of the nation—its old place. It has been written down until the Young South is ashamed & is ready to flop into any section that is not the beaten one. You, with your dreams and aspirations can hardly figure to yourself the weakly, silly, practical, prosaic creature the Southern young man is of the present day—striving after football contests instead of political championship.—

Let me know as soon as you find a publisher. I can get at least one or two good newspaper notices of it. That is, I can recommend the book as one for serious consideration. I am trying to get back to some work myself—taking up the threads of the story that I dropped in my anguish of last year.[20]

The publishers are always kind to me and encourage me along in every way they can. I advise you most earnestly to make friends with your publishers. Submit rather to what you feel is an injustice from them rather than quarrel with them. But on your side be frank & outspoken with them. They are a queer lot—sometimes a vindictive set. Did I ever ask you for your photograph? If not I do so now. I have a few—a very few in my study—and now I want to add your's to the little coterie.

Ever Sincerely and Cordially and even Affectionately your's

Grace King

To Warrington Dawson

Hill House, Newdigate, Surrey
15 March 1906

My dear Warrington—

Will you excuse this dreadful paper, whose only merit consists in its thinness & the fact that it is the only kind of thin paper we can buy hereabouts. I want to write to you about your book without any of the hampering limits of postage before my eyes.

Well, will you be surprised to learn that I read your book, not as a

20 "My anguish of last year" probably refers to the death of Sarah Ann Miller King, Grace King's mother, in 1904.

book, but as a document upon yourself. A first novel, you know, is a first revelation of one's self. As you once wrote me, it writes itself. Criticism is useless upon it because one can write a first novel only once. Never again will you be so much possessed by your characters. Hereafter you must be content with possessing them—but you will be freer to do as you please.

When I first wrote I was constantly asked by magazine authorities, "Why did you do this or that." My only answer was "I couldn't help it." Sometimes they would ask me to change something & I would try to gratify them, but I couldn't—any more than I could change my eyes. So as I read your book I felt that every line in it was inevitable; every twist & turn of the plot. I felt your feeling in it throughout. This to me is the great & abiding merit of the book. It is documentary evidence of the best kind. It is not a work of art, but a living reality. But in it you have shown possibilities of a great work of art. Strange to say, your characters to me are startlingly artistic (but I hate that word). The circumstances—the atmosphere—the environment—what you know as the real in your story—they have gone into it in all their crudity of a first impression on you. Five years ago I came to the crossing of this road & I am yet hesitating at it. Shall I or my experience be master in my stories? My "ideal" or my knowledge—my instinct for art—or my duty toward the real.

Eleanor is a fine conception, but you have not said the last word yet upon her. You will come back to her in some future story & in a maturer way. You have hardly more than projected her. In another & less tyrannous environment you will do more justice to her—and I predict the same about the Hadleighs.

How you have poured out your characters & incidents—rather how they have poured themselves out of you! It is a pity that the South has been so much written up in novels. I can see how the novelty of your story did not strike publishers surfeited with descriptions of the South. A cursory reading of it would class it with scores of other stories—but there is an immense difference between it & all the others—a difference as between Browning's "reach & grasp." [21] You have reached far in excess of your grasp.

Do you care for this sort of judgment. It is the only kind I can give a friend. I myself care so little for praise of anything "done." As soon as anything is done one is already beyond—past it. Perhaps I should say—one at your age.

21 Browning's "Ah, but a man's reach should exceed his grasp,/Or what's a heaven for?" is from "Andrea del Sarto," in *Men and Women* (1855).

I like your style very much. It is clear, direct, simple. You have a valuable gift in that. You say what you want to say—and you see things clearly.

Today is a windy, damp disagreeable day with no walk in it for me; only letter writing. I have written through my list—ending with your mother—a poor answer I am afraid to her kind offer—but when we know one another better she will find out how very hampered I am by the cloud that surrounds me.[22]

I like to write about your book—& I have thought about it so carefully. It has helped me to see my way through some of my own difficulties. I congratulate you heartily upon it. I thought it was written by some old, well trained hand at it. Your Cora di Brazza is simply inimitable—I am intimate with her. Several copies were sent to me. These things will make a good book one of these days.

I am so stupid today I should not write—yet I must write to keep my thoughts from harassing me to death. I have a dreadful cold & a racking cough—have been kept in the house three days. My eyes are too weak to read—but I can manage to see to write.

We came to London ten days ago. The weather has been lovely & we have been feasting our souls in St. Paul's & the Abbey. Unfortunately I missed the culminating feast Easter yesterday. We shall stay about two weeks longer & then go out into the country again—make a loitering excursion I fancy among the cathedrals. I wish now heartily in the torture of this cold that we had gone straight to France; where the people are so much more home-like than the English. My great comfort is that we need never come back to England. Does anyone ever come back to England? Your mother was quite right to call it sad. It is sad—heart-breakingly so.

I know none of the literary news here. Have not been in a book shop. On Wednesday (day after tomorrow) we move into a little hotel—No. 21 Bedford Place, Russell Square N.C.—just under the dome of the Museum—a quiet corner that I have been in before. We are now in Fensbury Park—an hour's distance from the city—in these ridiculous horse trains & "busses." I find the people I meet here so much in love with Roosevelt & the negro that I cannot sympathise with them about the horrors of the Education bill.[23] Maybe if religion were taken out of their

22 The reference to "the cloud that surrounds me" is probably to the neurotic illness of Grace King's youngest sister Nina.

23 The controversial and unsuccessful British education bill of 1906 failed to mention any change in state support for religious or even sectarian instruction.

education they would learn a little more about other things. There has not been such a turmoil raised over religion in Europe since the Crusades—when all along, nothing more is meant than the Church.

This is Bank holiday—all the shops closed—& all the shop people walking the streets. I am glad the weather is so fine. The newspapers say that in the memory of man, only once before has such weather been known in London at Easter. And we have it in New Orleans all the time!

My sisters are off at a picture gallery. Well—this is not an answer to your letters. I still owe you that—only a little token that I am thinking of you—in this horrible state I am in. If I were in France I should send for a doctor—but I once had an English doctor—

But it has eased me to talk a moment with you. I wish you could talk back.

Always Cordially
Grace King

To Warrington Dawson

London. 16 April 1906

My dear friend Warrington.

Your letter has given me many interesting moments of thought. There is nothing more interesting than one's self & one's ideals. I am anxious to see your next book—your next. You do books as I used to do short stories; my short stories I fear have spoiled my chance of ever writing a long one. I believe you have commenced at the better end of the dilemma.

The story I am now on[24] I wrote out impulsively—enthusiastically with my whole soul. It was sent back to me with the suggestion to revise at some calmer period. The calmer period condemned it, in toto—but I shall not abandon my idea—& so it lures me on, on—everlastingly. What I did was not art. I see that. I wonder if I shall ever find out what art is. I cannot write any more until I do. You see why, & how your letter interests me.

But do not look down upon your newspaper work. The first one—I mean article, I read—when I came to your name at the end I was transfixed with surprise and from it draw the happiest conclusions as to your future. Do not go too fast however—do not spend your fortune of

24 She probably refers to *The Pleasant Ways of St. Médard.*

imagination too recklessly. After all, I believe disagreeable publishers are our best friends.

Goodbye & God speed—
Always sincerely & Affectionately
your friend
Grace King

To John R. Ficklen

24 Chemin de la Station
Meudon, France
November 27, 1906

Dear Mr. Ficklen.[25]

. . . It will be two weeks tomorrow since we arrived in France. I came the day after to Meudon, where I expected to find Mme Blanc ready to go to Arcachon. But she has had a kind of relapse & cannot go. I fear she is dangerously ill. I shall stay here the rest of the winter. Nannie & Nina will remain in Paris;—Nina is getting strength very slowly & is painfully languid—but she has the compensation of being prettier than ever in her life before—as Mme B says, is full of exquisite charm. She & Nan & Dr. Sweet[26] all came to see me last week. . . . I am trying to take up the threads of former literary connections here—& to get into my work again. I do not have to go to Paris for society for there is a constant stream of visitors to see Mme Blanc—& I seem to be taken as a matter of course in her Salon. I enjoy the conversation very much—all about books & literary questions. The Church & politics are not discussed. Dreyfus is a sore & humiliating episode for them. His rehabilitation is for them, a slap in the face of the army. And now Brunetière is dying—& who is to succeed him on the Revue! That is a very grave question for all. I have a great deal of reading to do to get back into the literary current here. "Louis XIV & La Grande Mademoiselle" [27] (Hachette)—I can recommend to you & to Tulane Library. It is considered the strongest piece of historical work ever done by a French woman. I find it exceedingly interesting. . . .

25 John R. Ficklen (1858–1907) collaborated with Grace King in *A History of Louisiana* (New Orleans, 1902) and *Stories from Louisiana History* (New Orleans, 1905).

26 She probably refers to Dr. Henry Sweet (1845–1912), the English philologist.

27 *Louis XIV and La Grande Mademoiselle, 1652–1693* (1905), by Arvede Barine.

To John R. Ficklen

Convent St. Maur
12 Rue de l'Abbé Grégoire,
Paris

5 March 1907
Dear Mr. Ficklen.

Your letter of Feb. 13th reached me last night. I intended to write, thanking you for ordering the books so promptly. They came in time for New Year's week. But—about that time Mme Blanc became very much worse—& I lost count of the letters I owed. She died on Feb 5th. No one was with her at the time but her son, nurse & myself. Although she had been suffering extremely for three months—she was patient & calm to the end—& almost at the end loved to hear me talk of New Orleans—our life & the people there. The loss of such a friend as she had been for years is an irreparable one to me. A week later I came into Paris & was fortunate enough to find a room in this old Convent quite close to Nan's & Nina's pension—where there was no room. Do you remember the place? Quite in the heart of Paris—within a stone's throw of the Bon-Marché. The Dames de St. Maur have been teaching here since 1668. They at the first took charge of St. Cyr for Louis & Maintenon. The costume is the same—worn then—& worn by Mme de Maintenon in her retreat here and the manners & customs of the place are not much newer than the costumes. The School has been broken up & the property sequestrated—but until the Gov. actually siezes the "dames" hold on it these "dames pensionnaires"—a few, old, aristocratic & very pious ladies of the Faubourg St. Germain—who, some of them have been living here for years. I had to give references to get in, but the Baron de Pontalba,[28] & a few other friends as irreproachable as he on the score of religion vouched for me— & I find myself most comfortably—if not luxuriously housed. No other pension that I have seen over here compares with this convent. The service—& food—as well as rooms—are perfect. I can sympathise with the Catholics—in the robbery of their buildings without hypocrisy—& hear the abuse of the free-masons & Jews without demur—& so can bear my part in the conversation at table. We talk of nothing else.

28 Baron Édouard de Pontalba (1839–1919) was a scholarly French aristocrat and friend of Grace King. See her *Creole Families of New Orleans* (New York, 1921) 130–32.

Nina is going to England, to take charge of Carleton[29] during his Easter vacation—& then—we shall journey on to Switzerland for the summer. Nina is all that she ever aspired to be in health—in spirits & good looks. She is at last enjoying life. Nan, of course is well. . . .

To May King McDowell

15 Nov 1908

My journey was a most curious experience—although in appearance so natural & unimportant. To begin at the beginning—I telephoned to the telegraph Co—& had a messenger sent to take my wire to Mrs Gay & then I began to pack my "grip"—& shawl bag. Then Mrs R[30] came & took me a long drive. The weather was so hot, I thought I should melt. . . . Well, I had time to finish my packing after dinner—ask Hugh Wilson to see about my mail—put the private watchman in charge during my absence & write Mill Millikin. The[n] Mary & I went to bed. The next day, she gave me my coffee a little after 6 & I bathed—combed & dressed most carefully—as I had learned to do in Europe when travelling. By 8 oc the house was most carefully closed & locked . . . everything in order. Mary given the pass keys—I taking mine. Then with my darkie to carry my bags—I went to the station—& in short got off at 9.15. As I looked out of the car window, I thought of the old times, when we were so glad to get to Roncal [31]—things that I had completely forgotten came to me—& as if it were yesterday. I remembered how we all stood at Roncal to see you pass from your famous first trip North. The little rustic stations of those days are all flourishing towns, with plate glass windows in their shops. Kents' is "Kentwood" a great saw mill & brickyard place—simply humming with business and people. I watched for Terry's Creek with anxiety—& sure enough the train made the old rumbling noise in passing over it. I looked eagerly & found it was not changed. In the march of improvement it seems to have been stepped over. The station is no longer there—but the trees—& the sumach seemed most familiar—& I felt that if I tried hard—I could see the Judge somewhere among them—peering through his glasses to find his way.

29 Carleton King was the son of Grace King's youngest brother Will who had died in 1901.

30 Mrs. Gay was Mrs Charles Gayarré; Mrs. R was probably Mrs. Ida Richardson, wealthy benefactor of Tulane University.

31 Roncal: For Grace King's account of her first visit to the Gayarré country home Roncal, see *Memories of a Southern Woman of Letters*, 30–45.

Osyka has grown & become finer, like the other places—but I am sure that I saw the old row of buildings where the Cadis shop was—the old row of shops, that is. . . . The train reached Canton [Mississippi] about 3. The young Mr. Vivian Ricks was there with the carriage for me— & we drove nine miles through plantations & forests. The weather had begun to turn cold about mid-day, it was pretty sharp when we reached the great plantation house & the Ricks. I was warmly greeted by Mr. & Mrs Ricks and Mrs. Gay—her excitement was intense. It brightened her up so that she did not look in the least altered during the three years—since I last saw her. I was taken into the sitting room—where the biggest log fire I have ever seen was blazing. It was a very pleasant reception indeed. When I went up stairs to my room I found another great log fire blazing in another great big room—as big as three ordinary sized rooms. I furbished up considerably & came back into the sitting room looking so very Parisianised that Mrs Ricks could not keep her eyes off me. As for poor Mrs. Gay—she is now so blind that she could just distinguish me & that was all. The supper was on the same scale as the rooms—huge hot biscuits—hot waffles—beefsteak—honey—hominy corn bread—preserves—pickles—buttermilk—tea—coffee. Such waste I have read about —but I have never seen it before; the regular old Southern plantation prodigality. Mr. Ricks has all his old slaves working for him & he seems to be as much their master as he ever was. Mrs Gay & I talked until 10 oc & then commenced right after breakfast the next morning & talked straight through the day. The weather had become freezing cold—& I must confess that two log fires would not have warmed my big room, with its fine old mahogany furniture. When it dawned upon me the next morning (about 7 oc) that I was to have no early coffee I felt dismal indeed. It seemed to me with all the prodigality on the table—early coffee might well have been given. But I will say, the Ricks's drink the meanest coffee I have ever come across. They make it with a "percolator"—& pour it into ice-cold cups with cold cream & no boiled milk. . . . The more I saw of Mrs. Gay that day & the next—the more I exclaimed to myself "Poor Mrs Gay." She is now 88 years old; thin—weak—wrinkled —but her mind is just as bright as ever—& she maintains her old interest in politics. Her feeling toward our family has become a devotion. The Ricks are kind but, they are unsympathetic—& not at all intellectual—or religious. Mrs Gay cannot see to knit any more—even to play cards. She says she sits, sings hymns to herself—to keep from going crazy & repeats every thing she ever learned by heart. She was pathetically grateful to me for coming to see her—& the Ricks seemed very much pleased too—Mrs R most particularly so. They wanted me to stay longer—but I had prolonged my stay from Friday to Saturday & as I had written to Mary to meet me at the station—I had to go. But the letter I wrote to her never arrived. I suppose the young man who took it with him to Canton forgot all about posting it. So the poor old soul went on Friday night in all the cold & rain to meet me—& when I arrived Saturday she was not there. I got a little boy to carry my bags—& as I knew that even if I could go home alone & sleep there I would need Mary to get breakfast for me. I went to her home with her daughter. Fortunately it was near the station. Mary had been given a strong toddy by her daughter—& had gone to bed early on account of her exposure the night before. But as soon as she heard I was there inquiring for her she got up—dressed—& came home with me. Kelly the watchman was on the look-out for me—& so we three came into the dark silent house & lighted up. I found in my shawl bag—a box of beaten biscuits—& the most delicious partridge I ever eat—so—when I got off my dress—I sat down & eat it with my fingers & just as soon as I could get to bed—mighty thankful to be home once more. . . .

To Robert Underwood Johnson

1749 Coliseum Place
New Orleans
30 March 1909

My dear Mr. Johnson

The arrival of some proof from the Century caught me in the very thick of thinking about you.

I have a kind of story—written on the instigation of Mr. Brett [32] about reconstruction. That is, I wanted it to be a story—& most of it is purely fictitious—but it has unrolled itself in a most disgustingly real way—following life & nature instead of romance. I have my doubts about its being published first in book form—it seems to me to have dedicated itself ab initio to the service of a magazine—as a serial. I am under contract for the book to the Macmillan Co—and- but- if . . . Are you filled up too far ahead to consider such a thing. The country seems to be turning in heart again toward the South. I should say that my wayward offspring is a light—humourous lady—looking at reconstruction—more as a wife & mother than a politician—more moved by the slight than the grave troubles of it.

Ever Sincerely yours
Grace King

32 See Introduction, p. 23, for Mr. Brett and an account of the publication of *The Pleasant Ways of St. Médard.*

To Fred Lewis Pattee

1749 Coliseum Place, N.O.
19 January 1915

Professor Fred Lewis Pattee[33]
My dear Sir.

I am distressed at leaving your letter of Dec. 27th so long unanswered. But, frankly, I have been too busy to give you the answer you asked. And even now, I am obliged to refer you to the World's Best Literature for the dates you need.

Monsieur Motte appeared first in the New Princeton Review. (I really forget the date).

I was inspired to write by my love for the South & the feeling that justice was not being done her in the current literature of the country. Cable doubtless gave a true picture of the Creoles as he knew them (mostly quadroons)— I have always considered his works a libel on the Creoles I knew. However, he pleased the audience he wrote for, & he has made money. Harris & Page of course wrote from a different standpoint;—that of the white *gentleman* as I write from the standpoint of a white lady. Charles Gayarré influenced me in my writing & so did Lafcadio Hearn, but no one else. I am not a romanticist, I am a realist à la mode de la Nlle Orléans. I have never written a line that was not realistic—but our life, our circumstances, the heroism of the men & women that surrounded my early horizon—all that was romantic—I had a mind very sensitive to romantic impressions, but critical as to their expression.

My "New Orleans the Place & the People" I consider my best work, I may say the one work I have accomplished. My "Balcony Stories" are valuable for the light they throw on social conditions in New Orleans after the Reconstruction.

Hoping that I have written you something that may be of use to you—

Sincerely Your's
Grace King

33 Fred Lewis Pattee (1863–1950), professor of English, Pennsylvania State College, was collecting material for his *History of American Literature Since 1870* (1915).

To Carleton King

Covington
June 4, 1915

Dearest Carleton

My great day has come & gone—leaving the Tulane degree of Dr. of letters behind it. We had to get up at 5 in the morning to take the 6 oc train to the city. And of course I could not sleep during the night. But the morning was so cool & beautiful & all of us in such good spirits—that I soon forgot all discomforts & let my mind enjoy itself looking out of the car window. We reached the city on time at 9 oc & took a taxi to the house, where Maggie & Mary according to directions were waiting for us with a good breakfast prepared. Everything looked cool & clean there & in good order. While we eat, Maggie gave us her account of our tenants. . . . Then we went upstairs & for one hour were mistresses again of our rooms. We dressed most carefully for the ceremony ahead of us—& were looking our very best as we took a taxi again to the Opera House.[34] There we found a great crowd; & the usual excitement of families & friends over the graduates. My rendezvous was in the foyer—& there was a rousing welcome I had from Newcomb & Tulane. Really—I would not have believed they could be so nice. Giving the Hon. Degree to me seemed to be the distinction of the day to them. Tulane Board & the Professors from Mr. Walmsley, Bishop Sessums[35]—down to the latest professor made such a fuss over me! If I had been younger & foolish, my head would have been turned. But I managed to keep it in the proper position on my shoulders—& answered compliments with compliments, & very deftly turned the tables on the complimenters. Mrs. Stuart[36] who was to receive a degree too—was there but no one seemed to know her—& she stood aloof & silent—while I was receiving my ovation. We all walked in procession to the stage—I leading just after the Board—& on the stage—I was given the place of honour, & you know I enjoyed that—& beamed down my smiles on Nannie & Nina seated in a stage box. The

34 The French Opera House in the *Vieux Carré* was used by Tulane University for commencement exercises. It was destroyed by fire on December 3, 1919.

35 She probably refers to S. P. Walmsley, president of the New Orleans Cotton Exchange and of the Louisiana National Bank; Davis Sessums was Episcopal Bishop of Louisiana, 1891–1929.

36 Ruth McEnery Stuart (1849–1917) wrote dialect stories, chiefly of rural Louisiana and Arkansas.

proceedings were long and tiresome & I thought my turn would never come. For at every step—between every speech & announcement there was a long piece of music.

Finally—before the whole multitude and as will happen I suppose on the Day of Judgment—Mr. Dixon pronounced the eulogy on Mrs. Stuart that had gained her the honorary degree—(proposed by Newcomb). When he finished Prof. Peirce Butler gave my epitaph as I call it—very fine & dignified, I felt that I had earned it. Mr. Sharp[37] himself handed the precious papers to us. Nan & Nina say I looked very distinguished when I received mine. All on the stage stood while this was being done. Then the benediction & more music; & the break up—but all my friends crowding around me once more—to shake hands & congratulate. I wish you had been there to see it. Beautiful flowers were sent me—& my arms were full of them. When I left the Opera I could hardly get down the steps—for the crowd—waiting to greet the literary ladies. . . .

To Edward Garnett

1749 Coliseum Place
New Orleans
7 April 1916

Dear Mr. Garnett.[38]

Heartened by your praise of my story Henry Holt & Co. asked to read the ms. & then made an offer to publish it which I have accepted. I suppose it will be printed at once.

I was in hopes that the Macmillan Co. would be persuaded by your praise to reverse their former verdict & print the story as a kind of *Amende honorable*; for it was written at Mr. Brett's request, he himself suggesting Reconstruction as the period; & I wrote it over *five* times trying to suit him. This consumed years of my life & bled me of spirit & energy. But, Mr Brett I fancy was offended at your sharp criticism of the Harbor[39]—one of his books—& so would not pay you the compliment of agreeing with you about my story.

What you have accomplished for me seems a miracle. In the homely

37 Brandt Van Blarcom Dixon organized Newcomb College in 1887; Pierce Butler was professor of English, Tulane University, and dean of Newcomb College; Robert Sharp was 9th president of Tulane University (1912–18).

38 For Edward Garnett's evaluation of *The Pleasant Ways of St. Médard*, see Introduction, p. 24.

39 *The Harbor* (1915), the first novel of Ernest Poole.

old-fashioned phrase I can only thank God for it. The South has a few publishers—in progressive cities like Atlanta & Richmond, but they have not a good reputation for fair dealing. The literary quality of the books they put out is wretched. I have never had any trouble with Northern publishers until this last effort. Houghton Mifflin & Little, French of Boston[40] were frank enough to let me know that they did not care to publish any more about Reconstruction. But they would publish without hesitation a "best seller" about it.

What you say about the war is sorrowfully true. Even here we are living under the shadow of it. The German atrocities keep us in a constant state of horror.

I hope President Wilson is right in the stand (if you can call it *stand*) that he is taking. To me he is forcing a very ignoble position upon the U.S. The people here are not with him, as I hope he will find out one day. We are not neutrals in heart—if he is. We want to stand by England with the Allies—we want to strike a blow at Germany.

Always your grateful &
sincere friend
Grace King

To Edward Garnett

1749 Coliseum Place
New Orleans
3 Feb. 1917

Dear Mr. Garnett:

The Holts printed very small editions of St. Médard (1200)—so *three* printings sound bigger than they really were. But the book, tho' not a best seller, except in N.O., has been extraordinarily well received. I send you a few notices to show that the Yankees have not entirely overlooked their shameful Reconstruction achievement. It amuses me to see how they reproach *me* for rancor & bitterness—just as I suppose, one of these days the Germans will reproach the Belgians. As we have no *real* critics, we do not expect real critical appreciation of our novels.

The newspapers of the South, strange to say, have shown marked indifference to the book, wh. shows merely that the South has been too well whipped to have any longer any individual pride. But here in N.O. I

40 Undoubtedly "Little, Brown [and Company] of Boston" is intended.

have been amazed & touched by the remarkable outburst of sentiment that it has evoked. Every woman who lived during Reconstruction says it is her own story—& the best men here have thanked me for it in fine letters. They all repeat what you say—that the book will live. . . .

G.K.

To George W. Cable

1749 Coliseum Place
14 Oct. 1917

My dear Mr. Cable.

Your note is just what you meant it to be; graceful, agreeable, & warm hearted—just the note in fact to give me great pleasure & touch my heart.

St Médard was written so long ago! During the golden age of my memory when my dear mother was still with us, & my dear brother Branch. Life has been so dark without them—that I have not written anything worth while since they left us. And I have had so much *business* to think about & attend to!

I hope that you are still as ever sturdily employed—giving us the stories, that only you in all this great world can write.[41]

Praise from you is indeed praise from "Sir Walter." [42]

With many thanks
Cordially Your's
Grace King

To Warrington Dawson

August 5, 1924

Dear Warrington—

I was very glad to get your letter yesterday, & to know that you could make use of what I wrote about you. It seems to me very necessary to insist upon the fact that young Southern writers differ from the other variety by their higher standpoint. Patriotism & the most exalted love for our parents was our inspiration. We knew we cared for no other motive & our books are a part of the history of the Confederacy—as our lives are. I

41 For Grace King's opinions of George W. Cable, see Introduction, pp. 8–11.

42 Praise from "Sir Walter" is presumably an echo of "praise from Sir Hubert," from the original "Approbation from Sir Hubert Stanley is praise indeed." Thomas Morton, *A Cure for the Heartache*, V. ii.

hope the News & Courier will print your pretty review of Ste Hermine. Only one paper here reviewed it. Books are of no account in the South, I am sorry to say. The Macmillans do not count upon New Orleans at all in the estimated sale of my books. No *best* book has a chance here—only the flimsiest, & the most immoral best sellers.

I am very much disgusted about it. But I still work on. Our reward will come one of these days in the future.

I am glad that you are so cheerful & courageous. But do not work too hard. I feel that I have worked & am working beyond my strength, but there is nothing else in life for me.

I shall look forward eagerly to the book about you. What a loss! the death of Conrad. I thought of you at once. He was one of the great admirations of my life. I always hoped one day to know him. He cannot be replaced in literature.

Ever affectionately your old friend
Grace King

Do excuse my poor stiff cranky hand.

To Leonidas Warren Payne

1749 Coliseum Place
18 Oct. 1927

My dear Mr Payne—[43]

I shall be very grateful for a copy of the Dallas News with your review of my St. Médard. All that I can say—all that it would be discreet of me to say—is that I was a child during Reconstruction—& I wrote from my memories of that period. My father, Wm W King was a distinguished lawyer of N.O. His character lives in my memory as I describe him. My mother also was just what I describe her. They had a large family—& their struggle to feed and educate it was bitter. I wrote St. Médard at the request of a Northern publisher—who wanted to know about Reconstruction. I told him the problem was one of meat & bread.

The negro family I describe is taken from life.

This is for you personally. I have a horror of publicity from my books. Please do not quote me.

Sincerely Your's
Grace King

43 Leonidas Warren Payne (1873–1945) was professor of English, University of Texas.

To Warrington Dawson

New Orleans
4th November 1930

. . . As you see my hand is nervous, & it is a task to make it write a legible letter. In fact, I have about given up writing letters & walking also. The doctor says I am suffering from a nervous affection. That my dear Warrington, it is not that only. I am just reaching the end of my line That is all. And it is time.

I work a little every day. I will finish my interminable Memories—this winter—unless they finish me first. Tell me what you are doing—how you are feeling—"Watchman tell me what of the night—"[44] as says the Old Testament—[4 illegible words]—believe me—

Always your loving friend
Grace King

44 More accurately, the phrase is "Watchman, what of the night?" Isaiah, XXI. 11.

Bibliographical Note

Beer, William, "List of Writings of Grace King," *Louisiana Historical Quarterly,* VI (1923), 353–59.

Turner, Arlin (selected writings about Grace King), in Louis D. Rubin, Jr. (ed.), *A Bibliographical Guide to the Study of Southern Literature* (Baton Rouge, 1969), 234–35.

Vaughan, Bess, "A Bio-Bibliography of Grace Elizabeth King," *Louisiana Historical Quarterly*, XVII (1934), 752–70 (The most complete bibliography of Grace King).